Advance Praise
for Managing Intellectual Capital in Practice

"The approach presented by Göran Roos and his team in this book was the template for turning FOI into a world-class organization. I would recommend it to anyone responsible for value creation in the public sector."
—**Bengt Anderberg**, Director General [ret], FOI (Swedish Defense Agency)

"Göran Roos and his colleagues' interpretation of the value of managing intellectual capital correctly as a way of establishing differentiation and sustainable competitive advantages in a wide range of organizations is superb. This new book is a great stimulator for managers to adopt new ways of management with an excellent combination of theory and practical examples."
—**Sabin Azua**, Managing Director, BearingPoint, Spain

"The first book providing practical advice on how to extract more value from intangibles – highly recommended."
—**John J. Ballows**, Partner, Shareholder Value, Accenture

"Göran Roos is a leading light in the field of intellectual capital. I have had the great pleasure of being both a co-author and a student of his innovative work. The enclosed text is a must read for any academic or practitioner interested in a holistic review of the literature. The expertise of Professor Roos and his co-authors clearly shines in the way the arguments are meticulously laid out. Plus, their breadth of knowledge in a variety of interrelated areas including strategy, accounting, finance, organizational behavior, human resources and technology is refreshing when dealing with such a complex and multifaceted topic. Intellectual capital is the *de facto* currency of our millennium, and Göran Roos and his colleagues continue to effectively evangelize its importance."
—**Dr. Nick Bontis**, Director, Institute for Intellectual Capital Research Professor, McMaster University, Hamilton, Ontario, Canada

"The management of intangibles and organizational knowledge stands as a dynamic and creative perspective which will enable intellectual capital to be developed in organizations, an innovative viewpoint analyzed by Göran Roos and his co-authors, who have been able to contribute with their valuable experience on the subject in this recent work."
—**Eduardo Bueno Campos**, Director of Parque Científico de Madrid (PCM), Centro de Investigaciones sobre la Sociedad del Conocimiento (CIC) and Instituto Universitario de Administración de Empresas (IADE)- Universidad Autónoma de Madrid, Spain

"It is a pleasure to see how Göran Roos and his co-authors integrate the most recent models and concepts into a very comprehensive and practically oriented treatment of Intellectual Capital. With this book the ICS team has once again shown how competitive advantages can be built upon intellectual capital. As one of the founding fathers of Intellectual Capital, Göran Roos knows how intellectual capital works and what the challenges are in developing a knowledge-based strategy."
—**Per Nikolaj Bukh** (www.pnbukh.com), Professor, Aarhus School of Business, Aarhus Denmark; co-author of the *Danish Guideline for Intellectual Capital*

"Göran Roos and his co-authors have drawn on a wealth of experience in this path-breaking and insightful study of why intellectual capital matters and how intellectual capital management can be applied in organizations. Its lucid style, penetrating analysis of IC methods and numerous practical examples make it a valuable and accessible addition to the literature for business managers, academics and students alike."
—**Alan Burton-Jones**, CEO, Burton-Jones & Associates, South Brisbane, Australia, and author, *Knowledge Capitalism: Business, Work, and Learning in the New Economy*

"Although the value and importance of Intellectual Capital has been reported on extensively, Professor Göran Roos and his co-authors describe for the first time a methodology which could be applied to any organization. The process is practical and it works."
—**Dr. Stuart W. Carr**, Director, Radiopharmaceuticals, Australia Nuclear Science & Technology Organization, Radiopharmaceuticals and Industrials (ARI)

"Managing value creation in today's organizations that are based mainly on intangible assets with a clear analysis and understanding of all available resources – including intangibles. The Intellectual Capital Management movement has focused on this fact and promoted this message over the last one and a half decades. Göran Roos and his co-authors go much further in this book. The concept they present allows managers to not only put more rigor in systematic resource analysis, but to also understand how the different resource categories are transformed in the value creation process – which enables them to really manage the value creating process, both from a strategic and operational perspective. Thus, this book presents the missing building block for true Intellectual Capital Management (or Intangible Assets Management) and is a must read for everyone interested in modern business management."
—**Jürgen H. Daum**, CFO adviser, enterprise management expert and Chief Solution Architect, SAP AG, Waldorf, Germany

"**Managing Intellectual Capital in Practice** provides a very useable framework for managing intangibles. This text takes a deeper look at intangibles, their measurement and their management, and gives the reader some powerful ideas to drive strategic planning processes."
—**John Dean**, General Manager, Corporate Strategy Group, Department of Industry, Tourism and Resources, Australia

"**Managing Intellectual Capital in Practice** appears to be one of the best books regarding application of intellectual capital in contemporary organizations. The essence of the book is in the sequence of rather practical procedures- i.e., how to identify, value, measure and report on the intellectual capital of your business. Undoubtedly the personal experience of the author makes this book helpful for practitioners as well as researchers."
—**Vassily K. Dermanov, Ph.D**, Associate Professor, Vice-president, Stockholm School of Economics, Saint Petersburg, Russia

"Göran Roos and his co-authors give readers the benefit of their long and outstanding experience in intellectual capital and make this complicated concept easy to both under-

stand and put into practice. Their wisdom as relates to extracting value from intangibles is breathtaking. Strongly recommended as reading to all business leaders and managers."
—**Mehmet Gün**, Founder, Mehmet Gün & Co., Istanbul, Turkey

"Professor Göran Roos has together with his co-authors synthesized current professional and research knowledge about intellectual capital into this accessible book. I highly recommend **Managing Intellectual Capital in Practice** for practitioners and academics as it provides case studies and detailed illustration of various theoretical constructs and models for intellectual capital management, measurement and reporting."
—**Professor James Guthrie**, School of Business, University of Sydney, Australia

"Many people talk about the new economy and how the basis of value creation is fast shifting from physical to intellectual capital. Few people take us beyond the theory. In this important book, Göran Roos gives us the tools and the strategies we need to navigate businesses in this unfamiliar but exciting world."
—**Ian R. Harper**, Executive Director, Centre for Business & Public Policy, Melbourne Business School, Australia

"This dynamic work reflects the increasing scope and importance of extracting value from intangibles in our hypercompetitive environment. Professor Roos and his co-authors' deep understanding of intangibles and rich experience in applying it strategically are captured in this work of leading-edge practice. An invaluable guide for today's decision-making to deliver high performance results."
—**Dr. Werner Hoffmann**, Professor, University of Applied Sciences, Ludwigshafen, Germany

"Intellectual Capital is one of the central cornerstones of modern business life. Professor Göran Roos and his co-authors present this, sometimes difficult to understand, subject in a very clear, practical and compelling way, drawing on their strong scientific competence. The book is an important tool in every executive's library."
—**Professor Erkki KM Leppavuori**, President and CEO, Technical Research Centre of Finland, VTT

"This book is an important addition to the fast-growing literature on intellectual capital. Particularly worthwhile are the numerous practical examples and the extension to the not-for-profit and government sectors."
—**Baruch Lev**, Philip Bardes Professor of Accounting and Finance at New York University, Stern School of Business, and Director of the Vincent C. Ross Institute for Accounting Research, New York, USA

"Professor Roos and his team have once again shown that "the soft stuff" needn't be fluffy, but can actually be measured and managed in a meaningful and truly useful way. This book gives managers the language to work with all resources in their organization and the tools to make sure they contribute to achieving tangible results."
—**Lea Lillkåll**, VP, HR/Competence & Leadership, TeliaSonera, Finland

"Most managers recognize the significance of intellectual capital— **Managing Intellectual Capital in Practice** provides them with the practical tools to manage it. In a step by step fashion, the authors distill the essential principles of this complex field, helping managers better understand, define, value, and use their essential knowledge

assets for competitive advantage. This is not a casual read. This will become the primer on intellectual capital and knowledge management. It has been a long time coming but it is here. The serious practitioner will find it invaluable."
—**Sarah Mavrinac**, Assistant Professor of Accounting & Control, INSEAD, Fontainebleau Cedex, France

"Göran Roos and his co-authors bring fresh perspectives, well-researched concepts and excellent practical applications to the area of intellectual capital. Any organization that wants to succeed in the future needs to clearly understand the role of intellectual capital and the measurement of intangibles to determine future value. The book is clear and well thought through and brings out the interrelated concepts of strategy, innovation, technology and organizational behavior. This invaluable guide is a business essential for the future and necessity for any successful organization in the future."
—**Susan Mackie**, Chief Executive, de Bono Institute, Melbourne, Australia

"The management and measurement of Intellectual Capital is a major proportion of the value in 'new economy' companies and in many old economy ones too. In mergers and acquisitions, the intangible value of potential synergy is critical to the purchase decision. Göran Roos and his team are global leaders in understanding these issues and this book is a beacon for those wanting to understand the value to their organization of intangibles and Intellectual Capital. The case studies are invaluable practical lessons in IC."
—**Anne E Molyneux**, Director, CS International; Former Director Technical Affairs at the Institute of Chartered Accountants in England and Wales; Former Director Intellectual Capital at CPA Australia and was also CPA Australia's Finance Director

"Göran Roos is clearly a leading author in the field of intellectual capital, and this book testifies to this. It locates intellectual capital in a series of contexts and shows to students and advanced practitioners the merits of making intellectual capital not only a tool for management and reporting but also a framework for thinking about strategy. Göran Roos here mobilizes his academic talent as well as huge practical experience for the benefit of readers and advances the frontiers of intellectual capital."
—**Jan Mouritsen**, Professor, Copenhagen Business School, Denmark

"We have worked with Göran for six years and his practical thinking is continuously influencing the way we go about our business, with measurable success as a result. The content of this book reflects part of Göran's thinking and is highly recommended for anybody involved in FMCG."
—**John Murphy**, Managing Director, Fosters, Australia

"Göran Roos at his best. One of the few people working in the field of intangible assets that can actually make the concept tangible and actionable. Göran's wisdom, insight and intellect shines through this thought-provoking book."
—**Professor Andy Neely**, Cranfield School of Management, Cranfield, UK & Deputy Director, Advanced Institute of Management Research, London, UK

"In his new book, Göran Roos and his colleagues explore complex and innovative concepts and interrelationships in a territory yet to be charted. An excellent piece of work!"
—**Patricia Ordoñez de Pablos**, Professor of Business Administration, the University of Oviedo, Spain; Executive Editor of the International Journal of Learning and Intellectual Capital

"The term 'intellectual capital' denotes an emerging competitive landscape in which many companies feel lost and disorientated. In **Managing Intellectual Capital in Practice**, Göran Roos and his colleagues apply an impressive combination of practical experience and analytical insight to provide one of the most detailed and comprehensive maps yet available of this new landscape."
—**Professor Harry Scarbrough**, Warwick Business School, University of Warwick, Coventry, UK

"We have found during several client engagements in the Baltic States that managers are acknowledging the real importance of intellectual capital—it is the most important resource of the organization. The new book from intellectual capital guru Göran Roos and his colleagues gathers together the main theoretical concepts and their practical implications of intellectual capital. This is something that every manager should look into in order to be competitive."
—**Mati Sööt**, Chairman, Inscape Baltic, Tallinn, Estonia

"Göran Roos and his co-authors have laid out a comprehensive and compelling approach for identifying, measuring and valuing an organization's intellectual capital. This book is an important resource for organizational strategists, performance managers and business measurement practitioners alike."
—**Les Trudzik**, Ph.D., Executive Director, KPMG Risk Advisory Services, Australia

"The practical and useful approach presented in this book has simplified my task of turning around the European business of our organization – a very useful read for anybody in the telecoms business."
—**Derek Welford**, CEO, Cable and Wireless Europe

"Roos et al. provide a very readable and useful yet penetrating treatment of Intellectual Capital. Particularly important are the extensive and clear presentations of the nature and properties of IC and its relation to financial and physical capital, the highly practical approaches to assessing and developing IC within the enterprise, and the motivating analysis of how IC relates to value creation and business benefits.

The numerous examples make the text both readable and understandable and bring forth the reality of how and where IC becomes important in supporting the success of the enterprise. This is a book that not only should be on every manager's shelf—it should also be incorporated in their daily and strategic practices. Roos and his co-authors provide fresh new perspectives that at times are contrary to conventional and outdated wisdom. They model their analysis and synthesis on comprehensive yet pragmatic approaches and the perspective of the effective enterprise. They also incorporate advanced theoretical methods in their treatise to deal with the more complicated and subtle aspects that nevertheless play important roles and need to be brought to the surface to be of practical value."
—**Karl M. Wiig**, Chairman, Knowledge Research Institute, Inc., Arlington, Texas, USA

Managing Intellectual Capital in Practice

Göran Roos

Stephan Pike

Lisa Fernström

Routledge
Taylor & Francis Group

LONDON AND NEW YORK

First Published by Butterworth-Heinemann
This edition published 2011 by Routledge
2 Park Square, Milton Park, Abingdon, Oxon OX14 4RN
711 Third Avenue, New York, NY 10017, USA
Routledge is an imprint of the Taylor & Francis Group, an informa business

Notice
No responsibility is assumed by the publisher for any injury and/or damage to persons or property
as a matter of products liability, negligence or otherwise, or from any use or operation of any
methods, products, instructions or ideas contained in the material herein. Because of rapid
advances in the medical sciences, in particular, independent verification of diagnoses and drug
dosages should be made

British Library Cataloguing in Publication Data
A catalogue record for this book is available from the British Library

Library of Congress Cataloguing in Publication Data
A catalogue record for this book is available from the Library of Congress

ISBN 978 0 7506 7940 4

For information on all Routledge publications visit our website at
www.routledge.com

Typeset by SPI Publisher Services, Pondicherry, India

Contents

Foreword

The topic of this book, to work with intellectual capital in practice, is an issue that is very familiar to most business leaders. You may not use the term "intellectual capital" but in today's service- and knowledge-based economy you cannot do without managing intangible resources such as knowledge, networks, brands, and systems to create value for the firm's or organization's stakeholders. Despite this, there are no truly accepted routines and models for managing and measuring the intellectual capital. With this book, we want to fill that void and share our expertise and long-time experience of managing, measuring, and valuing intellectual capital.

This is the first book from recognized experts in the field, with an action-oriented and holistic perspective on how to increase value creation in companies and organizations by leveraging intellectual capital. It covers central management questions about how to ensure the availability of suitable resources and how best to employ them to successfully execute the strategy of the firm. Moreover, we show how to safely measure intellectual capital resources and discuss how to disclose this non-financial information. We also explain how to use intellectual capital thinking and tools to maximize value creation in mergers and acquisitions, knowledge management, and human resource management.

The book is designed to help business leaders and managers in practice and is as such supported by 25 cases from businesses in different industries and from different parts of the world, in order to illustrate various applications of intellectual capital thinking. It is also fundamentally grounded in theory with references to the most important academic publications in the field throughout, rendering it useful as supplemental course literature in strategy, management, management accounting, and other business administration subjects.

We would like to take this opportunity to thank a number of people who have contributed to this book. We extend our sincere appreciation to Roland Burgman of AssetEconomics for his contributions to

Chapters 1 and 5. Special thanks to Yoshikawa Katsuhiko of Recruit (Japan), Taru Rastas and Leena Piponius of IC Partners (Finland), Anne Fletcher of Growing your Knowledge (Australia), and Sanna Kuukkanen for their contributions with regards to the case studies. We would also like to thank Oliver Gupta for his assistance in the preparation work of this book.

London, June 2005

Göran Roos, Stephen Pike and Lisa Fernström

Intellectual Capital Services Ltd.
Visit our website at www.intcap.com

1

What is intellectual capital and why is it important?*

Over the last ten years we have seen a rapidly growing interest in and understanding of the role that intellectual capital resources play in the workings of all organizational forms. Concomitantly, there has been a realization that organizations should be managed differently, including the use of new methods for performance measurement and disclosure.

In a recent survey conducted by the Economic Intelligence Unit for Accenture,[1] 94% of CEOs agreed that it is essential to understand and manage intellectual capital. Out of these, 50% stated that intellectual capital management is one of the three most important challenges for managers and 13% stated that it is the most important challenge.

The purpose of this book is to create a better understanding of intellectual capital and its management and to discuss how intellectual capital management can be applied in practice in organizations. Throughout, the reader will be provided with solid and grounded foundations, including tools and techniques, for crafting an organizational strategy that takes into account intellectual capital. Our discussions in later chapters will be illustrated with examples from different types of organizations: private sector, public sector and third sector.[2] Cases will be used to illustrate how intellectual capital thinking is applied.

WHY INTELLECTUAL CAPITAL?

Listed firms[3]

We have heard much about the new economy and its management challenges. Interestingly, the discussion has diminished somewhat since the dot.com bubble burst in 1999. It should not have. That unhappy event for many investors has masked a serious consideration of what is

---

* In this chapter, we are grateful to AssetEconomics LLP for providing substantial amounts of data and analysis.

structurally new and different in developed economies generally. The United States economy in particular has changed radically. Stock market valuation underpinnings are seemingly irrevocably altered. There has been tremendous growth in expectations for the future earnings of U.S. companies.[4] We have forms of enterprise that, first, employ new business models and second, grow and compete by leveraging different resource forms than those on which we have conventionally relied. The responsibility for managing shareholder wealth now has new implications for understanding what resources are to be managed, how, and what is to be communicated to whom, under what conditions and through what media.

In this and the following chapters we will outline:

- The changed nature of the U.S. economy in terms of its constituent companies,
- The unavoidable and profound importance of future value in the market valuation of equity,
- The new challenges that confront management in their quest to manage for value,
- The nature of intellectual capital and a broader understanding of the ways in which value is created in companies that predominantly rely on intellectual capital, and finally,
- A new basis for managing for shareholder value.

The economy has changed. We are used to hearing about the New York Stock Exchange (NYSE), Dow, and National Association of Securities Dealers Automated Quotation (Nasdaq) indices and their growth over the last several years. The predominant indices are the Dow Jones Industrial Average ("the Dow"), the S&P 500, and the Nasdaq–100. The S&P 500 is often regarded as the bellwether index of the U.S. economy.

The best illustration of the fundamental changes that have occurred to the U.S. economy is the growth of the number and importance of Nasdaq-listed companies in the S&P 500. Typically there had been few Nasdaq-listed companies in the S&P 500; less than 25 before 1993, accounting for less than 5% of the S&P 500's equity market value. At the height of the dot.com boom in 1999, the then 47 Nasdaq-listed companies in the S&P 500 represented over 20.6% of its value. Even after the dot.com market implosion at the end of 1999, the number of Nasdaq-listed companies in the S&P continued to climb. At the end of 2003, 74 Nasdaq-listed companies were represented in the S&P 500, accounting for 16.7% of the index's value. These new economy[5] companies are among the U.S. economy's prime shareholder value creators[6] and include Microsoft, Cisco, Amazon, Yahoo!, Amgen, and eBay. eBay, a company

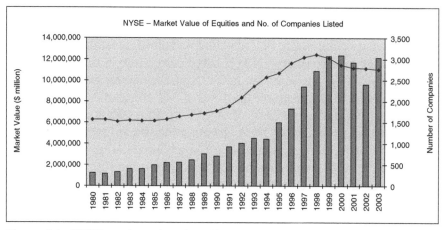

Figure 1.1. NYSE: market value of equities and number of listed firms, 1980–2003. *(Source: AssetEconomics LLP.)*

with a market capitalization of close to $60 billion in September 2004, which joined the S&P 500 in late 2003, was formed in 1995 and only had its IPO in 1997, the latter event a mere seven years ago.

The new economy is broadly identified in Figures 1.1 and 1.2.[7] These figures show a history of more than twenty years of the NYSE and Nasdaq exchanges by number of companies listed and their market value at year-end for the NYSE.

Broadly speaking, the NYSE is regarded as the home of the old economy, whereas the Nasdaq is regarded as the home of the new economy.

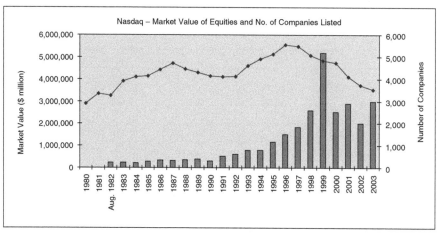

Figure 1.2. Nasdaq: market value of equities and number of listed firms, 1980–2003. *(Source: AssetEconomics LLP.)*

As we might expect then, the asset backing of companies listed on each of these exchanges is quite different. Taking the S&P 500 as an example, the market-to-book value of Nasdaq-listed nonfinancial companies in the S&P 500 is twice that of NYSE-listed companies in the index.

The S&P 500[8] represented some 67.9% of the market value of equities in the United States[9] out of the total 6,288 companies listed on the NYSE and Nasdaq at the end of 2003[10]. Nasdaq-listed companies are now a permanent feature of this bellwether index and many of these represent new forms of doing business, often relying on nontraditional business models and leveraging intellectual capital rather than strictly physical resources to create superior competitive advantage. The emergence and importance of the new economy in the United States is demonstrated by the number and value of Nasdaq-listed companies in the S&P 500, as shown in Figures 1.3 and 1.4. We will see that these companies are very important and represent a fundamental change in the make-up of the US economy.[11]

There have been extensive discussions about the new economy and its management. The economies in which businesses operate are in constant change. As a consequence, we cannot expect to excel managerially if we apply thinking developed for different economic dynamics than those in which we operate. This means that we constantly need to reappraise our mental models, our assumptions, and our practical approaches to managing organizations. To illustrate the point, we are not necessarily going to succeed by applying the tools and thinking developed for a manufacturing company assuming economies of scale to running a service organization grounded in economies of scope. Today's world has a greater

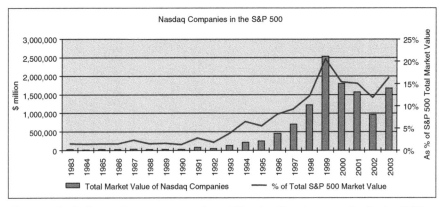

Figure 1.3. Dollar and percentage value of Nasdaq-listed companies in the S&P 500. *(Source: AssetEconomics LLP.)*

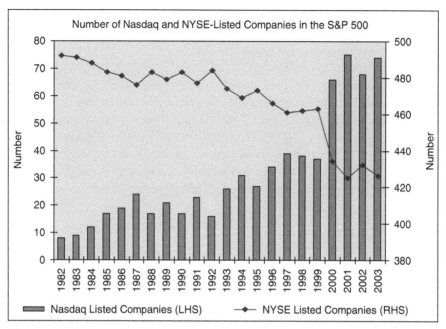

Figure 1.4. Number of NYSE versus Nasdaq-listed companies in the S&P 500. *(Source: AssetEconomics LLP.)*

focus on services and intangibles than ever before and therefore requires much more sophisticated management of issues such as processes, brands, IP, relationships and competence.

Today all companies are trying to improve their value, whether monetary or nonmonetary in nature—many with mixed success. A contemporary example of the problems that require new approaches is outsourcing. A company that is outsourcing a manufacturing facility is actually exchanging a physical resource for a relational resource. If the organization does not change its management practices and strategy to take into account the differing economic behaviors of plant and equipment as compared to external relationships, it is highly likely that the expected economic benefits will either never be realized or that the (net present) value of these benefits is either negative or substantially smaller than expected. The responsibility for these failures lies equally with both parties in the outsourcing relationship. To illustrate this, we may examine how often either party in a potential outsourcing relationship has brought up the issue of required changes in management processes so as to extract maximum benefit from a relational resource (that is not owned nor controlled, follows network economic behavior, and is nonadditive in nature). We argue that failure to plan for and implement necessary changes in management practices will account for many of the stated occasions when the benefits of outsourcing have not been realized in accordance with original expectations.[12]

Good managers have always been able to manage their intellectual capital resources well, but they have usually relied on intuition and experience rather than explicit tools, and have been frequently frustrated in their endeavors to monitor the effectiveness and efficiency of value creation from these intellectual capital resources. This book aims to provide managers with tools that are as well grounded and tested as those available for management of classical monetary and physical resources.

Valuation of the firm

The importance of intellectual capital resources is not only illustrated by surveys of senior executives in many countries but is also inherent in the valuation of publicly listed companies on stock exchanges globally.

Finance theory was identifiably born in 1961. At that time, the valuation model for the firm was established in two parts: the value of "assets-in-place" and the value of growth opportunities. This distinction is central to the valuation of firm equity.

1. The present value of the uniform perpetual earnings on assets currently held, and
2. The present value of the opportunities the firm offers for making additional investments in real assets that will yield more than the "normal" market rate of return.[13]

Both present value calculations are made using the same "cost of capital" discount rate. Subsequently, a model known as the KBM model was developed[14,15] which separated the overall market value of a firm into the value of assets-in-place and the value of growth opportunities (also known as growth options). So we have known (at least formally since 1961) that expectations about the future have been included in share prices.

The important question for us now is: How big a contribution to share prices do future growth expectations make? The answer for today's listed companies in the United States is: An enormous amount. As of December 2003, the future growth value (FGV) for the Russell 3000, an index that accounts for the equity value of over 98% of listed U.S. equities, represented an average 72.5% of companies' equity market value and an average of 46.3% of listed companies' enterprise value[16] (EV).

The FGV component of EV has grown over time and is now a fundamental part of the U.S. economy. The phenomenon varies by industry group.[17] Table 1.1 illustrates the FGV/EV percentages for the Russell 3000.

Of the 23 industry groups we have included in this review, there are three clusters that seem to emerge. The first cluster is of four industry groups with a FGV/EV percentage in the 70% to 90% range comprising semiconductors and semiconductor equipment, technology hardware and equipment, software and services, and media. The second cluster is of thirteen industry groups with an FGV/EV percentage range of 39% to 59%. The third cluster is of six industry groups with a FGV/EV percentage range 10% to 29% made up of utilities (10%), energy (13%), and banks (13%) at the low end, to food, beverage, tobacco (24%) and diversified financials (29%) at the high end.

The absolute value represented by FGV should also be put into perspective. The $7.277 trillion (46.3%) of FGV represented in the Russell 3000's $15.706 trillion of EV is greater than the gross domestic product of any country other than the United States[18] and is about the same as the U.S. federal debt.[19]

What we can conclude is that the responsibility for managing shareholder value has become greater (in terms of the husbanding of shareholder wealth), at the same time as the basis for managing that wealth has shifted, and continues to shift, from traditional economic assets to intangible and intellectual capital assets. This is true for many companies in both the U.S. economy's and the global economy's growth future. Companies such as Microsoft, Amazon, Amgen, PeopleSoft, and even eBay typify the future and the new management challenge. In Chapter 4 we will introduce a set of tools that allow us to better manage the future value component of share price, a task that is of the utmost importance if total shareholder returns are to be maximized on a sustainable basis by the management of firms with a high future value component.

An associated important issue is the disclosure of intellectual capital. Companies are already struggling with the rules around disclosure of goodwill, and further requirements are in the pipeline from, for example, the International Accounting Standards Board (IASB). In Chapter 5 we will discuss the present state of disclosure of intellectual capital.

Table 1.1. Enterprise Value and Future Growth Value of Firms Comprising the Russell 3000: 2003

Industry Group	CICS Code	Total Enterprise Value (EV)	Future Growth Value (FGV)	Current Operations Value (COV)	FGV as a Percent of EV
Energy	1010	$917,061	$115,557	$801,504	12.60%
Materials	1510	$666,546	$377,436	$289,110	56.63%
Capital Goods	2010	$1,173,597	$630,122	$543,475	53.69%
Commercial Services & Supplies	2020	$298,305	$144,488	$153,817	48.44%
Transportation	2030	$417,269	$235,073	$182,196	56.34%
Automobiles & Components	2510	$291,647	$145,947	$145,700	50.04%
Consumer Durables & Apparel	2520	$290,660	$59,327	$231,333	20.41%
Hotels, Restaurants & Leisure	2530	$269,976	$119,483	$150,493	44.26%
Media	2540	$933,210	$654,407	$278,803	70.12%
Retailing	2550	$767,247	$385,611	$381,636	50.26%
Food & Staples Retailing	3010	$507,686	$199,913	$307,773	39.38%
Food, Beverage & Tobacco	3020	$809,733	$196,764	$612,969	24.30%
Household & Personal Products	3030	$320,808	$157,450	$163,358	49.08%
Health Care	3510	$727,540	$317,559	$409,981	43.65%
Pharmaceuticals & Biotechnology	3520	$1,207,989	$715,197	$492,792	59.21%
Banks	4010	$1,022,036	$128,349	$893,687	12.56%
Diversified Financials	4020	$813,353	$234,304	$579,049	28.81%
Insurance	4030	$508,817	$209,573	$299,244	41.19%
Software & Services	4510	$738,089	$540,996	$197,093	73.30%
Technology Hardware & Equipment	4520	$947,334	$788,134	$159,200	83.19%
Semiconductors & Semiconductor Equipment	4530	$514,570	$468,077	$46,493	90.96%
Telecommunication Services	5010	$662,781	$362,508	$300,273	54.69%
Utilities	5510	$900,532	$90,897	$809,635	10.09%
Totals		$15,706,786	$7,277,172	$8,429,614	46.33%

Real Estate (4040) omitted – real estate investment trusts and real estate management & development companies. Source: AssetEconomics LLP.

Unlisted firms

The preceding section argues the importance of intellectual capital for listed firms. But what of unlisted firms? We argue here that the importance of intellectual capital is equal, but for different reasons.

All firms are responsible for maximizing value creation to their stakeholders. In a listed firm the intuitive understanding of this statement is relatively easy and primary stakeholders in a listed firm are, as was explained in the preceding section, mainly interested in total shareholder returns as a proxy for value. In the private firm, value is a bit more complex; it is whatever the owner decides that it is. Owners may see their firms as a means to allow them to regularly visit another country, engrave their names on the business community, pursue interesting hobbies, and so on. In essence, there are many possible interpretations of what value might mean in this scenario (more about this in Chapter 4). Whatever value is, the organization must ensure that it provides for the highest potential realization of value, as it is defined, and that the actual value realized lives up to this potential. Since, as a rule, dependence on intellectual capital increases with decreasing size (the one-person firm is solely made up of intellectual capital) and since dependence on intellectual capital increases with increasing service content and smaller firms generally have a high service component in their offering, it follows that small firms on average have a higher dependency on intellectual capital than large firms.

Privately held firms are usually smaller than listed firms, and as a consequence their dependency on intellectual capital is, as a rule, higher than that of listed firms. Privately held firms need to be able to identify, manage, and measure the way they create value from their intellectual capital in order to deliver the value that their stakeholders require. In addition, the value required by stakeholders is frequently composed of intellectual capital components. From this discussion then, it should be clear that the importance of intellectual capital is at least as high to privately held firms as it is to listed firms.

The not-for-profit sector

The reasoning becomes even clearer when we look at organizations that are not limited companies, be these cooperatives, not-for-profit organizations, or government departments. For these organizations, money is a means to an end and not an end in itself. We start by looking at not-for-profit organizations, using a recent Australian survey to illustrate the importance of not-for-profit organizations.

An Australian inquiry[20] concluded that not-for-profit organizations comprised charities, religious institutions and community service organizations (Figure 1.5). In our reasoning we will use the definition from this inquiry: "We regard an organization as being not-for-profit where, by its constituent documents or by operation of law (for example, a statute governing an organization), it is prevented from distributing its profits or assets for the benefit of particular persons...."[21]

The inquiry concluded that the not-for-profit sector contributed AU$14.6 billion, or 3%, to Australia's GDP (of this, charities contributed AU$9.9 billion, or 2%, of GDP).[22] These statistics established that the not-for-profit sector was larger than many others in the Australian economy in terms of contribution to national wealth, especially since the data did not account for the value of voluntary work. For example, the Australian Bureau of Statistics estimates that the gross value added at basic prices in 1998–1999 by the not-for-profit sector was AU$15 billion, which was just less than that of Australia's agricultural industries combined.[23]

Although it is sometimes argued that not-for-profit organizations do not compete and hence do not need to have a competitive advantage, such organizations do have to compete with each other to obtain community support, sustain community confidence, and attract government grants or contracts, as in the case of public–private partnerships. It can

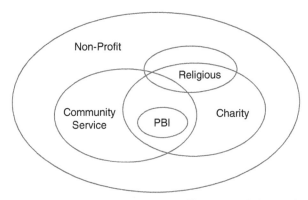

Figure 1.5. Scope of not-for-profit organizations.[24] (PBI: public benevolent institution.)

therefore be argued that clear competitive advantage is important for the not-for-profit sector.

Managerial research focusing on not-for-profit organizations is generally judged to be inadequate, requiring better understanding of internal and external influences on strategic planning.[25] This inadequacy must be understood in the context of continued growth of the sector, a dynamic external environment, and increasing challenges for management[26] since the voluntary sector has achieved an increased social, political, and economic significance worldwide.[27] In addition, the trend to modernize government and public services has led to a greater need for the not-for-profit sector to establish and maintain relationships with clients, suppliers and governments.

Studies on applying intellectual capital to not-for-profit organizations,[28,29,30,31] educational institutions,[32,33,34,35,36] and government departments and programs[37,38] have shown that the concepts of intellectual capital are just as important, if not more relevant and important, to the management and performance of third sector organizations as they are to for-profit companies (this is further illustrated by some of the specific disclosure documents that these types of organizations produce[39,40]). This is obviously due to the inherent complexity of these organizations, with many stakeholders of roughly equal importance to management (since they all can enhance or restrict organizational wealth or economic benefits—normally as a means to an end).[41] These types of organizations tend to have:

- A high reliance on relationships, especially in voluntary organizations
- A high intangibility component of the value created, e.g. in religious organizations
- A high dependence of trust and reputation, especially in donor financed organizations

All these resources are difficult to manage without resorting to some form of intellectual capital approach.

If, as clearly is the case in not-for-profit organizations, the concept of organizational wealth contains both tangible and intangible components,[42] it is necessary to include in the management process the determination and assessment of service value as perceived by stakeholders, including such elements as knowledge sharing, complementary resources, capabilities, and collaborations. This is a complex problem that requires sophisticated tools to be meaningful (more about this in Chapter 4).

Stakeholder management, if well executed, enables managers to ensure that the strategic and operational direction of an organization addresses stakeholder perceptions. However, key stakeholders may also use various types of "influence strategies," whereby they make known the priorities organizations should be attending to in their decision-making.[43] An understanding of different stakeholders' value perceptions will reduce the risk of an organization satisfying the stakeholder with the most effective influence strategy, at the expense of stakeholders with the highest influence on the organization's ability to continue its value creation. Stakeholders are recognized as being of particular importance in public and not-for-profit organizations, which commonly have a more diverse group of stakeholders than do private for-profit organizations, making it more difficult to identify strategic issues in not-for-profit organizations.[44]

Government organizations[45]

A lot of what we stated for the not-for-profit organizations is also valid for government organizations that are in the not-for-profit category. However, as we might expect, there are some additional (and interesting) issues that justify a special discussion about government agencies.

Globally, there are four government agency archetypes:

1. The fully corporatized government agency: The agency is incorporated as a listed company (subject to the governing company law of the land) and is operating under a specific enabling legislative act. An example of such an agency is Telstra Corporation Limited, a full-line telecommunications company that is Australia's largest company in terms of market capitalization. This company is listed, but is 50.1% owned by the Australian Commonwealth Government and 49.9% publicly owned.[46] Telstra has a representational board with all board members being appointed by the Australian government. Similar examples can be found in many other countries.

2. The corporatized government agency[47]: The agency is incorporated as an unlisted company (subject to the governing company law of the land) and is operating under a specific enabling legislative act. Examples of such agencies are Airways New Zealand, a company responsible for managing all domestic and international air traffic in two flight information regions that collectively make up one of the largest areas of airspace in the world: 34 million square kilometres.

Airways New Zealand is a public unlisted company with two (government) shareholders.[48] Another example is AMTRAK (the National Railroad Passenger Corporation), the national rail service provider in the United States.

3. The government agency: A department is created that is not incorporated and does not operate under company law but does operate under a specific enabling legislative act. Examples of such agencies are The Inland Revenue, which is responsible for Great Britain's revenue collection, and the Office of Management & Budget (OMB), the financial management arm of the executive office of the President of the United States.

4. The agency division: An entity is formed that has a certain administrative form and boundaries but is neither operating under company law nor under a specific enabling legislative act but rather under a more general act from which it draws its powers. Examples of such agency divisions are the United States Department of Agriculture (USDA) Forest Service and the USDA Food and Nutrition Information Centre (FNIC) at the National Agricultural Library in the United States.

The distinctions between these government agency types are important in light of the following questions:

- What is value?
- For whom?
- What obligations and responsibilities must the agency consider in creating and maximizing its value content?

These will have quite different answers depending on the circumstances of the agency, particularly the imposts placed on it and its operating environment.

Notwithstanding the different nature of government agencies, it is clear that there is ever increasing pressure on all agencies to demonstrate in a visible way that they create value and are prudently managed fiscally.[49] In counterpoint to this, publicly listed companies are seeking to demonstrate social relevance in a much more transparent way. Initiatives around triple bottom-line and sustainable development reporting are illustrative. These influences will see a convergence in social value and economic value reporting. These directional changes are shown in Figure 1.6.

We propose that the objective function for not-for-profit organizations be stated as:

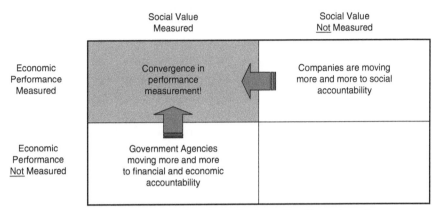

1. Companies with strong triple-bottom line (sustainable development) auditing and reporting programs include Dow Chemical, Royal Dutch Shell, Ford, Nike, BASF, British Telecom, Bristol-Myers Squibb, Canon, Electrolux, GM, KLM, Nokia and South African Breweries
2. The US, the President's Management Agenda, announced in the summer of 2001, is an aggressive strategy for improving the management of the Federal government. It focuses on five areas of management weakness across the government where improvements and the most progress can be made – the strategic management of human capital, competitive sourcing, improved financial performance, expanded electronic Government and budget and performance integration
3. A number of Government agencies have strong social and economic performance measurement disciplines – Airways New Zealand and Telstra Corporation are examples

Figure 1.6. The convergence of influences for social value and economic value reporting. *(Source: AssetEconomics LLP.)*

Maximize Sustainable Societal Value; Subject to achieving specified financial performance levels and/or staying within specified budgetary constraints.

In contrast, and consistent with theory, we propose that the objective function of for-profit organizations be stated as:

Maximize Sustainable Economic Profit; Subject to adhering to a set of societal imposed behavioral constraints.

The dilemma for government agencies is to articulate what the value outcomes are for their stakeholders and to demonstrate fiscal responsibility. This two-handed game occurs within a space where value is not necessarily determined by attempts to gain more of both value constructs. The zone of "maximum value" will be determined by the value perceptions and value weightings of the agency's stakeholders. In theory, this zone could be anywhere, but in practice it is likely that for most agencies, management's goal will be to deliver the maximum social value subject to a generally well understood set of financial goals and constraints.

Government agencies are instruments of the relevant government, its peoples, and its peoples' interests. As a government agency it is the means through which specific government policy is executed and set tasks accomplished.

The management task for government agencies then is to understand who their stakeholders are, what they value, how they value what they value, what values are ascribed to that which they value, and what trade-off in performance on attribute outcomes can be achieved in order to maximize overall value from the point-of-view of all stakeholders. This task is made more difficult when demands are made by stakeholders that are contradictory, competing, and incessant because these affect investment and operational decision choices.

In all government agencies there will obviously be some trade-off between the economic dimension and the rest of the value construct, such as the social dimension. The economic dimension can be addressed by applying our understanding of the economic profit construct (introduced in the preceding discussion on listed companies) to government agencies. This approach would see a government agency's outputs clustered and represented by, say, a strategic business unit (SBU), but where an income statement and balance sheet reflecting that cluster of outputs can be developed.

What should the economic profit of a government agency be? Assuming that government agencies are not in the business of being in business, then arguably target profitability is an economic profit of zero. At an economic profit of zero, all inputs have been paid for, including the required return for capital providers (both debt and equity). If this is not achieved for a government enterprise, there will be an implicit subsidization flowing from the owners of the enterprise (taxpayers) to the consumers of the product or service (the free rider problem). Indeed, to the extent that income does not provide for the replacement of infrastructure, there can also be an intergenerational transfer of wealth from the current generation of taxpayers and/or of current consumers to future ones (who will have to pay more when an infrastructure has to be replaced). The demise of Railtrack and its aftermath in the United Kingdom illustrates this point.

An important consideration for government is what financial goal/s or profit constraint/s to impose on its agencies. The answer from the above is that a government agency should target an economic surplus (or profit) that is equivalent to achieving an economic profit (EP) equal to zero.[50] This is impossible to achieve on a year-to-year basis, but a *policy* of achieving an average of an EP equal to zero *over time* is entirely possible.

If the pricing for government agency core outputs is such that the economic profit is negative, then we propose that social contracts be developed between a government agency service provider—the seller—and a government agency charged with the responsibility of acting as buyer on behalf of consumers of the products or services. It is important that the social contracts embedded in the continued provision of products and services at an economic loss be explicitly agreed to by the relevant stakeholders and funding bodies with a transparent set of transactions occurring which will permit the continuous evaluation of the "value for money" being provided to product and service consumers.

The economic decision logic that should be applied is shown in Figure 1.7, where the definition of a core business is one that the government agency is required to engage in and where specific products and/or services are mandated to be provided by legislation.

There are four possible business circumstances for a government enterprise, as shown in Figure 1.7:

I shows the best result, in which core businesses are earning above the cost of capital, like A and B—no problem here!

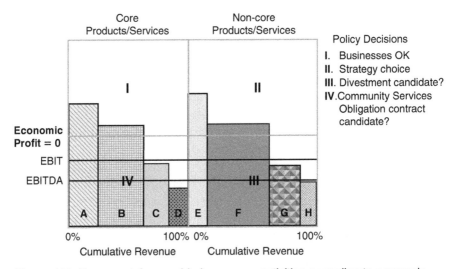

Figure 1.7. Framework for considering agency activities according to economic and financial returns criteria. *(Source: AssetEconomics LLP.)*

II shows businesses earning at or above the cost of capital but where they are not core—there will be a policy decision here, like for E and F (is a government enterprise in the business of business?)—but there is no economic reason not to keep carrying out the activity.

III shows the enterprise carrying out non-core activities that are not earning the cost of capital—clearly these activities, like for G, are divestment candidates (subject to analysis).

IV shows those core activities where the cost of capital is not being met—these activities, like C and D, are clearly community service obligation (CSO) candidates and should be subject to a CSO contract.

A COMMUNITY SERVICE OBLIGATION (CSO) CONTRACT LOGIC ILLUSTRATION: AMTRAK

The need for CSO contracts is based on the need to make the delivery of products and services, that are incapable of being delivered without subsidy, explicit and transparent, particularly for external decision-makers. The other benefit is that cross-subsidization begins to be eliminated. The method for doing this is to enter into a CSO contract with the government agency that is responsible for ensuring that the product or service is provided to the relevant customer classes.

The mechanism is shown in Figure 1.8. In this example we are using the U.S. national rail service provider—Amtrak—as an illustration. Amtrak does not have a CSO contract in place of the kind we are describing but serves to describe the entities that would likely be involved if a CSO contract were to be put into place.

The cash cycle in Figure 1.8 would be that Treasury supplies the Department of Transportation with the budget to provide the products or services in question. The Department of Transportation is then able to engage any product or service provider/s subject to normal supply contract provisions.[51] Often there is only one provider available (government monopoly) but this is not always the case. Where there are alternative provider possibilities, the contract can become a tender. Nonetheless, the Department will then pay the provider for the product/s or service/s provided (the basic transactional exchange). Assuming that the product/s or service/s are provided in accordance with the supply contract provisions, the provider should be "profitable" and dividends can then be paid back to Treasury, completing the cash cycle.

Figure 1.8. Illustrative CSO service delivery and contract cash cycle. *(Source: AssetEconomics LLP.)*

There will be issues of best practice performance remaining but these are different issues and also can be addressed. Presumably in Amtrak's case, an activity based costing (ABC) review can be carried out to establish the starting point for contract costing. This can be juxtaposed against best practice information to establish a price reduction path for the supply contract (for example, 5% reduction per annum in price to be paid for contract services over the contract life). This structure would acknowledge the starting point situation as a reality as well as providing an environment for operating performance improvement.

With the structure provided by Figure 1.8 an economic profit-type financial management framework can be introduced to drive the behaviors that will be needed to achieve the performance that is wanted from Amtrak by its stakeholders.

We have illustrated an approach that takes care of the economic aspects of a government agency's value creation. We are now left with the social dimension, which leaves us with the concomitant problem of output performance measurement. Given that the means to produce this social output is normally highly dependent on intellectual capital and that the output itself frequently contains a substantial part in the form of intellectual capital resources, the importance of developing intellectual capital approaches to management of government agencies becomes obvious.

INTELLECTUAL CAPITAL: A DEFINITION

The term *intellectual capital* has existed for a long time but the concept is not yet in common use throughout the business world. Intellectual capital (IC) can be defined as all nonmonetary and nonphysical resources that are fully or partly controlled by the organization and that contribute to the organization's value creation.

Intellectual capital resources contribute to an organization's potential to commence or continue to create value and are collectively known as intellectual capital or IC. Although there are many different ways of subdividing IC, the one favored by the authors is to divide intellectual capital into three categories based on their economic behavior. These are:

1. **Relational:** These include all relationships that the organization has, such as customers, consumers, intermediaries, representatives, suppliers, partners, owners, lenders, and the like.
2. **Organizational:** The intuitive definition was best articulated by Leif Edvinsson as "all those things that remain in the organization when the employees have left the building but that you cannot find in the balance sheet." This includes resources such as brands, intellectual property, processes, systems, organizational structures, information (on paper or in data bases), and the like.
3. **Human:** All the attributes that relate to individuals as resources for the company and under the requirement that these attributes cannot be replaced by machines or written down on a piece of paper. This includes resources such as competence, attitude, skill, tacit knowledge, personal networks, and the like.

These IC resources all form the basis for potential competitive advantage but few of them make it into any disclosure document in a verifiable form. Brand is sometimes found in the balance sheet but the value assigned to it is in no way correlated to its realizable market value at any given time (more about this in Chapters 4 and 5).

IC resources behave differently from monetary and physical resources and therefore must be managed in a different way. Monetary and physical resources, for example, are both additive in nature; that is, if one uses them, one has less left to use and if one invests in them, one has more left to use. Both follow the law of diminishing marginal returns and both are owned and controlled by the organization in whose balance sheet they appear.

Case 1.1 Radisson SAS Hotels & Resorts: Focusing on the Intellectual Capital Perspective

This case study is derived from a study by Westnes and Westnes[1] and refers to the work of Göran Roos.[2] The hotel chain Radisson SAS Hotels & Resorts decided to evaluate its intellectual capital resources. This project is briefly outlined in this case.

During the study, Radisson SAS Hotels & Resorts, part of Rezidor SAS Hospitality, operated in many countries worldwide. It was a high quality hotel brand where knowledge and intangibles were considered to be the most important assets. Even though Radisson SAS Hotels & Resorts had a strong focus toward the financials of its business, there was a need for a better understanding of managing and measuring its intellectual capital. Therefore, an evaluation of the intellectual capital resources was implemented covering 16 hotels within Radisson SAS Hotels & Resorts in Norway.

The study objective was to determine critical intellectual capital related to overall goals, assess critical intellectual capital at hand, make employee investments more efficient, provide a management tool for handling intellectual capital systematically and effectively, and explore the intellectual capital needed to improve performance and reach business objectives.

The findings at Radisson SAS Hotels & Resorts revealed that there was a strong relationship between human and organizational resources. This is understandable, as even though hotels are primarily seen as knowledge intensive, they are providers of service where both individual knowledge of employees working in the hotels (human resources) and organizational knowledge (organizational resources), expressed in routines, systems, customer databases, and so forth are considered important elements in effectively running hotels. As a result of the process, an organization-specific model for evaluating intellectual capital in a hotel chain was built and a greater understanding of the case organization's value creation path was created. In addition, it seemed that consciously focusing on managing intellectual capital was just as important as the actual success of implementing the process because it created awareness about the importance of intangibles among all employees. This awareness is in itself essential when competing in an economy where knowledge and intangibles are considered the most important assets.

IC resources, on the other hand, have different characteristics to relational, organizational, and human resources are additive in nature—just because one uses them, one does not have less left to use and just because one invests in them, one does not necessarily have more to use.

Relational and organizational resources follow the law of network economics. This means that initial investments tend to exhibit very little return and substantial cumulative investments are needed before returns

reach reasonable levels. After this the marginal return of further investment in these resources will increase until an inflexion point* is reached,
after which further marginal investments generate diminishing marginal
returns. Here we can use the example of fax machines. The first investor
in a fax machine had no use whatsoever out of his investment since
there was nobody to fax to. Subsequently, each new investor in fax
machines generated value for all existing users of fax machines since the
user base increased. Each subsequent investor in fax machines is here
generating more marginal value to the existing users of fax machines
than the preceding investor. This continues until there are so many fax
machines around and in use that it starts to get difficult to get a fax
through. After a given point, each subsequent investor reduces the
increase in value more than the preceding investors in fax machines, and
at the end of the day the final investor adds zero value to existing users
of fax machines. This is an example of network economics, an effect
that can be seen in all relational resources such as customer relationships and all organizational relationships such as brands.

Human resources tend to follow the law of increasing marginal
returns. This can best be illustrated by the statement "The more you
know about something the more you understand how little you know
as compared to what could be known." This also means that in a discourse between two individuals of high but differing levels of knowledge both will learn, but the knowledge distance between them will
have increased.

Relational resources are not owned and controlled by the organization. At best it can influence relationships. The organization does not
own its customer relationships but it can try to influence them.[52] A
relationship is, from each party's point of view, controlled by the other
party. No contract in the world can prevent a party from walking away
from a deal mentally and thereby preventing the success of its intent,
whilst still abiding by the letter of the agreement.

Organizational resources are owned and controlled by the organization. In effect, they are the only IC resources owned and controlled by
the organization. These resources can be traded, albeit often on inefficient markets. Many of these resources are complementary to either relational resources or human resources and are, both in this form as well as

---

*Inflexion point is a mathematical term. It means the point at which the first derivative
reaches infinity. In layman terms, it is the point at which the leaning stops to increase and
starts to decrease.

in their standalone form, an important basis for competitive advantage for most organizations.

Human resources are not owned by anyone but are controlled by the individual. Just because the individual comes to work does not mean that one has access to his/her competence. The gatekeeper between the individual's competence and the organization that wants to make use of that resource is the individual himself or herself.

Monetary and physical resources are rival resources. This means that they cannot simultaneously be used for different purposes. An airplane that is presently flying between Singapore and Sydney cannot at the same time fly between Los Angeles and London. IC resources, on the other hand, are nonrival. This means that they can simultaneously be used for many things. Three simple examples from each of the three types of intellectual capital resources illustrate this point:

- A customer relationship can simultaneously be used to earn money and to build the brand of the supplier (relational).
- A booking system can simultaneously confirm a booking on the Singapore–Sydney and the Los Angeles–London flights (organizational).
- A competent individual can simultaneously think about a business problem and drive a car to the airport to fly to Singapore (human).

Monetary and physical resources have full excludability. In other words, it is legally possible to prevent others from using these resources. IC resources, on the other hand, have only partial excludability, meaning that it is very difficult to legally prevent others from appropriating them and thereby drawing economic benefit from them. A relationship can be usurped, a brand can be emulated, and a patent can be innovated around using the information filed in the original patent. Additionally, all IC resources provide opportunities for free-rider effects.

IC resources, in contrast to monetary and physical resources, have higher than normal levels of information asymmetry. This means that there is uncertainty around these resources, both their volume and their quality, and that there are no really efficient markets for trading these resources.

These differing behavioral characteristics of IC resources give rise to differing economic behavior and thereby to differing value creating logics. A summary of the different characteristics of the three value logics is shown in Table 1.2.

Table 1.2. Value Logics and Their Explanation[53]

	Value Chain	Value Shop	Value Network
Technology	Long-linked technology	Intensive problem-solving technology	Mediating and facilitating technology
Business Problem	Transforming inputs into products	(Re)solving customers problems; mobilizing resources and activities to resolve unique customer problems	Linking customers; enabling direct and indirect exchanges between customers separated by time and/or space
Business Focus	Product or service	Problem solution (change from an existing to a more desired state—human, site, system or knowledge)	Service, service capacity, and service opportunity
Deliverable	Relative cost—customer value is defined either by cost reductions that the product can provide in the customer's activities or the performance improvements that the customer can gain by using the product	Relative benefit—although client problems sometimes involve more or less standardized solutions, the value creation process is organized to deal with unique cases	Relative value—the value of the service is dependent on who else adopts it

Continued

Table 1.2. (Continued)

	Value Chain	Value Shop	Value Network
Resources Leveraged	Firm scope, linkages, capacity to learn, inter-relationships, degree of vertical integration, and physical location/s	Firm reputation (signals value), relative certainty in solution to problem/s, quality of relationships and/or image, ability to recruit, retain, and develop high-quality personnel, strong information asymmetry with the client	Firm platform and process standardization, contract management, intercon-nectedness of structure, service provisioning
Competitive Focus	Scale, capacity utilization	Scope and personnel utilization	Coverage, capacity utilization
Technology	Performs a fixed set of activities that enable it to produce a standard product in large numbers	Performs the selection, combination and ordering of the application of resources and activities according to the requirements of the problem	Performs a simultaneous and layered performance of activities based on standards (standards are critical)
Value Creation Logic	Understood by disaggregating the value creation process of the firm into discrete activities that contribute to the firm's relative cost position and create a basis for differenti-ation; disaggregation must be complete in the sense that it captures all the activities performed by	Understood by recognizing that the flow of activities is not linear but iterative between activities and cyclical across the activity set resulting in a high degree of both sequential and reciprocal interdepen-dence between activities often involving multiple disciplines and specialties in spiraling activity sets (where each cycle implements the solutions that are the outcomes of the	Understood by recognizing that a concurrent and layered set of activities is required to service efficiently a random need for mediation services between a large number of customers

Medium for Transferring Value	■ Inbound logistics ■ Operations ■ Outbound logistics ■ Sales and marketing ■ Service ■ Control and evaluation	■ Problem finding and acquisition ■ Problem solving ■ Choice of problem solution ■ Execution	■ Network promotion and contract management ■ Service provisioning ■ Network infrastructure operation
Common Value Creation Focus	■ Procurement ■ Technology development ■ Human resource management ■ Corporate services (planning, finance, accounting, legal affairs, government affairs, TQM)	■ Human resource management	■ Network infrastructure development ■ Service development ■ Procurement ■ Contract management ■ Human resource management
Business Logic "Method"	Coordination of sequential activities	Co-performance of cyclical, spiraling and reciprocal activities	Synchronization of simultaneous, parallel activities
Role of Marketing	Two purposes—(i) develop and refine the value chain by providing product specifications and volume estimates, (ii) stimulate required level of demand for the chain's output to ensure stable operation and capacity utilization	Two purposes—(i) build the reputation of the firm's professionals (often the critical marketing resource), (ii) manage relationships for referrals from customers and colleagues	Two purposes—(i) grow the size and pervasiveness of the communities on either side of the mediation, (ii) encourage exchanges

Continued

Table 1.2. *(Continued)*

	Value Chain	Value Shop	Value Network
Industry Examples of Value Logics	Manufacturing and retail firms	Professional service firms (management consultant, legal, architectural, consulting engineering), health, resource exploration, property development and design firms	Airline, parcel delivery, insurance, retail bank, telecom operarors, Internet auction and many pure e-commerce firms
Companies Illustrating Value Logics	GM, Wal-Mart, Dell, Anheuser-Busch, Sun Microsystems, Sony, ConAgra Foods, Nokia, Starbucks, Best Buy, Bausch & Lomb, McDonald's (ex USA)	IDEO, McKinsey, Amgen, DreamWorks, PeopleSoft, CIENA, Apple Computer, Walt Disney, Paychex, Pixar	eBay, Orbitz, FedEx, Southwest Airlines, Verizon Wireless, Bank of New York, New York Times, AXA, Microsoft, Visa International, Yahoo!, Amazon, Avon, McDonald's (USA)

Source: AssetEconomics, Inc.
Our explanation in Table 1.2 has found a complementing interpretation in Table 1.4.

What can immediately be seen from this table is that the three value logics are compellingly different. It will also be obvious that many larger companies either (1) have a number of value logics that are being pursued (often through different businesses, business units or divisions), or (2) have moved away from a pure form (often as they have grown) and morphed toward an alternative form. This consequence of growth is most commonly observable as value shops become value chains. This means, of course, that we can position companies and/or their principal operating entities (businesses, business units or divisions) in a "fractal" space. We show this in Figure 1.9.

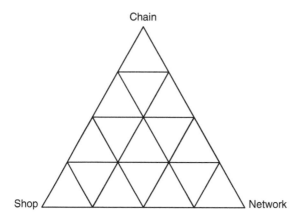

Figure 1.9. Fractal triangle representation of value chain, value shop and value network logics.

A fractal triangle helps us apply our value logic thinking to corporations. Typically, a position away from the extreme or "pure breed" points will be seen to require some form of balancing act: a series of compromises between competing interests played out in the company's structure and process designs. The key insight offered by the fractal triangle turns this notion on its head; intelligent organizational design, rather than balancing chain and/or shop and/or network value logics can employ their dynamic interplay to create business opportunities and maximize value in any of the value logics being applied. As we move around the fractal, the key design question is how to design so that value can be generated within and for each value logic. Managing internal coordination and transaction benefits and costs is the primary approach (more on this later).

At this juncture, if we look at three extreme organizations that are "pure breed" value chains, value shops, and value networks we would see the following attributes (most large organizations are a mix of pure value creating logics).

For value chains—a world dominated by monetary and physical resources—characteristics that will be evident will include:

1. Secrecy being paramount (since a small advantage will be rapidly caught up by competition)
2. Size mattering, and a push for monopoly inherent in the activities of the organization (since it is a world dominated by economies of scale)
3. Standardization, leading to a push attitude toward customers (since it is a world dominated by economies arising from experience and learning, requiring repetition and thereby standardization)
4. Relative certainty about short-term future value that can be realized from these resources.
5. Relative ease with which market prices are established for these resources.

For value shops—a world dominated by human resources—characteristics that will be evident include:

1. Openness, dialogue, and discourse being paramount (since a small advantage rapidly grows into a large advantage. If you have just developed new knowledge, you will invite your competitors to a discourse around this new knowledge, its foundations, and its consequences. This can clearly be seen in the academic world and in the behavior of people involved in research and development activities).
2. Larger size not necessarily being better and market share not necessarily being relevant, both rather being seen as irrelevant or being rapidly overturned (since it is a world dominated by economies of scope).
3. Standardization being counter productive, indeed there being a drive to solve the same problem differently the second time around to maximize learning, leading to a pull attitude toward customers (since it is a world dominated by economies of scope).
4. Relative uncertainty about short-term future value that can be realized from these resources.
5. Relative difficulty, perhaps impossibility, in establishing universal and verifiable market prices for these resources.

For value networks—a world dominated by relational and organizational resources—characteristics that will be evident include:

1. Cooperative efforts such as agreeing on standards and joint marketing having appeal (since in the early phase of building a resource, cumulative investments will have small returns). Once the marginal return on investment passes a certain level and continues to increase, a sharing of insights will become common (e.g., the exchange of internal benchmarking data). Once the resource enters into the area of decreasing marginal returns, organizational behavior will take on the characteristics of value chains, and operate much more as though in the world dominated by monetary and physical resources.
2. Size matters, but here the optimal market share is not 100% but rather around 40% in a world of many competitors, at which point maximum marginal return is to be expected since it is a world dominated by network economics.
3. Management of the different phases being paramount, leading to challenges around the phase changes since it is a world dominated by network economics.
4. Relative uncertainty about short term future value that can be realized from these resources.
5. Relative difficulty, not to say impossibility, in establishing universal and verifiable market prices for these resources.

These intellectual capital resource characteristics are summarized in Table 1.3.

IC and intangibles: The same or different?

There is a further distinction worth noting: that between intellectual capital resources and intangibles. The accounting discipline's debate about intangibles in the United States has long been about the definition of an asset for the purpose of recognizing the value on the balance sheet. Although important, this objective is not fundamental for managerial purposes. What is fundamental is management's need to identify, quantify, and measure the causal impact of IC resources and to manage these to create an optimal value outcome.

Why draw a distinction between intangibles and intellectual capital resources? The answer is that they are not necessarily the same thing, although many use the terms *IC* and *intangibles* interchangeably. We argue that whether a resource is tangible or intangible represents a debate about the recognizability of the resource while an argument about whether a resource is a traditional economic resource (monetary

Table 1.3. The Characteristics of the Five Resource Groups

	Monetary Resources	Physical Resources	Relational Resources	Organizational Resources	Human Resources
Description	Financial resources that take the form of cash or assets (such as marketable securities) that can easily be converted to pure cash.	Normally what would be found under the heading of plant and equipment on the balance sheet but also assets that have physical characteristics (e.g., any form of physical inventory or for a beer bottle: the paper that the label is printed on, the metal cap, the glass bottle itself as well as the physical liquid that fills it).	Any and all stakeholders that influence the operations of the organization be they customers, suppliers, donors or local government and pressure groups or the like.	Resources that the organization has developed or procured and that the organization legally owns that are not physical in nature, e.g., brands, image, reputation, IP, processes, routines, systems, structures and information in data bases or on paper.	Resources that are unique to the human being such as tacit knowledge, creativity, decisiveness, ability, attitude, motivation, etc.

Owned and Controlled by	The organization	The organization	The other party (from both parties point of view)	The organization	The individual
Economic Behavior	Decreasing marginal returns	Decreasing marginal returns	Network economics	Network economics	Increasing marginal returns
Additive	Yes	Yes	No	No	No
Information Asymmetry	Low	Low	High	High	High
Rivalry Resource	Yes	Yes	No	No	No
Excludability	Yes	Yes	No	Partial	No

or physical) or an intellectual capital resource (relational, organizational or human) represents a debate about the form and ultimately the economic behavior of the resource. This is not a semantic distinction. What we are proposing is that there is a broad class of resources that have not been properly acknowledged in management's lexicon: intellectual capital resources. This class of resources needs to be equally recognized alongside traditional economic resources. Not to do so opens up many companies to an erroneous view that somehow intellectual capital resources are inferior. Of course, the inequality of these resources makes it hard to argue for investing in them, hard to develop coherent strategies (Table 1.4 outlines some of the traditional strategies) around them, and makes them vulnerable to more ad hoc management attention and/or performance review (since there is no "logical" basis for evaluating their contribution to shareholder value outcomes).

Table 1.5 separates out the idea of resource form from accounting recognizability. From this, the argument that intangibles and intellectual capital resources are not the same thing is self-evident. There are plenty of intellectual capital resources that have a tangible expression. Likewise, there are plenty of traditional economic resources that have intangible expressions. Common sense and experience tell us that institutional investor (buy-side) and investment bank (sell-side) analysts take many nontraditional intangible resource considerations into account in their valuations (conditioning valuation models), analysts' reports, and recommendations.

Why is this classification important? Table 1.5 separates management of resource form from accounting recognizability. These are different classification dimensions. The recognition of the three intellectual capital resource forms (relational, organizational, and human) acknowledges that each of these resource forms represents different ownership, behavioral, and control phenomena (as discussed in the preceding section). Unlike the two traditional economic resource forms (monetary and physical), the three intellectual capital resource forms have nonlinear returns to scale, do not exhibit diminishing return behaviors, and are not necessarily owned or controlled by the firm. A traditional economic and accounting-based asset classification potentially captures only a small aspect of the resources a firm has available and is leveraging. From these insights, it will be clear that the management skills required to manage intellectual capital resources are fundamentally different from skills conventionally required (and taught in many business schools). We argue that for many companies, a new managerial dawn has arrived.

Table 1.4. Summary of the traditional Porterian type corporate strategies[54]

Name	Outpacing	Differentiation	Cost Leadership	Rest in Peace
Main Strategic Elements	Superior understanding of what drives value in the mind of customers and superior ability to deliver on these drivers. Superior ability to operate with low costs.	Superior understanding of what drives value in the mind of customers. Concentrate on branded goods and brand advertising, design, service and quality. Alternatively concentration on innovation, functionality and first mover advantage.	Superior ability to operate with low costs. Investment in volume production; product design that simplifies production [standardization]; tight cost control in for example R&D.	Low or no understanding of what drives value in the mind of customers and/or no or inferior ability to deliver on these drivers. High operating costs and no or low ability to reduce operating costs.

Continued

Table 1.4. (Continued)

Name	Outpacing	Differentiation	Cost Leadership	Rest in Peace
Resource Needs and Organizational Needs	Same as differentiation + Same as cost leadership + Organizational and human resource flexibility.	Marketing competence, product design competence; creativity; basic research competence; incentive systems based on objective targets instead of quantitative; strong cross-functional co-ordination. Fast mover.	Access to capital; process technology competence; fast reporting; tight cost control; structured organization and structured responsibilities; incentive system based on quantitative objectives.	None
Principle	Perceived value is higher than price and price does not relate to cost.	Perceived value is higher than price and price may or may not relate to cost.	Price is lower than perceived value and price relates to cost.	Perceived value is lower than price and price relates to cost or cost and thereby price is higher than perceived value.
Reject/Accept Question for Changes	Does it increase the perceived value in the eyes of our customers at the same time as it reduces costs?	Does it increase the perceived value in the eyes of our customers more than it impacts cost?	Does it reduce our costs more than it reduces perceived value in the eyes of our customers?	None

Table 1.5. Complete Resource Classification System[55]

Resource Form

	(Traditional) Economic Resources		Intellectual Capital Resources		
	Monetary	Physical	Relational	Organizational	Human
Tangible					
Intangible					

Resource Recognizability (left axis label)

Although the world does not need a new classification system, there are benefits from using this conceptualization. These are (1) that any resource can be allocated according to its form and accounting recognizability, and (2) that functional management will have resources that represent more than one form. The latter is shown in Table 1.6 for human resources. Here we see that human capital resources are predominately intangible. We also see another phenomenon: the codification of a human capital resource results in it becoming an organizational tangible resource. Further, we see that the management of human resources as a function traverses a number of resource forms. Although we do not explore this in this book, at the functional level there are substantial implications for the management and measurement of performance.

Table 1.6. Resource Classification for a Company Highlighting Human Capital Resources at a Higher Level of Detail

	Monetary	Physical	Relational	Organizational	Human
Tangible	✓ Cash ✓ Investments ✓ Receivables ✓ Payables ✓ Compensation and benefits incl. long term incentive schemes (incl. option schemes)	✓ Property, plant & equipment ✓ Inventories (raw materials, WIP, finished goods) ✓ Standard assets ✓ Physical work environment		✓ Documented systems ✓ Documented processes ✓ Patents ✓ Brands ✓ Mastheads ✓ Access rights ✓ Management contracts ✓ Employee contracts ✓ Employee development & training programs ✓ Performance management systems ✓ Customer lists ✓ Customer contracts ✓ Supplier contracts ✓ Formal alliances	✓ Leadership ✓ Problem solving ability ✓ Work environment (interaction) ✓ Recruitment & selection ✓ Career paths ✓ Rewards and recognition ✓ Employee satisfaction ✓ Employee retention ✓ Employee relations ✓ Knowledge (incl. tacit) ✓ Functional skills ✓ Experience
Intangible	✓ Credit ratings ✓ Accruals ✓ Balance sheet strength ✓ Cash flow volatility	✓ Plant location	✓ Stakeholder support ✓ Preferred status ✓ Organizational reputation ✓ Rights to tender, to design, to participate ✓ Networks ✓ Regulatory imposts	✓ Organizational structure ✓ Culture	

The recognition of these managerial realities is fundamental since the ability to manage IC resources comprehensively and consistently (in the context of a prevailing business model and intended strategy) is key to delivering shareholder value for many of the largest and most important firms and organizations driving both the U.S. and other economies today. Managing all relevant resources in an integrated way is the basis for achieving competitive advantage in organizations with high dependency on IC resources. Managing by instinct can no longer be acceptable since economies will increasingly be made up of companies representing business models that primarily leverage intellectual capital resources.

LINKING STRATEGY AND RESOURCES

Our discussion on linking strategy and resources will be somewhat theoretical but is included since it introduces a set of useful and grounded concepts around causalities that are drawn upon later in this book.

Corporate strategy has many definitions, but the one that is favored by the authors is as follows[56]:

The pattern of decision-making in a company that determines and reveals its objectives, purposes, or goals, produces the principal policies and plans for achieving those goals, it defines the range of business the company is to pursue, the kind of economic and human organization it is or intends to be, and the nature of the economic and non-economic contribution it intends to make to its shareholders, employees, customers, and communities.

There have been major changes since the 1980s in the way strategy is approached. Many of these changes have reflected an increased importance placed on understanding the role of IC resources as a basis for competitive advantage.

The basic axioms of strategy that we accept are as follows:[57]

- Firms are rent-seekers. This is to say that firms strive to achieve a return above and beyond the level required by the market for an investment of similar level of risk. This is equally true of organizations that generate nonmonetary value, but for these firms it means generating more value per unit of commitment than is required by stakeholders to maintain their commitment to the organization.

- Strategy is a deliberate set of actions taken to create rents. In other words, it is heavily reliant on human creativity and is highly context specific. This means that there are no simple recipes to follow that always provide a good result.
- Rent creation involves obtaining a strategic fit between the organization and its environment. This means that it is easier to sell something to people that they want rather than to try to sell them something that they do not want.
- The degree of fit changes over time due to competitive and other (exogenous) influences. This means that just because one has achieved a good fit at a point in time, this does not automatically mean that one will achieve a good fit at a later point in time. Crafting strategy is a constantly ongoing process.

There are basically two schools of strategy that have relevance for us. The first is the competitive forces paradigm, represented by Michael Porter and expressed in his seminal contributions to the strategy field. The competitive forces paradigm argues that it is possible to increase industry profitability by purposefully engaging with one's industry structure. The basic strategic decisions here are entry/exit decisions and decisions that change the firm's ability to modify the industry structure. As is well known, Porter has defined industry profitability as the interaction of five forces: buyers, substitutes, suppliers, entrants, and existing competition*. The stronger these forces, the lower industry profitability. This model has empirical support in several studies[58,59,60,61] that have shown the existence of sustained profitability differences between industries. This view is then further strengthened by the strategic groups construct[62,63,64,65,66] which argues that the reason firms in the same industry have different profitability is a set of forces known as mobility barriers that prevent some firms from imitating the strategy of the most successful firms in the industry. The logical extension of this reasoning is that the smallest level of granularity is the group of a single firm and only this level of granularity will explain why intra-industry profits vary three to five times as much as inter-industry profits.[67,68,69]

The problem is the high number of forces that must be identified to create the barriers necessary to explain these profitability variances.

---

*The need for a sixth force has arisen in industries with heavy dependence on complementary services and products. This sixth force is known as "complementors" and can be illustrated by the way the VHS video standard won the market battle aganist Betamax by ensuring a better availability of films in VHS format [the complementor component] from third parties and thereby ensuring a higher desirability of the main product.

Erecting a barrier to entry allows for the extraction of monopoly rents (monopoly rents arise when supply is artificially constrained to levels below demand by one player and supply cannot be immediately expanded by other players). As a consequence, the competitive forces paradigm is about creating monopoly rents. Monopoly rents require the presence of resources that can form the basis of comparative advantage. Such resources are, for example, regulatory protection, resource monopoly, and the like.

The second school is the resource based view of the firm. The resource based view argues that the difference in profitability between firms is grounded in differences in their resource portfolios. If one firm holds a valuable resource that other firms lack, then this firm can achieve higher profitability. Resources are defined as inputs[70] into the firm's operations rather than products and services. Examples of resources include IP, plant and equipment, capabilities of different kinds, and competent people. These resources must, at the end of the day, be embedded in the end products or services that create value for the customers.[71,72] In this school it is imperative that the benefits of being able to apply resources to a wide range of products, services, and activities are realized.[73,74] When this is done, strategic value is delivered to customers. The strategic value delivered to customers is a mix of four distinct value dimensions:[75]

1. Reduced costs (defined as all the things the customers have to give up in return for what they get; for example, time, money, existing relationships, and the like).
2. High fit functionality (defined as all those attributes linked to the deliverable that can be objectively measured; for example, color, weight, speed, and the like).
3. High distinctness (defined as all those things that build mindshare as a precursor to market share; for example, brand, reputation, image, and the like).
4. Mental proximity (defined as all those things that contribute toward lowering the barriers to building person-to-person trust; for example, shared language, shared values, shared looks, and the like).

The more rare a resource is, the greater its probability of creating scarcity rents. Scarcity rents arise when demand exceeds supply and supply cannot be rapidly expanded. As a consequence, the resource based paradigm is about creating scarcity rent. Durability (i.e., the extent to which the benefits that the strategic asset provides do not decline over time) inimitability (i.e., the extent to which the strategic asset can be copied by others) and unsubstitutability (i.e., the difficulty in substituting one asset for another) of a strategic asset are important attributes in determining the sustainability of a scarcity rent producing period.[76]

The most important strategic assets tend to be intangible.[77,78,79,80,81] Identification and management issues of these intangibles have not been satisfactorily addressed in traditional strategy literature. The view that competitive advantage of firms in today's economy does not result from market position, but from difficult to replicate knowledge based assets and the manner in which they are developed[82] and deployed arguably represents the current dominant view. This has led to the development of another concept in strategic management—that of dynamic capability, which is the ability to achieve new forms of competitive advantage by appropriately adapting, integrating, and reconfiguring organizational skills, resources, and competencies to match the requirements of a changing environment.[83] Another contribution to this field argues that the development or evolution of organizational resources and competencies is path-dependent—that is, is influenced by past decisions and actions and that organizational routines (i.e., all regular and predictable patterns of behavior in firms) could be viewed as inherited competencies of firms.[84] Intellectual capital management emerges as a synthesis of these insights in strategy.

Before we define the concept of intellectual capital management however, it is worthwhile understanding the insights that have generated this definition. Value generation is a function of the way resources are managed. In the 1980s the concept of invisible assets was introduced and defined as information based assets, which included technology, consumer trust, brand image, corporate culture, and management skills. In conjunction with this definition, these assets were identified as the most important resources for long-term success because only invisible assets can be used simultaneously in several areas.[85] In the late 1980s assets and skills were identified as the basis of competition[86] and at the same time the concepts of intellectual assets and later intangible assets were introduced as critical value drivers. Intangible assets were defined as those assets that have as their essence an idea or knowledge, the nature of which can be defined and recorded in some way.[87] These intangible assets were split into intellectual property (those assets for which the organization has property rights) and knowledge assets (those assets for which the organization does not have property rights). Intangible assets were argued to drive capability differentials, which in turn drove sustainable competitive advantage, which is why organizations needed to bring intangible resources and core competences into their strategic thinking.[88]

In his 1991 *Fortune* article, Tom Stewart wrote:[89] "Every company depends increasingly on knowledge—patents, processes, management skills, technologies, information about customers and suppliers, and old-fashioned experience." He continues: "Added together, this knowledge is intellectual capital." Stewart defined intellectual capital as the sum of everything everybody in the company knows that gives the company a competitive edge in the marketplace. Simultaneously, it was put forward that the majority of economic and production power of an organization lies in its intellectual capability.[90] The classification of intangible resources was subsequently split into assets and skills: assets included trademarks, patents, copyrights, registered designs, contracts, trade secrets, reputations, and networks (personal and commercial relationships); whereas skills comprised know-how or culture.[91] In a survey of 95 firms reported in 1992, company reputation, product reputation, and employee know-how were identified as the most important contributors for overall success.[92]

Following these articles, various authors have defined taxonomies for intellectual capital.[93,94,95,96,97,98] Although many authors agree on the significance of intellectual capital as a resource underpinning organizational performance, there is considerable lack of consensus on the definition of intellectual capital.[99] Based on an extensive literature review of intellectual capital taxonomy,[100] we have put forward the taxonomy used in the early parts of this chapter. This taxonomy was first introduced in 1997[101] and has been adapted by many other authors. We ourselves have extended this taxonomy, with our recommended change[102] to use the term *resource* rather than *capital*, to avoid confusion with accounting language and definitions. The aim of this classification is to facilitate the identification of resources in firms and to provide a language to discuss the topic of resource management. Resources, as stated earlier in this chapter, are classified as traditional economic resources (divided into monetary and physical resources) and intellectual capital resources (divided into human, relational, and organizational resources.)

The taxonomy of organizational resources we propose provides a static picture of resource architecture. Having access to these resources is a necessary but not sufficient requirement for value creation. In order to create value these resources need to be deployed, to be put into a structure where one type of resource is transformed into another type of resource. The decisions made to deploy these resources in a meaningful structure and the management of the ongoing value creation that takes place in such a deployment structure, including and integrated with traditional economic resources, is what we mean by intellectual capital management.

However, we strongly emphasize that from a strategy perspective it is more important that organizations identify all their context-specific value drivers, including but not limited to a consideration of resources (the other aspects are activities and deployment or allocation decisions), disregarding differences in language or taxonomy.

It is now finally time for our definition of intellectual capital management (ICM):

Intellectual capital management is the deployment and management of intellectual capital resources and their transformations (into other intellectual capital resources or into traditional economic resources) to maximize the present value of the organization's value creation in the eyes of its stakeholders.

Many studies show the importance of these types of transformation systems. Intellectual capital resources such as employee skills and customer relationships often deliver the attributes of customer satisfaction and loyalty, which in turn deliver shareholder value.[103,104] It is essential that managers have the tools at their disposal that allow them better control of the effectiveness of the resource deployment structure as well as the tools at their disposal for managing the efficiency of the resulting value generation.

According to the resource based paradigm, resources exist as a bundle and these resource bundles affect performance with causal ambiguity.[105] It is therefore difficult to identify how individual resources contribute to success without taking into account the interdependencies with other resources.[106,107] For example, the latest technology is worth little without the right knowledge and competencies to use it. In turn, all the latest understanding and knowledge of how to operate technology is worthless if users do not have access to the technology.[108] A balance-sheet approach to intellectual capital is inherently a snapshot in time and does not provide information on the transformation from one resource category into another.[109] It has also been pointed out that intangibles are frequently embedded in tangibles and in labor, leading to considerable interaction between resources in the creation of value.[110] These arguments all underpin the need for tools that assist managers in better understanding how their resources interact to create value and a competitive advantage. Tools are needed that capture the complex interactions of resources both on the level of influencing value creation and on the level of tracking actual transformations while fulfilling the measurement requirements of completeness, independence, distinctness, agreeability, and scaling (more about this in Chapter 4). This last is something that existing management tools do not do; none of the tools such as the balanced scorecard, strategy maps, and success maps fulfill these requirements. These tools can still be useful, but they have built-in weaknesses which mean that their predictive power is very low. This is true for most tools that exist in the marketplace today.[111,112,113]

VALUE-CREATING LOGICS

The economic behavior of firms is a function of the economic behavior of the resources they deploy. If a firm deploys only resources with the same economic behavior, the economic behavior of the firm will be clearly observable and clearly recognizable. Since there are three types of economic behavior—decreasing marginal returns, increasing marginal returns, and network economic marginal return—we would expect to be able to observe three types of economic behavior of firms. This behavior is described as value-creating logic. We will here look more closely at the three value-creating logics (called value chain, value shop and value network) we have identified previously.

The value chain

In Porter's[114] conventional value chain, the product or service output tends to embody everything that brings value to the customer.

The activities executed in a value chain logic are sequential and linear; the overall process has a clear beginning and a clear end. This type of value creation relies on standardized processes and repetition (economies of learning) and mass production (economies of scale). This means that the resources that form the basis for competitive advantage in these types of organizations will at some stage show diminishing marginal returns. Human resources can never be a basis for a competitive advantage in these types of organizations. This logic has an inherent drive toward efficiency (this does not mean that it is efficient, it just means that efficiency is what occupies management's focus of attention) and as a consequence there is great focus on trying to reduce transaction costs (which are associated with efficiency). Classically, manufacturing plants tend to fall into this category. When these organizations fail, they do so not because they become inefficient, but because they become ineffective (i.e., they produce very cheaply something that nobody wants). The organization will

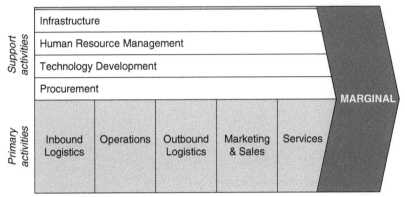

Figure 1.10. The value chain logic.

often perceive the symptoms of ineffectiveness (such as sales volumes and margin pressures) as symptomatic of inefficiency and will address the ineffectiveness problem with an efficiency solution (such as cost cutting), thereby exacerbating the original problem. It does not take many turns for this vicious circle to become terminal.

Another interesting characteristic relating to this logic is that all subunits in larger organizations should also follow this logic to optimize overall efficiency. An example of the chain organization is any manufacturing sub-supplier to the automotive industry.

The value shop

In a value shop, the main focus is on solving a previously unsolved problem for the client. In contrast to the value chain, the value in a value shop logic resides not only in the solution itself—the output—but also in the individuals who came up with the solution and the way they reached it.

The activities executed in this logic are sequential and circular; the overall process does not necessarily have a clear beginning and end. This type of value creation relies on the ability to continuously reconfigure a given resource portfolio to address completely new problems: economies of scope. This means that the resources that form the basis for competitive advantage in these types of organizations must at some stage show increasing marginal returns and, as a consequence, monetary or physical resources can never be the basis for a competitive advantage

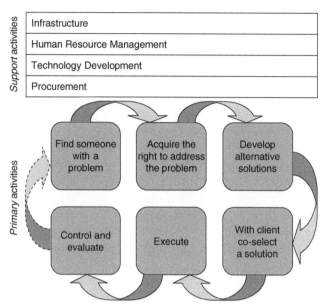

Figure 1.11. The value shop logic.[115]

in value shop organizations. This logic has an inherent drive toward effectiveness (this does not mean that it is effective, it just means that effectiveness is what occupies it) and as a consequence there is great focus on trying to reduce coordination costs (which are associated with effectiveness). A classical research facility is an example of this logic. Most of these organizations, when they fail, do so not because they become ineffective but because they become inefficient (i.e., they solve an important problem so expensively that nobody can afford to pay for the solution) and the organization perceives the symptoms of inefficiency (such as a lack of new client engagements) as symptomatic of ineffectiveness, and therefore addresses the inefficiency problem with an effectiveness solution (such as an increased sophistication in the solutions identification process), thereby exacerbating the original problem. Again, it does not take many turns for this vicious circle to become terminal. As an analogue to the value chain, to optimize overall effectiveness in larger organizations that follow this logic, all subunits should also follow this logic.

The value network

In a value network the basis for value creation lies in connecting people or organizations who wish to be temporarily interdependent while remaining independent. The actual enabling of this connection constitutes the basis for value creation.

The activities executed in a network organization are parallel and nonlinear; the overall process does not have a clear beginning or end, and connections between different activities are almost random. This type of value creation relies on balancing network economic resources at the point of maximum marginal return. This means that the resources that form the basis for competitive advantage in these types of organizations must show network economic behavior; as a consequence, only relational and organizational resources can form the basis for competitive advantage. The inherent drive for this logic is neither toward efficiency nor toward effectiveness. This means that network organizations have a higher propensity than the other two logics of doing the wrong thing badly.

Another interesting characteristic relating to this logic is that, to optimize overall effectiveness and efficiency, the subunits in larger organizations have to follow the logic that best achieves this objective; they can be either value chains or value shops. An example of the network organization is eBay, the globally dominant Internet auction company.

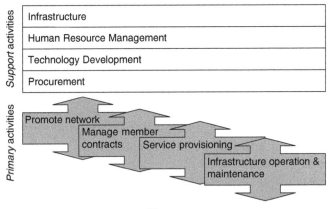

Figure 1.12. The value network logic.[116]

Summary on value logics

Firms are not genetically predisposed to any one of the three value logics we have described. However, firms make choices that cause them to represent and be reliant on one or more of these logics. A bank may serve as a good example to illustrate this, because banks can and do represent each of the three value logics.

A bank can be a value chain when it converts inputs to outputs, in which case the focus will be on efficiency (transaction costs minimization through economies of scale and standardization). In this case, it will look upon itself as a factory that processes loans, applications, or something similar. A bank can also be a value shop in which it views itself as a financial services operator or a financial advisor that also has the ability to provide money. It would identify the problems of a client, address them, and select a solution together with the client and help to implement it. It would have highly qualified staff and stringent quality controls. As part of its offering, it could (and often wants to) supply clients with some debt and/or equity capital in the form of investment. The focus here would be on economies of scope. Finally, the bank can be a value network, in which case the bank would act solely as a conduit between people who do not have money and people who do. The bank would then arrange for the flow of cash between them. Table 1.7 summarizes the resources that can form the basis for a competitive advantage in the different value creating logics.

For each of the activities in the different logics, there is a requirement that the transformation activity is done well. Transforming resources well is the ability to transform different types of intellectual capital resources effectively and efficiently. For example, for a consulting firm applying the value shop logic, it boils down to transforming the knowledge that resides in the individual into effective, useful solutions for the client. Having the knowledge within the organization is not enough. There is a crucial distinction between having a resource—be it competencies, processes, systems, intellectual property, relationships, machines, or cash—and putting it to value-creating use, which is the ability to transform one resource into another.

THE INTELLECTUAL CAPITAL MANAGEMENT PROCESS

The purpose of the intellectual capital management process (ICMP) is to increase the value creation of the organization. This process becomes

Table 1.7. Possible Resources as a Basis for Competitive Advantage in the Different Value-Creating Logics

Resource Type	Value Chains	Value Shops	Value Networks
Monetary	Normal		
Physical	Normal		
Relational	Possible but requires sophisticated management approach	Possible but requires sophisticated management approach	Normal
Organizational	Possible but requires sophisticated management approach	Possible but requires sophisticated management approach	Normal
Human		Normal	

more appropriate as the organization's dependence on intellectual capital resources increases. To achieve this objective, the ICMP identifies relevant dimensions that can be used to discuss the organization's strategy. One of the first requirements is to identify what value creation means for the organization and who are the primary stakeholders for the value created. This is followed by an identification of which resources are required to create value today and which resources are required to achieve the desired future position of the organization. Once the desired resources are identified, existing and future deployment structures for resources are identified. This deployment structure is then evaluated for possible effectiveness improvements. The resources that form the basis of the organization's competitive advantage are then evaluated against the value-creating logic of the organization for possible effectiveness issues.

Once an effective deployment structure has been identified that fits with the organization's overarching strategic objective, the focus moves to efficiency issues. This requires the identification of a performance measurement system that can consolidate the different transformations into performance measures on different levels of integration, to operate as an early warning system for future changes in the organization's ability to generate value. Through the ICMP, management will get a better understanding of both the potential for value creation and how well actual value is created. In addition, the ICMP provides the necessary tools for following up the organization's value creation, including identification of issues (for example, coordination cost issues versus transaction cost issues). The ICMP also provides tools for valuation of the organization or any subpart thereof.

By using the IC perspective, the value creation path in the organization can be determined. An example of Company A and Company B will illustrate the point.[117] Both companies are consulting firms. Company A is made up of very bright people with a minimal set of physical resources (such as computers) and some working capital to keep the business going. They need numerous personal relationships with customers and other people, and they need to have an enormous amount of competence as individuals. There is no structure and there are no processes in this company. Every time they do something they tend to reinvent the wheel. They make money from two transformations: (1) by converting their time to cash, which is based on their competence, meaning that they can charge considerable amounts for their time, and (2) since they have very strong personal relationships, they have opportunity revenue in the form of higher prices due to lack of competition and/or lower selling (search) costs. That is, the relationship's contribution to the charging level is the second transformation.

Company B has a different approach and provides packaged solutions. They have some averagely skilled people whom they can leverage through excellent structure and processes and thereby produce high quality deliverables. Their processes, systems, brands, and intellectual property allow them to use average people to provide good solutions. For Company B, relationships between itself and client organizations are based on the Company B brand rather than individual relationships. They charge a certain amount for man-hours, although they cannot charge at very high rates for average people. Instead, they make their money by supplying a packaged solution. Hence, there are three contributing transformations to cash flow: (1) a small amount from man-hour sales, (2) significant amounts from sales of standardized solutions, and (3) some opportunity revenue amount from the organizational relationship (brand) that they have with the client organization.

Looking at these two firms from a financial perspective, they may appear exactly the same. They can have the same turnover, gross margin, and balance sheet. Even if one extends this to asking clients about how satisfied they are, the companies may appear very similar, with the same customer satisfaction and retention ratio levels. However, when examining the intellectual capital resources of the two firms—looking at the type of competencies, processes, structure, systems, brands and IP resources they have and how these are used—the difference between the two companies will be quite apparent. In conclusion, the only way to discover the difference between these two firms is to analyze the approaches by which each actually creates value, and by taking the intellectual capital perspective.

In illustrating the value creation of these firms graphically, the deployment of resources can be shown in an intellectual capital navigator.[118] Here, the key resources are represented by circles, the size of the circle reflecting the influence the resource has on value creation-the larger the circle the greater the influence. The transformation of one type of resource to another is represented by the connecting arrows, the thickness of which represents the influence of the transformation on the value creation of the organization. In the two diagrams in Figure 1.13, the difference between Company A and Company B is immediately obvious. The reliance of Company A is reflected in the size of the human resources circle (reflected in attitude, competence, and intellectual agility) and the resulting transformations. In contrast, Company B relies more on written processes, part of organizational capital. This is because they have chosen different value creation logics for their activities.

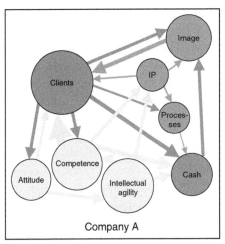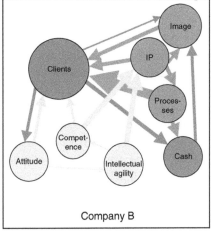

Figure 1.13. The value creation paths of two advisory firms (modified).

The preceding example with the two advisory firms shows how differently seemingly similar companies within an industry can operate. Indeed, the financial statements of the companies can seem remarkably similar, especially if standard financial ratios are used as a basis for performance comparison.

An overview of the ICMP

We will here briefly present the steps that are part of the ICMP. Chapters 2 to 4 will cover these steps in more details. The steps in the ICMP are as follows:

1. **Analyze the strategy of the organization and present and future desired strategic positions.** Define the strategic intent of the organization. What type of value is to be created? What right of existence does the organization have? Who are the stakeholders of the organization and what is their relative importance? It is essential that the answers to these questions are clear and unambiguous.
2. **Construct a resource distinction tree for the organization.** Identify the resources the organization has at its disposal and break them down to a suitable level of precision. Use this listing to build a resource distinction tree (see Chapter 2). Evaluate the quality and quantity of the resources and their relative importance for the organization's value-creating potential given the organization's strategic intent.
3. **Decide how the resources are to be deployed to achieve the organization's desired position.** Identify and map which transformations originate and end in each of the resources identified at the lowest level in the resource distinction tree. The end result will be an intellectual capital navigator (see Chapter 3).
4. **Analyze and evaluate the effectiveness of the intellectual capital navigator.** Execute an analysis to identify value sinks and value sources among the resources in the suggested deployment structure and as a consequence identify how the intellectual capital navigator can be improved to achieve higher effectiveness. Also ensure that the intellectual capital navigator is aligned with at least one identified value-creating logic of the organization and its identified improvement opportunities. If need be, identify coordination cost drivers in the suggested deployment structure (see Chapter 3 for more on this).
5. **Create a performance management tool for tracking the efficiency with which value is created in the organization.** There are two principal ways

forward here. The first is the creation of a performance management system for internal use; this is known as the IC-index. The second is the creation of a performance valuation system for external disclosure that will stand up to third-party evaluation; this is known as the conjoint value hierarchy, or CVH (see Chapters 4 and 5 for more on this).

Benefits of the ICMP

One of the issues around intellectual capital resources is that they make up a large part of most organization's resource portfolio and thereby become very important to the success of the organization, but at the same time they tend to be poorly documented and poorly managed. The IC resources are of special importance since they are the primary drivers of the organization's future value generation. In other words, a change in the organization's IC resource portfolio is an early warning for a change in the organization's ability to generate value in the future. Most organizations already manage their IC resources, but they do it using gut feelings and intuition rather than well-documented and transparent processes. Add the fact that most companies are very good at managing their monetary and physical resources and it becomes clear that the organization's success, when compared to its competition, is going to be highly dependent on the organization's ability to manage its IC resources.

The problem organizations face is that most available management tools and models are either developed for value chain logic thinking (and are built around monetary or physical resources) or make assumptions about the characteristics of the resources that are not valid for IC resources. If traditional management tools are used for the management of IC resources the result will be at best unpredictable, at worst erroneous.

The ICMP provides a fuller picture of the organization, taking into account, as it does, all the resources that the organization has at its disposal and how these interact with each other to create value. The ICMP not only incorporates intellectual capital resources but also monetary and physical resources. The ICMP provides a unifying language for the discussion of intellectual capital resources both inside and outside the organization. This makes it easier for management to communicate within its own fora and with employees about how to implement strategies that maximize value creation using IC resources, and also to communicate with external stakeholders around how value is created within and by the organization.

Like all measurement approaches, the measurement of intellectual capital resources requires judgment when it comes to identifying indicators, weighting these indicators, and synthesizing them in order to make trade-off decisions. In spite of this, the use of sophisticated measurement approaches that take into account the IC resources will visualize a larger part of the organization, which allows for more precise performance tracking, performance communication or valuation.[119]

By using the potential for value creation as its starting point, the ICMP will provide a complement to traditional transaction based accounting and traditional management accounting. The former will provide an excellent basis for studying costs associated with historical transactions, while the ICMP identifies value sources and how the creation of value actually happens, irrespective of the accounting recognizability of the different resource types and independent of whether or not the resources are owned and controlled by the organization. In addition, the ICMP focuses on the potential for value creation and is not limited to historical data.

The ICMP and the balanced scorecard approach (see Chapter 5) differ in their assumptions about what is to be measured and managed in organizations. The ICMP has its roots in the resource based theory of the firm whereas the balanced scorecard has its roots in strategic consequences.[120] The creators of the balanced scorecard simply want managers to have a more balanced view of the organization. In one of their books the creators of the balanced scorecard claim that the scorecard complements financial measurements of historical performance with measures of future performance. Targets and measures in the balanced scorecard are derived from the organization's vision and strategy.[121] This means that the balanced scorecard approach focuses on what the organization wants to be and what the organization wants to do without taking into account what it does or what it will have to do in the existing business reality. The ICMP does not suffer from these weaknesses.

Using the ICMP to evaluate and manage the organization provides a structure for understanding the unique complexities that are associated with any given organization. The ICMP provides context-specific insights that are missing from many standardized approaches to managing intellectual capital resources.

Case 1.2 AP*i*ON Telecommunications Software Solutions: Using an Intellectual Capital Approach to Design and Implement a Growth Strategy

This example is derived from two papers by Peppard and Rylander.[1] AP*i*ON's management had been presented with an objective to maximize shareholder value within 5 years. To reach this goal, a coherent growth strategy was needed that would focus on leveraging intangible resources. By adopting the IC perspective, it was possible for AP*i*ON's management to formulate and implement a growth strategy that could capture the full value-creating potential of their intellectual resources, which in turn allowed for a more effective deployment of resources. The IC process and its outcome are depicted in a general level in this case study.

Based in Belfast, Northern Ireland, AP*i*ON Ltd. was formed in 1995 to function as a project house for Aldiscon and Ericsson for joint development work. When Denis Murphy took over as CEO in July 1996, AP*i*ON had 20 employees, mainly involved in developing switching software. In 1997, Logica bought Aldiscon for $100 million and AP*i*ON was spun off as a separate company. With the purchase of Aldiscon, Murphy was presented with an explicit objective: maximize shareholder value. The strategic intention was to successfully utilize leading edge technology in the commercial exploitation of "first to market" computer based network infrastructure components in the convergent space. Although Murphy had a firm belief that software companies and not traditional telecommunications companies would be the key players in the telecommunications industry in the next century, he faced the challenge that the necessary knowledge and skills were not in great supply and sourcing them would be particularly difficult in Northern Ireland. As a result, he put in place a strategy to build the required competencies; a central feature was the acquisition and development of this skill and knowledge. Essential to this knowledge acquisition program was a focused strategy to "aggressively develop people" both through training and education, and the strategic rotation of staff between both technologies and different types of projects.

Despite the fact that a range of different initiatives was set up to support the building of necessary skills, Murphy was uneasy with this range of activity, not because he believed them to be inappropriate but because they were based on gut feelings rather than a tried and trusted formula. He was also frustrated with the traditional strategy process and model as well as management information and reporting systems, which he found inadequate to support him in developing and implementing a strategy so heavily dependent on building and leveraging knowledge. Without a structured framework for describing strategy or even a common language within the organization for communicating strategy it was difficult to take action. For Murphy, the IC framework provided a complementary perspective on strategy, and its strong focus on action and implementation was appealing. In early 1998 he decided to take his management team through an IC process.

Articulating the value creation path is an iterative process where consensus within the group is achieved through discussion and argumentation. During a series of IC workshops the management team worked through the implications of their strategic intent in terms of how to focus and prioritize their investments, activities, and resources.

Insights from the Process

Applying the IC perspective enabled management to understand the particular characteristics, value-creating behavior, and importance of different intangible resources within the context of the organization and to develop a common language around their strategy. This allowed tailoring of and executing a growth strategy that could capture and exploit the full potential of AP*i*ON's intangibles. The IC process revealed particularly two insights that came to modify the focus and implementation of the strategy. The first was that structural capital (made up of organizational and relational resources) was most important for creating value, and not human resources, as had been thought. This led to a change of focus by putting mechanisms in place to extract the experience and tacit knowledge of employees and turn it into structural capital, instead of focusing on building the knowledge of different individuals (human capital). In this way AP*i*ON could leverage or even multiply the value of knowledge and competencies of employees at the same time as it enabled a much faster product development. The following figure illustrates schematically the conversion of the skills and knowledge of employees into organizational competencies.

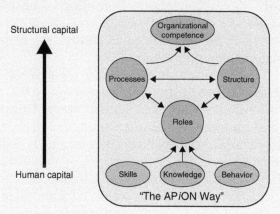

Harnessing intellectual capital at AP*i*ON

The second influential insight was the understanding that transformations between resources are key to value creation. This insight led AP*i*ON to shift the focus from mere building of the resource base into the deployment of resources.

These insights reached during the IC process drove AP*i*ON to become a process driven, learning organization, which helped to achieve its strategic intent of being first to market in the convergent space. As a result, AP*i*ON was the first to launch its WAP gateway product ahead of competition in February 1999. The IC approach also allowed AP*i*ON to accelerate the execution of its strategy and to achieve its strategic intent at a remarkable pace, leading to an astonishing end result; Phone.com bought AP*i*ON for $263 million on 21 October 1999 (of which $100 million was the articulated value of AP*i*ON's intellectual capital), thus confirming rise and development of a small telecommunications software house into a major-league player over a period

Continued

of less than three years. AP*i*ON not only achieved its shareholder value objective but also exceeded it. Interestingly, when Phone.com purchased AP*i*ON they only acquired part of the company because they were solely interested in the intellectual capital the company had built to develop WAP products.

The ICMP has been developed in a dynamic process of interaction and learning between organizational managers and academic researchers, drawing on the best of both worlds.[122,123] As a result, the ICMP is, from a management perspective, practical and easy to operationalize and implement. The ICMP allows managers to gain insight into the IC resource consequences and thereby the value creation consequences, of a proposed strategy. It also allows for comparing and contrasting alternative strategies from a value creation perspective.

The theoretical roots of the ICMP lie in a synthesis of several theories, including finance theory, strategy, epistemology, axiology, measurement theory, behavioral science, and system theory. This wider eclectic approach to the problem of value creation is also becoming more accepted in, for example, strategy literature where there is an articulated need to better understand the characteristics of resources and how to integrate them,[124,125] since it is through the allocation and integration of all resources that the potential for value creation is increased and nurtured.[126,127]

The concepts, tools, and techniques presented throughout this book have been researched and developed by the authors over a period of fifteen years, based on theoretical work, consultation in organizations, and best practice studies. During this fifteen-year period we have reached many dead ends, stumbled, and fallen, but have now reached a level of understanding and grounding which makes us comfortable in presenting a set of approaches that have worked and have generated useful and actionable insights on every occasion in which they have been applied, as will be evidenced through the numerous illustration cases presented throughout this text. This book is the summary and synthesis of hundreds of academic papers and case studies (many written by the authors) drawing on experiences from numerous countries, industries, and organizational types.

LEARNING CASES

In addition to a large number of illustrative case studies distributed in all the chapters throughout this book, we will use three learning cases. These cases are built on real existing organizations but they have been made anonymous to better present the issues. Each of the three organizations illustrates one of the three value-creating logics. These cases will in a step-by-step process apply the concepts and ideas presented in this book. This means that the reader will be able to read about the theories and concepts with some illustrative cases and in addition see how these three case companies have applied these theories and concepts.

Here follows a brief introduction to the three organizations.

A manufacturing company

This firm produces food products. It has 115 employees and a turnover of approximately $30 million. The company operates solely in a national market. The strategic intent of the firm is to achieve superior consumer loyalty and high profitability through high product quality combined with a strong brand.

The firm is a typical value chain, and it buys raw materials and executes all production and value adding steps in-house. The finished products are sold to customers (e.g., supermarkets, convenience stores, etc.) who act as channels to market. These channels include both on-premise (e.g., catering companies) and off-premise organizations (e.g., retailers). The company is focused on achieving economies of scale and bases its activities primarily on physical (raw materials, finished products, plant and equipment), organizational (processes, brand, recipes), and relational (customers, partners, and suppliers) resources.

The firm has, through excellent execution of its strategy, managed to avoid its products becoming commoditized. Most consumers buy on distinctness (brand) and/or functionality (taste), although there is increasing but not yet disturbing pressure on price from customers. This has produced a firm that is well recognized among consumers and customers alike—sometimes the word *admired* could be used—with a profitable business and a strong balance sheet.

A research organization

The research organization was originally a government laboratory financed by the country's national budget. After a major administrative and budget reform, the laboratory is now a government agency, according to the definition we provided earlier. The major impact of this reform was that the organization's budget, with the exception of 20%, was removed from the organization and handed to its customers, who were given complete freedom of action as to where to spend these funds to get best value for money. The 20% was retained for work in which the government was the sole customer and the organization the sole provider. These changes obviously created a major upheaval in the organization. We are looking at the organization in this period of transition.

The research organization is active internationally but does have a heavy national emphasis. It has about 1,000 employees and a turnover of around $130 million.

The strategic intent of the organization is to build applied knowledge that will allow its customers to address a clearly articulated problem. This applied knowledge is based on basic research executed at universities and research institutions worldwide. The deliverables come in the form of written material, verbal presentations, and prototypes.

The research organization's primary resource is human in the form of competent people, complemented by relational (customers, knowledge, suppliers and partners), organizational (past deliverables, databases, processes, reputation and brand), and to some extent physical (laboratory buildings and specialized experimental equipment) resources—in other words a typical value shop.

A network organization

The network organization is a listed financial market with regional focus. The organization has around 400 employees and a turnover of $95 million. Its strategic intent is to build trust so as to provide a customer-oriented, effective and efficient trading environment.

The primary resources for this organization are organizational (systems, processes, brand and reputation) and relational [sellers, buyers, regulators, suppliers and many other stakeholders] resources—in other words, a typical value network.

Table 1.8 summarizes the three organizations.

Table 1.8. Some Introductory Facts about the Three Learning Case Organizations

	The Manufacturing Company	The Research Organization	The Network Organization
Turnover ($ '000)	30 000	130 000	95 000
Number of employees	115	1 300	400
Industry	Consumer products	Applied R&D	Financial market
Value-creating logic	Value Chain	Value Shop	Value Network

Key Points in Chapter 1

- Organizations are today more dependent then ever before on intellectual capital resources. This is evidenced by, for example, the future value components of the share price of listed companies.
- Intellectual capital resources frequently form a basis for competitive advantage. This means that the need for formal and transparent management of the value extraction of intellectual capital resources is great as evidenced by several surveys.
- Intellectual capital resources can be defined as: all nonmonetary and non-physical resources that fully or partly are controlled by the organization and that contribute to the organization's value creation.
- Intellectual capital management can be defined as: the deployment and management of intellectual capital resources and their transformations (into other intellectual capital resources or into physical or monetary resources) to maximize the present value of the organization's value creation in the eyes of its stakeholders.
- Intellectual capital resources are subdivided into relational resources, organizational resources, and human resources, and have fundamentally different characteristics and economic behavior from the traditional monetary and physical resources.
- By using the intellectual capital management process an organization can increase its value creation and establish suitable systems for performance measurement of all its deployed resources.
- There are important issues around the fit between value-creating logics (value chains, value networks, and value shops) and the resources that form the basis for competitive advantage.
- Customers perceive four categories of value drivers in some combination: cost, functionality, distinctness, and mental proximity.

ENDNOTES

1. Molnar, Michael J., Executive Views on Intangible Assets: Insights from the Accenture/Economist Intelligence Unit Survey, Research Note, Intangible Assets and Future Value, Issue One - April 13, 2004, Pp. 2.
2. We use third sector organization as a synonym for not-for-profit organizations.
3. Part of this section has been presented in R. Burgman and G. Roos: "The New Economy—A New Paradigm for Managing for Shareholder Value," paper accepted for presentation at the International IC Congress at Hanken Business School in Helsinki, I & C of IC: "Interpretation and Communication of Intellectual Capital," Helsinki, on 2–3 September, 2004.
4. The S&P 500 price earnings (P/E) multiple has climbed steadily around a strong upward trend since a P/E low of 6.9 times in May 1980 through a peak P/E of 45.7 in March 2002 to a P/E multiple in January 2004 of 23.2. Refer to Neil Davis Research Inc. @ http://www.comstockfunds.com/files/NLPP00000/026.pdf
5. The term *new economy* is a multifarious one. In recent years, the term has generally arisen in connection with the rapid technical developments in the information and telecommunications sector and the subsequent greater use of related technologies and products. Definitions vary. A broadly useful definition has been provided by Lars Jagran and Erik Morell (2001), who describe a new economy as one arising from the combination of a number of ongoing changes and trends. These include, *inter alia*:
   - New basic technologies
   - New deregulated and increasing global markets
   - The higher importance attached to knowledge and intellectual capital
   - New organizational structures in companies
   - New economic policies
   - Low inflation
   - New values and attitudes

   Clearly, others have preferred to define the new economy more narrowly, focusing on a particular aspect of change and labeling it accordingly. Thus we have had such terms as the knowledge economy, the digital economy, the new-look economy, the postindustrial economy, and so on.
6. Here, shareholder value creation is measured as the difference between enterprise value and current value where enterprise value is the sum of the market value of equity plus net debt (interest bearing debt obligations including off-balance-sheet debt obligation less surplus cash and marketable securities), and current operations is the sum of net capital employed plus the perpetuity value of current economic profit. The difference between enterprise value and current value is the market value added, and represents the shareholder value retained within the company at a point in time.
7. It should be noted that the focus on "new economy" companies listed on Nasdaq is meant to be illustrative. The methodology we are describing is relevant to all companies, just more relevant to some than others. Included in the broader group will be companies that represent consumer products (brand value), pharmaceutical products (R&D value), and media (masthead value), to name but a few industry groups.
8. The Standard & Poor's web site states the following: "Although the S&P 500 focuses on the large-cap segment of the market, with over 80% coverage of U.S. equities, it is also an ideal proxy for the total market". For a description of the S&P 500, refer to http://www2.standardandpoors.com/NASApp/cs/ContentServer?pagename=sp/Page/IndicesIndexPg&r=1&b=4&s=6&ig=48&I=56
9. S&P value of $10.285 trillion vs. NYSE value of $12.158 trillion and Nasdaq value of $2.988 trillion (total value of $15.146 trillion) at the end of 2003.

10. The S&P 500 accounted for 67.9% of the value of the NYSE and Nasdaq exchanges with 7.6% of the companies listed at the end of 2003. Source: AssetEconomics, Inc. analysis.

11. When financial companies are separated out of the S&P 500, nonfinancial companies show quite different traits when each listing group to the other. The 380 NYSE-listed and 66 Nasdaq-listed nonfinancial companies in the S&P 500 are valued differently. This is most noticeable when the market value of equity to sales revenue average multiples are considered. For NYSE-listed nonfinancial companies this multiple is 1.4 times; for Nasdaq-listed nonfinancials it is 4.3 times (versus an average for the entire S&P 500 of 1.6 times). Another market multiple of interest is the market value of equity to invested capital multiple. For NYSE-listed companies this multiple is 2.3 times; for Nasdaq-listed companies it is 4.3 times (versus an average for the entire S&P 500 of 2.5 times). Source: AssetEconomics, Inc. analysis.

12. This claim is supported by merging the arguments of K. Pavitt (2001), "Can the large Penrosian firm cope with the dynamics of technology," Electronic Working Paper Series No 68, SPRU and V. Mahnke (2000), "Limits to Outsourcing and the evolutionary perspective on firm boundaries," Department of Industrial Economics and Strategy, Copenhagen Business School, 2 ed. Preliminary draft, October 10.

13. Merton Miller and Franco Modigliani (1961), "Dividend policy, growth and the valuation of shares," *Journal of Business*, 34 (October), 411–433.

14. W. Carl Kester, (1984) "Today's options for tomorrow's growth," *Harvard Business Review*, 62(2) (March–April), 153–160.

15. Richard A. Brealey and Stewart C. Myers (1981), *Principles of Corporate Finance*, 1st Edition, McGraw-Hill.

16. Net interest bearing debt obligations (NIBDOs) are added to equity market value to establish enterprise value.

17. Standard & Poor's uses the Global Industry Classification Standard (GICS) of 10 sectors and 24 industry groups for its S&P 500 index (as well as for all its other indices). We use this second level of industry group classification here. The ten sectors are energy, materials, industrials, consumer discretionary, consumer staples, health care, financials, information technology, telecommunication services, and utilities. The twenty-two industry groups contained in this database in 2002 were energy; materials; capital goods; commercial services & supplies; transportation; automobiles & components; consumer durables & apparel; hotels; restaurants & leisure; media; retailing; food & drug retailing; food; beverage & tobacco; household & personal products; health care equipment & services; pharmaceuticals & biotechnology; banks; diversified financials; insurance; software & services; technology; hardware & equipment; telecommunication services and utilities.

18. World GDP data include the following: world GDP $49.000 trillion, U.S. GDP $10.450 trillion and China GDP $5.989 trillion. Refer to *The World Factbook* at http://www.cia.gov/cia/publications/factbook/rankorder/2001rank.html

19. The U.S. federal debt was estimated at $7.1 trillion as at March 1, 2004. Refer to US National Debt Clock at http://www.brillig.com/debt_clock/

20. Commonwealth of Australia (2001), Report of the Inquiry into the Definition of Charities and Related Organizations, AGPS, Canberra.

21. Commonwealth of Australia, 2001:92.

22. Commonwealth of Australia, 2001:46.

23. Commonwealth of Australia, 2001:47–48.

24. Commonwealth of Australia, 2001:2.

25. W.F. Crittenden and V.L. Crittenden (2000), "Relationships between organisational characteristics and strategic planning in not-for-profit organizations," *Journal of Managerial Issues*, 12(2), 150–168.

26. R. Bush (2002), "Effective not-for-profit leadership: the leadership factor," *Not-for-profit Management and Leadership*, 12(3), 327–333.
27. J. Myers and R. Sacks (2001), "Harnessing the talents of a loose and baggy monster," *Journal of European Industrial Training*, 25(9), 454–464.
28. A. Fletcher, J. Guthrie, P. Steane, G. Roos, and S. Pike (2003), "Mapping stakeholder perceptions for a third sector organization," *Journal of Intellectual Capital*, 4(4), 505–527.
29. A. Fletcher, J. Guthrie, P. Steane, G. Roos, and L. Fernström, "Valuing a blood service from the perspective of its stakeholder," paper presented at 25th McMaster World Congress Managing Intellectual Capital, Hamilton, Ontario, Canada, January 14–16, 2004.
30. Studies on the Application of Intellectual Capital Approaches to FOA by Roos & Anderberg (unpublished case); VTT regarding Intangible Assets And Technology Portfolio Management by Kenneth Holmberg, Varpu Lindroos, Rolf Rosenberg, and Pekka Silvennoinen (unpublished paper); VTT regarding Application of Intellectual Capital Navigator at VTT by Markku Auer, Pentti Grönberg, Tomi Mattila, Maria Saarela, and Harri Soininen (unpublished notes); ANSTO by Roos & Kuukkanen (unpublished case).
31. J.-H. Leitner and M. Bornemann. Development and implementation of the first enterprise wide intellectual capital report for a European contract research organization: Background, main ideas and experiences. In: *Proceedings of International Conference on Knowledge Management in Research and Technology Organisations: Policies and practices to make your RTO competitive in the 21st Century*, pp. 40–61, 11–13 October 2000, The Haag, The Netherlands, 2000.
32. L.A. Joia (2000), "Using intellectual capital to evaluate educational technology projects," *Journal of Intellectual Capital*, 1(4), 341–356.
33. J. Guthrie, and E. Vagnoni (2001), "Intellectual capital and intellectual property in Australian and Italian universities," The Health Policy Forum, Ferrara, Italy, 19 November, 2001.
34. H. Biedermann, M. Graggober, and M. Sammer (2002), "Die Wissensbilanz als Instrument zur Steuerung von Schwerpunktbereichen am Beispiel eines Universitätsinstitutes." In: *Wissensmanagement: Konzepte und Erfahrungsberichte aus der betrieblichen Praxis,* M. Bornemann and M. Sammer (Eds.), Wiesbaden 2002 S. 53–72.
35. K.-H. Leitner, M. Sammer, M. Graggober, D. Schartinger, and C. Zielowski (2001), "Wissensbilanzierung für Universitäten, Auftragsprojekt für das Bundesministerium für Bildung, Wissenschaft und Kunst," 2001. URL: http://www.weltklasse-uni.ac.at.
36. K.-H. Leitner (2002), "Intellectual capital reporting for universities: conceptual background and application within the reorganisation of Austrian universities," Paper presented at The Transparent Enterprise. The Value of Intangibles, 25–26 November,. Madrid, Spain.
37. N.C. Dragonetti and G. Roos, "La evaluación de Ausindustry y el business network programe: una perspectiva desde el capital intellectual," *Boletín de Estudios Económicos*, Vol. LIII Agosto 1998 Núm. 164.
38. G. Roos and K. Jacobsen (1999), "Management in a complex stakeholder organisation; a case study of the application of the IC-process to a branch of the Commonwealth public service," *Monash Mt. Eliza Business Review*, 2(1), 82–93.
39. Risø National Laboratory Optics and Fluid Dynamic Department (1999): Intellectual Capital Accounts, Roskilde.
40. Deutsches Zentrum für Luft- und Raumfahrt DLR (2001), Intellectual Capital Report 2000, Köln 2001.
41. L.E. Preston and T. Donaldson (1999), "Stakeholder management and organisational wealth," *Academy of Management Review*, 24(4), 619–620.

42. As claimed in K.E. Sveiby (1997), *The New Organizational Wealth: Managing and Measuring Knowledge Based Assets*, Berrett– Koehler Publishers, San Francisco.
43. J. Frooman (1999), "Stakeholder influence strategies," *Academy of Management Review*, 24(2), 191–205.
44. J.M. Bryson (1995), *Strategic Planning for Public and Not-for-profit Organizations,* Jossey-Bass, San Francisco, CA.
45. Parts of this section have been presented in R. Burgman and G. Roos, "Measuring, managing and delivering value performance in the public sector," paper presented at the International IC Congress at Hanken Business School in Helsinki, I & C of IC, Interpretation and Communication of Intellectual Capital, Helsinki, on 2–3 September 2004.
46. Telstra Corporation has 1.8 million shareholders from 1.2 million households (out of Australia's estimated resident population of 19.7 million and estimated household population of 7.1 million at mid-2002), representing 9.1% of individuals and 16.9% of households, respectively.
47. It is often argued that the only purpose of corporatization is as a prequel to privatization (transfer of the ownership of the agency into private hands by way of a "trade sale" or listing of shares by way of an initial public offering (IPO)). This is not strictly true, as company law generally requires an independent board, accrual accounting, and transparency of commercial dealings, among other things. The benefits of a stricter and independent governance regime have been a major driver for creating value from government agencies hitherto managed in a more cloistered environment.
48. Airways New Zealand is a state-owned enterprise, wholly owned by the New Zealand Government. Its two shareholders are the Minister for Finance and the Minister for State Owned Enterprises.
49. The imperatives for "Excellence in Government" in the United States are embedded in the Government Performance Results Act of 1993 and in the President's Management Agenda, Office of Management & Budget, The Executive Office of the President, Fiscal Year 2002, pp. 64.
50. The logic of economic profit is what matters here. The economic profit thinking assumes a capital charge equal to the net capital employed in creating the output cluster multiplied by the weighted average cost of capital (WACC) for the enterprise. And yes, government agencies can and should calculate and apply their WACC to investment decisions.
51. These could include performance standards, performance penalties, cost reductions, take or pay provisions, internal audit provisions, and inspection rights.
52. Here the customer franchise view can be helpful.
53. After J.D. Thompson (1967), *Organizations in Action*, McGraw-Hill, New York: New York; and C.B. Stabell and O.D. Fjelstad (1998), "Configuring value for competitive advantage: on chains, shops and networks," *Strategic Management Journal*, 19, 413–437 and drawing on a synthesis of Chatzkel, Jay *"A Conversation with Göran Roos"*, Journal of Intellectual Capital Vol. 3 No. 2, 2002, pp. 96–117, Roos, G., von Krogh, G., and J. Roos with L. Femström *"Innføring i Strategi, 4th edition"*, Fagbokforlaget, Norway, 2005, and Computer Sciences Corporation, *Chains, Shops and Networks: The Role of IS in New Models of Value Creation,* Foundation Strategic Innovation Report, Computer Sciences Corporation, 1998, at http://www. cscresearchservices.com/foundation/library/value/RP19.asp
54. Roos, G., von Krogh, G., and J. Roos with L. Femström *"Innføring i Strategi, 4th edition"*, Fagbokforlaget, Norway, 2005
55. The importance here is the framework (i.e., the dimensions along the two axes), and not What is in the boxes, which is why the table is not populated with examples in this table.

56. K. Andrews (1971), *The Concept of Corporate Strategy*, Homewood, Ill: Richard D. Irwin.
57. S.E. Phelan (1997), "Using artificial adaptive agents to explore strategic landscapes," Ph D-thesis, La Trobe University, Bundoora, Australia.
58. R.M. Grant (1991), *Contemporary Strategy Analysis*, Cambridge, MA: Blackwell.
59. S.M. Oster (1990), *Modern Competitive Analysis*, New York: Oxford University Press.
60. D.J. Ravenscraft and C.L. Wagner (1991), "The role of the FTC's line of business data in testing and expanding the theory of the firm," *Journal of Law and Economics*, 34, 703–730.
61. R. Schmalensee (1985), Do markets differ much? *The American Economic Review*, 75(3), 341–351.
62. R.E. Caves and M.E. Porter (1977), "From entry barriers to mobility barriers: Conjectural decisions and contrived deterrence to new competitors," *Journal of Economics*, 91, 421–434.
63. A. Fiegenbaum, D. Sudharshan, and H. Thomas (1990), "Strategic time periods and strategic groups research: concepts and an empirical example," *Journal of Management Studies*, 27(2), 133–148.
64. K.J. Hatten and M.L. Hatten (1987), "Strategic groups, assymetrical mobility barriers and contestability," *Strategic Management Journal*, 8, 329–342.
65. J. McGee and H. Thomas (1986), "Strategic groups: Theory, research and taxonomy," *Strategic Management Journal*, 7, 141–160.
66. S. Oster (1982), "Intra-industry structure and the ease of strategic change," *Review of Economics and Statistics*, 64, 376–383.
67. R.P. Rumelt (1984), "Towards a strategic theory of the firm." In: R.B. Lamb (Ed.), *Competitive Strategic Management* (pp. 556–570), Englewood Cliffs, NJ: Prentice-Hall.
68. K. Cool and D. Schendel (1987), "Performance differences among strategic group members," *Strategic Management Journal*, 12, 49–68.
69. R.P. Rumelt (1991), "How much does industry matter?" *Strategic Management Journal*, 12, 167–185.
70. B. Wernerfelt (1984), "A resource-based view of the firm," *Strategic Management Journal*, 5, 171–180.
71. C.K. Prahalad and G. Hamel (1990), "The core competence of the corporation," *Harvard Business Review*, no 3 (May–June), 79–91.
72. B. Wernerfelt (1984), "A resource-based view of the firm," *Strategic Management Journal*, 5, 171–180.
73. E. Penrose (1959), *The Theory of the Growth of the Firm*, London: Basil Blackwell.
74. C.K. Prahalad and G. Hamel (1990), "The core competence of the corporation," *Harvard Business Review,* no 3 (May–June), 79–91.
75. As quoted in G. Roos and F. Lövingsson (1999), "*El Proceso CI en el «Nuevo Mondo de las Telecomunicacione».*" In: A.M. Güell (Ed.), *Homo faber, homo sapiens – La gestión del capital intelectual,* Ediciones del Bronce; and as further outlined in G. Roos, S. Pike, and L. Fernström (2004), "Intellectual Capital Management, Measurement and Disclosure." In: P. Horváth and K. Möller (Eds.), *Intangibles in Management,* Verlag Frans Vahlen, Munich.
76. M.A. Peteraf (1993), "The cornerstones of competitive advantage: a resource-based view," *Strategic Management Journal*, 14, 179–191.
77. H. Itami (1987), *Mobilizing Invisible Assets*, Cambridge, Mass.: Harvard.
78. D.J. Teece (2000), *Managing Intellectual Capital: Organizational, Strategic, and Policy Dimensions*, Oxford: Oxford University Press.
79. J. Nahapiet and S. Ghoshal (1998), "Social capital, intellectual capital, and the organizational advantage," *Academy of Management Review*, 23(2), 242–266.

80. S.L. McGaughey (2002), "Strategic interventions in intellectual assets flows," *Academy of Management Review*, 27(2), 248–274.
81. A. Delios and P.W. Beamish (2001), "Survival and profitability: the roles of experience and intangible assets in foreign subsidiary performance," *Academy of Management Journal*, 44(5), 1028–1038.
82. D. Teece (1998), "Capturing value from knowledge assets: the new economy, markets for knowhow and intangible assets," *California Management Review*, 40(3), 55–79.
83. D. Teece (1997), Capturing value from technological innovation: integration, strategic partnering and licensing decision, in Tushman, M. and P. Anderson (Eds.) *Managing Strategic Innovation and Change*, Oxford University Press, 287–306.
84. R.R. Nelson and S. G. Winter (1982), *An Evolutionary Theory of Economic Change*, Cambridge, Mass.: Harvard University Press.
85. H. Itami (1987), *Mobilizing Invisible Assets*, Cambridge, Mass.: Harvard University Press.
86. D. Aaker (1989), "Managing assets and skills: the key to a sustainable competitive advantage," *California Management Review*, 31, 91–106.
87. R. Hall (1992), "The strategic analysis of intangible resources," *Strategic Management Journal*, 13(2), 135–144.
88. R. Hall (1993), "A framework linking intangible resources and capabilities to sustainable competitive advantage," *Strategic Management Journal*, 14, 607–618.
89. T. Stewart (1991), "Brainpower," *Fortune*, 123, 44–50.
90. J.B. Quinn (1992), *The Intelligent Enterprise: Knowledge and Service-Based Paradigm for Industry*, The Free Press.
91. R. Hall (1992), "The strategic analysis of intangible resources," *Strategic Management Journal*, 13(2), 135–144.
92. R. Hall (1992), "The strategic analysis of intangible resources," *Strategic Management Journal*, 13(2), 135–144.
93. W.J. Hudson (1993), *Intellectual Capital: How to Build It, Enhance It, Use It*, New York: Wiley.
94. J. Nahapiet and S. Ghoshal (1998), "Social capital, intellectual capital, and the organizational advantage," *Academy of Management Review*, 23(2), 242–266.
95. A. Brooking (1996), *Intellectual Capital: Core Assets for the Third Millennium Enterprise*, London: Thompson Business Press.
96. A. Brooking (1997), "The management of intellectual capital," *Long Range Planning*, 30(3), 364–365.
97. L. Edvinsson (1997), "Developing intellectual capital at Skandia," *Long Range Planning*, 30(3), 320–331.
98. J. Roos and G. Roos (1997), "Measuring your company's intellectual performance," *Long Range Planning*, 30(3), 325.
99. B. Marr and J. Chatzkel (2004) Intellectual Capital at the Crossroads: managing, measuring, and reporting of IC, *Journal of Intellectual Capital (editorial)*, 5(2), 224–229.
100. B. Marr, G. Schiuma, and A. Neely (2004), "The dynamics of value creation: Mapping your intellectual performance drivers," *Journal of Intellectual Capital*, 5(2), 312–325.
101. J. Roos and G. Roos (1997), "Measuring your company's intellectual performance," *Long Range Planning*, 30(3), 325.
102. A. Bainbridge, K. Jacobsen, and G. Roos (2001), "Intellectual capital analysis as a strategic tool," *Strategy and Leadership Journal*, 29(4), 21–26.
103. A.J. Rucci, A.P. Kirn, and R.T. Quinn (1998), "The employee–customer profit chain at Sears," *Harvard Business Review*, 76(1), 82–98.

104. C.D. Ittner and D.F. Larcker (1998), "Are nonfinancial measures leading indicators of financial performance? An analysis of customer satisfaction," *Journal of Accounting Research*, 36(Supplement), 1–35.
105. S.A. Lippman and R.P. Rumelt (1982), "Uncertain imitability: an analysis of inter-firm differences in efficiency under competition," *Bell Journal of Economics*, 13(2), 418–438.
106. I. Dierickx and K. Cool (1989), "Asset stock accumulation and sustainability of competitive advantage," *Management Science*, 35(12), 1504–1511.
107. A.W. King and C.P. Zeithaml (2001), "Competencies and firm performance: examining the causal ambiguity paradox," *Strategic Management Journal*, 22(1), 75.
108. B. Marr, G. Schiuma, and A. Neely (2004), "The dynamics of value creation: mapping your intellectual performance drivers," *Journal of Intellectual Capital*, 5(2), 312–325.
109. J. Roos and G. Roos (1997), "Measuring your company's intellectual performance," *Long Range Planning*, 30(3), 419.
110. B. Lev (2001), *Intangibles: Management, Measurement, and Reporting*, Washington, DC: The Brookings Institution.
111. S. Pike and G. Roos (2004), "Mathematics and modern business management," *Journal of Intellectual Capital*, 5(2), 243–256.
112. D. Andriessen and R. Tiessen (2000), *Weightless Weight—Find your Real Value in a Future of Intangible Assets*, London: Pearson Education.
113. D. Andriessen (2004), *Making Sense of Intellectual Capital—Designing a Method for the Valuation of Intangibles*, Burlington, Mass: Butterworth-Heinemann.
114. M.E. Porter (1985), *Competitive Advantage: Creating and Sustaining Superior Performance*, New York: The Free Press.
115. C.B. Stabell and O.D. Fjeldstad (1998), "Configuring value for competitive advantage: on chains, shops, and networks," *Strategic Management Journal*, 19, 413–437.
116. C.B. Stabell and O.D. Fjeldstad (1998), "Configuring value for competitive advantage: on chains, shops, and networks," *Strategic Management Journal*, 19, 413–437.
117. This example has been used in class over several years to illustrate the value of the intellectual capital perspective and the graphical representation language that the ICMP uses. The case has also been published as a part of the chapter "in the *Handbook of Strategy*. Roos, G. *"Intellectual Capital and Strategy; a primer for today's manager"*, in Coate (eds.) *Handbook of Business Strategy*, Vol. 6. No.1, 2005, pp. 123–132.
118. G. Roos and K. Jacobsen (1999), "Management in a complex stakeholder organisation," *Monash Mt. Eliza Business Review*, July, 82–93.
119. G. Roos, L. Edvinsson, and J. Roos, J. with N.C. Dragonetti (1997), *Intellectual Capital: Navigating the New Business Landscape*, London: Macmillan.
120. A. Fink, B. Marr, A. Siebe, and J.-P. Kuhle (2005), "The future scorecard: combining external and internal scenarios to create strategic foresight," *Management Decision*, 43(3), 360–381.
121. Kaplan, R and D. Norton, 1996, The Balanced Scorecard: translating strategy into action, Harvard Business School Press, page 8.
122. Larsen, Heine T., Jan Mouritsen & Per Nikolaj Bukh (1999), "Intellectual capital statements and knowledge management: measuring, reporting and acting," *Australian Accounting Review*, 9(3),15–26.
123. J. Mouritsen (1998), "Driving growth: economic value added versus intellectual capital," *Management Accounting Research*, 9, 461–482.
124. J.A. Black and Boal K. (1994), "Strategic resources: traits, configurations and paths to sustainable competitive advantage," *Strategic Management Journal: Special Summer Issue on New Paradigms*, 15, 131–148.

125. Haanes, Knut and Fjeldstad, Øystein (2000), "Linking intangible resources and competition," *European Management Journal*, 18(1), 52–62.
126. Amit, Raphael and Paul J. Schoemaker. 1993. "Strategic assets and organisational rent," *Strategic Management Journal* 14 (January): 33-46.
127. Grant R.M. 1996. Toward a knowledge-based theory of the firm. *Strategic Management Journal*, 17, 109–122.

CASE 1.1 ENDNOTES

1. P. Westnes and S. Westnes (2002), "Evaluating Intellectual Capital in the Hotel Industry. A Case Study of Radisson SAS Hotels & Resorts." Master's thesis, The Norwegian School of Hotel Management, Stavanger University College, Norway.
2. E.g., N. Bontis, N.C. Dragonetti, K. Jacobsen, and G. Roos (1999), "The knowledge toolbox: A review of the tools available to measure and manage intangible resources," *European Management Journal*, 17(4), 391–402; B. Roos and J. Roos (1997), "Measuring your company's intellectual performance," *Long Range Planning*, 30(3), 413–426; and G. Roos, J. Roos, N.C. Dragonetti, and L. Edvinsson (1997), *Intellectual Capital: Navigating the New Business Landscape*, London: Macmillan Press Ltd.

CASE 1.2 ENDNOTES

1. J. Peppard and A. Rylander (2001), "Leveraging intellectual capital at APiON", *Journal of Intellectual Capital*, 2(3), 225–235: and J. Peppard and A. Rylander (2001), "Using an intellectual capital perspective to design and implement a growth strategy: The case of APiON," *European Management Journal*, 19(5), 510–526.

2

How to identify the organizations' intellectual capital resources*

In Chapter 1 we discussed what intellectual capital is and how the different types of intellectual capital resources behave as compared to traditional economic monetary and physical resources. We also discussed the necessity for the organization to have access to a given portfolio of resources to be able to achieve its strategic objectives and that intellectual capital resources normally form a, if not the, basis for competitive advantage in most organizations. In this chapter we will further explore the resource portfolio of the organization.

The stakeholders of an organization are all expecting management to do its utmost to increase value in the eyes of the stakeholders. So, it is essential to start by exploring and evaluating the organization's resource portfolio to ensure that the right resources, in sufficient quantity and of sufficient quality, are available. Understanding the resource issue is the first step of the intellectual capital management process (ICMP).

Through this initial step in the ICMP the organization will be able to judge if it can directly pursue its chosen strategy, or if action such as the acquisition of resources is necessary before it is able to pursue its chosen strategy (as intended, or modified).

---

* In this Chapter, we are grateful to Intellectual Captial services Ltd. for providing substantial amounts of data and analysis.

Case 2.1   Proteome Systems: Using an Intellectual Capital Approach to Build Value in a Start-Up Biotechnology Company

By Anne Fletcher

This case study is based on an analysis by Growing Your Knowledge, which provides consulting services in Australia based on an intellectual capital approach.

There are common challenges facing start-up companies, including securing sufficient establishment capital, developing a strategy for achieving the business model, and establishing a cash flow to support operations, research, development, and marketing. In addition, the founders may not be experienced in business. Start-up companies are very dependent on the intellectual capital of their founders and staff.

Biotechnology start-up companies face additional hurdles in that their capital requirements may be considerably higher than in other industries, due to the cost of R&D, and there may be a long lead time until cash-generating activities commence. Moreover, the overall success rate in commercializing biotechnology ideas (especially those leading to drugs) is known to be low. Traditionally, raising capital in Australia for new biotechnology companies has been difficult, partly due to the lack of early phase investment funds. Potential investors may have difficulty in understanding the science on which the biotechnology is based. Biotechnology companies will generally need to trade and compete in a global marketplace. Finally, investment sentiment about the sector may be influenced by both global and local trends.

Proteome Systems is an Australian biotechnology company that aims "to become a leading supplier of proteome technologies to biotechnology, pharmaceutical, and government funded organizations around the world."[1] The proteome is the complete set of proteins that is expressed at a given time in a cell, tissue, organ, or organism. Proteomics (a term coined by one of the six founders of the company) is the study of the proteome using technologies for the large-scale separation, identification, and characterization of proteins and their interactions. Many scientists see proteomics as the successor to genomics (the study of genomes using molecular biology to identify all the genes in an organism). Professor Keith Williams, with a team of people who had worked together as pioneers in defining and promoting the field of proteomics at Macquarie University, established Proteome Systems in January 1999. These founders are the innovators whose ideas, knowledge, and competencies have been translated into a business in the emerging industry of proteomics.

Proteome Systems has adopted an intellectual capital approach to build value over a relatively brief time span. It has a patent portfolio comprising 51 patent families (including 7 granted patents and 130 pending patent applications). In addition, it has trade secrets and know-how on which its products are based. Proteome Systems achieved sales in the global marketplace in its second full year of operations and in subsequent years. It has established successful relationships with major international companies. In just over five years the company has grown from a handful of people to over 120 employees. As it developed, it strengthened its board with business expertise. In August 2004 it lodged a prospectus with the Australian Securities and Investment Commission for a fully underwritten initial public offering, and it listed on the Australian Stock Exchange on September 30.

How has Proteome Systems demonstrated that it utilizes an intellectual capital approach? In its prospectus it recognizes its core assets as "people, IP, and alliances." However, an examination of its track record reveals a comprehensive focus on developing its human, organizational, and relational intellectual capital assets and on linking them effectively together.

The human intellectual capital assets of an organization comprise the knowledge, competency, intellectual agility, relational agility, and attitude of its employees. Proteome Systems employed a people-focused business strategist from its early days who has been influential in implementing a range of strategies and policies to support and retain key staff and to attract valuable new employees. These include Change Tracking[R], a diagnostic tool[2] for understanding people and their emotional responses, which affect business responses, and a performance management system. Incentives have been implemented to reward staff with cash or share ownership benefits. A major strength in Proteome Systems is its strong R&D expertise and the ability of its research staff to build and maintain global personal networks. Proteome Systems has demonstrated stable and high quality management, success in executing its strategy, success in meeting R&D goals and major milestones, a high degree of employee loyalty, and positive employee motivation and attitude. All of these are indications of Proteome Systems' success in managing its human assets.

A major strategy employed by Proteome Systems has been to establish and develop its relational assets. From its inception it sought to identify appropriate partners and to develop sound relationships with significant global organizations. It has established alliances with leading industry partners such as systems supplier IBM, the Japanese instrument manufacture Shimadzu, C-Qentec, and Thermo Electron. It has a large number of discovery partnerships, including those with the Public Health Research Institute (USA), Eukarion Inc., High Q Foundation, The Cystic Fibrosis Foundation Therapeutics, CSIRO, Nestle, World Anti-Doping Authority, Buck Research Institute, Iberica, The University of Missouri, Children's Hospital Westmead, and the University of Sydney. Commercialization partners include Sigma, Millipore, and SGE. It has established joint ventures with the Japanese supplier and distributor ITOCHU. In addition, stakeholder support has been strengthened by close attention to investor needs and to federal and state government relationships. Customer needs are met by professional installation and support services and by providing solutions through collaboration. Proteome Systems sees itself as providing problem-solving solutions rather than simply selling equipment.

The patent portfolio often dominates the organizational assets of a biotech company. Proteome Systems has considerable strength in this area with over 130 patents—some granted and others pending, almost all invented within the company since 1999—and with additional assets relating to know-how and trade secrets. This reflects the organization's R&D productivity. Proteome Systems has effectively leveraged its patent portfolio to develop a suite of new products. These products are based on technology (instruments, tools, software, consumables), diagnostics (in agriculture and potentially in medicine for point-of-care use), and drug discovery (with the objective of out-licensing or partnering in drug development). However, Proteome Systems has many other organizational resources in addition to its intellectual property. Other

Continued

Case 2.1 Proteome Systems: Using an Intellectual Capital Approach to Build Value in a Start-Up Biotechnology Company—cont'd

assets include proprietary software (for example, software programs that support its systems and instruments), database management systems, and IT systems. Information from projects is captured. Sharing of information is actively encouraged and is supported by software technology. Weekly seminars assist in transferring important information to staff, including news about discoveries and innovations. The organizational structure has evolved to meet the needs according to the company's stage of development. Despite its relatively brief life, Proteome Systems has developed a strong reputation (or brand) as an innovative and successful company. This reputation has been enhanced by the many awards the company has received (e.g., The Frost and Sullivan Technology Award, 2003; the Nikkei Award for Xcise, 2003; and the US R&D award for ChIP) as by Keith Williams becoming a state finalist in the Australian Entrepreneur of the Year Award for 2003.

Thus, Proteome Systems has established and understood its value creation pathway and has leveraged its resources effectively. It has achieved a competitive advantage by utilizing strategic resources, primarily based on the skills and competencies of its founders. It has created a valuable technology that is difficult to imitate, thus creating a barrier against competition. It has closely linked its human assets with its organizational assets (the technology and products) and the relational assets of its joint ventures, alliances, and collaborations. The challenge now is for Proteome Systems to translate its strong intellectual assets into full commercial development, to maximize the company's full value, and to realize this in the marketplace.

RESOURCE IDENTIFICATION: WHAT RESOURCES DOES THE COMPANY HAVE ACCESS TO?

In Chapter 1 we stated that the resource portfolio of the organization can be divided into five categories. Traditional economic resources are divided into two categories—monetary and physical—while intellectual capital resources are divided into three categories—relational, organizational, and human. The logic behind these distinctions is that each group of resources has different managerially important characteristics from the other.

The best way to visualize the organization's resource portfolio is to express the portfolio in the form of a resource distinction tree (RDT). This helps the organization to identify, prioritize, and evaluate the most important resources necessary for its value creation efforts. An RDT is a structure that in a step by step way breaks down overarching resources into constituent resources until a suitable level of granularity is achieved. There are four criteria for identifying a resource on each level of a hierarchy. On each level:

1. Each resource must be **distinct** (i.e., the definition of a resource must be clear and separate from the definitions of all other resources at that level).
2. Each resource must be **complete** (i.e., there must be no relevant resources missing from a given level of the distinction tree).
3. Each resource must be **independent** from other resources (i.e., if one of the resources changes there must be no automatic and immediate change in any of the other resources).
4. Finally, the resource distinction tree must be **agreeable** (i.e., it must be broken down to a level that is suitable for the purpose we intend to use it for).

If these requirements are adhered to, the RDT will, in a structured and easily accessible way, show all resources, broken down to a suitable level of granularity, that the organization has access to in order to create value. The highest levels of the RDT are shown in Figure 2.1.

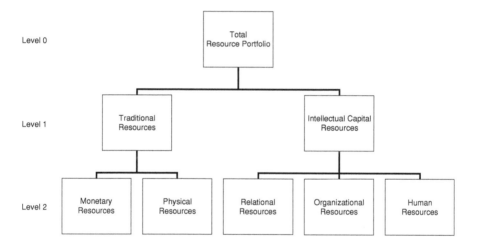

Figure 2.1. The generic beginning of a resource distinction tree.

The resource distinction tree visualizes and facilitates the evaluation of the resource portfolio that is at the disposal of the organization. The resource distinction tree is, as is indeed the whole intellectual capital management process, agnostic when it comes to legal structure of the organization and its objectives. It works equally well for a listed company, a privately held company, a government agency, a charity, or a cooperative. The reason for this is that all organizations are, from this perspective, a bundle of resources that has been deployed in a given way. The objective of the ICMP is to ensure that maximum value (whatever that means for the given organization) is achieved from the resources the organization has at its disposal.

One of the many advantages of expressing the resource portfolio in the form of a resource distinction tree is that all resources in the resource portfolio are gathered in the same structure. This is not the case with any other management approach. Another advantage is that the process of identifying resources enhances understanding of not only the individual resource but also the resource portfolio as a whole. A further advantage is that resource evaluation is not limited to resources that the organization owns but takes into account all resources that the organization has at its disposal and that have the potential to continue to contribute to the organization's value creation. A good example of resources that otherwise normally get overlooked is things like partner relationships, supplier relationships, pressure group relationships, and the like.

All organizations are unique in the combinations in their resource portfolios and how they have chosen to deploy them. It is essential that the resource distinction tree is developed to a level that allows this uniqueness to become visible. Whether this is Level 3, Level 5, or Level 7 depends on the organization. Our recommendation is to never stop at a level before Level 3 in this step of the ICMP.

To facilitate the development of the resource distinction tree we will here illustrate in a nonexhaustive way potential components of the resources that appear at the generic level (i.e., at Level 2 in the RDT).

RELATIONAL RESOURCES

Relational resources encompass all those relationships the organization has with entities outside the organization and that influence the organization's ability to create value. Examples of subdivision of these resources are listed in Table 2.1. This table is not complete and is for illustrative purposes only. The individual organization will, as for organizational and human resources, have to define the dimensions that are relevant to it when it comes to creation of value.

Again, any structure will do, as long as the requirements of completeness, distinctness, independence, and agreeability are fulfilled. The end result will be a function of six key parameters:

- The business in which the organization operates.
- The value-creating logic the organization follows.
- The value the organization is trying to generate.
- The legal form and ownership of the organization.
- The age of the organization.
- The size of the organization.

Table 2.1 Main Resource Components of Relational Resources

Potential Resources on Level 3 for Relational Resources	Potential Resources on Level 4 for Level 3 Resources under Relational Resources
Directly Business Related	<ul><li>Customers</li><li>Suppliers</li><li>Partners</li><li>Unions</li><li>Channels to market/representatives</li><li>Sources of new knowledge (e.g., universities)</li></ul>
Indirectly Business Related	<ul><li>Owners</li><li>Media</li><li>Regulatory bodies</li><li>Pressure/interest groups</li><li>Local government</li><li>National government</li><li>Educational institutions</li></ul>

ORGANIZATIONAL RESOURCES

Organizational resources, as quoted from Leif Edvinsson in Chapter 1, are "those resources that remain in the organization when the employees have left the building but that cannot be found on the balance sheet" (we substituted the word "cannot" for "may or may not," but the spirit is the same). These resources make up the nonhuman embodiment of the accumulated knowledge that has been developed by the organization and suppliers to the organization that are contributing to the organization's value creation. In other words, these are the developed structures, systems, and other tools of the organization's trade. These resources are owned and controlled by the organization and require continuous and thought-through investments to develop.

Examples of subdivision of these resources are listed in Table 2.2, and like Table 2.1, this table is not complete and is for illustrative purposes only. The individual organization again will have to define the dimensions that are relevant when it comes to creation of value. Any structure that meets the requirements of completeness, distinctness, independence, and agreeability will work.

As with relational resources, the end result will be a function of the six key parameters: the business the organization operates in, the value-creating logic the organization follows, the value the organization is trying

Table 2.2 Main Resource Components of Organizational Resources

Potential Resources on Level 3 for Organizational Resources	Potential Resources on Level 4 for Level 3 Resources under Organizational Resources
Externally Oriented	• Brands • Trademarks • Service offerings • Product concepts • Patents and other IP
Internally Oriented	• Processes • Organizational structures • Systems • Information on paper • Information in databases • Software • Organizational culture.

to generate, the legal form and ownership of the organization, the age of the organization, and the size of the organization.

We expect that there will be clear differences between firms such as a small consulting firm and a large consulting firm and a newly started printing company and one that has been in existence for 100 years.

HUMAN RESOURCES

Human resources relates to all the resources embodied in the individuals employed by or linked to the organization in a way that makes it possible for the organization to deploy these resources. Examples of a subdivision of these resources are listed in Table 2.3. Again, this table is not complete and is for illustrative purposes only, and the individual organization will have to define the dimensions that are relevant when it comes to creation of value. Again, any structure will do as long as the requirements of completeness, distinctness, independence, and agreeability are fulfilled. Here though, the end result will be a function of four key parameters: the business the organization operates in, the value-creating logic the organization follows, the value the organization is trying to generate, and the legal form and ownership of the organization. The age and size of the organization are far less important.

Again we will expect to see clear differences between organizations such as a dairy that is a limited company and a dairy that is a cooperative;

Table 2.3 Main Resource Components of Human Resources

Potential Resources on Level 3 for Human Resources	Potential Resources on Level 4 for Level 3 Resources under Human Resources
Competence	• Specific knowledge fields that encompass tacit aspects • Specific abilities that encompass tacit aspects • Brain power or processing capacity (IQ) • Empathy • Ability to build personal networks • Ability to participate in (maintain) personal networks • Ability to use (leverage) personal networks
Attitude	• Behavioral traits including social intelligence • Motivation • Pace—sometimes known as sense of urgency • Endurance or perseverance
Intellectual Agility	• Ability to innovate • Ability to imitate • Ability to adapt

a not-for-profit contract research organization and a for-profit contract research organization; a department store that is a value chain and a department store that is a value shop; a pharmaceutical company and a media company, and so on.

Case 2.2 Ericsson Business Consulting Norrköping (EBCN): Creating a Unique Distinction Tree with Four Resources

This case study builds on the paper by Göran Roos and Fredrik Lövingsson.[1] The management team of EBCN faced a challenge when it had to align its business to Ericsson's new customer oriented strategy and at the same time keep delivering value to its owners. By piloting the IC process, it was possible to achieve a clearer picture of the discrepancies between the outlined strategy and the articulated value creation path. Instead of describing the whole IC process, the following case is limited to describing only the creation of the company's distinction trees (first and second iteration) since it was perceived as a very valuable exercise in the IC process by the management team. This case illustrates the uniqueness of the value creation path and shows that the determination of the relative importance of resource categories in line with strategic intent often takes time and the final outcome can differ from the first iteration of the distinction tree.

Continued

Case 2.2 Ericsson Business Consulting Norrköping (EBCN): Creating a Unique Distinction Tree with Four Resources—cont'd

Ericsson Business Consulting was a new unit for Ericsson when the IC process was carried out in 1999. EBCN had approximately 160 employees and was part of the business unit's Nordic region, which was further divided into four service areas. Being a profit driven subunit in corporate Ericsson, the main task for EBCN was to deliver value to the owners. During that time the management team of EBCN faced a great challenge: aligning its business to Ericsson's new customer oriented strategy whilst at the same time maintaining growth rate, profitability, and innovation. As EBCN had been in the forefront of working with IC, it was a natural step for the company to pilot the IC process to improve its strategy, management, and measurement systems. This took place over a five-month period, including a total of ten workshops with the management team.

After identifying stakeholders, defining value creation, and outlining strategic intent, the management team faced the next stage of defining necessary resources that create value at a future steady state, determined by the strategic intent. Because all organizations are distinctive in the combination of their resource portfolios, it is important that the distinction tree is developed to reflect this inimitability. The outcome from the exercise was a unique distinction tree where physical resources were classified as negligible in the company's value creation path by the management team, and for this reason this resource was excluded from the distinction tree.

Next the management team was asked to determine the relative importance of different resource categories in line with the strategic intent. The distribution showed an organization focused on relational (36%) and human resources (31%), with low focus on monetary (17%) and organizational (16%) resources. See the following figure.

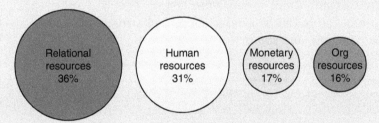

Relative importance of the resources after first iteration.

This figure depicts a consulting organization dependent on its individual employees (human resources), who are not governed by predetermined processes and concepts (organizational resources). However, this idea was challenged by the facilitator, who argued that EBCN would probably not look like this due to the lack of scalability, associated costs, and risk structure in the company. In addition, consulting companies hosted in big corporations tend to be locked into existing processes and structures, and Ericsson is traditionally dependent on its organizational resources. The management team was asked whether EBCN wanted to sell standard solutions or one-off solutions. This initiated an intense discussion where the outcome was that EBCN should focus on selling combinations of standard components within the framework provided by the organizational resources. The management team was urged to make a new tradeoff, since focusing on human resources and organizational resources represents two fundamentally different management philosophies. After this, a new distinction tree of the company was created (presented in the following figure) where organizational (31%) and relational (31%) resources were identified as most important, followed by human resources (25%) and monetary (13%) resources (in order of

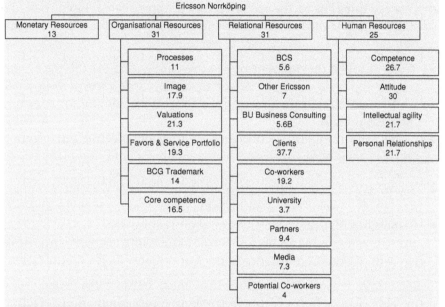

A distinction tree for EBCN after the second iteration.

priority). This depicts a traditional consulting company focused on selling prepackaged concepts and processes performed by skilled consultants, which illustrates EBCN's management philosophy better than the outcome of the first iteration.

A possible explanation for the rather contradictory results within the management team may be the fact that EBCN hosts different service areas with different business logics. Therefore, the IC process should ideally be performed at the highest organizational unit with a single business logic and coherent strategy. Nevertheless, the creation of distinction trees was essential for EBCN because it facilitated the building of taxonomy for discussing value creation within the organization. This illuminates also the importance of performing the IC process in iterations, allowing participants to redefine terms and reconsider opinions.

One of the most important outcomes resulting from the creation of distinction trees was the need for management to prioritize activities and get focused by bringing hidden disagreements to the surface. In addition, the exercise was perceived as valuable by the management team because it showed them the importance of focusing on the vital few strategically important areas and made it easier to carry on with the next step in the IC process.

RESOURCE IDENTIFICATION

To identify and structure the resources to which the organization has access is not an easy task, but both the process of identification and the resulting RDT are useful in their own right in addition to being an essential first step in the intellectual capital management process. This approach requires a fundamental shift from the more common activity or process thinking to the resource based approach of looking at the organization. For those who are new to this way of looking at an organization the following advice may be useful:

- Think through the different types of resources that exist in the organization and try to identify each of them with as few words as possible while ensuring that the descriptions are still meaningful for someone from the outside.
- Check your results with colleagues in other parts of the organization and get their views on the understandability and completeness of your list.
- Try to ask as many different people as practically possible how they perceive the organization and what is important for it to do well.
- Remember that different parts of the organization may have different strategies and that this needs to be taken into account since strategy will determine which resources are valuable to the organization.

Sometimes it is useful to go through these steps of the process as a team. This ensures that a common language and a common understanding are developed among the participating team members. It also increases the probability that the requirements of completeness, distinctness, independence, and agreeability are fulfilled.

Useful Sources in the Creation of the Resource Distinction Tree

- All types of in-house documents that discuss resources
- Industry statistics
- Any type of resource-specific information
- Industry (multi-client) studies
- Analysts' reports
- Regulatory review reports
- Reports from industry associations
- Academic articles, papers, and theses
- Examples of RDTs from other organizations

Example 2.1 The Value Chain Distinction Tree

An initial distinction tree for the value chain company was developed through interviews and workshops and resulted in the following figure.

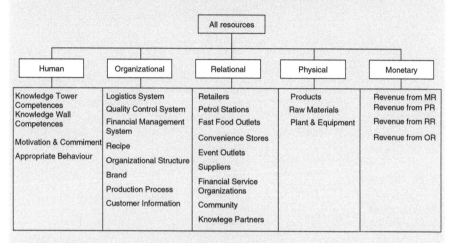

The initial tree was revised and reduced to one with only 13 subresources. Thereafter, the resources were weighted according to their importance for the company's value creation. The revised and weighted tree is shown below.

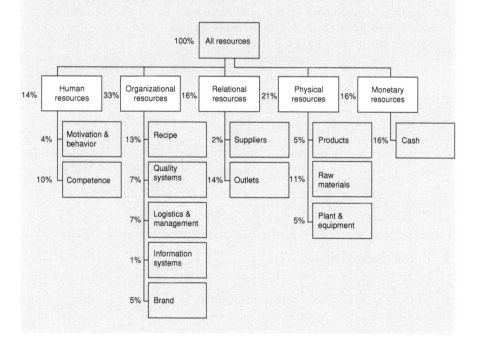

Example 2.2 Value Shop Distinction Tree

A distinction tree of the organization was constructed by means of interviews and workshops. The first round of interviews sought to determine the scope of the resources used by the company. A workshop was then held to gain a consensus on the nature of the resources and their meanings. The resulting distinction tree is shown below.

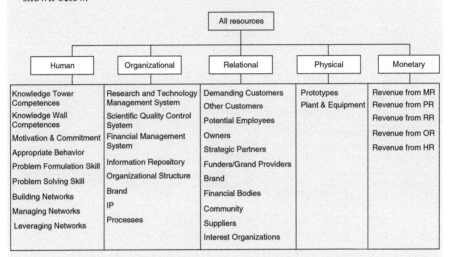

This tree contained 35 resources and it was felt that many of these could be combined without undue loss of detail. This was done and the tree reduced to 13 resources as shown in the following tree. The consensus view on the relative importance of these resources in generating value for the company was also determined at the workshop. These are also shown in the diagram.

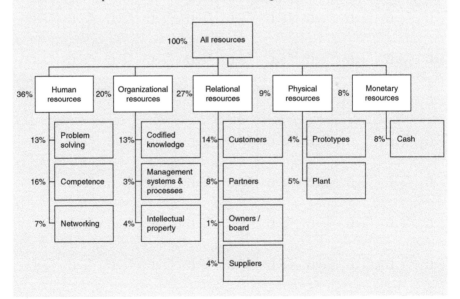

Example 2.3 A Distinction Tree for the Network Organization

The Value Network organization's distinction tree ended up with 13 subresources, as shown in the following RDT. The consensus view on the relative importance of these resources in generating value for the company was also determined and is also shown in the following diagram.

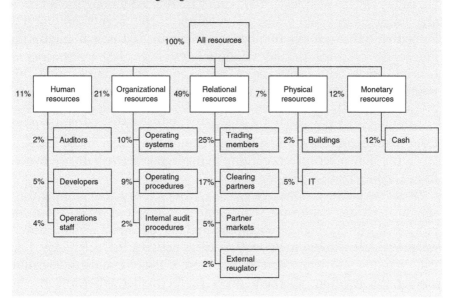

WEIGHTING THE RESOURCES

Once resources have been identified and mapped it is time to judge their relative importance for the organization's ongoing ability to create value. It is essential to keep in mind that identified resources are not equally important for the organization's future value creation. It is while making these judgments that different views as to how the organization is supposed to create value become clearly visible. Judgments have to be made on three dimensions:

1. How influential is a given resource on the organization's ability to create value?
2. What level of quality does the resource hold compared to the ideal?
3. What quantity of the resource does the organization have access to, compared to the ideal situation?

It is normal to start by judging the relative influence of the different resources on the organization's future value creation. This is always done under the assumption that both quality and quantity are sufficient for all resources. One way of doing this is to divide 100 points among the five resource categories—monetary, physical, relational, organizational, and human—in such a way that twice as many points means the categoryis twice as influential for the organization's future ability to create value. On the next level, 100 points are divided among the immediate subcategories of monetary resources, 100 points among the immediate subcategories of physical resources, 100 points among the immediate subcategories of relational resources, 100 points among the immediate subcategories of organizational resources, and 100 points among the immediate subcategories of human resources. This division of points then continues on the next level down in the RDT.

In Figures 2.2 through 2.5 we show an example of a weighted RDT from a telecommunications software company. There are no physical resources shown because, according to management, they do not matter from a value creation perspective.

If this weighting is done as a group activity it is essential that there are several iterations before the final numbers are agreed on and that the individual with the highest weightings and the individual with the lowest weightings are allowed to argue their cases between the weightings. This will lead to a better understanding and a lower standard deviation among the resulting numbers, allowing for higher reliability of end results.

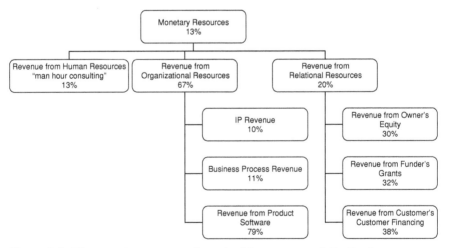

Figure 2.2. The monetary resource branch of the resource distinction tree.

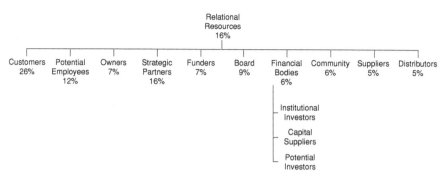

Figure 2.3. The relational resource branch of the resource distinction tree.[1]

Once the weightings are agreed on, it is appropriate to evaluate each resource for its quality and quantity. This is normally done using a judgment traffic light system where green means clearly sufficient, orange/yellow means borderline, and red means clearly insufficient. This is done on the lowest level in the RDT only. Once this is done, the resources are grouped together in a table that shows potential problem areas (see Table 2.4).

The actions indicated in Table 2.4 are proposed under the assumption that the influence weightings of the resources are equal. This is not normally the case, and one would expect the weightings to decrease from top left to lower right. As a consequence, one would not normally have to take any major activity in the lower right-hand corner of Table 2.4 since the resources in this corner normally do not influence the organization's value creation in any meaningful way. On the other hand, if many of the resources found in the lower right-hand corner of Table 2.4 do influence the organization's value creation in a substantial way the articulated strategy of the firm must be queried since its probability of success is very low.

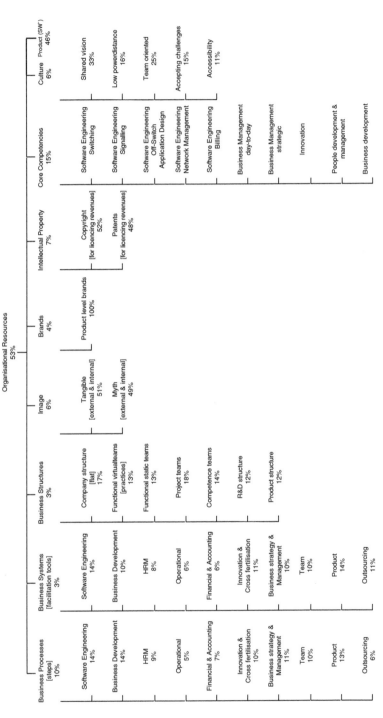

Figure 2.4. The organizational resource branch of the resource distinction tree.

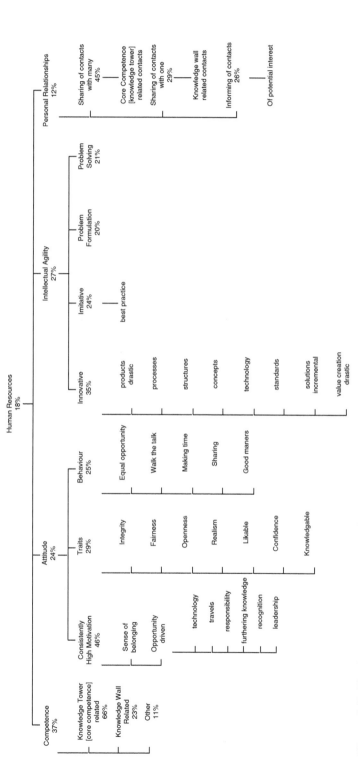

Figure 2.5. The human resource branch of the resource distinction tree.

Table 2.4 Action Table for Quality and Quantity of Resources in the Resource Distinction Tree with Principal Recommended Actions

	Quality Judgment		
	Green	Orange/Yellow	Red
Quantity Judgment			
Green	No action	1. Ensure that quality does not deteriorate, and 2. Initiate some quality enhancing activities	Initiate forceful quality improvement activities
Orange/Yellow	1. Ensure that quantity does not deteriorate 2. Initiate some quantity enhancing activities	Ensure that neither quality nor quantity deteriorate and initiate some quality and quantity enhancing activities	1. Initiate forceful quality improvement activities; 2. Ensure that quantity does not deteriorate; and, 3. Initiate some quantity enhancing activities
Red	Initiate forceful quantity improvement activities	1. Initiate forceful quantity improvement activities, 2. Ensure that quality does not deteriorate; and, 3. Initiate some quality enhancing activities	Initiate forceful qualitative and quantitative improvement activities

Case 2.3 Saku Brewery: Two Levels of Distinction Trees

With the Estonian beer market becoming more competitive and presenting several pressing challenges, the management team of market leader Saku Brewery realized the need to be proactive in order to survive. By implementing the IC process, management wanted to understand how the brewery could most efficiently and effectively implement its strategy in its domestic market and how resources could be leveraged to achieve Saku's strategic intent most effectively. To analyze Saku's value creation process, it was important to break down, to a suitable level of granularity, the value-creating resources the organization had access to. Therefore, this case depicts a development of Saku's distinction tree, broken down into four levels, with the purpose of capturing Saku's specific resources. This allowed the uniqueness of Saku to become visible, which was a necessity in order to apply the IC process successfully.

Saku Brewery has been a leading Estonian brewery for the past 100 years, producing a variety of beer brands in addition to seasonal beers and mineral water. In 1991 Baltic Beverages Holding AB (joint venture of Pripps Ringnes AB and Oy Hartwell AB[1]) took a majority shareholding in Saku Brewery, owning 75% of the shares, with the remainder in the hands of private shareholders. When the IC process was carried out, Saku Brewery was Estonia's largest brewery, with a 48% market share of the total beer market in Estonia. At the end of the 1990s the market was becoming more aggressive with several pressing challenges from competing breweries such as Tartu and Carlsberg who were actively developing new products that could have seriously affected Saku's market share. The management of Saku understood that a competitive advantage in the future beer market lay in the different aspects of intellectual capital. Hence, to meet the strategic goal of maintaining Saku's position relative to competitors as the lowest delivered cost and highest perceived value producer of beer in Estonia, they needed to identify what resources provided them with a competitive advantage and how to leverage these resources to achieve their strategic intent most effectively. At the suggestion of Baltic Beverages Holding, the brewery implemented a full IC process that had a focus on the aforementioned issues.

During the IC process, the management team went through many workshops and stages where they determined the value creation path and identified actions for improvement. One of the cornerstones of the IC process was the development of Saku's distinction tree which clarified the links and relative importance of each type of resource. It took a fairly lengthy iterative process to reach consensus on the different resources and on their importance to value creation. Although some of the more senior executives took a very broad view of processes in their company, others tended to focus disproportionately on the contribution of their own particular disciplines. However, with the help of the facilitator, management was able to combine the perceptions concerning the relative standalone importance of different resources within the organization, and distinction trees for different levels were created. In the following figure, Saku's distinction tree is presented at Level 3. It is then broken down into Level 4, depicted in the second figure, where the distinction tree for organizational resources is presented.[2]

Continued

Case 2.3 Saku Brewery: Two Levels of Distinction Trees—cont'd

It was essential to break down Saku's resources into their constituent resources because it facilitated the understanding not only of the individual resources but also of the resource portfolio as a whole, which takes into account all the resources having potential to continue Saku's value creation. The development of the distinction trees through all four levels was in itself a valuable process because it facilitated a common understanding of Saku's unique resource portfolio. In addition, the distinction trees as part of the whole IC process brought the management to a better common view on what really drove value to the organization and thus needed to be managed and measured. These outcomes made it easier to carry on with the next step of the IC process, where Saku's deployment of resources was defined and visualized by the navigator. This step will be depicted in Chapter 3 along with the outcome of the IC process applied at Saku.

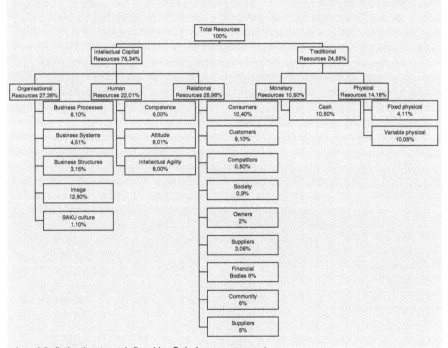

Level 3 distinction tree defined by Saku's management.

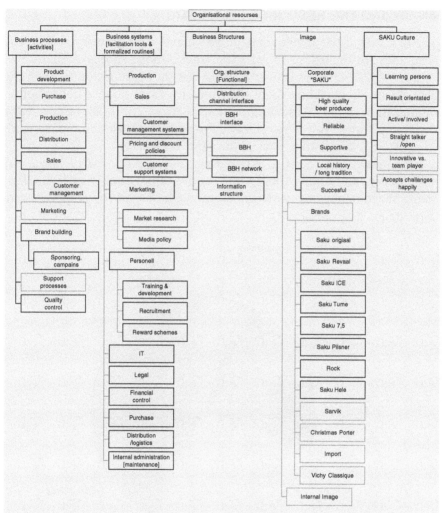

Level 4 distinction tree of organizational resources defined by Saku's management.

ANALYZING THE RESOURCE PORTFOLIO

The first step of the analysis is to judge whether the resource portfolio and weighting are aligned, or fit, with the organization's strategy. What do we mean by fit? In Chapter 1 we articulated that the organization exists to create value for its stakeholders in some priority order. For the not-for-profit organization, value takes on a nonmonetary form (this will be covered in detail in Chapter 4), whereas for the for-profit organization money tends to make up a dominating part of the value construct.

This means that the first requirement is to identify the organization's stakeholders and to give them some relative importance. Figure 2.6 illustrates the outcome of such an exercise for a part of a government department.

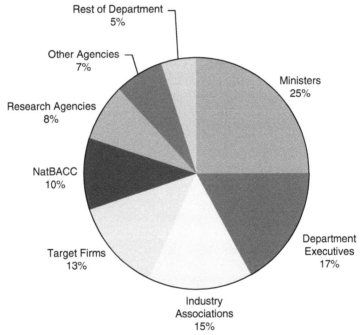

Figure 2.6. Stakeholder identification and weighting within a delineated part of a government department.

The second task is to identify the components of, or forms that, value takes from the primary stakeholders' points of view (i.e., what is the output?). In a listed firm we can assume that value equals shareholder financial returns,[2] but in not-for-profit organizations this is not likely to be the case. Sometimes the value construct becomes very complicated and this is espe-

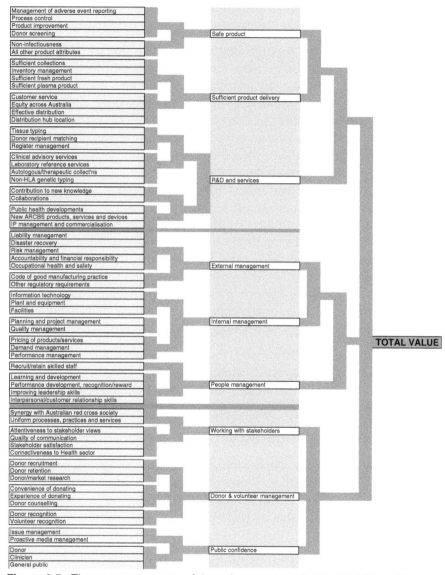

Figure 2.7. The component parts of the value construct for the Red Cross Blood Service.

cially true for not-for-profit organizations. Figure 2.7 illustrates the valued attributes for the Red Cross Blood Service (more on how to arrive at a structure like this and how to interpret and use it will be covered in Chapter 4).

Once we know the stakeholders, their relative importance, and what we mean when we use the term *value*, we have to start looking at resources.

For each of the resources identified in our portfolio we have to make a judgment as to what extent the resource fulfills the requirement for being:

- Valuable in allowing the organization to address threats or opportunities in the organization's environment (as determined by the strategy).
- Durable[3] (i.e., it must be possible to use/deploy the resource frequently). A resource is durable to the extent that the benefits it conveys do not decay over time (i.e., the resource is self-sustaining) and as a consequence durable resources must demonstrate a degree of factor immobility or be linked to complementary resources that demonstrate a degree of factor immobility.
- Rare (i.e., not all competitors[4] must have access to this type of resource; in fact the fewer that have access to this type of resource the better it is).
- Inimitable[5] (i.e., a resource is difficult to imitate when the organization that tries to copy or duplicate it will incur sizeable cost disadvantages compared to those organizations that already have access to the resource).
- Unsubstitutable[6] (i.e., a resource that is difficult to substitute will have a longer life as a basis for a competitive advantage and therefore will have a higher value to the organization).

Again, it is useful to classify the resource portfolio according to which resources possess which of these traits. Table 2.5 is a summary of which resources possess which traits, to what extent, and the actions needed to increase the traits.

INCREASING THE STRATEGIC VALUE OF RESOURCES

We will now make a few clarifying comments on the actions outlined in Table 2.5. It is essential to remember that only resources that have green status in all five areas can form a basis for a competitive advantage for the organization (See Table on page 105).

Value

If the resource is not valuable given the articulated strategy, then there is no reason for the organization to keep it in its resource portfolio and it may be better to exchange it for other resources by, for example, selling it.

Durability

If the resource is not durable, then either its durability must be improved (e.g., a person knowledgeable in a foreign language; this

Table 2.5. Action Table for Which Resources in the Resource Distinction Tree Possess What Traits to What Extent, with Principal Recommended Actions

	Judgment		
	Clearly Is	Borderline	Clearly Is Not
Resource Traits			
Valuable	Do nothing	Marginally relevant for the strategy. Nothing to do unless a change in strategy is contemplated.	Not relevant for the strategy. Nothing to do unless a change in strategy is contemplated. May be worth disposing of the resource in exchange for other resources.
Durable	Do nothing	Make a judgment if something needs to be done to improve durability and, if so, ensure bundling with durable resources so that the bundle as a whole becomes durable.	Ensure bundling with durable resources so that the bundle as a whole becomes durable.
Rare	Do nothing	Nothing to do	Nothing to do
Inimitable	Do nothing	Make a judgment if something needs to be done to improve inimitability and, if so, increase the cost of imitation by ensuring maximum benefit from: • Scale • Information asymmetry • Time • Inertia	Try to increase the cost of imitation by ensuring maximum benefit from: • Scale • Information asymmetry • Time • Inertia

Continued

Table 2.5. (*Continued*)

Unsubstitutable	Do nothing	Make a judgment if something needs to be done to improve unsubstitutability and, if so, increase the cost of substitution by ensuring maximum benefit from: • Scale • Information asymmetry • Time • Inertia	Try to increase the cost of substitution by ensuring maximum benefit from: • Scale • Information asymmetry • Time • Inertia

knowledge skill embodied in the person is not automatically durable. We all know that if we do not use what we know it tends to decay over time. If the language knowledge embodied in the person is put to use, we will have increased the durability of this resource), or it must be linked with a co-specialized resource that is durable. Examples of such pairings are human resources (normally not durable) that are linked with organizational resources such as firm-specific, idiosyncratic, and embedded resources such as routines or IT-systems, or firm-specific, idiosyncratic, embedded and tacit resources such as corporate culture.[7] As another example, banks that innovated with ATMs first gained control of the best locations (an intangible physical resource), a co-specialized resource necessary for a bank's electronic banking service network (an organizational resource) to achieve durability, since the IT part could be made obsolete by someone else innovating or developing a better system.[8]

Scarcity

Obviously, if a strategic resource is one-of-a-kind it is able to generate scarcity rents, but resources do not need to be one-of-a-kind. A relatively rare resource can be shared among a limited number of competing firms and still generate scarcity rents (see Figure 2.8) as long as the total output, Q_s, is less than the equilibrium output, Q_e.[9] If the resource is not scarce, very little can be done to increase scarcity.

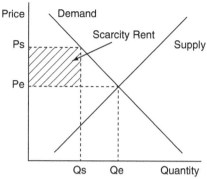

Figure 2.8. The concept of scarcity rents.[10]

Inimitability

The inimitability of a resource can be increased in the following ways:

- "Adding increments to an existing asset stock is facilitated by possessing high levels of that stock . . . the underlying notion is that success breeds success."[11] This is normally true in economies of scale, experience curve effects, and economies of scope situations. Inimitability is increased if these economies are exploited.
- There are benefits of first mover advantage or lags in imitation. Inimitability is increased if these opportunities are exploited.
- Cost of entry is high enough to exclude others from participating. In this case access to capital (i.e., the monetary resource) can be said to fulfill the requirements of being inimitable.
- In markets where network economics are at work these can enhance the inimitability of resources. In cases where consumer utility is an increasing function of a firm's or technology's market share, then a slight advantage in initial market share will result in market domination and the locking out of competitors. The effect is often strong enough to lock out superior technologies from the market.[12]
- Inimitability can also be increased if switching costs can be increased.
- If information asymmetry can be increased to the advantage of the firm to the level where causal ambiguity[13,14] arises (i.e., when the link between a firm's resources and its sustained competitive advantage are poorly understood), then inimitability is increased.[15]
- In some situations it is possible to fully understand what underpins competitive advantage and still not have enough information to

imitate it, for example, when socially complex resources such as a firm's reputation or corporate culture may play an understandable role in underpinning the competitive advantage but be impossible to imitate.[16,17] So if competition can be made to say "we know what to do but not how to do it," inimitability has been achieved.

- Inimitability of human resources is inherent since the knowledge they hold, according to our definition, is tacit.[18,19,20]
- It is also feasible that the owner of a resource can be completely ignorant of how the resource was created; it may have been accidentally created or the original creator may have left the company and left no record of the process, or the resource could have emerged from the complex interactions of members of the organization. In this situation the resource is by default inimitable.[21]
- If the costs of acquiring, analyzing, and acting on information about the resource to be imitated outweigh the benefits of imitating those resources, the resource is de facto inimitable.[22]
- If for some resources there are time constraints. Some organizational resources such as reputation, corporate culture, and key firm routines evolve over long periods of time. The inimitability of these types of resources is based on the fact that doubling the flow of inputs that created a resource will not lead to the accumulation of a given level of resource stock in half the time.[23] As a consequence, if you want to imitate a resource of this type you have to follow the same timeline as the original developer, thereby making the resource de facto inimitable.
- There are situations where inimitability arises from path dependencies (i.e., future choices are constrained by the history of past decisions). Once a certain path is taken, the size of the (irreversible) commitment locks the firm into its chosen (investment) strategy. In practice, the costs of changing paths are generally significant, if not insurmountable.[24] This means that firms that have not taken the same paths historically will find some of the resources that arise out of these paths inimitable. There are aspects of first mover advantage that arise out of path dependencies due to the fact that the actions of earlier entrants change the choices available to late entrants (i.e., they appropriate the best locations or the best representatives). These appropriated resources then become inimitable to the late entrants.
- Sometimes inimitability is due to the lack of ability to respond.[25,26,27] This lack of ability to respond is frequently due to the ways of think-

ing that have been ingrained in managers and that make it impossible for them to see all alternatives. As the reality of the firm moves further from the reality that generated the mindset of managers, the possibility of an inappropriate response increases and the response time to new opportunities increases. The ability to change is being constrained by five groups of behaviors:[28,29]

1. Distorted Perception

   o Myopia. The consequence of individual myopia may be organizational inertia.

   o Hubris and denial. A serious source of perceptual distortion is denial—the rejection of information that is contrary to what is desired or what is believed to be true. Denial may stem from hubris—overwhelming pride in past accomplishments—or it may derive from fear. Hubris is also explainable as superstitious learning—learning based on associating past success with factors that were coincidental to it but bear no causal relationship to the success.

   o Grooved thinking. There are three aspects of this: (i) restricted thinking that groups impose, punishing or rejecting ideas and information that deviate too much from orthodoxy, (ii) patterns of thinking as mental habits whose structure and function are the same as physical habits and are therefore difficult to change even if one is aware of them, and (iii) the use of the "wrong" metaphor, a wrong metaphor that, once accepted, acts as a powerful restriction on future thought.

2. Dulled Motivation

   o Direct costs of change. It is likely that change temporarily increases the risk of organizational failure, disrupts operations, and involves a great deal of expensive effort. Even more important is that change may imply the abandonment of costly sunk specific investments (note that an impediment to change may be rational).

   o Cannibalization costs. When a new product's success eats into the sales and profits of an older product, the older product is said to have been cannibalized. Cannibalization problems may be rational or simply reflect subgroup interests. Rational cannibalization problems occur under conditions of buyer loyalty (or switching costs). Loyal buyers will stay with a firm's old product despite competitors' introductions of new versions, but will switch to the new version when it is offered by the firm they favor.

○ Cross-subsidy comforts. The motivation to change is inhibited when a problem business is subsidized by rents from another business. The subsidy may be direct, in the form of management's toleration of losses in a business that are compensated for by gains elsewhere, or it may be indirect, obtained through artificial transfer prices or through bundling businesses together so that separate measures are not obtained.

3. Failed Creative Response

○ Speed and complexity. Analysis is blocked or frozen when things happen too quickly. If a competitor can take action faster than an opponent, the opponent may not simply struggle along but may freeze up or collapse. In military terms this is known as "seizing and holding the initiative." The pace of events tends to overtake resource allocation systems and the complexity of judgments required tends to exacerbate the situation.

○ Reactive mindset. Change is inhibited when people adhere to the view that their problems are natural and inevitable. The most common reactive mindsets are that the industry is "mature" and that the problems are industry problems and not the fault of the firm. These points of view often have great validity behind them, including the weight of expert advice and analysis. They are also self-fulfilling. If all competitors define the market as mature, then their collective actions will often cause the outcome.

○ Inadequate strategic vision. Even when analysis and choice have not been blocked, the direction chosen—and especially its articulation— may be so flawed that change is blocked. Vision (direction) also may be inadequate because it is hypocritical. Hypocritical vision is dishonest, claiming values and goals that are known to be false.

4. Political Deadlocks

○ Departmental politics. Managers rarely act to unseat themselves or to terminate their own departments.

○ Incommensurable beliefs. These arise when different individuals or groups hold sincere but differing beliefs about the nature of the problem or its solution. What happens when these managers are asked to reach a consensus? Four basic patterns can emerge:[30] First, a leader may simply impose a decision, eliminating the illusion of group choice. Second, the choice process may cycle for some time without generating an outcome. Third, the managers may recognize the irrationality of the situation and withdraw from participation (essentially colluding to avoid choice). Finally, other considerations or "games" may change the relative influence the managers have, resolving the paradox.

○ When managers disagree, there is often no rational way to combine their beliefs (forums or processes do not exist). If speed is important, leadership may have to abandon the group decision process. When process is important and beliefs differ, inertia may well be the outcome.

○ Vested values. Unlike the cases of differing interests or beliefs, here individuals, departments, and business units or divisions are taken to have strong emotional or value attachments to products, policies, or ways of doing things. These vested values and interests can easily be the greatest impediments to change. Vested values lie at the heart of institutions. The defenders of vested values are usually the informal leadership network—the defenders of the group and its norms. The paradox of change is that these same people, perhaps the best and the brightest, easily become the source of inertia. The problem of vested values is not with simple foot dragging, but with the organizational equivalent of patriotism.

5. Action Disconnects

○ Leadership inaction. For change to begin, leadership must articulate a vision for change, must alter incentives, must take direct action where possible, and must shift the power base. If it fails to do these things, change will be inhibited. Major change requires a leader to repudiate prior commitments, thus lessening his or her ability to lead in the future. Hence, entrenched leadership is normally a source of inertia.

○ Embedded routines. The life functions of a business are its processes—its ways of doing things. Complex processes possess great inertia. The knowledge of how certain steps are performed may be tacit; no one may have a complete understanding of the process, and changing one aspect of a process may have significant unanticipated consequences on other parts of the organization. Finally, the various routines that make up a process take on the force of habit. From a purely economic perspective, organizational change only requires a change in incentives. However, the habitual patterns of work have an inertial force that can be much stronger than any practical incentives.

○ Collective action problems. Action can be blocked by a variety of collective action problems. The simplest is the first mover problem: if senior management has called for new initiatives, does it pay to be a first mover? In many situations the incentives are clearly in favor of waiting to see how the first mover does. In such cases, the equilibrium is for no one to move at all. There are also analogous problems of free-riders that inhibit change even when first movers have led the way. The more complex collective action problem is that best described as cultural. A dysfunctional culture may block change and itself be virtually impervious to alteration. Because culture depends on mutual expectations, it is not easily changed. A culture that resists change or that does not fit the direction the firm needs to take can be an insurmountable source of inertia.

○ Capabilities gaps. The final action blockade is simply a gap or disconnect between the tasks that need to be performed and the competencies and capabilities within the firm. Whilst a small gap may be positive, too great a gap is discouraging and is more likely to inhibit than induce change.

Any activity that the organization can initiate that generates these types of inertia in competing organizations increases the inimitability of the organization's resources generally.

Unsubstitutability

The way to increase the unsubstitutability of a resource is very similar to the way to increase its inimitability. Special emphasis should be put on customer loyalty to achieve customer retention in the face of substitutes.

CONCLUSION

Based on the preceding analysis, it is possible for the organization to evaluate whether its resource portfolio is well aligned with what the organization is trying to achieve and, if the alignment is not perfect, what actions are suitable to take. At this point it should become clear that the organization's ability to create value is not only a function of its resource portfolio but also of its ability to deploy or use these resources. This is the topic of Chapter 3.

Key Points in Chapter 2

- The intellectual capital management process not only encompasses the resources that the firm owns but also all resources that the firm can access to create value. As a consequence, it gives a better picture than more traditional approaches of the firm's resource portfolio.
- The resource portfolio is subdivided into five categories: monetary, physical, relational, organizational, and human. The reason for this subdivision is the differing economic behavior of these resource categories.
- The resource distinction tree is introduced as a useful tool to map the resource portfolio of the organization. A resource distinction tree is mapped out to a suitable level of detail—normally at least to Level 3. This allows for the capture of organization specific resources—a necessity for being able to evaluate the resources.
- Once the resources are mapped into a resource distinction tree they are weighted based on their influence on the organization's ability to create value. Subsequently, each resource is evaluated for its quality and quantity.
- The final step in the resource portfolio evaluation is the evaluation of which resources can form a basis for the organization's sustainable competitive advantage. This entails an evaluation of each resource for its strategic value, durability, scarcity, inimitability, and unsubstitutability.
- Once deficiencies have been identified in this analysis, action programs to rectify these are outlined and initiated.
- By linking the evaluated resource portfolio to the organization's strategy, objectives, and perception of its environment and the future, it is possible to judge if the resource portfolio has a good fit and enables the achievement of the organization's strategic intent. If there is no good fit, there needs to be either a set of actions to change the content of the resource portfolio or a reevaluation of the organization's strategy, objectives, or perceptions of the environment or the future.

If the book is being used as a workbook, then the following results should have been achieved so far:

- A resource distinction tree at least down to level 3 should have been produced.
- Each of the resources should have been weighted.
- Each of the resources should have been evaluated for quality and quantity using the traffic light style table.
- For those important (derived from the weighting) resources that have insufficient quality and/or quantity, action plans should have been outlined and possibly initiated to rectify the situation.
- Each resource should have been evaluated for its potential to form a basis for a sustainable competitive advantage for the organization.
- For those resources lacking in ability to form a basis for a sustainable competitive advantage, action plans should have been outlined and possibly initiated to rectify the situation.

Key Points in Chapter 2—cont'd

- An opinion should have been formed about whether the organization's strategy and objectives can be achieved given the present resource portfolio. If not, a plan to either change the organization's strategic intent (or its perception of the environment or future) or to modify the resource portfolio should have been outlined and possibly initiated.

The following table summarizes the theoretical consequences of not fulfilling all five requirements:

The Resource is:					Competitive consequence	Performance consequence
Valuable	Durable	Rare	Inimitable	Unsubstitutable		
No	Yes	No	Yes/No	Yes/No	Competitive Disadvantage	Sub-normal Returns
Yes	Yes	No	Yes	Yes	Competitive Parity	Normal Returns
Yes	Yes	Yes	Yes	No	Temporary Competitive Advantage	Supra-normal Returns declining to Normal Returns
Yes	Yes	Yes	No	Yes	Temporary Competitive Advantage	Supra-normal Returns declining to Normal Returns
Yes/No	No	Yes/No	Yes/No	Yes/No	No Competitive Consequence	No Performance Consequence
Yes	Yes	No	No	No	Table Stake	No Performance Consequence
Yes	Yes	Yes	Yes	Yes	Sustainable Competitive Advantage	Sustainable Supra-normal Returns
Yes	Yes	Yes	No	No	Temporary Competitive Advantage	Supra-normal Returns declining to Normal Returns
Yes	Yes	No	Yes	No	Table Stake	No Performance Consequence
Yes	Yes	No	No	Yes	Table Stake	No Performance Consequence
No	Yes	Yes	Yes	Yes	Competitive Disadvantage	Sub-normal Returns
No	Yes	Yes	Yes	No	Competitive Disadvantage	Sub-normal Returns
No	Yes	Yes	No	Yes	Competitive Disadvantage	Sub-normal Returns
No	Yes	Yes	No	Yes	Competitive Disadvantage	Sub-normal Returns

ENDNOTES

1. Please note that due to rounding the top level adds up to 99% instead of 100%.
2. Conventionally, this is identified as total shareholder return (TSR), the compound annual return (measured over 3, 5, or 7 years) that is the annualized return of dividends received during the period plus share price appreciation over the period measured either as an arithmetic or a geometric progression
3. M.A. Peteraf (1993), The cornerstones of competitive advantage: a resource-based view, *Strategic Management Journal*, 14, 179–191.
4. We here define the term *competitor* to be a potential supplier of products and/or services that from the customer's point of view are substitutable. For example, if I want to travel from New York to Hartford, Connecticut, I may chose between airlines and limousine service companies, all of which are competitors to each other.
5. M.A. Peteraf (1993), "The cornerstones of competitive advantage: a resource-based view," *Strategic Management Journal*, 14, 179–191.
6. I. Dierickx and K. Cool (1989), Asset stock accumulation and sustainability of competitive advantage, *Management Science*, 35(12), 1504–1511.
7. D.J. Teece, G. Pisano, and A. Shuen (1997), "Dynamic capabilities and strategic management," *Strategic Management Journal*, 18(7), 509–533.
8. B. Dos Santos and K. Peffers (1995), "Rewards to investors in innovative information technology applications: a study of first movers and early followers in ATMs," *Organization Science*, 5(2), 241–259.
9. Directly from S.E. Phelan (1997), "Using artificial adaptive agents to explore strategic landscapes, Doctoral Dissertation, School of Business, Faculty of Law and Management, La Trobe University, Bundoora, Australia, November".
10. Directly from S.E. Phelan (1997), "Using artificial adaptive agents to explore strategic landscapes, Doctoral Dissertation, School of Business, Faculty of Law and Management, La Trobe University, Bundoora, Australia, November".
11. I. Dierickx and K. Cool (1989), Asset stock accumulation and sustainability of competitive advantage, *Management Science*, 35(12), 1507.
12. W.B. Arthur (1988), Self reinforcing mechanisms in economics. In: P. W. Anderson, K. J. Arrow, and D. Pines (Eds.), *The Economy as an Evolving Complex System* (pp. 9–32), Redwood City, CA: Addison-Wesley.
13. S. Lippman and R.P. Rumelt (1982), "Uncertain imitability: an analysis of interfirm differences in efficiency under competition," *Bell Journal of Economics*, 13, 418–453.
14. R.P. Rumelt (1984), "Towards a strategic theory of the firm." In: R. B. Lamb (Ed.), *Competitive Strategic Management* (pp. 556–570), Englewood Cliffs, NJ: Prentice-Hall.
15. J. Barney (1991), "Firm resources and sustained competitive advantage," *Journal of Management*, 17(1), 99–120.
16. I. Dierickx and K. Cool (1989), "Asset stock accumulation and sustainability of competitive advantage," *Management Science*, 35(12), 1504–1511.
17. P.J.H. Schoemaker (1990), "Strategy, complexity and economic rent," *Management Science*, 36(10), 1178–1192.
18. M. Polanyi (1962), *Personal Knowledge: Towards a Post-Critical Philosophy*, New York: Harper.
19. R.R. Nelson and S.G. Winter (1982), *An Evolutionary Theory of Economic Change*, Cambridge, Mass.: Harvard University Press.
20. D. Teece (1982), "Towards an economic theory of the multiproduct firm," *Journal of Economic Behavior and Organization*, 3, 39–63.
21. S.E. Phelan (1997), "Using artificial adaptive agents to explore strategic landscapes, Doctoral Dissertation, School of Business, Faculty of Law and Management, La Trobe University, Bundoora, Australia, November".

22. S.E. Phelan (1997), "Using artificial adaptive agents to explore strategic landscapes, Doctoral Dissertation, School of Business, Faculty of Law and Management, La Trobe University, Bundoora, Australia, November".
23. I. Dierickx and K. Cool (1989), "Asset stock accumulation and sustainability of competitive advantage," *Management Science*, 35(12), 1506.
24. D.J. Teece, G. Pisan, and A. Shuen (1994), *Dynamic capabilities and strategic management* (CCC Working Paper 94–9): University of California at Berkeley.
25. P. Ghemawat (1991), *Commitment: The Dynamic of Strategy*, New York: Free Press.
26. M.T. Hannan, and J. Freeman (1984), "Structural inertia and organizational change," *American Sociological Review*, 49, 149–164.
27. C.K. Prahalad and R.A. Bettis (1986), "The dominant logic: the new linkage between firm diversity and performance," *Strategic Management Journal*, 7(6), 485–501.
28. R.P. Rumelt (1995), "Inertia and transformation." In: C.A. Montgomery (Ed.), *Resource-Based and Evolutionary Theories of the Firm: Towards a Synthesis*, Boston: Kluwer Academic Publishers.This section is based on R.P. Rumelt (1995), a revised and abridged version of the full article, which appeared in: C.A. Montgomery (Ed.), *Resources in an Evolutionary Perspective: Towards a Synthesis of Evolutionary and Resource-Based Approaches to Strategy*, Norwell, Mass.: Kluwer Academic Publishers, 101–132. Located at http://www.anderson.ucla.edu/faculty/dick.rumelt/Docs/Papers/berkeley_précis.pdf.
29. The main content of the bullet points are take straight from R.P. Rumelt (1995) "Precis of Inertia and transformation," a revised and abridged version of the full article, which appeared in: C.A. Montgomery (Ed.), *Resources in an Evolutionary Perspective: Towards a Synthesis of Evolutionary and Resource-Based Approaches to Strategy*, Norwell, Mass.: Kluwer Academic Publishers, 101–132. Located at http://www.anderson.ucla.edu/faculty/dick.rumelt/Docs/Papers/berkeley_precis.pdf. Any modifications, removals and additions are solely the authors'.

CASE 2.1   ENDNOTES

1. Proteome Systems prospectus.
2. Change Track resource.

CASE 2.2   ENDNOTE

1. "El Proceso CI en el "Nuevo Mondo de las Telecomunicacionel" in Güell, A. M. (ed.), Homo faber, homo sapiens – La gestión del capital intelectual, Ediciones del Bronce, 1999, pp. 141–169.

CASE 2.3   ENDNOTES

1. Since 2002 BBH has been a 50:50 joint venture between Scottish & Newcastle and Carlsberg Breweries.
2. The other four resources have been broken down in the same manner but are not presented here due to lack of space.

3

Putting intellectual capital resources to value-creating use*

This chapter deals with the effectiveness problem: how can I ensure that my resources are put to use in such a way that I have maximized my potential to create value?

It is important to be aware that there is no correlation between the amount of a given resource the organization has at its disposal and the value the organization can create. Just because the organization is provided with more money, more machines, more customers or suppliers, more or better processes or IP, or more competent people does not mean that it automatically will produce more value. The value it manages to produce is a function of how it puts its resources to use—sometimes we use the term *resource deployment*. This all boils down to the decisions the firm makes as to which resources are going to be transformed into which other resources and in what order.

In chapter 2 we identified and evaluated the organization's resource portfolio. Now we must likewise identify and evaluate the organization's resource transformation structure.

Any given organization is made up of a unique resource portfolio deployed in a unique transformation structure; no two organizations are the same. All resources in an organization are interconnected in one way or another, and value is created through the transformation of one resource into another (e.g., products into money, competence into new processes, relationships into reduced search costs, brands into increased revenues, etc.). Figure 3.1 illustrates a simple transformation example in which a competent development group comes up with a prototype for a

*In this chapter, we are grateful to Intellectual Capital Services Ltd. for providing substantial amounts of data and analysis.

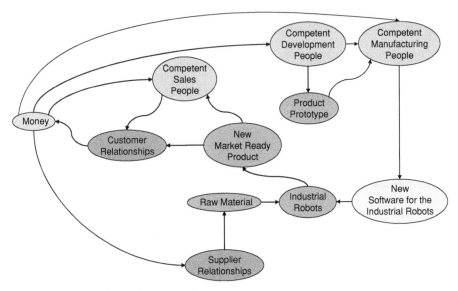

Figure 3.1. Transformation example.

new product which is then discussed with the competent manufacturing team that writes new software for the industrial robots that enable them to produce this product. Raw material is then procured from suppliers and the product is produced and handed to the competent sales people, who go to the existing customer base and sell them the product. The resulting money is used to pay for the firm's input and its people.

This is obviously a far too simple example to be a real case, but it illustrates that the resources (ellipses) in the diagram are necessary but not sufficient; what is necessary and sufficient are the transformations (arrows). The arrows are what actually happens in the firm and the arrows are what managers spend most of their time managing.

What we are interested in is identifying and evaluating the organization's unique transformation structure. Here is where we run into our first set of problems:

- Problem 1: Not all resources are additive, as we saw in Chapter 2, so just because we put more of something real into a resource we do not necessarily end up having more of the resource.
- Problem 2: Every arrow in our diagram is actually a set of different transformations. Some are representing a physical flow, some are representing a monetary flow, some are representing some knowledge transfer, some are representing some reputation or trust transformation, and so on. Most of the arrows are actually made up of several

of these different types of transformations and for practical purposes become difficult, if not impossible, to identify and map.

The conclusion here must be that we cannot operate in the *reality* of what happens but must move to the *principle* of what happens.

We will here use a trick from system dynamics and move to influence space. Influences can be treated as additive—if I influence you by both persuading you through talking to you (competence, time, power, trust, etc.) and by paying you to do something, you will be more influenced than if I just paid you or just tried to persuade you. This illustrates that we can deal with problem 1 in the preceding list. If we then introduce the generic term, *effort* to encompass all the different forms that influence can take, we have a concept that will take care of problem 2. We now have the means of identifying, sizing, and mapping the transformations.

What about the objection "you are talking about the principle not the reality"? Here we run into a behavioral effect that actually is on our side. If I ask someone to describe a complex system to me, they will not describe the actual system but will instead describe the system as they perceive it. If I therefore ask someone who controls the boundary condition of the firm to describe to me the desired future position of the firm and the present position of the firm, it does not matter if the resulting description of the present position of the firm is a true representation; this person will act as if it is a true representation and will therefore drive the firm from wherever it is to what is described as the desired position. Hence a methodologically sound approach to capturing the principle of something is as good as trying to catch the actual reality of this something and is a much easier task. This is actually what we do every time we try to model something on a higher level of abstraction than the reality we describe.

What we are interested in is identifying and mapping for further evaluation the organization's unique transformation structure—how the organization deploys its resources to create value. The tool for doing this is called an intellectual capital navigator.[1]

THE INTELLECTUAL CAPITAL NAVIGATOR

The intellectual capital navigator (ICN) is a numeric and visual representation of how management views resource deployment to create value in the organization. The ICN is about identifying transformations from one resource into another. This is a somewhat different way of thinking, and Figure 3.2 provides a set of examples of such transformations. It is important to remember that all transformations are possible but may not all be relevant in a given organization. Figure 3.3 provides a

	MONETARY	PHYSICAL	RELATIONAL	ORGANIZATIONAL	HUMAN
MONETARY	Investment in financial instruments	Investment in assets	Investment in building relationships	Investment in brands, image and systems	Investment in competent people
PHYSICAL	Sales of products	Equipment generates products	Features build loyalty or addiction	New equipment generates new working processes	New equipment generates new competence in user
RELATIONAL	Strong relationships generate lower selling costs	Use of other company's equipment	Leveraging existing relationships to generate new relationships	Access to someone else's processes or brands	Competence building from joint projects
ORGANIZATIONAL	Sales/licensing of IP, systems, processes, SW or information Brand generates higher sale price	Drawing or recipe converts to product	CRM systems increase customer loyalty	Patent application process generates IP	Computer SW that trains users in how to use other SW
HUMAN	Sales of competence frequently using the proxy of man-hours	Developing prototypes or artist creating a work of art	Building & developing relationships	Knowledge codification, creating new processes, SW, IP, etc.	Mentoring, apprenticeship

Figure 3.2. Examples of transformations on Level 2 in the distinction tree.

	MONETARY	PHYSICAL	RELATIONAL	ORGANIZATIONAL	HUMAN
MONETARY		Investments in physical facilities	Discounts to visitors and commission to travel agencies	Investment in image [through advertisement], investments in systems and processes	Staff salaries, bonus and training costs to retain and build competence
PHYSICAL	Sale of physical merchandising and art and craft products, renting rooms, entry fees		Attractive and comfortable rooms, gifts to selected visitors	Guide routines driven by climate and weather	Operating equipment [e.g. lifts] drive competence
RELATIONAL	Repeat visitors provide higher gross margin		Word of mouth generating new visitors	Improvement suggestions from staff and visitors	
ORGANIZATIONAL	The share of merchandise revenue, room rates, entry fees attributed to the branding, licensing of the brand	Special recipes for location, specific food and templates for souvenirs	CRM systems increase customer loyalty	Trade marking and branding	Written checklists etc. that generate competence for new or casual staff
HUMAN	Sale of guide services	Art and craft production	Staff attitudes and behaviors build customer loyalty	Writing new checklists	Mentoring, apprenticeship

Figure 3.3. A non-exhaustive illustration of transformations on Level 2 in the distinction tree for a mountain village selling destination tourism.

non-exhaustive example of transformations for a mountain village selling location tourism.

By mapping how resources influence each other, the ICN provides an overall map of the logic used by management when it comes to resource deployment in a given organization. The ICN must not be confused with different types of models that try to map the real flow of things in the organization. These real-flow models are insufficient to capture what goes on in organizations. They can actually only capture well the transformations in the white area in Figure 3.2. They are able to capture either the input or the output, but not both, in the light gray area in Figure 3.2 and they are not able to capture anything in the dark gray area. This is due to the multidimensional nature of the transformations and the non-additiveness of the transformations that include intellectual capital resources. The ICN is on a higher level of abstraction than these flow models but is simultaneously more useful (as we will see) since it provides a total picture of all transformations and resources that contribute to the organization's value creation.

All managers have a more or less articulated model of how value is created in the organization. This model frames the thinking and the decisions that are made as a consequence. This is especially noticeable when managers are under severe time pressure that does not allow them long enough to go through a rational decision process. They will then make the decision on gut feeling using the mental models they have. These mental models are based on personal experience and will therefore differ between members of a management team. A team that has worked together for a long time probably has a more unified model than one that has just started to work together. In the authors' experience, a major benefit of the ICN is that it unifies the models of how value is created within the management team that participates in the ICN development process. As a consequence, critical assumptions surface and can be discussed, leading to better strategy implementation or sometimes a change in strategy itself. The authors have seen some dramatic outcomes here; a recent case revealed that the core competence was to *build* plants, rather than operating plants, which led to a dramatic shift in strategy.

The visual language of the ICN is unmatched in its ability to make complex organizations understandable and thereby provides an excellent tool for strategic discussions. The ICN is actually a very useful bridge between strategy crafting and strategy implementation.

Case 3.1 VTT: An Intellectual Capital Navigator Approach

This Case builds upon the draft notes "Application of Intellectual Capital Navigator at VTT" by Markku Auer, Pentti Grönberg, Tomi Mattila, Maria Saarela, and Harri Soininen at VTT, Technical Research Centre of Finland, P.O.B. 1200, FIN-02044 VTT, Finland.

VTT Technical Research Centre of Finland is an impartial expert organization that carries out technical and techno-economic research and development work and produces information services. With around 2700 employees (in the year 2000), VTT provides a wide range of technology and applied research services. The most important customer sectors are domestic industry, private sector services, and the domestic and European public sector. With a turnover of about 210 million euros, VTT actively works in partnership with companies, universities, employment and business centers, technology centers, centers of expertise, and other regional and international actors.

VTT seeks to be the engine of technological development in Finland. This requires development and cultivation of their own knowledge capital, especially in those spearhead fields where they believe the future competitiveness of the Finnish economy can be built. As a consequence, VTT approached the Helsinki School of Economics/JOKO for the provision of a program that would expose all its senior and middle management to modern management thinking relevant for an R&D organization heavily dependent on intangibles. The intellectual capital navigator approach was used in this program.

The following abbreviated example of an intellectual capital navigator application does not necessarily represent the corporate view of VTT, but is the result from one of VTT's learning groups. First, the group identified how VTT creates value. For them, the main component of value is simply problem solving (used here in a generalized meaning including, for example, innovative solutions for customer needs). Therefore, VTT can be seen as mainly a value shop. Secondly, the group was asked to evaluate the importance of different resources now and in the future. To simplify the complicated organizational RDT, only the most important transformations were included in the third step. The resulting graphic Intellectual Capital Navigators, VTT present and VTT desired, are shown in the figure below.

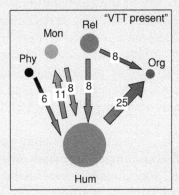 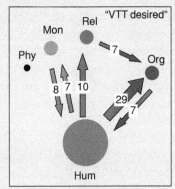

"VTT Present" and "VTT Desired" (the present and desired situation of VTT according to the group).

Case 3.1 VTT: An Intellectual Capital Navigator Approach—cont'd

The human-to-organizational transformation clearly got the highest weight in both the present and the future situations. This is no surprise since the value provided by VTT is created through problem solving that takes the form of developed processes, solutions, reports, and so on. According to the group, it is increasingly important to use new processes and systems to develop competence, and thus the transformation from organizational to human was given more weight in the future situation. The group thought it increasingly important for VTT to use its world class competence to strengthen relationships with relevant organizations and individuals. Therefore, the transformation from human to relational resources was given more weight in the future.

Fourth the "VTT Desired" navigator was refined further by comparing it with VTT's strategy. VTT's strategic emphasis is increased collaboration with customers and other research establishments, both domestic and abroad. This is why the weight for relational resources increased. The weight for physical resources was also increased. However, the iterative changes done to the weights did not change the priorities obtained in the "VTT Desired" picture. The principal transformations emerging from the transformation matrix are presented in the navigator diagram in the following figure.

The IC navigator revealed VTT to be predominantly human oriented, which was expected, and is a typical result for a research organization. In order to achieve the strategic intent, organizational and relational resources needed to be further developed. VVT perceived group work to be an essential part of the IC Navigator process. The delphi-like approach allows for the merging of viewpoints into a meaningful consensus enabling commitment to the strategy and facilitating the implementation of the strategy.

The IC navigator was found to be a good modeling tool to assist in higher-level strategic decision making since it provides a convenient method to investigate how changing the resource weights will change the organizational output. The transformation process assisted in participants' thinking and contributed to the way activities were reorganized at VTT.

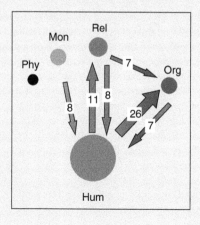

HOW TO CREATE AN INTELLECTUAL CAPITAL NAVIGATOR

The process used to create an ICN is a consensual process aimed at capturing the tacit knowledge in the management team as to how value is perceived to be created in the organization. In Chapter 2 we covered the necessary first steps in this process:

1. Identification of the resource distinction tree down to at least Level 3;
2. Weighting of the resources as to their ability to influence value creation in the organization;
3. Evaluation of the identified resources as to their suitability to form the basis for competitive advantage, and evaluation of the quality and quantity of each resource.

We now need to address the dynamics of how these resources are deployed, and then we can evaluate the resulting deployment (transformation) structure.

Case 3.2 Recruit, *Jutaku-Joho Towns* Division: Using the IC Approach to Improve Performance[1]

This case study is based on the information from Recruit Co. Ltd. in Japan, that provide consulting services using the IC approach.[2]

Recruit Co. Ltd., based in Japan, is a leading provider of a wide range of classified advertisement magazines and websites. One of its magazines, *Jutaku-Joho Towns* (JJT), offers real estate information for the potential buyers of properties and houses in their neighborhood. To meet the buyers' needs, many local editions of JJT are published, and each of them lists advertisements of real estate in a limited area. For example, more than ten local editions of JJT were published in the Tokyo metropolitan area in 2004. The revenue of JJT's business totally depends upon the advertisement fee from ad sponsors such as real estate dealers.

JJT was first published in 2003 in Tokyo, and grew very quickly. Due to its speed in launching new local editions, there were some problems in its organization. Shinya Nakamura, the division officer of the JJT division, found there was confusion among sales managers in local branches about how to run the business. Sales managers seemed unsure about the Key Success Factors (KSFs) of JJT business, and there was some redundancy and irrelevance in their activities. Nakamura decided to introduce the IC approach in an attempt to solve this problem and improve the performance of JJT.

First, Nakamura and his right-hand person, Noriyuki Ueno, joined the IC process to identify intellectual capital resources and the illustrated Intellectual Capital Navigator. Through the process, they found some transformations were not as important as sales managers had thought. Other resources and transformations were quite important, but no sales manager took care of them. Even between Nakamura and Ueno there was conflict about how to prioritize resources and transformations, and who was responsible for each of them. After some concentrated meetings, they finally defined core resources and transformations and activities (or KSFs).

Case 3.2 Recruit, *Jutaku-Joho Towns* Division: Using the IC Approach to Improve Performance—cont'd

Second, they tried to create a vision statement and code of conduct for JJT. Through the vision statement, they aimed to show their passion for the value that JJT delivers to customers, both potential buyers and ad sponsors. And through the code of conduct, they aimed to tell people about the KSFs of the business. They did this work based on the Intellectual Capital Navigator. (About the code of conduct, see the following figure.)

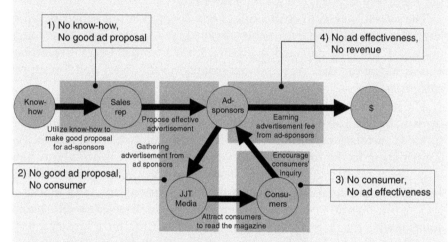

Code of conduct derived from the Intellectual Capital Navigator.

Third, they held a workshop with sales managers in the JJT division to share their thoughts in the IC process. In the workshop, sales managers discussed how to prioritize the resources and transformations, and drew the Intellectual Capital Navigator by themselves. After that, Nakamura showed the Intellectual Capital Navigator that Nakamura and Ueno had illustrated, and explained their thoughts behind it. At the end of the workshop, Nakamura introduced the vision statement and the code of conduct. Through the workshop, sales managers understood the KSFs of the business and why they were important. Even more important, they were motivated to improve the performance of their business based on the Intellectual Capital Navigator, vision statement, and code of conduct.

Through these efforts, Nakamura succeeded in making his vision explicit and involving sales managers in realization of the vision. For example, a couple of weeks after the workshop, sales managers launched some spontaneous projects inspired by the Intellectual Capital Navigator, such as a best practice competition and knowledge management initiative.

Normally, two ICNs are built: the current one and the one we want to have as a steady state in the future (the future here is defined by the firm's strategy and strategic time horizon). Sometimes these two ICNs are one and the same.

The first step is to take the resource distinction tree in Chapter 2 and convert it to serve as a basis for developing an ICN. This is done by converting the weightings in a branch of the tree, from weightings as a percentage of the node to absolute percentage weightings. This is a simple but necessary step. Figure 3.4 illustrates this.

The second step is to create, out of the distinction tree's most detailed level (e.g., Level 3 or even more detailed; see Figure 3.5), a resource matrix of the type depicted in Figure 3.6, where the Level 3 resources appear along the two axes and are grouped in the five Level 2 resource categories.

The next step is to weight the resource transformations on each row by distributing 100 points across them. This is done by asking the question, "How relatively influential is this transformation when it comes to contributing to the organization's value creation?" It is not about how large the transformation is, it is about how much it matters—this is a very important distinction since small transformations may matter a lot (e.g. the creation of a new concept based on a discussion with a consumer), whereas large transformations may not matter a lot (e.g., paying rent for a large service organization in a city location). The result of this step is a matrix where every row adds up to 100 and where each transformation that has been assigned a weight greater than zero is defined (i.e., the question "what do we mean by this transformation?" is answered).

The next step in the process is to convert the ICN from a row-based description of the transformations to a total picture (i.e., all the transformations in the matrix must add up to 100). We can do this since the influence matrix (i.e., our matrix) is additive whereas a matrix that tries to capture real flows would not be additive, making this step close to impossible in the latter. We do this by viewing the numbers on a given row as percentages of the weighting of the resource that is the starting point of the transformations. Figure 3.7 illustrates this principle.

Figure 3.8 shows a total weighted transformation matrix for an advisory firm. As can be seen from this figure, most of the possible transformations are zero. This is normally the case, hence the advice of starting with the

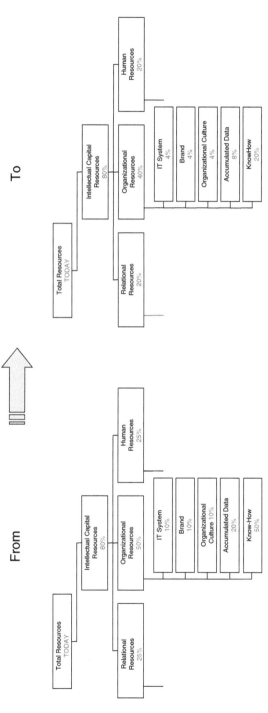

Figure 3.4. Example of transforming a weighted resource distinction tree from a node-based weighting to a tree-based weighting.

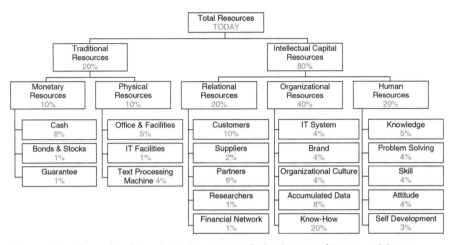

Figure 3.5. Example of a weighted resource distinction tree from an advisory organization.

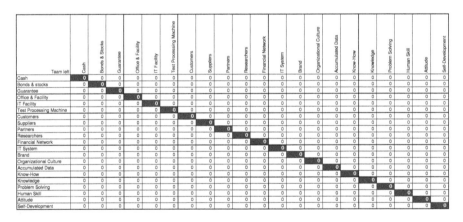

Figure 3.6. Example of a resource matrix from an advisory organization building on the Level 3 resources in the resource distinction tree depicted in Figure 3.5. (To avoid confusion the resource weights are not shown here.)

transformations that either are irrelevant for the organization's value creation or the transformations that have no influence on the organization's value creation.

This Intellectual Capital navigator can be a bit confusing to interpret, so we begin by removing all transformations that fall below a boundary.

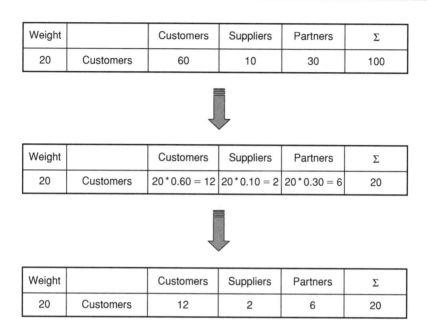

Weight		Customers	Suppliers	Partners	Σ
20	Customers	60	10	30	100

Weight		Customers	Suppliers	Partners	Σ
20	Customers	20 * 0.60 = 12	20 * 0.10 = 2	20 * 0.30 = 6	20

Weight		Customers	Suppliers	Partners	Σ
20	Customers	12	2	6	20

Figure 3.7. Converting the matrix from row-based weighting to a total weighted picture of the transformation.

The boundary can be calculated using a statistical approximation, assuming normal distribution over an infinite matrix, as equal to half the average per possible transformation. This equals a boundary of 0.12 [0.5*100/21*21] in our case, so everything below this level is removed as noise. The other way to remove transformations is by using the Pareto rule, removing all transformations from the smallest and upwards until the cumulative sum is 20 or just below. Having done this, we then blank out everything that has been removed. To further enhance clarity we use a color code as follows: 0–1 sized influences are black, 1–2 sized influences are orange, 2–3 sized influences are **purple**, 3–4 sized influences are blue gray, 4–5 sized influences are green 5–6 sized influences are **blue**, and 6– sized influences are red. These color codings are made based on increasing (or decreasing) cumulative influence on value creation. The resulting matrix for the advisory firm is illustrated in Figure 3.9.

Figure 3.8. The normalized transformation matrix for an advisory organization.

Resource / weighting	Cash	Bonds&Stocks	Guarantee	Office&Facility	IT Facility	Text Processing Machine	Customers	Suppliers	Partners	Researchers	Financial Network	IT System	Brand	Organizational Culture	Accumulated Data	Know-How	Knowledge	Problem Solving	Human Skill	Attitude	Self-Development	Σ
weighting	0.00	0.00	0.00	0.00	0.50	0.50	1.60	0.40	0.40	0.00	0.00	0.70	0.70	0.00	0.40	0.80	0.40	0.40	0.40	0.40	0.40	
8.00 Cash	0.00	0.00	0.00	0.00	0.00	0.00	0.00	0.00	0.00	0.00	0.00	0.00	0.00	0.00	0.00	0.00	0.00	0.00	0.00	0.00	0.00	8.00
1.00 Bonds&Stocks	1.00	0.00	0.00	0.00	0.00	0.00	0.00	0.00	0.00	0.00	0.00	0.00	0.00	0.00	0.00	0.00	0.00	0.00	0.00	0.00	0.00	1.00
1.00 Guarantee	1.00	0.00	0.00	0.00	0.00	0.00	0.00	0.00	0.00	0.00	0.00	0.00	0.00	0.00	0.00	0.00	0.00	0.00	0.00	0.00	0.00	1.00
5.00 Office&Facility	0.00	0.00	0.00	0.00	0.19	0.50	0.38	0.00	0.13	0.00	0.13	0.19	1.50	0.13	0.13	0.13	0.25	0.25	0.25	0.63	0.25	5.00
1.00 IT Facility	0.00	0.00	0.00	0.03	0.00	0.07	0.07	0.03	0.03	0.00	0.00	0.28	0.04	0.00	0.10	0.10	0.12	0.05	0.03	0.05	0.03	1.00
4.00 Text Processing Machine	0.00	0.00	0.00	0.10	0.00	0.00	1.10	0.20	0.30	0.00	0.00	0.00	0.30	0.00	0.60	1.40	0.00	0.00	0.00	0.00	0.00	4.00
10.00 Customers	1.50	0.00	0.00	0.00	0.00	0.00	0.00	0.00	0.13	0.00	0.38	0.00	3.25	0.13	0.75	1.00	0.63	0.63	0.63	0.50	0.50	10.00
2.00 Suppliers	0.10	0.00	0.00	0.00	0.00	0.10	0.60	0.00	0.10	0.00	0.00	0.00	0.15	0.00	0.05	0.90	0.00	0.00	0.00	0.00	0.00	2.00
6.00 Partners	0.45	0.00	0.00	0.00	0.00	0.00	3.30	0.15	0.00	0.00	0.00	0.08	0.60	0.00	0.00	1.05	0.00	0.00	0.00	0.00	0.00	6.00
1.00 Researchers	0.00	0.00	0.00	0.00	0.00	0.00	0.06	0.00	0.00	0.00	0.00	0.00	0.29	0.03	0.13	0.30	0.15	0.04	0.01	0.00	0.00	1.00
1.00 Financial Network	0.53	0.00	0.00	0.00	0.00	0.04	0.06	0.00	0.00	0.00	0.00	0.00	0.34	0.00	0.04	0.04	0.00	0.00	0.00	0.00	0.00	1.00
4.00 IT System	0.20	0.00	0.00	0.00	0.20	0.10	0.30	0.05	0.20	0.05	0.00	0.00	0.05	0.30	0.40	0.70	0.70	0.20	0.25	0.10	0.20	4.00
4.00 Brand	1.10	0.00	0.00	0.00	0.00	0.00	1.08	0.19	0.27	0.19	0.09	0.00	0.00	0.24	0.00	0.05	0.10	0.10	0.10	0.29	0.20	4.00
4.00 Organizational Culture	0.20	0.00	0.00	0.00	0.00	0.00	1.00	0.20	0.20	0.00	0.00	0.00	0.60	0.00	0.00	0.30	0.30	0.10	0.20	0.60	0.30	4.00
8.00 Accumulated Data	1.80	0.00	0.00	0.20	0.20	0.20	1.20	0.20	0.00	0.50	0.00	0.00	1.60	0.00	0.00	1.20	0.90	0.20	0.20	0.00	0.00	8.00
20.00 Know-How	6.00	0.00	0.00	0.50	0.50	0.00	3.00	0.00	0.00	0.25	0.00	0.25	2.50	1.00	1.25	0.00	1.50	1.75	1.25	0.50	0.25	20.00
5.00 Knowledge	1.00	0.00	0.00	0.00	0.13	0.00	0.88	0.00	0.00	0.31	0.00	0.06	0.44	0.25	0.25	1.00	0.00	0.44	0.13	0.06	0.06	5.00
4.00 Problem Solving	1.10	0.00	0.00	0.00	0.10	0.00	0.80	0.05	0.05	0.00	0.00	0.00	0.40	0.15	0.10	0.60	0.30	0.00	0.20	0.10	0.05	4.00
4.00 Human Skill	1.00	0.00	0.00	0.00	0.00	0.00	0.80	0.10	0.10	0.00	0.00	0.00	0.30	0.20	0.00	0.60	0.25	0.30	0.00	0.60	0.15	4.00
4.00 Attitude	0.60	0.00	0.00	0.00	0.00	0.00	0.80	0.15	0.15	0.00	0.00	0.50	0.50	0.70	0.00	0.30	0.20	0.15	0.15	0.00	0.30	4.00
3.00 Self-Development	0.15	0.00	0.00	0.00	0.00	0.00	0.15	0.00	0.00	0.00	0.00	0.25	0.08	0.30	0.00	0.30	0.20	0.56	0.41	0.49	0.00	3.00
100.00	17.73	0.00	0.00	0.13	2.11	1.50	17.17	1.72	2.05	1.30	0.67	1.55	13.63	3.42	4.15	10.76	6.36	5.16	4.00	3.92	2.69	100

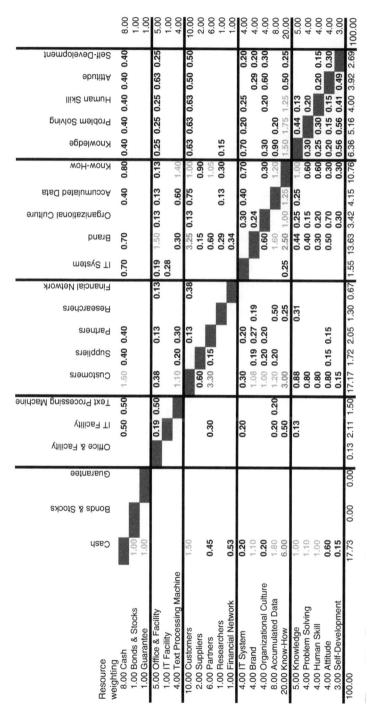

Figure 3.9. The normalized and cleaned transformation matrix for an advisory organization.

Case 3.3 Zurich Small Business Solutions: Creation of a Visual Model of the Value Creation Path

For a knowledge intensive company like Zurich Group's Small Business Solutions unit (ZSBS), physical and monetary resources will not be the primary basis for business success. Instead, intellectual capital resources and the organization's ability to make use of these resources in the most effective way to achieve its strategic intent of becoming a more volume based business, is the key to success. The IC process was implemented as the ZSBS management team recognized that its work on IC-based strategy lacked focus and that traditional management systems could not help them to identify or manage the organization's intellectual capital. Therefore, the objective with the IC process was to lay the foundation for an increase in ZSBS's business performance and market share. This was to be achieved by creating a better understanding of ZSBS's value creation path and developing a practical tool to help ZSBS to better manage the achievement of its strategic intent. A key activity of this process was to develop an Intellectual Capital navigator based on the management team's notion of how the organization creates value, a process depicted in the following case study.

At the time the IC process was implemented, ZSBS was a strategic business unit of Zurich Small Business (ZSB), a specialized insurance company based in Baltimore, Maryland, and serving the property and liability insurance needs of small businesses. Increased competition and growing sophistication of its customers required the organization to rethink its strategic intent and to develop a new approach to the way it carried out its business with the intention of becoming a more volume based company. ZSBS had been using Zurich's established strategic planning approach, but recognized that its work on IC-based strategy lacked focus and that traditional management systems could not help to identify or manage its intellectual capital. A new approach was needed and, at the suggestion of the Zurich's head office, the IC process was implemented.

After identification of value-creating resources and creation of weighted distinction trees, the process carried on by mapping value-creating relationships between resources for different resource levels. For ZSBS, the Intellectual Capital Navigators were used to visualize what was needed in order to achieve its strategic intent. In the figure below, the Intellectual Capital Navigator visualizing ZSBS's desired future state is depicted for Level 2 resources.

As can be seen, there is no circle for physical resources. This is because the physical resources of ZSBS were not considered important enough for value creation to merit a place on its value creation path. The first important insight from the process was that the organization has a heavier emphasis on human resources than would have been expected. Most large organizations have a very heavy dependence on organizational resources and/or relational resources where people perform their tasks according to well-defined processes and systems, which means that they are relatively easy to substitute. However, the heavy dependence on human resources may be explained by the fact that during the IC process, ZSBS was in the phase of rapid development and was therefore heavily dependent on the creative ability of its employees. This means that with time, the importance of human resources will decrease in parallel with the increase of both organizational and relational resources. It is important to notice that in order to avoid an insecure and unprofitable scenario the challenge becomes to develop the organizational and relational resources rapidly.

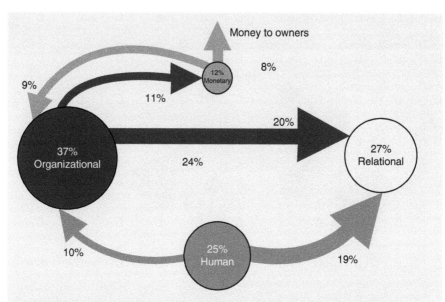

The Zurich Small Business Solutions Intellectual Capital Navigator for Level 2 resources.

According to the Intellectual Capital Navigator, human resources were used to build structures and relationships, which makes perfect sense given the situation just described. Relational resources were transformed into organizational resources, which in turn were used to build and sustain relationships and to generate money (e.g., through sales of service concepts). This reinforced the picture of an organization in a build-up phase, heavily dependent on its people to build up structures, systems and processes, and long-term relationships with agents and partners to make the value creation process more efficient. The ZSBS team agreed that this value creation path is a snapshot in time and not a picture of a desired future steady state. To analyze the value creation path of ZSBS further, a Intellectual Capital navigator for a more detailed level of resources was created, as depicted in the figure below.

In the preceding Intellectual Capital Navigator, only the most important transformations were included to make it simpler and easier to understand. At this level, it became clear that the most important transformations were the one from agents to products and from products to money. This makes sense as in essence this depicts that the core of ZSBS's recipe for creating value was to sell products through agents. To support this transformation and the core relationship with agents, ZSBS used their field organization (structures), the attitude and competence of the people, their processes, and Zurich Information Services. There was also another important transformation structure: agent relationships to customers to money. This represents the recurring payments made by existing customers having a relationship with agents and thereby being users of ZSBS's service concepts (products). The outgoing arrows from money show where ZSBS was focusing its investments. According to this figure ZSBS's monetary resources

Continued

Case 3.3 Zurich Small Business Solutions: Creation of a Visual Model of the Value Creation Path—cont'd

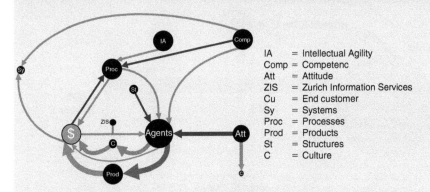

IA	= Intellectual Agility
Comp	= Competenc
Att	= Attitude
ZIS	= Zurich Information Services
Cu	= End customer
Sy	= Systems
Proc	= Processes
Prod	= Products
St	= Structures
C	= Culture

The Zurich Small Business Solutions Intellectual Capital Navigator for Level 3 resources.

were primarily dedicated to building organizational resources (processes and systems) and secondly to generating and sustaining relationships with agents. Another interesting feature depicted from the Intellectual Capital Navigator was the large flow to culture, which was a relatively unimportant resource being only a small contributor to value creation. Upon reflection, the team wanted to change the importance of culture based on the reasoning that when there is a culture in which the employees are happy, there is no need to spend a lot of time and money on it. The group concluded that this was acceptable at this stage, but if they did not pay attention to it now, they would be in trouble in a couple of years. Interestingly, there was no transformation from human resources to product. This meant that product development was driven by obvious suggestions from agents and customers, which were then validated by the team.

The findings illustrated by the Intellectual Capital Navigator helped ZSBS to redirect their program and enhance their business results. It further highlighted that in the short term ZSBS expected to draw on the existing pool of experience inside the organization rather than invest in building up the skills of all employees. However, for long-term sustained success ZSBS needed to consider how its resources could be used to nurture competence in new and less experienced staff. The outcome of the IC process was a revelation to the ZSBS team and it was only when implications were visualized in the Intellectual Capital Navigators that the management team realized the gaps and inconsistencies in their thinking. ZSBS managers were surprised by the lack of fit in several key areas between their aspirations for the future of the business and what the Intellectual Capital Navigators showed. It also helped ZSBS to reach the final output of the IC process, the IC index, which was created to better manage the achievement of their strategic intent. This final step of the IC process will be further described in Chapter 4. In general, the insights gained from the process were crucial to the development of an action plan to change the way ZSBS worked and to transform knowledge and expertise held by individuals into workable processes accessible to others in

Case 3.3 Zurich Small Business Solutions: Creation of a Visual Model of the Value Creation Path—cont'd

the organization. Craig Fundum, who was the managing director of ZSBS during the IC process, emphasized the relevance of the IC process for ZSBS:

The process delivered on all our expectations by validating our strategy and actions, pointing out areas for further improvement, generating actionable insights, establishing a common understanding of how ZSBS creates value, and helping the ZSBS management team to prioritize and focus on the issues that matter the most. In addition, the IC process was complementary to the established strategic management approach of ZSBS, the Roadmap process

If we want to, we can now construct the transformation matrix on any of the preceding levels in the distinction tree by summing up the transformation in the respective groups so, for example, the transformation in Figure 3.8 would look like Figure 3.10 when consolidated up to Level 2 in the resource distinction tree.

The row sum in the right-most column equals the weighting of the resources by definition, so Figure 3.10 excludes the weighting column on the left to show the result more clearly.

What we have now is the numerical representation of the ICN, and we will use this when we evaluate the effectiveness of the resource deployment structure. Before we go to the analysis phase we need to find a more accessible way of presenting results, and this is the pictorial representation of the ICN, which is created by illustrating resources as circles and transformations as arrows. The circle surface areas are proportional to the resource weightings and the width of the arrows are proportional to the transformation weightings. Figure 3.11 illustrates the pictorial ICN representation of the corresponding numerical ICN representation shown in Figure 3.10.

Figure 3.11 gives us a better feel for what actually happens in this organization. If we now clean up the matrix in Figure 3.10 using the Pareto approach, we get the matrix depicted in Figure 3.12. The pictorial representation of Figure 3.12 is shown in Figure 3.13.

Just by looking at Figure 3.13 it is possible to hypothesize what type of organization this is. There are some obvious characteristics that shine through:

1. Money is primarily generated through organizational resources, probably through selling some combination of standardized solutions in the form of processes or software complemented by reputation and/or brand.

Hints for Filling Out the Matrix

- If it is difficult to understand a given transformation, try to put a verb in front of the resource category (i.e., you *invest* money, you *leverage* relations, you *use* processes and equipment, you *deploy* competence, etc.).
- If there are several respondents (as is normally the case in a team), a Delphi process as outlined for the resources in Chapter 2 should be used. This means that an interactive process where the lowest and highest scoring members for a given transformation argue their case before a rescoring takes place. Once the differences are minimal between the team members an averaging can be made.
- Some aspects of value creation may be difficult to formulate initially, especially if they are seen as problems (e.g., regulators and competitors). It is important to formulate these in positive terms; for example, "creating a policy for influencing regulators." This positive phrasing tends to facilitate the intuitive understanding of the transformation.
- To simplify what is normally perceived as a complex matrix with lots of numbers to fill in, start with the zeroes (i.e., those transformations that are either irrelevant or that have no influence on the organization's value creation). There are normally quite a few of these, and this will simplify the remaining task substantially.
- Once all that remains on a given row is relevant and influential for the organization's value creation, divide the transformations into those that have a higher than average influence and those that have a lower than average influence. The sum of those that have a higher than average influence is normally between 70 and 80, and the sum of those that have lower than average influence is normally between 20 and 30. This further facilitates the task.
- It is important to remember that the ICN, like all other models, is highly dependent on the quality of the data that is used to populate it. It is therefore important that the people used to populate the matrix are insightful as to the way in which the organization goes about creating value.

2. The processes or ways of operating drive the competences and behaviors in the organization, so one can expect a strong socialization culture where the individual initiative is subordinated to existing processes and where apprenticeship seems to operate, leading to a fairly hierarchical structure based on tenure.
3. The reputation and/or brand combined with the solutions delivered are the primary drivers of relationships with the outside world (e.g., customers and partners).
4. New solutions are built on documented deliveries and/or brand and reputation is built on the solutions provided.

	Monetary	Physical	Relational	Organizational	Human	Σ
Monetary	2.00	1.00	2.40	2.60	2.00	10.00
Physical	0.00	0.88	2.34	4.88	1.90	10.00
Relational	2.58	0.44	4.85	9.06	3.08	20.00
Organizational	9.30	1.20	8.97	10.44	10.09	40.00
Human	3.85	0.23	4.34	6.53	5.06	20.00
Σ	17.73	3.74	22.90	33.51	22.12	100.00

Figure 3.10. The normalized transformation matrix consolidated to Level 2 for an advisory organization.

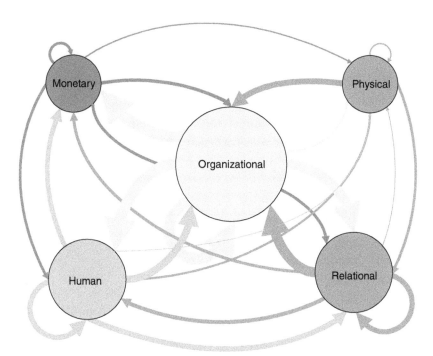

Figure 3.11. The pictorial representation of Figure 3.10.

	Monetary	Physical	Relational	Organizational	Human
Monetary	0.00	0.00	0.00	0.00	0.00
Physical	0.00	0.00	0.00	4.88	0.00
Relational	0.00	0.00	4.85	9.06	3.08
Organizational	9.30	0.00	8.97	10.44	10.09
Human	3.85	0.00	4.34	6.53	5.06

Figure 3.12. The normalized and cleaned transformation matrix from Figure 3.10.

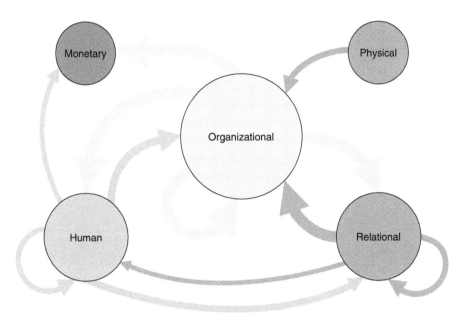

Figure 3.13. The pictorial representation of Figure 3.12.

5. There are some development activities, probably by some form of R&D unit that develops new standardized offerings.
6. There is some type of relationship-building activity by sales people generating new customers or R&D people generating new partners. Most new customers seem to come through word-of-mouth rather than personal selling.
7. There are some earnings from sale of man-hours but it is clearly subordinate to the earnings generated by the sale of the standardized solution.
8. There is some use of physical equipment, probably computers, to develop and/or automate the solutions into software form.

Based on these statements, we can hypothesize that the dominating value-creating logic (see Chapter 1) for this organization is a value chain with components that operate as value shops. Note that these statements are made solely from looking at the pictorial representation of the ICN. Imagine the level of analysis that can be made when the context is known and understood!

Case 3.4 Department of Industry, Science and Trade: Application of the IC Process to a Nonprofit Organization

This study is derived from a paper by Jacobsen and Roos[1] and is built on the Department of Industry, Science and Trade (DIST), which was a branch of a major Commonwealth government department in Australia that, in turn, was accountable to the Australian Parliament through its relevant minister. The trend towards outsourcing and privatization of traditional public sector activities had focused the attention of public sector organizations onto performance management. In the case organization, where the largest portion of value was generated through the interaction of intellectual capital, the measurement of financial performance alone seemed a poor management tool. The desired outcome of applying the IC process was to develop a tool for achieving more efficient value creation for all stakeholders and reaching a closer strategic alignment between performance measurement, organizational strategy, and value creation. This case depicts some distinctive issues involved when the IC process is applied to a nonprofit organization. However, it only describes the process at a general level, mainly focusing on the identification of the branch's value creation path visualized by the Intellectual Capital Navigator in relation to each stakeholder.

At the time the IC process was implemented, the branch was divided into three main areas of responsibility and was staffed by around 30 officers. It served the government by providing advice, briefing, and support for the activities of the minister; delivering advice and assistance to its stakeholders; and representing its stakeholders to other government departments and agencies. Most of the value created by the public service was generated through its people. Although there were well-established mechanisms for measuring the financial management performance of the branch, no processes were designed to measure the effectiveness of the management of its human capital. However, the desired outcome of applying the IC process to the branch was not to create a measurement system but to develop a tool for achieving more efficient value creation for all stakeholders and reaching a closer strategic alignment between performance measurement, organizational strategy, and value creation. The IC process is somewhat more complex for a stakeholder organization than for a profit generating organization because the value a profit driven organization delivers through maximizing shareholder wealth does not translate to a public sector stakeholder organization. Further, the delivery of valued services to stakeholders under budget and government appropriation constraints results in the necessity for tradeoffs between the different stakeholders.

This complexity emphasizes the importance of the first steps of the IC process where different stakeholders and the value the organization delivers in relation to each of the key stakeholders are identified. Once these phases were completed, the strategic intent for each stakeholder was agreed on and their relative importance articulated by the branch as well as by the key stakeholders. This was a vital part of the process, especially as the most important value dimension, "provide broad perspective," expressed by the stakeholders was not included in the initial list of dimensions identified by the branch. See the figure below which depicts the relative importance of value dimensions by stakeholders.

The next step was to outline the strategic intent by stakeholder. This perspective was then used to identify two sets of variables for each stakeholder: the set of key success factors and indicators as well as the branch's value creating path, which is described in the following paragraphs.

Continued

Case 3.4 Department of Industry, Science and Trade: Application of the IC Process to a Nonprofit Organization—cont'd

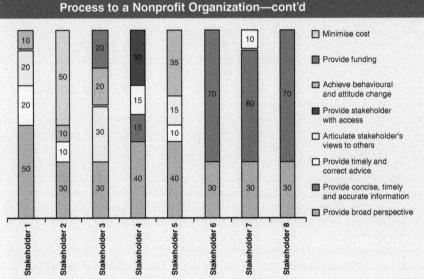

Relative importance of value dimension by stakeholder.

The aim of this step was to extract the tacit knowledge about both the present and the desired future value creation path residing in the officers of the branch. Working with this issue, the management group of the branch identified human resources as the most important driver both for present and future value creation. After that, the participants identified and prioritized what resources were needed to create value for the identified stakeholders and considered how these resources were transformed. The discussions surrounding the deployment of resources generated many different opinions and the process was performed in iterations. To avoid paralyzing information overload and to act upon new insights, it was essential to think in terms of tradeoffs and focus on the transformations that were important. The final outcome was an Intellectual Capital Navigator for each of the eight stakeholders visualizing the branch's value creation path. The Intellectual Capital Navigator for the desired situation with scaled resources and transformations of one of the stakeholders is depicted in the figure below.

For the purposes of this case we have chosen to look at the Intellectual Capital Navigator on an aggregate level even though a Intellectual Capital Navigator like this is created for every stakeholder. The most important transformation of resources is from human resources to organizational resources. This is not surprising since human resources to a large extent create processes, structures, and systems (the output to stakeholders). Another flow of almost equal importance is the transformation from human resources to relationship resources, implying that much of the work is to build and maintain relationships with stakeholders by using competent individuals. As the Intellectual Capital Navigator depicts, the branch invests money in competent people, which is rather logical as human resources are the branch's most essential resources for value creation.

The interpretation of context specific Intellectual Capital Navigators visualized the branch's fundamental business recipe and provided large amounts of information about hidden resources deemed important by the participants of the IC process. Thereby it pre-

Case 3.4 Department of Industry, Science and Trade: Application of the IC Process to a Nonprofit Organization—cont'd

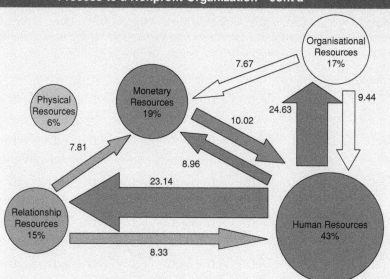

Intellectual Capital Navigator with rescaled weighted resources on Level 2 after removal of unimportant transformations.

sented a tool to communicate the branch's value creation strategy both internally in the organization and to different stakeholders and also helped in the creation of the IC index[2] which was the last phase of the IC process. The process provided the participants with several surprising results. For example, the participants initially did not identify the most important value dimension. As a consequence of this, the participants realized the importance of communicating and maintaining close relationships with stakeholders to raise and maintain perceived value. Another revelation was the understanding of the transformations between the different resources and that they are the key for value creation. This shows that it is not the knowledge residing in the individuals in the branch that is the most interesting, but how the branch managers transform that knowledge into processes, structures, and systems: in other words, establishing and developing systems to capture the value produced by human resources and to improve the value delivered to stakeholders consistently and over time. The process resulted in the development of a common language for discussing the vital importance of human capital contributions. This, in turn, facilitated more effective value creation for all stakeholders and a closer strategic alignment between performance measurement, organizational strategy, and value creation. Michael Dillon, Executive General Manager at DIST, further argued the applicability of the IC process:

"Getting a grasp on the changing state of the intangible resources in an organization is a major challenge for managers. The IC approach is an approach to measuring organizational performance which provides insights beyond what financial reporting alone provides, in a disciplined and structured way."

Overall, the participants "agreed" that the greatest value lay in the process itself—taking the time and effort to consider the relevant issues.

Example 3.1 The Value Chain Intellectual Capital Navigator

An IC-navigator for the value chain company was developed through a number of interviews and workshops, using the distinction tree as a starting point. This process led to a consensus view on how the company's core operations create value, and is shown in the figure below. The diagram on the left shows all transformations between the resources and the one on the right has been filtered to leave only the most significant transformations.

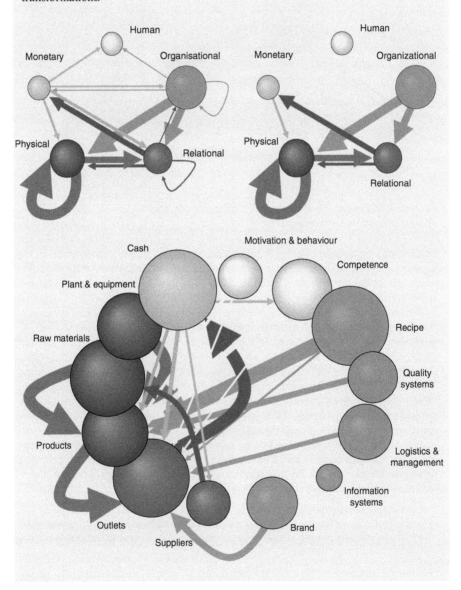

Example 3.1 The Value Chain Intellectual Capital Navigator—cont'd

From this simple picture of the company, it can be deduced that physical resources – raw material, the product itself and the plant and equipment to manufacture it – are the key things. Organizational resources are dominated by the recipe – the know-how of how to make food products. Quality and logistics systems are also important. People and cash are less important and in the middle sit the relational resources of the suppliers and outlets. The customer in this case is not the consumer but is represented by a group of outlets.

The crucial thing is the (filtered) Level 2 Intellectual Capital Navigator because this shows the classic value chain of a manufacturer (see the figure below). The first things to look at are the weak links through which outlets are influenced by brand, human resources, and recipe. This is the promotional process in action that preserves the customer (outlet) base.

The main transformations are in the physical resource area. The value chain starts with the suppliers who affect raw materials. These, in turn affect the product (as does plant and equipment). Organizational resources, in the form of recipe and quality control systems, also affect the product, as do human resources in the form of operator competance. The product then affects outlets that, finally, affect cash. In an Intellectual Capital Navigator, a value chain appears as a linear process, usually in the physical area with branches to allow for the input of human and organizational resources. The following diagram is what to look for in general:

Process information   Operators

Supplier → Raw materials → Manufacturing → Finished product → Customer Cash

Example 3.2 Value Shop Intellectual Capital Navigator

An intellectual capital navigator was constructed following a series of interviews and workshop sessions in the manner described in Chapter 3. This led to a general consensus on the nature of the organization should it be required to evolve to meet a situation in which most contracts were to be competively tendered for. From the assembled data, an Intellectual Capital Navigator was constructed at Level 1 (the level of the five top level resources) and is shown in the following diagrams. The left hand diagram shows all transformations between resources, and the righthand diagram has been filtered to leave only the most significant transformations. What is immediately apparent is that the managers foresaw that they would have to operate as a value shop; this can be seen by the classical triangular disposition in which human and organizational resources influence the relational resources (dominated by the customers) which may be interpreted as winning the work.

Relational resources influence human and organizational resources as the nature of contract work influences the development of human skills and the organization's knowledge base. Human resources influence organizational resources in problem solving and execution of work. Note that there are actually two main human contributions: one dominated by problem solving, the other competence-led consulting.

Continued

Example 3.2 Value Shop Intellectual Capital Navigator—cont'd

There is also a third but smaller loop involving the development of prototypes which mirrors the "consulting" process. Finally, the results in organizational, human, and physical form are delivered to customers, who then pay. The more detailed transformations are shown in the intellectual Capital Navigator below and similar loops can now be identified on this more detailed level.

Example 3.3 Value Network Intellectual Capital Navigator

An IC-navigator for the value network organization was constructed through a series of interviews and workshops. This process led to a consensus view on how the company's core operations create value and is shown in the figure below. The diagram on the left shows all transformations between the resources and the one on the right has been filtered to leave only the most significant transformations.

This Level 1 Intellectual Capital Navigator is typical of a systems-based value network. In this case, there is a massive interplay in the relational resource area, which reflects the stock exchange trades and clearing. These relational resources in turn influence the cash situation. The relational resources themselves are influenced by organizational resources i.e. operating systems and operating procedures. There is a small input from IT which is the effect of actual hardware used. The physical buildings in which the organization sit are relatively unimportant.

There are other types of value networks; telecom companies are good examples. In addition to systems and processes resources, telecom companies are far more influenced by physical hardware in the form of exchanges, base stations, cables and so on.

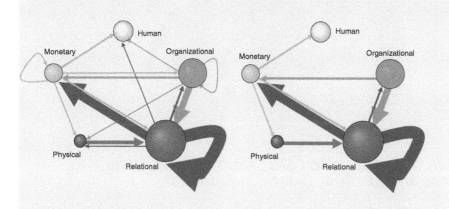

Thus the typical value network shows large relational-to-relational transformations influenced by either or both of organizational and physical resources. Relational resources are transformed into cash and this is where the users pay the bills. This can be seen in the filtered Level 2 Intellectual Capital Navigator shown in the figure above. Just out of view is the audit process and lost in the noise is the renewal cycle in which systems and hardware are updated. These too affect users. A quick inspection of the Intellectual Capital Navigator matrix will show all the transformations.

Continued

Example 3.3 Value Network Intellectual Capital Navigator—cont'd

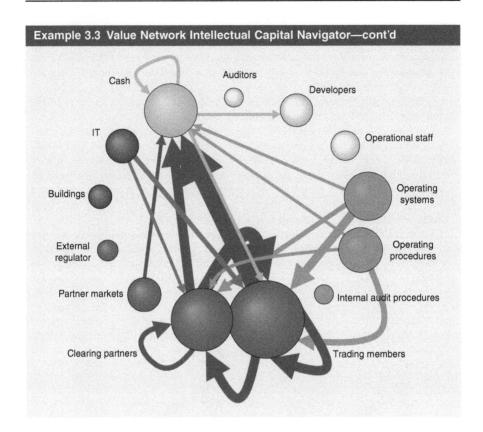

WHAT IS NEEDED FOR ANALYZING AND EVALUATING THE INTELLECTUAL CAPITAL NAVIGATOR?

To begin our evaluation we need to have the following information at hand:

1. The numerical representation of the resource transformation matrix (creation of the numerical representation of the resource transformation matrix is discussed in detail in the preceding section.)
2. The pictorial representation of the resource transformation matrix known as the intellectual capital navigator (also discussed in detail in the preceding section)
3. A judgment on the dominating value-creating logic of the organization, i.e., value chain, value shop or value network. (The definitions and reasoning around the value-creating logics are given in Chapter 1—our advisory firm in this example is operating as a value chain.)

4. A statement of the form that the resulting value (i.e., the outcome of what the organization is trying to achieve) takes (i.e., money, knowledge embodied in written articles, esthetic beauty embodied in paintings, stronger relationships with stakeholders, etc.)
5. A statement of the strategic intent[2] of the organization.

Case 3.5 Nihon Unisys: Using an Intellectual Capital Approach to Promote Transformation[1]

This case study is based on information from Recruit Co. Ltd. in Japan, that provide consulting services using the IC approach.[2]

Nihon Unisys, based in Japan, is an information technology company providing hardware, software, and services (such as consulting, system integration, and support). They originally provided mainframe hardware and related software and services in the 1950s and played a key role in the emergence of the Japanese IT industry.

In the mid 1990s a downsizing revolution occurred and many companies started to replace their big mainframes with small servers. Nihon Unisys was faced with a serious challenge because the organization was optimized to run mainframe business and did not fit the server business at all. In the early 2000s, struggling to reform their business to this downsizing, Nihon Unisys faced a second challenge from the market: the e-business revolution, where many companies started to combine their IT systems with their business strategy more closely. Therefore they required system providers to have strategic insight into their business. Although they had not yet fully overcome the first challenge, Nihon Unisys had to adapt to the second challenge.

In 2003 Seiichi Shimada, President and CEO of Nihon Unisys, decided to launch a new strategy and transform their organization to make it suitable for the new environment. He planned to establish a new organization that would take on business consulting and business development, and to restructure the existing organization.

But there was a problem: how to involve people? There were two major objections from managers. First, the new strategy did not seem differentiated enough from competitors. Managers thought the strategy was targeting the same position as all its competitors, and so would lead to price competition. Second, managers found it difficult to assume their respective new roles: "What is my mission?" "How should I collaborate with other divisions?"

To solve this problem, a corporate planning team, under Shimada, decided to utilize the IC process to identify their intellectual capital resources and to define the value-creating path which illustrates how and who will utilize each resource in line with the new strategy.

First, they identified both existing and new resources they should possess to pursue the strategy, and evaluated the competitiveness of each existing resource. They realized that they had competitive resources related to system implementation and support activities. For example, they had many explicit and tacit rules that enabled project managers to prevent major implementation trouble in advance. Also, they had a "don't stop the system" culture, which encourages all the people to prioritize prevention of and recovery from

Continued

Case 3.5 Nihon Unisys: Using an Intellectual Capital Approach to Promote Transformation[1]—cont'd

system troubles. This culture allowed them to react and solve customer's problems quickly. The advantage of these resources was proven by a customer survey. Identifying these resources enabled the corporate planning team to state their differentiation strategy clearly. "We target a system provider with both business insight and robust system service."

Second, they laid out the IC navigator to illustrate how to utilize each resource and define which division had the responsibility to develop and maintain which resource and which transformation. In this process, the key discussion was to design the collaboration among organizations such as sales, system implementation, and so on. Because they restructured the existing organization, streamlining collaboration was the key factor in delivering the transformation successfully. To achieve this goal, the Intellectual Capital Navigator was illustrated on a very detailed level, which included many resources (approximately 60), and the responsibility of each division was also illustrated in it. Collaboration with a newly established division, which took on business consulting and business development, was also defined (see the following figure). After depicting the Intellectual Capital Navigator, they made a list that explained the

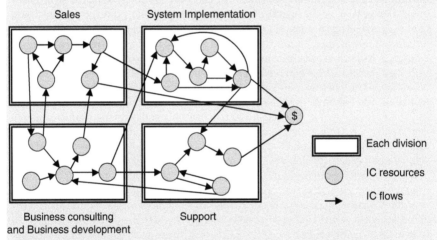

Illustrating the responsibility of each division on the Intellectual Capital Navigator.

mission of all divisions and the way to collaborate among divisions. This was the answer for managers who were having difficulty in assuming their new roles.

Finally, the corporate planning team built a presentation pack that explained business environment, new strategy, and new roles of each division, based on the insight derived from the IC process. With this presentation pack, president Shimada and other executives started a tour to explain the transformation plan to all managers in Nihon Unisys.

After the tour in April 2003, Nihon Unisys achieved some transformation milestones within one year. The new organization started up quickly and new deals were generated from the collaboration between the new organization and the sales division.

The embodiment of resulting value created by the organization

The primary stakeholders of an organization listed on the stock exchange are the shareholders. They are looking for total shareholder returns, which are driven by the free cash flow the organization is generating and the growth in this free cash flow. So here the value created by the organization is embodied in the form of monetary resources.

For other organizations the answer is not so straightforward. In order to be able to articulate how the organization embodies the value it delivers to different stakeholders we have to understand how value is perceived by stakeholders from an operational and strategic point of view (in Chapter 4 we will extend this to include an axiological or valuation point of view). This perceived value also has a direct effect on the profit in a for-profit organization since the organization's revenue stream is driven by the number of customer relationships, customer lifetime cycle, the amount of each purchase, and purchase frequency. These drivers are all affected by the customer's perceived value of offerings. The organization's margin is driven by the relative perceived value of the customers, because this drives willingness to pay and internal costs in the organization associated with providing offerings. Since net cash contribution is a function of revenue times margin it is essential, in order to manage net cash contribution, to have an in-depth understanding of cost drivers and perceived value drivers. Most organizations have rigorous control of cost drivers, and this information is usually readily available in a company. This is not normally the case for value drivers. In not-for profit organizations the reasoning is analogous, since you will not be provided with any operational (or working) capital unless you are able to provide value to your stakeholders.

The conclusion of the preceding reasoning is as follows: to deliver value to your stakeholders, whatever form value may take, you need to know and understand what drives value. Based on several years of research on executive MBA programs executed by the authors, four categories of value drivers have been identified:

1. The first is price, which is defined as all resources the organization has to give up in return for the service or product it purchases. This can be actual money, time, existing relationships, or something else.
2. The second is functionality, which is defined as everything objectively measurable surrounding the delivery of a product or service, such as on-time delivery, specification match (color, features, and functionality), and so on.

3. The third is distinctness, which is defined as everything that generates mindshare as a precursor to market share (brands, reputation, references, etc.).
4. The fourth and final value driver category is mental proximity, which is defined as those attributes that provide a basis for lowering barriers for building person-to-person trust (such as shared values and beliefs).

These four value driver categories are not equally important in any given situation. Their relative importance will depend on the situation and the buyer and supplier. The drivers of the situational relative importance of these drivers have been identified in the same research as:

1. The relative importance of the purchase from the customer's point of view. Is the purchase mission critical (i.e., if they do not get it their business stops)? Or is it just nice to have but they can live without it?
2. The customer's perceived information asymmetry of the customer–supplier relationship as it relates to the offering procured. On the one extreme the customer believes him or herself to know at least as much as the supplier, and on the other extreme the customer believes the supplier to know substantially more than the customer does.

The relative importance of the four categories of value drivers are depicted in Figure 3.14 using the two drivers of situational importance as the two axes.

The four numbered areas in Figure 3.14 illustrate four fundamentally different customer behavior zones.

1. This is the "commodity" zone. Here the customer is convinced that it knows at least as much as the seller. The customer therefore need not write down any specifications of the products in any detail in the belief that he or she understands the offering better than the supplier. The customer will normally ask for competitive tenders and will evaluate the offerings primarily on price (remember that the definition of price was not solely money but also time, existing relationships, etc.) and will procure the offering with the lowest price. If the tendering process is by auction, which is the case at some Internet-based exchanges, a version of the winner's curse[3] will operate, with the consequence that all surplus inherent in the transaction is appropriated by the customer (buyer). For suppliers operating in and intending to remain in this zone, there is one primarily feasible strategy, which is *cost leadership*. Outpacing is also possible but it is likely that the return on the differentiating investments in this strategy are low or negative.

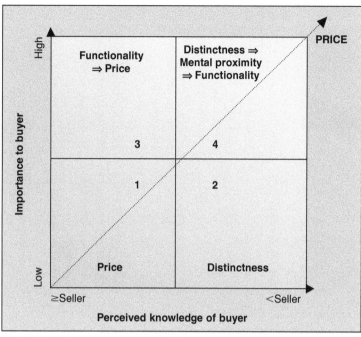

Figure 3.14. Situational importance of different perceived value driver categories.

2. This is the "branded products" zone. Here the customer believes him or herself to know less than the supplier, but the offering is not that important to the customer, so he or she is looking for a simple pseudo variable in order to reduce search cost and reach a quick decision. This is where brands, reputation, image, and all other distinctness attributes play a major role. In this zone we know that for many branded food products, for example, the taste of the product is in the brand rather than in the product itself; this can easily be verified by comparing blind tasting notes of a given group with tastings where the brand is revealed. The answers are frequently different between the two situations, although the participants think they have given the same answers. If the tendering process is not by auction, which is normally the case, most surplus inherent in the transaction is appropriated by the supplier (seller). For suppliers operating in and intending to remain in this zone, the most feasible strategy is that of *outpacing* albeit differentiation is also possible normally resulting in lower profitability (see Table 3.1).

Table 3.1. Outline of the Traditional Strategies

Name	Outpacing	Differentiation	Cost Leadership	Rest in Peace
Main Strategic Elements	Superior understanding of what drives value in the minds of customers and superior ability to deliver on these drivers.	Superior understanding of what drives value in the minds of customers.	Superior ability to operate with low costs.	Low or no understanding of what drives value in the minds of customers and/or no or inferior ability to deliver on these drivers.
	Superior ability to operate with low costs.	Concentrate on branded goods and brand advertising, design, service and quality. Alternatively concentration on innovation, functionality and first mover advantage.	Investment in volume production; product design that simplifies production [standardization]; tight cost control in for example R&D.	High operating costs and no or low ability to reduce operating costs.

Continued

Resource Needs and Organizational Needs	Same as Differentiation + Same as Cost Leadership + Organizational and human resource flexibility	Marketing competence, product design competence; creativity; basic research competence; incentive systems based on objective targets instead of quantitative; strong cross-functional coordination; fast mover.	Access to capital; process technology competence; fast reporting; tight cost control; structured organization and structured responsibilities; incentive system based on quantitative objectives.	None
Principle	Perceived value is higher than price and price does not relate to cost.	Perceived value is higher than price and price may or may not relate to cost.	Perciived value is higher than price andprice relates to cost.	Perceived value is lower than price and price relates to cost, and thereby price end up being higher than perceived value.
Reject/Accept Question for Changes	Does it increase the perceived value in the eyes of our customers at the same time as it reduces costs[4]?	Does it increase the perceived value in the eyes of our customers more than it impacts cost?	Does it reduce our costs more than it reduces perceived value in the eyes of our customers?	None

3. This is the "industrial procurement" zone. Here the customer is convinced that he or she knows at least as much as the seller, but at the same time, the offering is mission critical. The customer therefore writes down the specifications of the offering, to minimize risk, and asks for competitive tenders. The customer will evaluate the offerings primarily on functionality and will procure the one with the lowest price (remember that the definition of price was not solely money but also time, existing relationships, etc.), given fulfillment of specifications (i.e., functionality). The higher the complexity of the required offering, the fewer the potential suppliers and the higher the surplus that can be retained by the winning supplier. If the offering has low complexity and the tendering process is by auction with many potential suppliers—which is the case at some Internet-based exchanges—a version of the winner's curse will operate, with the consequence that most surplus inherent in the transaction is appropriated by the customer (buyer). For suppliers operating in and intending to remain in this zone, there is one primary strategy, which is *cost leadership* although both differentiation and outpacing are feasible if it is possible to influence either the perceived competence of the buyer or the content of the tender document or both.

4. This is the "trust" zone. Here the customer believes him or herself to know less than the supplier, and the offering is also mission critical to the buyer. We here find an interesting interaction between the value driver categories. Based on distinctness (reputation, image, brand, etc.), potential suppliers are invited to come and present to the buyer (sometimes known as a beauty parade). Here there is a common misperception of what is expected. Many potential suppliers assume the potential buyer to be interested in detailed information about the offer, but this is not normally the case since the potential buyer assumes him or herself incapable of understanding the offering. Instead the potential buyer is primarily interested in finding someone to trust (i.e., mental proximity). Once the potential buyer locates someone he or she can trust, the buyer normally instigates a feasibility project (i.e., it basically says, "Mr. Supplier A, you seem like you understand these things. Could you please assist us in specifying what we need to procure in order for us to achieve our objective? We are willing to pay you a small amount for your work." Potential Supplier A obviously agrees and provides a deliverable that fulfills the requirements). Now one of two things happens:

○ The not so sophisticated potential buyer will say, "This is a great feasibility study. Can your organization please deliver it?" and Supplier A has achieved its objective of providing a delivery without any competition on the monetary component of price. In this situation, all of the potential surplus inherent in the transaction is appropriated by the supplier. For suppliers operating in and intending to remain in this zone, there are two feasible strategies, which are *differentiation* and *outpacing*.

○ The sophisticated potential buyer will say, "This is a great feasibility study. I would like your organization to procure this delivery for me, but you cannot deliver it yourself and I will reward you on the savings you make for me as relates to the difference between the monetary component of the price of the deliverable and the budget I have for the project." The sophisticated buyer has moved the project from zone 4 to zone 3, where Supplier A operates. In this situation the potential surplus inherent in the transaction is divided between the chosen supplier [for the main project], supplier A [the supplier of the pre-feasibility study], and the buyer. For suppliers operating in and intending to remain in this zone, there are again two feasible strategies, which are *differentiation* and *outpacing*.

The embodiment of the value created by an organization that is not profit maximizing can be in any resource form. It can be in the excellent content of written academic papers (zone 3), which is an organizational resource. It can be in the brand of an awarded MBA (zone 2), which is an organizational resource. It can be in the trust that the electorate has in the government (zone 4), which is a relational resource. It can be in the competence that the apprenticeship process has imparted to the craftsman (zone 3), which is a human resource. It can be in the highest number of syringes per dollar spent (zone 1), which is a physical resource.

Also, different stakeholders may want different embodiments of the value delivered. It is essential that the value delivered is articulated clearly. In our advisory service example, the company operates in zone 4 and they are a for-profit company, so the value is embodied in monetary (cash) resources.

Having established the form that the value delivered takes, we need to understand what the concept of strategic intent entails before we can go on and analyze the ICN in a meaningful way.

Case 3.6 Saku Brewery: Identification of Perceived Value Drivers for Customers

A Baltic brewery facing a tougher competitive environment in its domestic market initiated an IC process to secure its future competitive position. With the aim of meeting the strategic goal of maintaining its position as a market leader, the management needed to understand not only what resources provided the brewery with a competitive advantage but also how to leverage these resources to achieve its strategic intent. As a foundation for the IC process and in order to better understand the evolving segmentation of consumer preferences in the domestic market, a sophisticated customer value driver study was implemented. This process is depicted at a general level in this case study.

A value driver study was implemented with the purpose of (1) identifying the factors that matter most for the brewery's customers in their relationship with the organization, (2) identifying the relative importance of these perceived value drivers, and (3) evaluating the brewery's performance relative to main competitors on these perceived value drivers.

The value driver study started with the identification of four main value driver categories—price, functionality, distinctness, and mental proximity—which in this study were operationalized through economic factors, functionality, image and service aspects (see the figure below). These were then further analyzed through field research. A questionnaire was prepared in cooperation with the brewery's sales department and interviews were implemented with diverse customer groups through a postal survey and telephone interviews.

As seen from the figure below the results of the value driver study showed that, economic factors and services aspects were the two most important value driver categories. Within the economic factors category, flexibility, price level, and discount were seen as the most important value drivers. In addition, the critical importance of brands and having the right brand portfolio was pinpointed by the study.

Then, the four main value driver categories were further analyzed and evaluated relative to the brewery's main competitors. Flexibility was seen as the most important economic factor, but when economic performance was evaluated, it turned out that one competitor was catching up, through good performance on flexibility and price change plan. In the service aspects category, the brewery's order processing factors such as quality of invoice and flexibility in order system were highly valued value-drivers. Even though the brewery outperformed competitors in this category, it was noticeable that the main competitor was closing the performance gap through service and a relationship oriented approach. Looking at the image category, brand awareness had a strong impact on customers' value perception and here the brewery had a highly significant performance advantage. Product quality was ranked as the most important factor in the functionality category, where the brewery had a very strong position. A customer comparison was also implemented where customers were divided into five categories (stores, wholesalers, HoReCa, gas stations, and kiosks). However, on most value drivers there was no significant difference between customer categories. Nevertheless, it was shown that both large and other customers perceived the brewery as the best performer.

Case 3.6 Saku Brewery: Identification of Perceived Value Drivers for Customers—cont'd

The results revealed what drives value most in the minds of customers and consumers, and showed that the brewery outperformed its main competitors on every value driver category rated in the survey. The study also revealed that competitors were catching up in some important value creation categories. The brewery got valuable information on its value drivers and management gained a better understanding of customer preferences in the brewery's domestic market. As a consequence, the brewery improved its performance on perceived value drivers for customers as outlined in the study with a focus on areas where the competitors were catching up. They also implemented a segmented service offering by packaging service components based on segment characteristics and value drivers. These improvements assisted the brewery in meeting the strategic intent of maintaining its position, relative to competitors, as the highest perceived value producer of beer in the domestic market. The study resulted in the launch of a new beer targeted at the domestic blue-collar market. In addition, the value driver exercise facilitated successful implementation of the IC process.

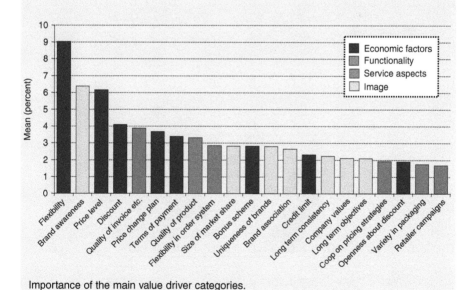

Importance of the main value driver categories.

Articulating the strategic intent of the organization

The strategic intent represents the strategic position the firm aspires to, relative to competitors. This is normally expressed as an aspirational position in terms of perceived value by customers and delivered cost. In not-for-profit organizations it is normally expressed as the target level of value to be delivered to a given stakeholder, within budget constraints.

Strategic intent is normally made up of the following four components:

1. Some form of an aspirational statement as to where the organization wants to be in the real world at some future point
2. A principle strategy normally expressed in the delivered costs/perceived value space. Traditional strategies are illustrated in Figure 3.15 and some characteristics are outlined in Table 3.1.
3. A direction normally expressed in customer/offering space. The traditional directions are illustrated in Figure 3.16.
4. Some principle discussion of the means by which the strategic intent is to be achieved (e.g., organic growth, acquisition, cooperation, etc.)

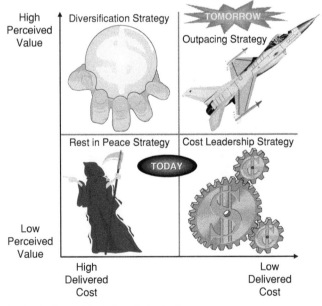

Figure 3.15. Illustration of traditional strategies.

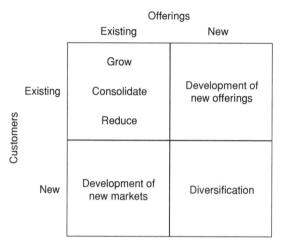

Figure 3.16. Illustration of traditional directions.

An example could be something like: "We are to become the dominant player (*aspirational statement as relates to global market share*) in the earth moving equipment industry (*defines the scope of the aspiration*) by constantly developing new innovative offerings (*the means is organic development*), each of which will have a higher value for our customers at a lower production cost to us (*the principle strategy is outpacing*)."

The strategic intent of our advisory firm is: "To achieve a dominating position in market share terms in the national market through a differentiation strategy using a directional and means strategy of fast conversion (academic ideas quickly converted to standardized service offerings) through internal conversion competence and external partnerships."

Having had the preceding discussion about value drivers and strategic intent, we can move on to the first step in analyzing the ICN.

Analysis step 1: construct an effector plot

The first tool we need at our disposal is one that will assist us in understanding which resources are value sinks (i.e., absorb more effort than they generate), and which resources are value sources (i.e., generate more effort than they absorb). This will allow us to relate this information to how influential the resources are. In a well-run organization all the influential intermediary resources are value sources (i.e., you get more out of them than you put into them).

On the x-axis of the effector plot we plot the influence of the resource, and on the y-axis we plot the effector ratio of the resource. The effector ratio of a resource is the sum total of all transformation streams going out of the resource divided by the sum total of all transformation streams coming into the resource. We always use the normalized but uncleaned resource transformation matrix to make these calculations. In our advisory firm case we will construct the effector plot for the resource transformation depicted in Figure 3.11, and then we will show the effector plot for the resource transformation matrix depicted in Figure 3.10.

The effector ratio is calculated by taking the row sum for the resource in question divided by the column sum for the resource in question. This is shown in Figure 3.17, with the resulting effector ratios shown in Figure 3.18.

	10/17.73	10/3.74	20/22.9	40/33.51	20/22.12	
	Monetary	Physical	Relational	Organisational	Human	Σ
Monetary	2.00	1.00	2.40	2.60	2.00	10.00
Physical	0.00	0.88	2.34	4.88	1.90	10.00
Relational	2.58	0.44	4.85	9.06	3.08	20.00
Organisational	9.30	1.20	8.97	10.44	10.09	40.00
Human	3.85	0.23	4.34	6.53	5.06	20.00
Σ	17.73	3.74	22.90	33.51	22.12	100.00

Figure 3.17. The principle calculation of effector ratios based on the resource transformation matrix in Figure 3.10.

	0.56	2.67	0.87	1.19	0.90	
	Monetary	Physical	Relational	Organizational	Human	Σ
Monetary	2.00	1.00	2.40	2.60	2.00	10.00
Physical	0.00	0.88	2.34	4.88	1.90	10.00
Relational	2.58	0.44	4.85	9.06	3.08	20.00
Organizational	9.30	1.20	8.97	10.44	10.09	40.00
Human	3.85	0.23	4.34	6.53	5.06	20.00
Σ	17.73	3.74	22.90	33.51	22.12	100.00

Figure 3.18. The resulting effector ratios based on the resource transformation matrix in Figure 3.10 using the principle calculation outlined in Figure 3.17.

We now have the y-axis values of the effector plot. The x-axis is easier since, by definition, the row sums of the respective resources are equal to the normalized weightings of these resources, so we will use the row sums for the respective resources as our x-axis values for the effector plot. The resulting effector plot is shown in Figure 3.19. In this plot, the more influential a resource is the further to the right it appears. Also in this plot, value sinks appear below the x-axis (i.e., have y-axis values below 1.0) and value sources appear above the x-axis (i.e., have y-axis values above 1.0).

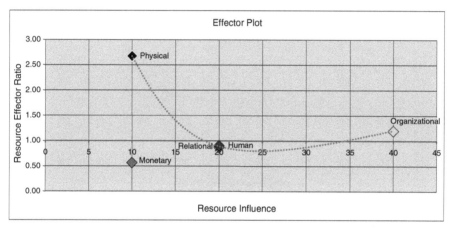

Figure 3.19. The resulting effector plot based on the resource transformation matrix in Figure 3.18.

Example 3.4 The Value Chain Effector

For the value chain company, an effector plot was made to further analyze resources. The following diagram shows the distribution, and that physical and organizational resources contribute most to value creation.

In the more detailed effector diagram it can be seen that recipe is a resource that is dangerously placed. Investment in alternatives and recipe development would move the recipe resource downwards and out of the danger zone. The company appears to be profitable since money is a value sink. Similarly, products make up a value sink since these also are an output resource (a lot is invested in it and then it gets sold). Quality systems are often left untouched for years and are just used as they are. Thus they are influential but their isolation from development means that they appear as a major source of value. If the company would have to invest in quality systems to meet new standards or to go with a new product then the investment in the systems would move the resource downwards.

Continued

Example 3.4 The Value Chain Effector—cont'd

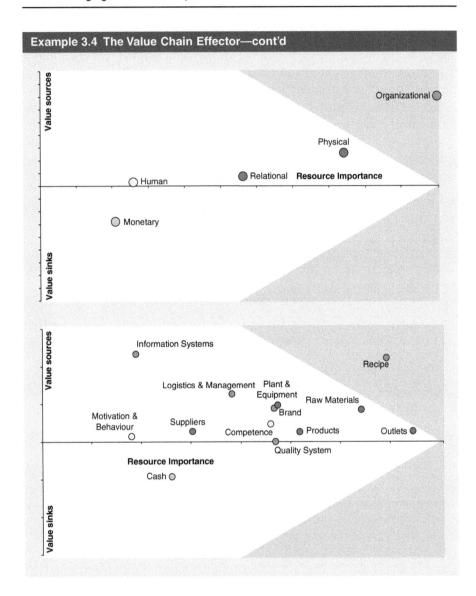

Example 3.5 Value Shop Effector

An effect plot was drawn. The following diagram shows the plot with human resources delivering most value. The plot deviates a little from the "ideal" in which resources line up on a bottom-left to top-right diagonal, but not seriously so. Organizational and physical resources contain the bulk of delivered value to the customers and so have a tendency to appear as sinks of value.

Example 3.5 Value Shop Effector—cont'd

Further analysis was then carried out at a more detailed level to determine whether there were any problems with the Intellectual Capital Navigator at Level 2. Further analysis was also carried out on the effector plot at Level 2 to see if any of the resources where vulnerable in any way (i.e., they were important sources of value that might cause collapse if they were unduly degraded). Only the problem-solving skills fell into this category (the were just inside the category). No resources appeared to be inefficiently used in the new model.

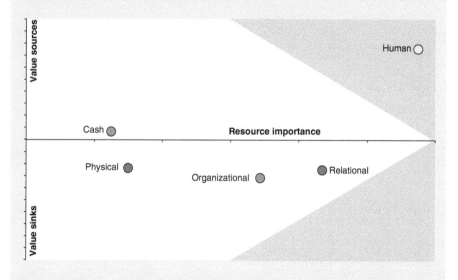

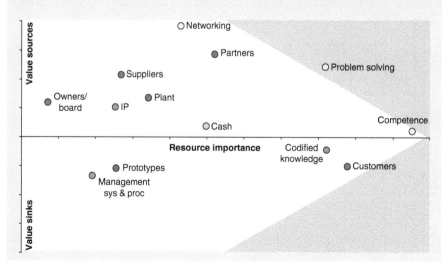

Example 3.6 Value Network Effector

An effector diagram was drawn. The following diagram shows the distribution and shows that relational resources contribute most value relative to others. This is typical for a value network.

From the effector plot on Level 2 it can be seen that the most important relational resource, trading members, is a value source. Buildings are not so important, so it does not really matter that these appear as a value sink. Most important, the diagram tells us that there are no resources in immediate danger that require urgent attention.

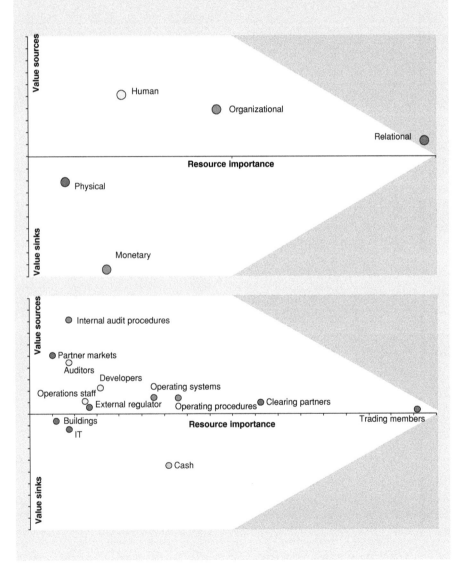

Analysis step 2: evaluate the effector plot

An ideal effector plot has the following set of characteristics:

- The output resource (i.e., the resource form that embodies the value the organization is delivering) should be one of the left-most resources (i.e., one of the least influential).
- The output resource should also always be a value sink (i.e., appear under the x-axis) that crosses the y-axis at 1.0. This is because a sustainable resource transformation system needs to generate more effort into the output resource than it must draw from the output resource to keep the system working. If this is the case, then there is an accumulation of effort in the output resource that can be used for other things (e.g., influencing the shareholders through paying dividends).
- The more influential an intermediary resource is (i.e., all resources except the output resource), the higher its effector ratio should be. This means that the resources that have the highest influence on value creation should be best leveraged (managed). This also means that the more uninfluential an intermediary resource is (i.e., the further toward the left it appears in the effector plot), the less critical becomes its position on the y-axis in the effector plot.
- The order in which the resources appear is determined by the value-creating logic (see Chapter 1) of the organization. The most influential resource is the one that forms the primary basis for the organization's competitive advantage. Table 1.3 provides an overview of the possible resource combinations that exist, but the main conclusions are:
  - In a value chain the human resource cannot be the right-most if the organization is in the business of making money.
  - In a value shop physical resources cannot be the right-most if the organization is in the business of making money.
  - In a value network you would expect some combination of organizational and relational resources to appear as the right-most if the organization is in the business of making money.

Figure 3.20 gives us further guidance in evaluating the effector plot. The figure shows a dotted line illustrating a line fit to the resources plotted (excluding the output resource) and delineator lines of three areas named 1, 2, and 3. The delineator lines are asymptotic to the least square fitted line and the y-axis respectively.

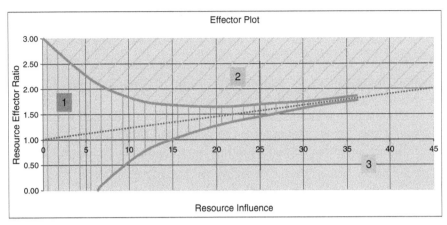

Figure 3.20. Effector plot evaluation guidance.

- Resources that appear in area 1 are no cause for concern.
- Resources that appear in area 2 are a potential cause of concern, and the question that must be asked relating to each resource in this area is: Is the value extraction from this resource sustainable over time or am I reinvesting too little (be it money, competence, reputation, or anything else) to maintain the value extraction at its current level?
- Resources that appear in area 3 are a potential cause of concern, and the question that must be asked relating to each resource in this area is: Is there a performance problem? Can I extract more value from this resource or can I reduce the investment in this resource without destabilizing the deployment system (transformation matrix) as a whole?

If we interpret this in the case of the effector plot (in Figure 3.19) of our advisory firm, we would expect:

1. The monetary resource (i.e., our output resource) to appear toward the left side of the effector plot, and this is the case.
2. The monetary resource (i.e., our output resource) to appear under the x-axis in the effector plot, and this is also the case.
3. The intermediary resource to appear above the x-axis in the effector plot, and we see that this is not the case for the relational and human resources. This provides us with our first improvement potential.
4. To be able to draw a continuously rising curve (or line) from left to right through the intermediary resources (the dotted line in

Figure 3.19 and Figure 3.21, respectively, represents the curve that can be drawn). We can see that this is only possible if we exclude the physical resources and ignore the small difference between the effector ratio for the human and relational resource. This provides us with our second improvement potential.

5. To see the organizational and relational resources (in decreasing marginal return mode) appear as the right-most resources in the effector plot because our advisory firm is a value chain operating in the business service sector. This provides us with our third improvement potential—to increase the influence of the relational resource at the expense of human resources.

If we then interpret the associated effector plot (in Figure 3.21) of our advisory firm we can ask the following questions:

1. Is the value extraction from physical resources sustainable? The answer is probably no. This provides us with our fourth improvement potential.
2. Is the value extraction from organizational resources sustainable? The answer is probably yes.
3. Can the value extraction from relational and human resources be improved? The answer is probably yes. This provides us with our fifth improvement potential.

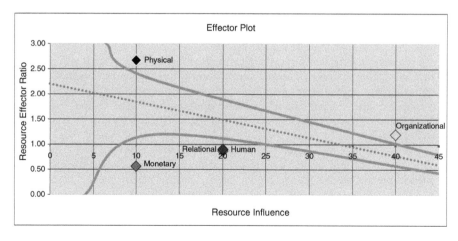

Figure 3.21. The resource transformation matrix in Figure 3.19 with inset least square fit line and area delineators.

Case 3.7 Saku Brewery: Securing the Future Competitive Position

Saku Brewery, the firm illustrated in both case 2.3 and case 3.2, continued its work with the IC Process by taking its developed Resource Distinction Tree to a Resource Transformation Matrix. This last step, described here, was done with the intention of capturing the deployment of all essential resources and the uniqueness of Saku's transformation structure. In order to achieve this, Intellectual Capital Navigators were created for the different levels in the Resource Distinction Tree.

At this stage, Saku's management defined the company's deployment of resources and visualized it in an Intellectual Capital Navigator that maps the organization's unique transformation structure and shows how to leverage Saku's resources to achieve its strategic intent most effectively. Reaching consensus on how different resources within the organization interact was a lengthy process. However, it was extremely valuable because final outcome from these discussions was a focused Intellectual Capital Navigator illustrating the present deployment. Transformations connecting the Level 2 resources showed an organization that was based on organizational and relational resources, which is rather normal in a company like Saku, operating predominantly as a value chain involved in branded consumer goods, where processes and competencies relating to brand building are paramount. The Intellectual Capital Navigator also showed that even though selling products generated the main income, base revenue was enhanced by customer satisfaction, increasing market share, strong brands, and efficient processes.

To capture the deployment of essential resources at a more detailed level, the figure below illustrates an Intellectual Capital Navigator showing Saku's most important Level 3 resources and transformations.

As the Level 3 Intellectual Capital Navigator shows, Saku's brand and image enhanced its relationship with its customers (retailers) and consumers. In turn, customers also strengthened the consumers' relationship with Saku. This allowed Saku to promote and sell more products at a better margin. In addition, Saku's strong brand and image contributed to higher margins. At the same time, Saku's products impacted its relationship with suppliers as well as its processes resulting in more cash, e.g. through procurement savings and/or increased market share. Saku also invested cash in building competence as well as continuously developing the corporate culture by taking into account employee attitudes Corporate culture was also impacted by empolyees' ability to innovate and imitate. However, in spite of market leadership, Saku's present resource deployment was not felt to be good enough to reach their strategic goal.

In the next step, the desired Intellectual Capital Navigator for Level 3 resources (depicted in the figure below) was created keeping in mind Saku's strategic intent and a few boundary conditions.

As Saku's base revenue was enhanced by customer satisfaction, increasing market share, strong brands, and efficient processes, it highlighted the importance of constant improvement and innovation based on continually enhancing competence. Therefore, such Level 3 human resources as competence, intellectual agility, and attitude were given more weight in the desired situation. The transformation from image to competitors was increased, thus implying that by strengthening its brand Saku was able to influence competitors in a way beneficial to Saku. There was an

Case 3.7 Saku Brewery: Securing the Future Competitive Position—cont'd

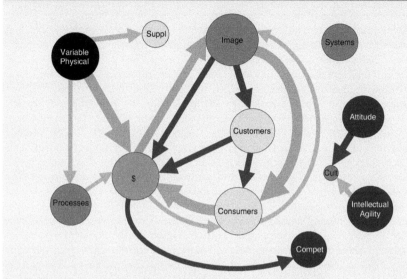

Saku's present Intellectual Capital Navigator for Level 3 resources.

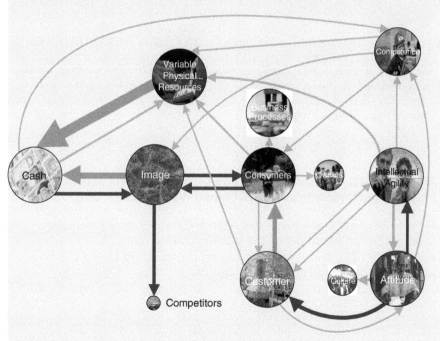

Saku's desired Intellectual Capital Navigator for Level 3 resources.

Continued

Case 3.7 Saku Brewery: Securing the Future Competitive Position—cont'd

important transformation from consumers to image as well as from image to cash, implying that a closer relationship with consumers results in a stronger brand that allows for a higher margin. The Intellectual Capital Navigator also shows an interesting transformation loop: attitude to intellectual agility to customer and back to attitude. An interpretation of this loop could be that employees are receptive to signals from the market (customers), which has a positive affect on their ability to innovate. This also enhances customer relationships in the form of better service. Moreover, transformations from cash, consumer, customer, and competence were given more weight, which implied that Saku got to benefit from higher revenue thanks to a better perceived value from consumers and from larger volumes. This can be achieved by investing in understanding which attributes drive value in the minds of customers and consumers and using employees' competence to develop and select products according to these attributes.

The creation of Intellectual Capital Navigators for different resource levels brought management to a more unified view as to what really drove value in Saku and thus needed to be managed and measured. It also enhanced the development of a coherent strategy and a better understanding of Saku's value creation path by encouraging management to stand back from their individual roles and agree what was important for the business as a whole. The created Intellectual Capital Navigators contributed to the way activities were reorganized by moving Saku from being a predominantly product based organization where marketing was used to sell the products, to a company that has a balance between product push and market pull in the make-up of brand portfolio and marketing approach. This shift has helped Saku to maintain and strengthen its position as a market leader in the domestic market. Through the IC process, Saku's management realized that the traditional categories on which its marketing and promotional campaigns had been based were no longer sufficient for long-term success. To better understand the evolving segmentation of consumer preferences in the Estonian market, a sophisticated market segmentation and brand positioning study was implemented.

Analysis step 3: improve the transformation matrix and plot the pictorial representation and accompanying effector plot

If these improvement potentials were acted upon we would change[5] the numerical representation of the transformation matrix to something like Figure 3.22. The corresponding pictorial representation of the transformation matrix would look like Figure 3.23.

Optimized	0.31	1.00	1.54	3.08	1.40	
	Monetary	Physical	Relational	Organizational	Human	Σ
Monetary	3.91	3.46	3.06	2.28	5.03	17.7
Physical	3.03	0.00	1.48	0.00	0.00	4.5
Relational	16.32	0.00	0.00	3.57	0.00	19.9
Organizational	22.44	0.48	5.97	4.95	5.95	39.8
Human	11.01	0.56	2.43	2.13	1.95	18.1
Σ	56.7	4.5	12.9	12.9	12.9	100.0

Figure 3.22. The numerical representation of the transformation matrix in Figure 3.18 after improving according to the identified improvement potentials.

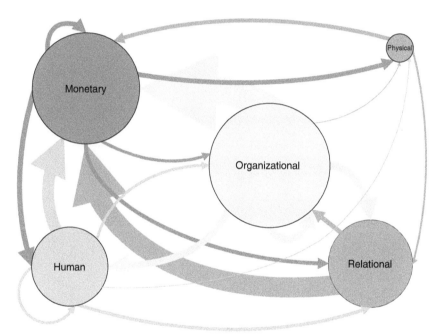

Figure 3.23. The pictorial representation of the transformation matrix in Figure 3.22.

The corresponding effector plot with a curve connecting the intermediary resources shown in the plot looks like Figure 3.24, and the corresponding effector plot with inset least square fit line and area delineators is shown in Figure 3.25.

We can see and interpret some of the changes in resource and transformation influence.

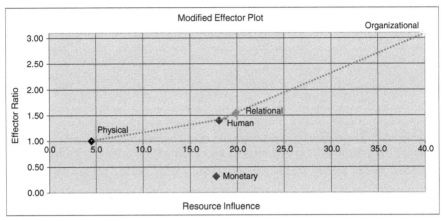

Figure 3.24. The resulting effector plot based on the resource transformation matrix in Figure 3.22.

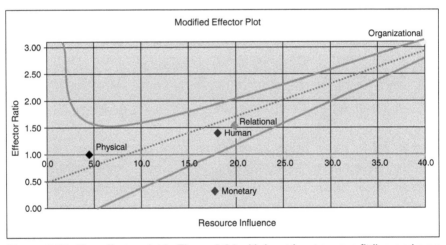

Figure 3.25. The effector plot in Figure 3.24 with inset least square fit line and area delineators.

Resources

All resources are within the upper area.

- Monetary (the output resource): This resource is now more influential than it was, but is still the least influential of the main resources, and its effector ratio has decreased, which is positive. The importance of the monetary resource is still too high, but this is probably due to profitability being insufficient at the moment, which tends to generate a higher influence in the ICN.

- Physical: This resource is now the least influential of all resources, which makes sense since this is a service producing organization. The effector ratio has now decreased to a break-even level, which is more reasonable for a relatively uninfluential resource.
- Organizational: This is still the most influential resource, which makes sense in a service organization providing standardized offerings. The effector ratio has increased and is now the highest among the resources. Again, this makes sense since we want the most influential resource to have the highest effector ratio.
- Relational: This is now clearly the second most influential resource and the effector ratio is well above one. Again, this makes sense since this organization's relationships are critical and must be well leveraged in a competitive market for standardized offerings.
- Human: This resource is now the second most uninfluential resource, but its effector ratio is still clearly above one. This makes sense in an organization that requests most of its people to follow a prescribed process in delivering services and where most of the fee relates to the offering delivered and not to the man-hours provided in its delivery.

Transformations

We include key comments and possible interpretations only (the reader can work out the meaning of the other changes).

- From monetary:
  - We see that there is an interesting transformation loop: monetary → physical → relational → monetary. This could be interpreted as the cost of a well-located high image office that generates more or better relationships that allow for higher income.
  - We see an increased size in the monetary → human transformation. This can be interpreted as higher investment in competent people.

- From physical:
  - All transformations from physical, with the exception of physical → monetary, have decreased dramatically. This makes sense since the influence of physical has decreased generally, and is in line with being a service providing organization.

- ○ Physical → monetary. This can be interpreted as the ability to charge customers for use of the high quality facilities the organization has access to.

- From organizational:

  - ○ All transformations from organizational, with the exception of organizational → monetary, have decreased dramatically. This makes sense since the primary business of the organization is to sell standardized solutions.
  - ○ Organizational → monetary. The increase in this transformation indicates a clearer focus on making money based on the price that can be charged for the organization's service offerings and its reputation/image/brand in combination with the costs that can be saved due to its well-functioning processes.

- From relational:

  - ○ All transformations from relational, with the exception of relational → monetary, have decreased dramatically. This makes sense since the primary business of the organization is to sell standardized solutions based on organic development from internally identified learning and opportunities.
  - ○ Relational → monetary. The increase in this transformation can be interpreted as benefits of economies of scale as the customer base/market share increase as well as a reduction in search cost (and thereby customer acquisition cost) through strong relationships.

- From human: The key changes here are in three transformations:

  - ○ Human → monetary: This transformation has increased. This can be interpreted as separating out those individuals that are versatile enough to be charged for separately and running them as a separate high value business dealing with customized solutions development/problem solving.
  - ○ Human → organizational: This transformation has decreased. This can be interpreted as more emphasis on standardized solutions and less emphasis on customer-specific modifications using competent individuals.
  - ○ Human → relational: This transformation has decreased. This can be interpreted as a higher emphasis on building and maintaining relationships based on reputation/image/brand combined with

excellent standardized service offerings rather than using competent individuals to build and maintain relationships.

We can see that all these changes are in line with a focused strategy of the type used by many larger service providers in the advisory industry.

Case 3.8 The Case of the Pharmaceutical Enterprise: Understanding the Value-Creating Resources Through the IC Process

This example is derived from a paper by Fernström, Pike, and Roos.[1] The pharmaceutical enterprise (hereafter referred to as the company) presented in this case is a globally operating organization with emphasis on discovering, developing, manufacturing, and marketing leading prescription medicines for humans and animals as well as many worldwide known consumer brands. The R&D function of the company went through the IC process with the initial objective of developing a more commercially oriented R&D function with improved alignment toward long-term strategic thinking. In addition, the IC process was expected to provide the necessary foundation to help the company better communicate the R&D function's role in meeting the business objectives within the department as well as their role and structure within the whole company. This would facilitate the development of a new generation of management and measurement thinking based on the key drivers of value. In order to meet the objective, it was a necessity to map and evaluate the company's resources and their interaction with one another. When these steps of the IC process were executed, the analysis of efficiency and effectiveness with which the company's resources were used was implemented and the company's effector plot was created, which is the step depicted in the figure below.

Once the strategy of the project group had been clarified, the nature of the resources at the company's disposal were determined and the interactions between resources were visualized in Intellectual Capital Navigators, the IC process extended to assess also the effectiveness and the efficiency with which the resources are deployed. The data used to generate the IC Intellectual Capital Navigators were further analyzed to produce an effector plot that is a graphic representation of the importance of a resource against a measure of its effectiveness. The effector plot for the company's second level resources is shown in the figure below.

The order in which resources appear in the effector plot is determined by the value-creating logic of an organization. The company's strategic logic is based on the value shop model (see Chapter 1 for information on generic business logics), which is to be expected from an R&D organization. The graph depicts that R&D capability is the most important Level 2 resource, since it is right-most at the x-axis, and the basis for competitive advantage, while the 10 discarded resources are least important and are found on the left extreme. It is rather common in value shop organizations that human resources, including R&D capabilities, are the basis for competitive advantage. All the resources located below the x-axis are value sinks that absorb more effort than they generate. The company's effector plot depicts that organizational resources such as organizational strategy and organizational culture are value sinks that do not make any meaningful contribution to value creation. By contrast, in an effective organization, strategy and structure indeed influence how value is created, and therefore the company's management needs to draw more attention to the effective deployment of these resources.

Continued

Case 3.8 The Case of the Pharmaceutical Enterprise: Understanding the Value-Creating Resources Through the IC Process—cont'd

At the righthand end of the plot are two triangular gray zones, which roughly cover one third of the plot area between them. Resources that fall in the upper triangle represent resources of importance. However, as they are also displaced high above the x-axis, this means that they are high net sources of value, implying that the resources might suffer from under-investment (investment can here be represented by any trans-

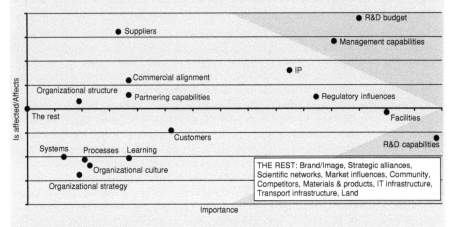

Effector plot of the company's Level 2 resources.

formation into the resource). In the case of the company, R&D budget and management capability are dangerously placed sources of value, by being important but not supported by other resources. Therefore, the managers should consider whether enough is invested in them and what the overall effects on value creation of a sudden loss or significant degradation in these resources might be. Resources in the lower triangle are again important as they are at the righthand side of the graph, but being below the x-axis are net sinks of value, implying that these resources are underused or over-invested in (investment can here be represented by any transformation into the resource). The effector plot shows that the R&D capability is a misused resource, and therefore management should consider carefully whether or not it is properly utilized.

The visualization of the company's resources through the effector plot helped management to develop a better understanding of the tacit value creation path. The IC process as a whole generated many conclusions that the company could act upon. For example, as shown in the effector plot, a degree of ineffectiveness in the R&D department was identified, in that a number of organizational resources such as culture and structure made little or no contribution to value creation. Also, some of the most important resources such as R&D capabilities, R&D budget, and management capabilities appeared to be mismanaged over- or under-invested in, or underused. In addition, the company's Intellectual Capital Navigator pointed at inefficiencies in the deployment of the company's external relational resources.

Case 3.8 The Case of the Pharmaceutical Enterprise: Understanding the Value-Creating Resources Through the IC Process—cont'd

Results from the IC process were shown to be of critical value in determining the nature of the minimum set of metrics necessary to follow the progress of the business from the company's current position to that of its strategic future. Overall, the objective of the intellectual capital study at the company was achieved with participants having been shown a new way of managing their business toward long-term strategic thinking. This was reinforced by the focus on strategy and all relevant resources, including external relational resources, which contribute to the development of greater commercial awareness of the value in R&D staff at the company through improved alignment.

Analysis step 4: taking into account the time dynamics

Organizations, like most things, go through some type of life cycle.[6] This is worth exploring further to identify intellectual capital navigator archetypes. Let's look at the development of three types of organizations from inception to maturity and possible decline. The first organization would be a manufacturing company. Figure 3.26 illustrates the stages a manufacturing company normally goes through from a value-creating logic perspective, and Figure 3.27 illustrates the same stages from a strategic perspective.

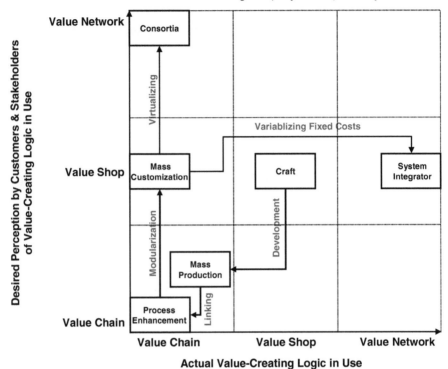

Figure 3.26. Stages in the life of a manufacturing company: value-creating logic perspective.

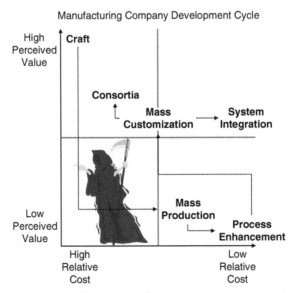

Figure 3.27. Stages in the life of a manufacturing company: strategic perspective.

Craft stage

All entrepreneurial firms tend to have an initial phase, no matter how short, as a craft type organization. This is the phase in which the idea or concept is tried out (proof of concept phase) and proven to work. It is natural that in this phase many things will be done for the first time, and therefore it is very much effectiveness focused (i.e., it is about doing the right things, in this case in the form of customization for initial or reference customers).

In this stage firms pursue the deployment of the following resources:

- Flexible manufacturing systems (made up of part physical resources such as used and/or non-specialized production equipment and part human resources such as skilled operators, in addition to the add-on customization services that are part of product offerings) are developed that will allow for production of customized goods (customization is limited only by man-hour constraints imposed by the presence of skilled operators) at costs higher than those in the mass production stage.
- Information (an organizational resource) is accumulated as a consequence of ascertaining and serving the individual customer's needs and then deployed to design suitable product offerings (physical resource).
- These customized product offerings (physical resource) are then deployed together with personal relationship building competence (human resources) to build up strong customer relationships (relational resource).
- The value creation process starts only when the customer's order is received.

The perceived value of the offering must exceed the cost in producing the offering. Both transaction costs and coordination costs are high in this stage. If we describe a typical manufacturing organization in this phase of its development it will look something like Figures 3.28 through 3.31.

From ＼ To	Effector Ratio: 0.20 Monetary	2.42 Physical	2.20 Relational	1.00 Organizational	2.66 Human	Σ
Monetary	**6.9**	**3.9**	**0.0**	**0.0**	**1.0**	11.7
Physical	**23.2**	**0.0**	**0.0**	**1.4**	**1.1**	25.8
Relational	**15.7**	**2.9**	**0.3**	**3.2**	**1.4**	23.4
Organizational	**1.1**	**0.0**	**2.8**	**5.0**	**1.8**	10.7
Human	**10.4**	**4.0**	**7.6**	**1.0**	**5.4**	28.4
Σ	57.3	10.7	10.7	10.7	10.7	100.0

Figure 3.28. Numerical representation of the transformation matrix on Level 2 for a typical manufacturing firm in the craft stage.

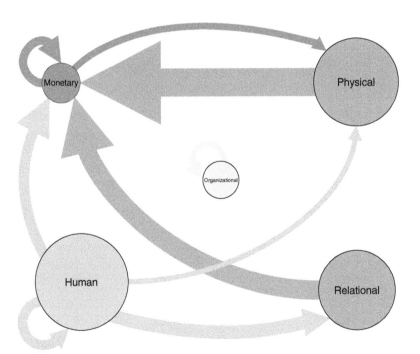

Figure 3.29. Pictorial representation of the Pareto cleaned transformation matrix (Figure 3.28) on Level 2 for a typical manufacturing firm in the craft stage.

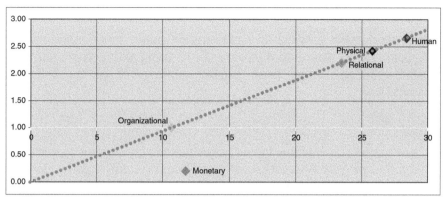

Figure 3.30. Effector plot based on the numerical transformation matrix in Figure 3.28 for a typical manufacturing firm in the craft stage.

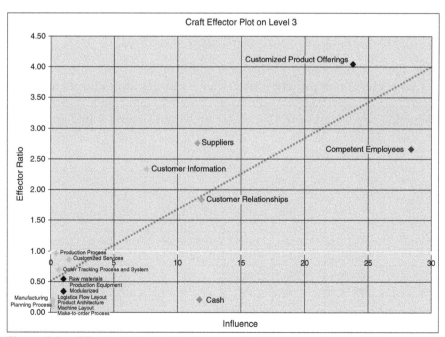

Figure 3.31. Effector plot based on the numerical transformation matrix in Figure 3.28 broken down to Level 3 for a typical manufacturing firm in the craft stage.

Mass production

Mass production is based on increasing efficiency by taking advantage of economies of scale and economies of learning at the expense of effectiveness. In this stage firms pursue deployment of the following resources:

- An efficient manufacturing system is made up of part physical resources (i.e. specific production equipment) and part organizational resources (i.e., machine layout, manufacturing planning process, production process, order tracking process and system, logistics flow layout) that will allow for production of standardized goods at costs lower to those in the craft stage.
- Information is accumulated (an organizational resource) as a consequence of ascertaining and serving customers, and then deployed to design suitable product offerings (physical resource).
- These standardized product offerings (physical resource) are then deployed to build up strong earnings (monetary resource).
- Make-to-estimated-demand processes (organizational resource) are developed. This means that most of the value-creating activities are performed before the customer's order is received.

The decrease in perceived value of the offering must be compensated for by a decrease in transaction cost (due to integration and standardization) and close to zero coordination costs. We describe a typical manufacturing organization in this phase of its development in Figures 3.32 through 3.35.

Effector Ratio:	0.21	1.70	1.21	1.56	1.00	
From To	Monetary	Physical	Relational	Organisational	Human	Σ
Monetary	1.7	0.1	0.0	4.0	2.1	7.9
Physical	19.5	9.4	3.6	4.5	1.0	38.0
Relational	5.6	6.4	0.0	3.8	0.0	15.8
Organisational	9.8	6.3	9.5	3.8	2.3	31.7
Human	1.1	0.1	0.0	4.3	1.1	6.6
Σ	37.6	22.3	13.1	20.3	6.6	100.0

Figure 3.32. Numerical representation of the transformation matrix on Level 2 for a typical manufacturing firm in the mass production stage.

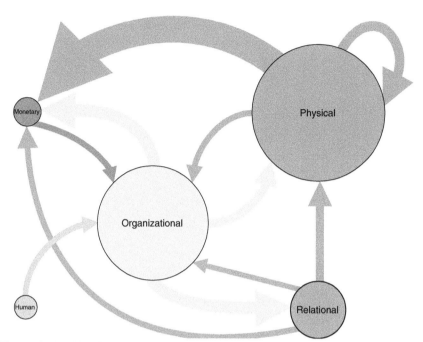

Figure 3.33. Pictorial representation of the Pareto cleaned transformation matrix (Figure 3.32) on Level 2 for a typical manufacturing firm in the mass production stage.

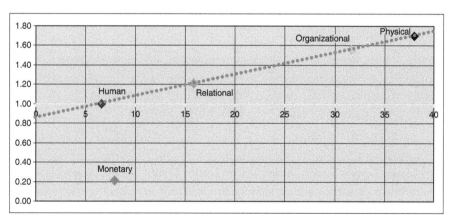

Figure 3.34. Effector plot based on the numerical transformation matrix in Figure 3.32 for a typical manufacturing firm in the mass production stage.

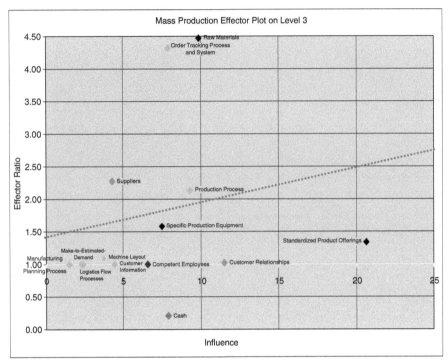

Figure 3.35. Effector plot based on the numerical transformation matrix in Figure 3.32 broken down to Level 3 for a typical manufacturing firm in the mass production stage.

Process enhancement

Process enhancement is based on increasing efficiency even further as compared to mass production by taking advantage of economies of scale and economies of learning at the expense of effectiveness. In this stage firms pursue deployment of the following resources:

- An efficient manufacturing system is made up of part physical resources (i.e. specific production equipment) and part organizational resources (i.e. machine layout, manufacturing planning process, production process, order tracking process and system, logistics flow layout) that will allow for production of standardized goods at costs lower to those in the mass production stage.

- Information is accumulated (an organizational resource) as a consequence of ascertaining and serving customers and then deployed to design suitable product offerings (physical resource).
- These standardized product offerings (physical resource) are then deployed to build up strong earnings (monetary resource).
- Make-to-estimated-demand processes (organizational resource) are developed. This means that most of the value-creating activities are performed before the customer's order is received.

There is no change in perceived value of the offering, but transaction cost (due to integration and standardization) is still decreasing and there are still no zero coordination costs. We describe a typical manufacturing organization in this phase of its development in Figures 3.36 through 3.39.

Effector Ratio:	0.14	1.64	1.28	1.68	1.00	
From To	Monetary	Physical	Relational	Organisational	Human	Σ
Monetary	2.7	0.1	2.0	0.0	0.3	5.2
Physical	15.1	8.8	3.1	8.6	0.1	35.7
Relational	10.6	1.7	2.4	2.0	1.1	17.8
Organisational	9.1	11.0	4.3	10.8	2.3	37.5
Human	0.6	0.0	2.1	1.0	0.1	3.9
Σ	38.1	21.8	13.9	22.4	3.9	100.0

Figure 3.36. Numerical representation of the transformation matrix on Level 2 for a typical manufacturing firm in the process enhancement stage.

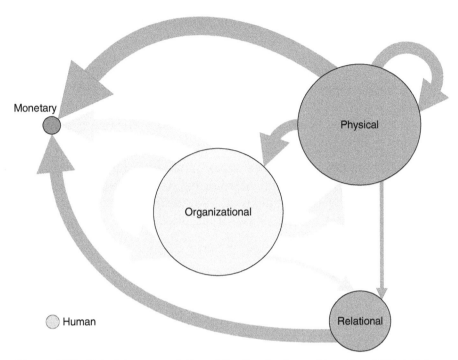

Figure 3.37. Pictorial representation of the Pareto cleaned transformation matrix (Figure 3.36) on Level 2 for a typical manufacturing firm in the process enhancement stage.

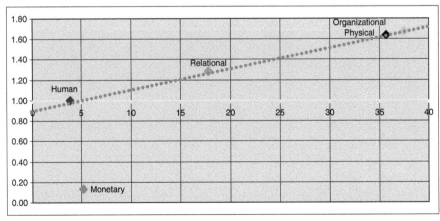

Figure 3.38. Effector plot based on the numerical transformation matrix in Figure 3.36 for a typical manufacturing firm in the process enhancement stage.

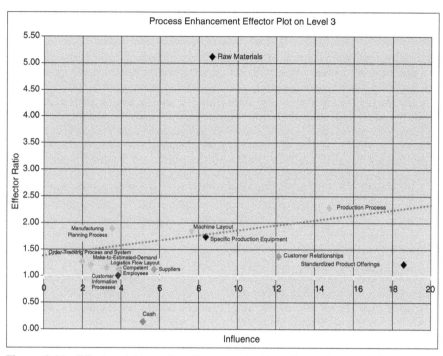

Figure 3.39. Effector plot based on the numerical transformation matrix in Figure 3.36 broken down to Level 3 for a typical manufacturing firm in the process enhancement stage.

Case 3.9 Ashi Breweries Alcoholic Beverages Business Unit: Utilizing an IC Approach at the Time of Strategic Change[1]

This case study is based on information from Recruit Co. Ltd. in Japan, that provide consulting services using the IC approach.[2]

Established in 1889, Asahi Breweries, Ltd. is a prestigious brewery in Japan with over 100 years of history. As a leading company in the beer market, it developed Asahi Super Dry into a product that boasted the highest market share (38.4% by volume) in Japan during 2002.

Beer has been a core business for Asahi Breweries since it was founded. In 2000, with ever-diversifying consumer tastes, it became clear that the beer market had stopped growing while other beverages, including low-alcoholic products were on the rise. To adapt, Asahi Breweries decided to shift its strategy in 2001 to being a total alcoholic beverage provider. It extended its product lineup from exclusively beer to other liquors such as whiskey, wine, spirits, and liqueurs, by forming sales alliances as well as through mergers and acquisitions.

Two years later, in the fall of 2003, government deregulated licensing of liquor sales. As store numbers had been traditionally capped by government, this deregulation

Continued

Case 3.9 Ashi Breweries Alcoholic Beverages Business Unit: Utilizing an IC Approach at the Time of Strategic Change—cont'd

caused a significant increase in liquor distribution channels. The sales division of Asahi Brewery was faced with a big challenge. Despite their long experience in selling a single product category-beer-to limited distribution channels, they had to establish a new sales approach to sell various product categories to various types of distribution channels, from supermarkets to drug stores to DIY stores. Asahi seemed it necessary to propose tailored product mixes, properly chosen from their various product lineups, for each distribution channel. In addition, new entry distribution channels required specific advice on how to procure, display, and sell alcoholic beverages. But sales managers were uncertain how to handle these new activities.

Under the leadership of the general business manager, HRD division took the initiative to use the IC process to establish a new managerial approach for this new environment. HRD set up a team of sales managers and they drew up an Intellectual Capital Navigator in line with corporate goals. Based on this, they determined a specific list of activities required by sales managers.

These processes brought two findings: the first was that end consumers are vital. Asahi Breweries has two kinds of customers: one is the consumer, and the other is the distribution channel. Before deregulation, sales managers' primary importance was in building relationships with distribution channels. This was key to increasing the number of distribution channels selling Asahi's beer and the share-of-shelf, as consumers has only limited outlets to buy alcoholic beverages from. However, now that there were various types of distribution channels selling alcoholic beverages, all easily accessible by consumers, increasingly sophisticated consumers could buy whatever they wanted wherever they liked. Consequently, for Asahi it was critical to consider customer needs and to propose a product mix for each distribution channel based on its customer base. In addition, it was important to offer marketing advice such as effective displays and appealing sales messages enabling distribution channels to attract consumers. In other words, it was necessary for the sales division to focus on

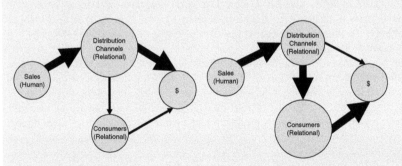

(a) Old Intellectual Capital Navigator; (b) new Intellectual Capital Navigator (extracts)

Case 3.9 Ashi Breweries Alcoholic Beverages Business Unit: Utilizing an IC Approach at the Time of Strategic Change—cont'd

the consumer more than on the distribution channel, whose customer is also the consumer (see the following figure).

The second finding was the importance of knowledge management. In the beer only days, the most important thing was the communication ability or personal skill of each sales person (human capital) to build better relationships with distribution channels. Now it was necessary to propose product mixes and explain how to attract customers for distribution channels based on consumer tastes. From this perspective, it becomes more important to collect and accumulate customer specific marketing know-how and good case studies (organizational capital) from sales persons all across the nation so that all sales people could easily share information and experience anytime they wanted to (see the following figure). Some years ago Asahi had

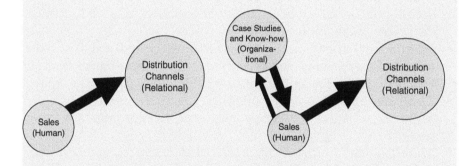

(a) Old Intellectual Capital Navigator; (b) new Intellectual Capital Navigator

launched a knowledge management initiative, and the findings from the IC process project contributed to improving this initiative.

Finally, these findings revealed the ideal sales management approach. Traditional sales managers used to build strong relationships with distribution channels, and required their subordinates to achieve sales goal through emulating them which worked well at that time. Now sales managers are required, instead of visiting distribution channels by themselves, to grasp consumer trends as quickly as possible, draw up sales strategies based on them, and instruct/develop subordinates by leveraging the accumulated successful case studies and know-how properly.

Asahi Breweries is implementing various measures based on these findings. Companywide changes are underway, including workshops for sales managers to learn their new roles and encourage action using the IC approach, reviews of assessment systems and knowledge management infrastructure.

Mass customization [7]

Mass customization is based on increasing efficiency by combining economies of scale and economies of learning, driven through the effectiveness increasing opportunities presented by customization. In this stage firms pursue deployment of the following resources:

- A flexible manufacturing system is made up of part physical resources (i.e. specific production equipment, reusable product platforms that provide communality) and part organizational resources (i.e., modularized product architecture, machine layout, manufacturing planning process, production process, order tracking process and system, logistics flow layout, and add-on customized services that are part of product offerings) that will allow for production of customized goods (customization is limited only by technological constraints imposed by requirements for stable processes and the decision on size of product family) at cost levels similar to those in the process enhancement stage.
- Information (an organizational resource) is accumulated as a consequence of ascertaining and serving the individual customer's need and then deployed to design suitable product offerings (physical resource).
- These customized product offerings (physical resource) are then deployed to build up strong customer relationships (relational resource).
- Make-to-order processes (organizational resource) are developed. This means that not all value-creating activities are performed until the customer's order is received.

The increase in perceived value of the offering must exceed the increase in transaction costs (information costs resulting from increased information handling in identifying and transferring individual customer configurations to manufacturing and increased costs due to individual distribution of the product offering) and increased coordination costs (increased complexity in production planning and control and increased coordination of external suppliers that are used for individual customization prefabrication). We describe a typical manufacturing organization in this phase of its development in Figures 3.40 through 3.43.

Effector Ratio:	0.27	1.37	1.18	1.27	1.00	
From　　　　To	Monetary	Physical	Relational	Organizational	Human	Σ
Monetary	0.0	6.9	0.3	0.0	0.1	7.3
Physical	15.4	7.8	6.8	6.0	1.9	37.9
Relational	5.9	6.0	1.5	6.3	1.2	20.9
Organizational	5.6	3.9	9.0	10.5	0.0	29.0
Human	0.2	3.0	0.1	0.0	1.5	4.8
Σ	27.1	27.6	17.7	22.8	4.8	100.0

Figure 3.40. Numerical representation of the transformation matrix on Level 2 for a typical manufacturing firm in the mass customization stage.

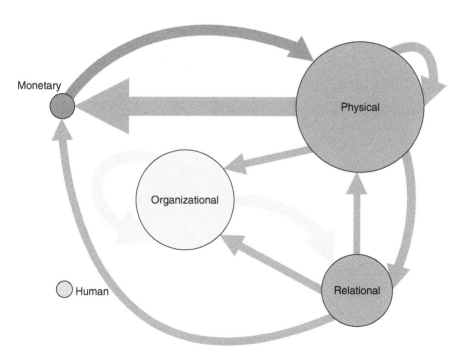

Figure 3.41. Pictorial representation of the Pareto cleaned transformation matrix (Figure 3.40) on Level 2 for a typical manufacturing firm in the mass customization stage.

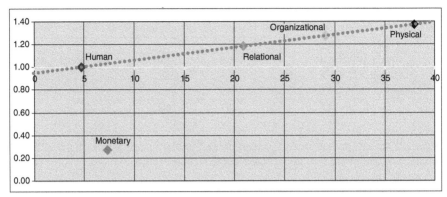

Figure 3.42. Effector plot based on the numerical transformation matrix in Figure 3.40 for a typical manufacturing firm in the mass customization stage.

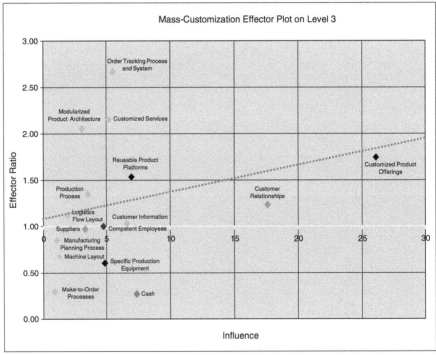

Figure 3.43. Effector plot based on the numerical transformation matrix in Figure 3.40 broken down to Level 3 for a typical manufacturing firm in the mass customization stage.

Consortia

Consortia are based on increasing effectiveness by ensuring a wider portfolio of capabilities at a somewhat reduced efficiency due to increasing coordination costs while transaction costs remain unchanged or increase somewhat. In this stage firms pursue deployment of following resources:

- A flexible manufacturing system is made up of part physical resources (i.e., specific production equipment, reusable product platforms that provide communality) and part organizational resources (i.e. modularized product architecture, machine layout, manufacturing planning process, production process, order tracking process and system, logistics flow layout), plus add-on customized services that are part of the product offerings and a flexible and efficient management system for managing the consortia (made up of part organizational resources such as quality control systems, design-for-manufacture processes, design distribution systems, order tracking process and system, logistics flow management systems, and all the consortia relationships) that will allow for production of customized goods (customization is limited only by technological constraints imposed by requirements for stable processes at the consortia members) at cost levels somewhat higher than those in the mass customization stage.
- Information (an organizational resource) is accumulated as a consequence of ascertaining and serving individual customers' needs and then deployed to design suitable product offerings (physical resource).
- These customized product offerings (physical resource) are then deployed to build up strong customer relationships (relational resource).
- Make-to-order processes (organizational resource) are developed. This means that not all value-creating activities are performed until the customer's order is received.

The increase in perceived value of the offering must exceed the increase in transaction costs (information costs resulting from increased information handling in identifying and transferring individual customer configurations to manufacturing and increased costs due to individual distribution of the product offering) and increased coordination costs (increased complexity in production planning and control, increased coordination of external suppliers, and increased coordination of consortia members used for individual subassembly manufacturing). We describe a typical manufacturing organization in this phase of its development in Figures 3.44 through 3.47.

Effector Ratio:	0.14	1.33	1.39	1.36	1.10	
From ＼ To	Monetary	Physical	Relational	Organizational	Human	Σ
Monetary	0.0	1.2	1.4	1.3	0.3	4.1
Physical	13.9	4.8	5.2	2.5	0.6	27.1
Relational	8.5	8.3	5.3	8.1	2.7	32.8
Organizational	6.0	3.7	10.2	9.8	0.1	29.8
Human	0.1	2.4	1.6	0.3	1.9	6.1
Σ	28.5	20.4	27.2	22.0	5.6	100.0

Figure 3.44. Numerical representation of the transformation matrix on Level 2 for a typical manufacturing firm in the consortia stage.

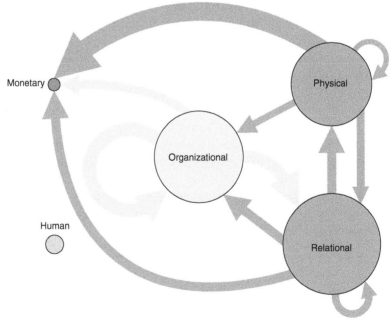

Figure 3.45. Pictorial representation of the Pareto cleaned transformation matrix (Figure 3.44) on Level 2 for a typical manufacturing firm in the consortia stage.

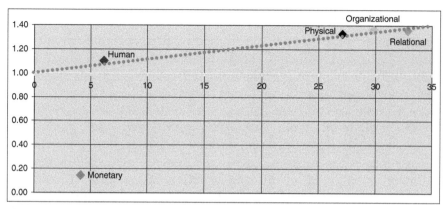

Figure 3.46. Effector plot based on the numerical transformation matrix in Figure 3.44 for a typical manufacturing firm in the consortia stage.

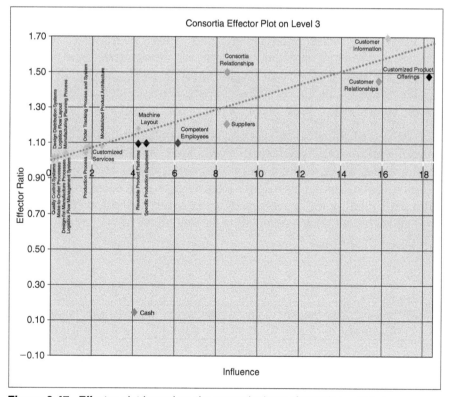

Figure 3.47. Effector plot based on the numerical transformation matrix in Figure 3.44 broken down to Level 3 for a typical manufacturing firm in the consortia stage.

System integration

System integration is based on variabilizing fixed cost through outsourcing of all major activities except final assembly. This maintains or increases efficiency while maintaining effectiveness. In this stage firms pursue deployment of the following resources:

- A flexible and efficient management system for outsourced activities is made up of part organizational resources (i.e., quality control systems, design-for-manufacture processes, design distribution systems, order tracking process and system, logistics flow management system, and all subsupplier relationships) that will allow for production of customized goods (customization is limited only by the capacity and capabilities of subsuppliers) at cost levels similar to those in the process enhancement stage.
- Information (an organizational resource) is accumulated as a consequence of ascertaining and serving the individual customer's need and then deployed to design suitable product offerings (physical resource).
- These customized product offerings (physical resource) are then deployed to build up strong customer relationships (relational resource).
- Make-to-order processes (organizational resource) are developed. This means that not all value-creating activities are performed until the customer's order is received.

The perceived value of the offering is unchanged compared to the mass customization stage whereas the cost level is similar to the process enhancement stage. Almost all of the costs are now coordination costs relating to managing subsupplier relationships with some small transaction costs relating to final assembly and delivery activities. We describe a typical manufacturing organization in this phase of its development in Figures 3.48 through 3.51.

Effector Ratio:	0.37	1.10	1.52	1.27	1.22	
From To	Monetary	Physical	Relational	Organisational	Human	Σ
Monetary	0.0	1.6	5.2	3.0	2.6	12.4
Physical	8.4	0.8	1.9	0.0	0.0	11.1
Relational	8.9	7.2	5.9	6.2	8.6	36.8
Organizational	4.3	0.2	8.7	7.6	0.5	21.2
Human	12.3	0.3	2.5	0.0	3.4	18.5
Σ	33.8	10.1	24.2	16.8	15.2	100.0

Figure 3.48. Numerical representation of the transformation matrix on Level 2 for a typical manufacturing firm in the system integrator stage.

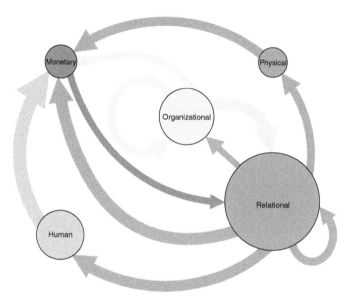

Figure 3.49. Pictorial representation of the Pareto cleaned transformation matrix (Figure 3.48) on Level 2 for a typical manufacturing firm in the system integrator stage.

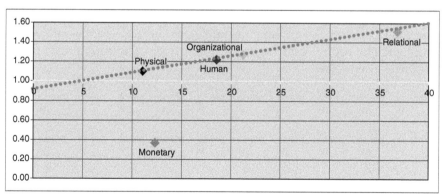

Figure 3.50. Effector plot based on the numerical transformation matrix in Figure 3.48 for a typical manufacturing firm in the system integrator stage.

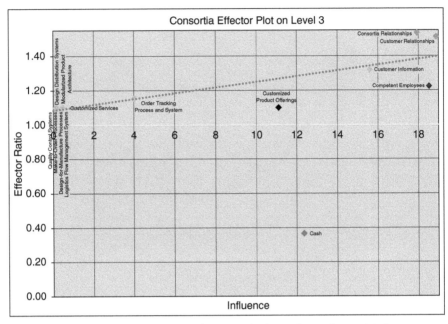

Figure 3.51. Effector plot based on the numerical transformation matrix in Figure 3.48 broken down to Level 3 for a typical manufacturing firm in the system integrator stage.

The second example would be a service company. Figure 3.52 illustrates the stages a service company normally goes through from a value-creating logic perspective and Figure 3.53 illustrates the same stages from a strategic perspective.

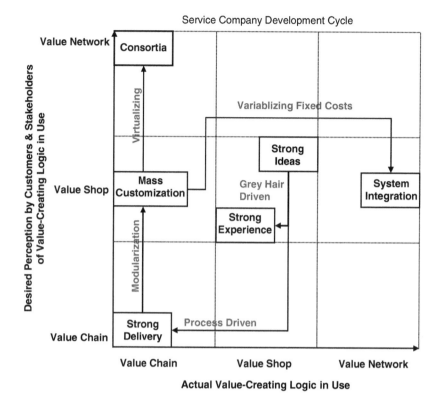

Figure 3.52. Stages in the life of a service company: value-creating logic perspective.

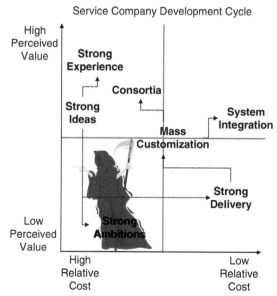

Figure 3.53. Stages in the life of a service company: strategic perspective.

Strong ideas

Strong ideas[8] leverage reputation and distinctive competencies. These organizations charge higher then average fees, have a reputation for original and exciting ideas, and will be important players in the professional community. They serve clients who are either themselves knowledgeable in the field or who rely on peer review for evaluating quality. They are usually organized in project form with a strong figurehead. The limited market is even further limited by strongly identifiable models developed in-house and these organizations tend to operate internationally and even globally in spite of their small size to compensate for this limited market. In this stage firms pursue the deployment of the following resources:

- A flexible service delivery system is made up of part human resources, (i.e., innovative and competent individuals) and part relational resources (i.e., the right partners and suppliers) that will allow for development and delivery of customized service offerings (customization is limited only by man-hour constraints imposed by the presence of the right individuals).
- A strong reputation is based on part organizational resources (i.e., brand and past service offerings) and part relational resources (i.e., existing customer relationships).
- These customized service offerings (organizational resource) are then deployed together with service delivery and relationship building competence (human resources) to build up strong customer relationships (relational resource) that can then be converted to cash.
- The value creation process starts only when the customer order is received.

The perceived value of the offering must exceed the cost of producing it. Both transaction costs and coordination costs are high in this stage. We describe a typical service organization in this phase of its development in Figure 3.54 through 3.57.

Effector Ratio:	0.36	1.10	1.41	1.17	1.38	
From　　　　　To	Monetary	Physical	Relational	Organizational	Human	Σ
Monetary	1.5	0.0	4.7	3.0	3.0	12.3
Physical	0.1	0.1	0.1	0.0	0.0	0.3
Relational	9.6	0.0	9.6	9.6	9.6	38.3
Organizational	13.4	0.0	6.7	2.2	2.2	24.6
Human	9.2	0.1	6.1	6.1	3.1	24.6
Σ	33.7	0.2	20.9	20.9	17.9	100.0

Figure 3.54. Numerical representation of the transformation matrix on Level 2 for a typical service firm in the strong ideas stage.

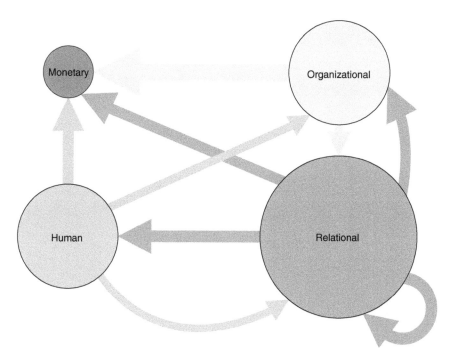

Figure 3.55. Pictorial representation of the Pareto cleaned transformation matrix (Figure 3.54) on Level 2 for a typical service firm in the strong ideas stage.

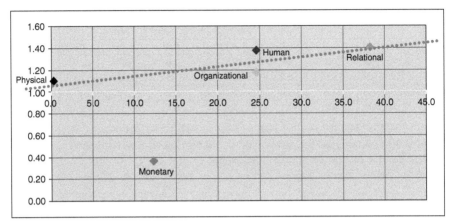

Figure 3.56. Effector plot based on the numerical transformation matrix in Figure 3.54 for a typical service firm in the strong ideas stage.

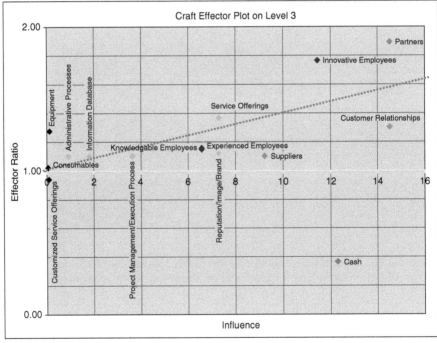

Figure 3.57. Effector plot based on the numerical transformation matrix in Figure 3.54 broken down to Level 3 for a typical service firm in the strong ideas stage.

Strong experience

Strong experience[9] deploys experience to meet clients' more demanding requirements (complex or unusual projects, execution difficulties, size of project or ability to value engineer the solution). Fees are higher then average grounded in clear value contribution to the project. This stage is typical for specialist or multidisciplinary firms. The difference from the strong ideas type firm is more in some of the details rather then the overall concept. In this stage firms pursue deployment of the following resources:

- A flexible service delivery system is made up of part human resources (i.e., experienced and competent individuals) and part relational resources (i.e., the right partners and suppliers) that will allow for effective and efficient provision of the service offerings. This is complemented by good systems and processes.
- A strong reputation is based in part on organizational resources (i.e., brand and past service execution) and in part on relational resources (i.e., existing customer relationships).
- These service offerings (organizational resource) are then deployed together with service delivery and relationship building competence (human resources) to build up strong customer relationships (relational resource) that can then be converted to cash based on successful execution.
- The value creation process starts only when the customer order is received.

The perceived value of the offering must exceed the cost of producing it. Both transaction costs and coordination costs are high in this stage, although transaction costs tend to dominate. We describe a typical service organization in this phase of its development in Figure 3.58 through 3.61.

Effector Ratio:	0.36	1.10	1.41	1.17	1.38	
From To	Monetary	Physical	Relational	Organizational	Human	Σ
Monetary	1.5	0.0	4.7	3.0	3.0	12.3
Physical	0.1	0.1	0.1	0.0	0.0	0.3
Relational	9.6	0.0	9.6	9.6	9.6	38.3
Organizational	13.4	0.0	6.7	2.2	2.2	24.6
Human	9.2	0.1	6.1	6.1	3.1	24.6
Σ	33.7	0.2	27.2	20.9	17.9	100.0

Figure 3.58. Numerical representation of the transformation matrix on Level 2 for a typical service firm in the strong experience stage.

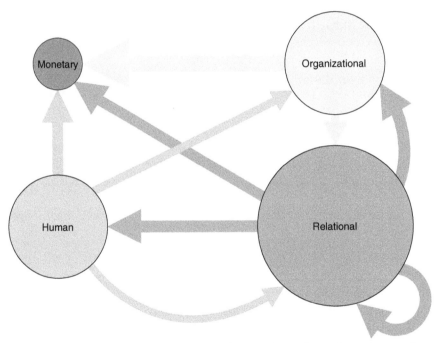

Figure 3.59. Pictorial representation of the Pareto cleaned transformation matrix (Figure 3.58) on Level 2 for a typical service firm in the strong experience stage.

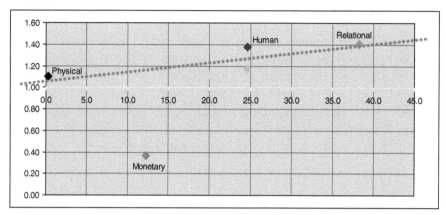

Figure 3.60. Effector plot based on the numerical transformation matrix in Figure 3.58 for a typical service firm in the strong experience stage.

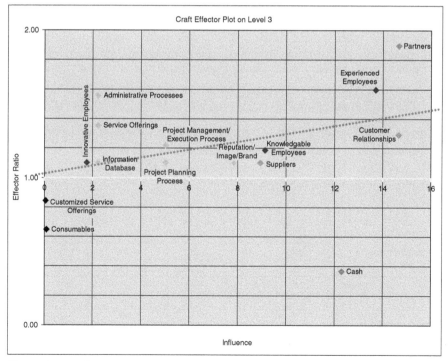

Figure 3.61. Effector plot based on the numerical transformation matrix in Figure 3.58 broken down to Level 3 for a typical service firm in the strong experience stage.

Strong delivery

Strong delivery[10] provides standardized solutions to well-known problems at less then average fees, but at a relatively high level of profitability through effective organization of the delivery process. These organizations make extensive use of standardized solutions components, rely heavily on IT, and have a high rate of juniors to seniors or simply low overheads. This form is typical for integrated larger service provision firms. In this stage firms pursue the deployment of the following resources:

- A standardized service delivery system is made up primarily of organizational resources (i.e., processes and systems) and secondarily of relational resources (i.e., the right partners and suppliers) that will allow for efficient provision of the service offerings. This is complemented by well-trained delivery people.
- A strong reputation is based on part organizational resources (i.e., brand and past service execution) and part relational resources (i.e., existing customer relationships).
- These service offerings (organizational resource) are then deployed together with service delivery processes and systems (organizational resources) and relationship building competence (human resources) to build up strong customer relationships (relational resource) that can then be converted to cash based on successful execution.
- The value creation process starts only when the customer order is received.

The perceived value of the offering must exceed the cost in producing it. Transaction costs are high and coordination costs are low in this stage. We describe a typical service organization in this phase of its development in Figures 3.62 through 3.65.

Effector Ratio:	0.46	1.10	1.20	1.51	1.10	
From \ To	Monetary	Physical	Relational	Organisational	Human	Σ
Monetary	2.9	0.1	6.6	6.6	0.9	17.0
Physical	0.0	0.1	0.0	0.4	0.0	0.5
Relational	12.9	0.1	12.9	12.9	0.0	38.7
Organisational	21.1	0.1	10.5	3.5	3.5	38.7
Human	0.2	0.1	2.3	2.3	0.2	5.0
Σ	37.0	0.5	32.2	25.7	4.6	100.0

Figure 3.62. Numerical representation of the transformation matrix on Level 2 for a typical service firm in the strong delivery stage.

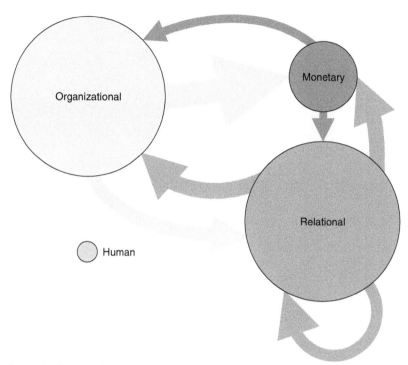

Figure 3.63. Pictorial representation of the Pareto cleaned transformation matrix (Figure 3.62) on Level 2 for a typical service firm in the strong delivery stage.

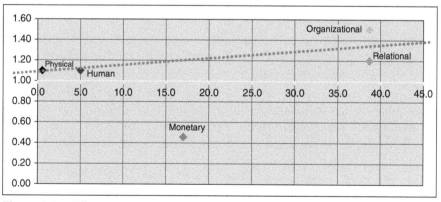

Figure 3.64. Effector plot based on the numerical transformation matrix in Figure 3.62 for a typical service firm in the strong delivery stage.

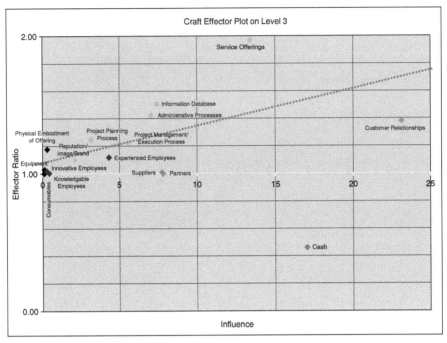

Figure 3.65. Effector plot based on the numerical transformation matrix in Figure 3.62 broken down to Level 3 for a typical service firm in the strong delivery stage.

Mass customization, consortia, and system integration are similar to the organizations outlined in the manufacturing cycle, with the obvious difference that we are talking about services rather than products. Strong ambitions is a self-explanatory failure strategy that will not be described here.

The third design would be an intermediary type company. Figure 3.66 illustrates the stages an intermediary company normally goes through from a value-creating logic perspective, and Figure 3.67 illustrates the same stages from a strategic perspective.

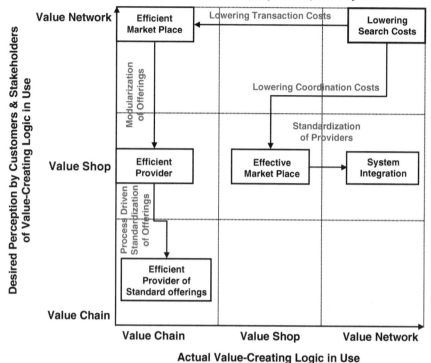

Figure 3.66. Stages in the life of an intermediary type company: value-creating logic perspective.

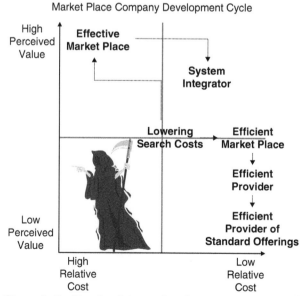

Figure 3.67. Stages in the life of an intermediary type company: strategic perspective.

Lowering search costs

The lowering search costs strategy enables potential buyers to compare offerings from more potential suppliers without incurring high search costs (e.g., through online auctions). The service is heavily dependent on reputation and systems, and requires high investments to generate sufficient participation for a profitable business. This is typical for early players in the e-business area. In this stage firms pursue deployment of the following resources:

- A standardized service delivery system is made up primarily of organizational resources (i.e., processes and systems) and secondarily of relational resources (i.e., the right partners and suppliers) that will allow for development and maintenance of processes and systems.
- Strong reputation based on part organizational resources (i.e., brand and past service execution) and part relational resources (i.e., existing customer relationships).
- These service offerings (organizational resources) are then deployed together with service delivery processes and systems (organizational resources) and relationship building competence through branding (organizational resources) to build up strong customer relationships (relational resource) that can then be converted to cash based on successful execution.
- The value creation process starts before any potential customer is involved.

The perceived value of the offering must exceed the cost in producing it. Transaction costs and coordination costs are both high at this stage. We describe a typical organization in this phase of its development in Figures 3.68 through 3.71.

Effector Ratio:	0.90	0.39	1.35	1.23	0.39	
From To	Monetary	Physical	Relational	Organizational	Human	Σ
Monetary	0.0	0.8	11.8	1.7	0.8	15.0
Physical	0.0	0.0	0.0	5.0	0.0	5.0
Relational	14.0	2.1	14.0	7.0	11.5	48.5
Organizational	2.5	10.0	10.1	3.3	0.7	26.5
Human	0.2	0.1	0.1	4.5	0.1	5.0
Σ	16.7	13.0	35.8	21.6	13.0	100.0

Figure 3.68. Numerical representation of the transformation matrix on Level 2 for a typical firm in the lowering search costs stage.

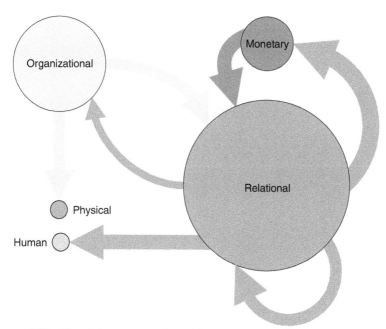

Figure 3.69. Pictorial representation of the Pareto cleaned transformation matrix (Figure 3.68) on Level 2 for a typical service firm in the lowering search costs stage.

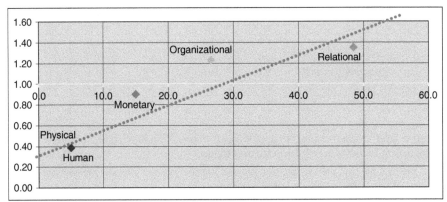

Figure 3.70. Effector plot based on the numerical transformation matrix in Figure 3.68 for a typical service firm in the lowering search costs stage.

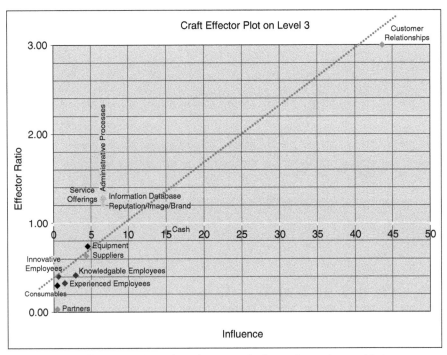

Figure 3.71. Effector plot based on the numerical transformation matrix in Figure 3.68 broken down to Level 3 for a typical service firm in the lowering search costs stage.

Effective marketplace

An effective marketplace strategy enables potential buyers to compare offerings from potential suppliers with high relevance without incurring high search costs (e.g., specialized procurement exchanges). The service is heavily dependent on reputation, systems, and prescreening of participants and requires high investments to generate sufficient participation to provide a profitable business. This is typical for industry specific players in the e-business area. The principle is very similar to the lowering search costs stage, with some small differences. In this stage firms pursue the deployment of the following resources:

- A standardized service delivery system is made up primarily of organizational resources (i.e., processes and systems, including prescreening processes) and secondarily of relational resources (i.e., the right partners and suppliers) that will allow for development and maintenance of processes and systems.
- A strong reputation is based on part organizational resources (i.e., brand and past service execution) and part relational resources (i.e., existing customer relationships).
- These service offerings (organizational resources) are then deployed together with service delivery processes and systems (organizational resources) and relationship building competence through branding (organizational resources) to build up strong customer relationships (relational resource) that can then be converted to cash based on successful execution.
- The value creation process starts already before any potential customer is involved.

The perceived value of the offering must exceed the cost in producing it. Transaction costs and coordination costs are both high at this stage but coordination costs tend to dominate. We describe a typical organization in this phase of its development in Figures 3.72 through 3.75.

The system integration stage is, for all practical purposes, the same as shown above for manufacturing companies.

Effector Ratio:	0.90	0.46	1.28	1.20	0.46	
From \ To	Monetary	Physical	Relational	Organizational	Human	Σ
Monetary	0.0	0.8	7.1	7.1	0.8	15.9
Physical	0.0	0.0	0.0	5.3	0.0	5.3
Relational	10.2	5.7	10.2	5.1	9.6	40.9
Organizational	7.3	4.9	14.6	4.9	1.0	32.7
Human	0.1	0.1	0.1	4.9	0.1	5.3
Σ	17.6	11.5	32.0	27.2	11.5	100.0

Figure 3.72. Numerical representation of the transformation matrix on Level 2 for a typical firm in the effective marketplace stage.

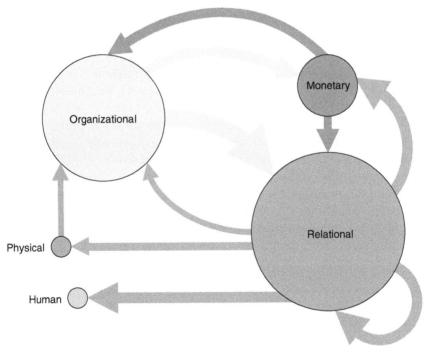

Figure 3.73. Pictorial representation of the Pareto cleaned transformation matrix (Figure 3.72) on Level 2 for a typical service firm in the effective marketplace stage.

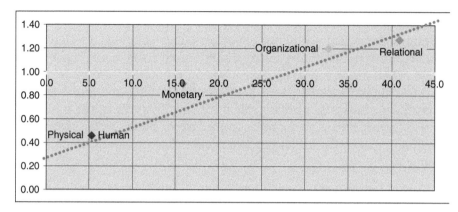

Figure 3.74. Effector plot based on the numerical transformation matrix in Figure 3.72 for a typical service firm in the effective marketplace stage.

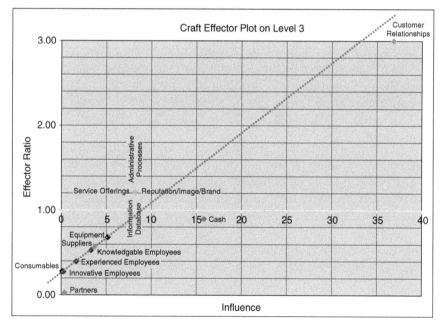

Figure 3.75. Effector plot based on the numerical transformation matrix in Figure 3.72 broken down to Level 3 for a typical service firm in the effective marketplace stage.

Efficient marketplace

The efficient marketplace stage enables potential buyers to compare offerings from many potential suppliers, and suppliers to find many potential buyers without incurring high search costs (e.g., large auction sites). The service is heavily dependent on reputation and systems, and requires high investments to generate sufficient participation to provide a profitable business. This is typical for large players in the e-business area. The principle is very similar to the effective marketplace with some small differences. In this stage firms pursue deployment of the following resources:

- A standardized service delivery system is made up primarily of organizational resources (i.e., processes and systems, including post-screening processes) and secondarily of relational resources (i.e., right partners and suppliers) that will allow for development and maintenance of processes and systems.
- A strong reputation is based on part organizational resources (i.e., brand and past service execution) and part relational resources (i.e., existing customer relationships).
- These service offerings (organizational resources) are then deployed together with service delivery processes and systems (organizational resources) and relationship building competence through branding (organizational resources) to build up strong customer relationships (relational resource) that can then be converted to cash based on successful execution.
- The value creation process starts before any potential customer is involved.

The perceived value of the offering must exceed the cost in producing it. Transaction costs and coordination costs are both high at this stage but transaction costs tend to dominate. We describe a typical organization in this phase of its development in Figures 3.76 through 3.79.

Effector Ratio:	0.90	0.40	1.20	1.36	0.40	
From ⟍ To	Monetary	Physical	Relational	Organizational	Human	Σ
Monetary	0.0	0.7	3.1	10.4	0.7	15.0
Physical	0.0	0.0	0.0	5.0	0.0	5.0
Relational	7.5	5.5	7.5	3.7	10.3	34.6
Organizational	9.1	6.0	18.1	6.0	1.2	40.4
Human	0.1	0.1	0.1	4.6	0.1	5.0
Σ	16.7	12.4	28.8	29.8	12.4	100.0

Figure 3.76. Numerical representation of the transformation matrix on Level 2 for a typical firm in the efficient marketplace stage.

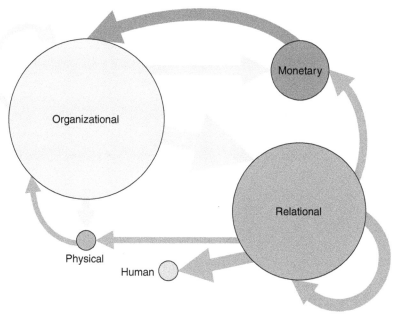

Figure 3.77. Pictorial representation of the Pareto cleaned transformation matrix (Figure 3.76) on Level 2 for a typical service firm in the efficient marketplace stage.

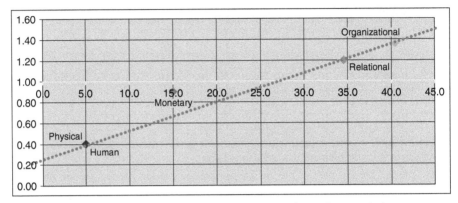

Figure 3.78. Effector plot based on the numerical transformation matrix in Figure 3.76 for a typical service firm in the efficient marketplace stage.

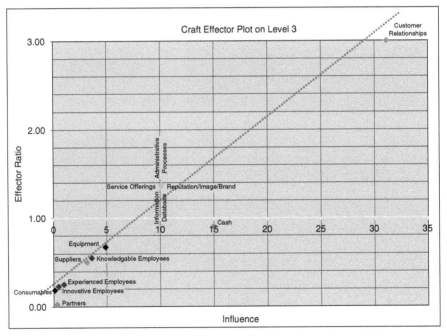

Figure 3.79. Effector plot based on the numerical transformation matrix in Figure 3.76 broken down to Level 3 for a typical service firm in the efficient marketplace stage.

Efficient provider

An efficient provider strategy enables potential buyers to use offerings from many potential suppliers through the provider at low search and transaction costs (e.g., a mobile phone operator). The service is heavily dependent on reputation and systems and requires high investments to generate sufficient participation to provide a profitable business. This is typical for large players in the infrastructure area. The principle is very similar to the efficient marketplace with some small differences. In this stage firms pursue deployment of the following resources:

- A standardized service delivery system is made up primarily of organizational resources (i.e., processes and systems) and secondarily of relational resources (i.e., right partners and suppliers) that will allow for development and maintenance of the service portfolio.
- A strong reputation is based on part organizational resources (i.e., brand and past service execution and part relational resources (i.e., existing customer relationships, or market share).
- These service offerings (organizational resources) are then deployed together with service delivery processes and systems (organizational resources) and relationship building competence through branding (organizational resources) to build up strong customer relationships (relational resource) that can then be converted to cash based on successful execution.
- The value creation process starts before any potential customer is involved.

The perceived value of the offering must exceed the cost of producing it. Transaction costs and coordination costs are both high at this stage, but coordination costs tend to dominate. We describe a typical organization in this phase of its development in Figures 3.80 through 3.83.

Effector Ratio:	0.78	1.05	1.05	1.25	0.57	
From To	Monetary	Physical	Relational	Organizational	Human	Σ
Monetary	5.0	2.9	5.7	4.8	0.9	19.3
Physical	0.1	0.1	0.1	9.3	0.1	9.7
Relational	10.0	0.1	10.0	5.0	4.3	29.4
Organizational	9.6	6.0	12.1	6.0	3.0	36.8
Human	0.1	0.1	0.1	4.4	0.1	4.8
Σ	24.9	9.2	28.0	29.5	8.4	100.0

Figure 3.80. Numerical representation of the transformation matrix on Level 2 for a typical firm in the efficient provider stage.

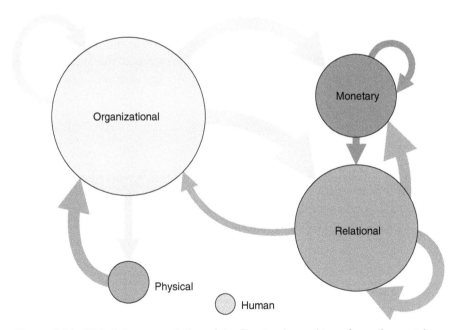

Figure 3.81. Pictorial representation of the Pareto cleaned transformation matrix (Figure 3.80) on Level 2 for a typical service firm in the efficient provider stage.

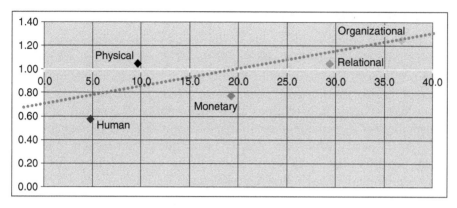

Figure 3.82. Effector plot based on the numerical transformation matrix in Figure 3.80 for a typical service firm in the efficient provider stage.

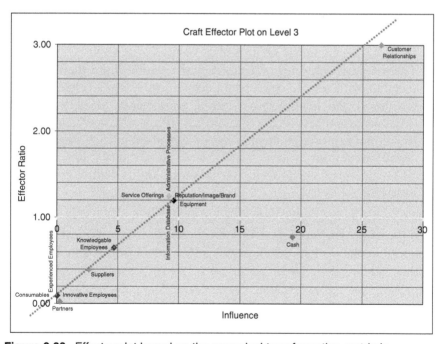

Figure 3.83. Effector plot based on the numerical transformation matrix in Figure 3.80 broken down to Level 3 for a typical service firm in the efficient provider stage.

Efficient provider of standard offerings

The efficient provider of standard offerings stage enables potential buyers to use offerings from a selected group of potential suppliers through the provider at low search and transaction costs (e.g., operators of the electricity distribution grid). The service is heavily dependent on reputation and systems and requires high investments to generate sufficient participation to provide a profitable business. This is typical for large players in the infrastructure area. The principle is very similar to the efficient provider stage with some small differences. In this stage firms pursue deployment of the following resources:

- A standardized service delivery system is made up primarily of organizational resources (i.e., processes and systems) and secondarily of relational resources (i.e., right partners and suppliers) that will allow for development and maintenance of the service portfolio.
- A strong reputation is based on part organizational resources (i.e., brand and past service execution) and part relational resources (i.e., existing customer relationships or market share).
- These service offerings (organizational resources) are then deployed together with service delivery processes and systems (organizational resources) and relationship building competence through branding (organizational resources) to build up strong customer relationships (relational resource) that can then be converted to cash based on successful execution.
- The value creation process starts before any potential customer is involved.

The perceived value of the offering must exceed the cost in producing it. Transaction costs are high at this stage. We describe a typical organization in this phase of its development in Figures 3.84 through 3.87.

Effector Ratio:	0.78	1.05	1.05	1.25	0.57	
From To	Monetary	Physical	Relational	Organizational	Human	Σ
Monetary	5.0	2.9	5.7	4.8	0.9	19.3
Physical	0.1	0.1	0.1	9.3	0.1	9.7
Relational	10.0	0.1	10.0	5.0	4.3	29.4
Organizational	9.6	6.0	12.1	6.0	3.0	36.8
Human	0.1	0.1	0.1	4.4	0.1	4.8
Σ	24.9	9.2	28.0	29.5	8.4	100.0

Figure 3.84. Numerical representation of the transformation matrix on Level 2 for a typical firm in the efficient provider of standard offerings stage.

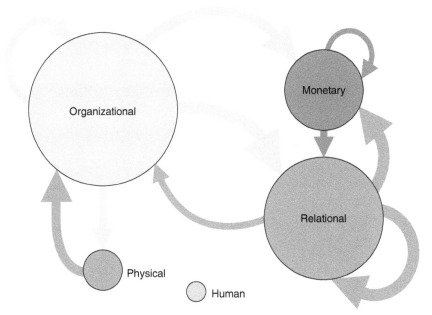

Figure 3.85. Pictorial representation of the Pareto cleaned transformation matrix (Figure 3.84) on Level 2 for a typical service firm in the efficient provider of standard offerings stage.

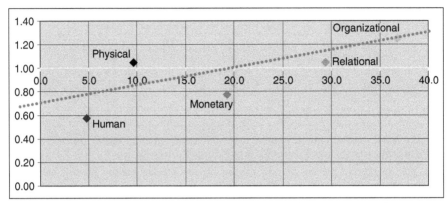

Figure 3.86. Effector plot based on the numerical transformation matrix in Figure 3.84 for a typical service firm in the efficient provider of standard offerings stage.

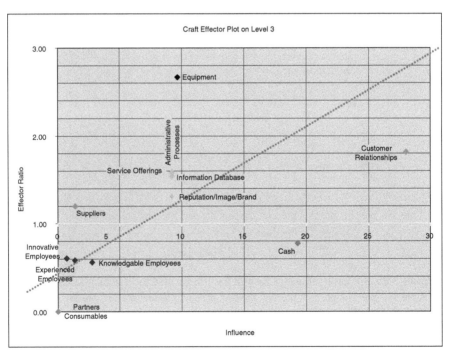

Figure 3.87. Effector plot based on the numerical transformation matrix in Figure 3.84 broken down to Level 3 for a typical service firm in the efficient provider of standard offerings stage.

CONCLUSION

Based on the preceding analysis it is possible for the organization to identify and evaluate its resource transformation structure. In order to do this, two tools from this chapter should be used. The first is the intellectual capital navigator, which allows us to formulate a set of hypotheses around the type of organization we have. If we do this in combination with the value-creating logics from Chapter 2 we can identify hypotheses around inconsistencies in the value creation structure and effectiveness improvement potentials in this value-creating structure. To execute this evaluation the following information must be available:

- The numerical representation of the resource transformation matrix (How the numerical representation of the resource transformation matrix is arrived upon is discussed in detail in this chapter.)
- The pictorial representation of the resource transformation matrix known as the intellectual capital navigator (How the ICN is arrived upon is discussed in detail in this chapter.)
- A judgment on the dominating value-creating logic of the organization (i.e., value chain, value shop, or value network) (The definitions and reasonings around the value-creating logics are given in Chapter 1 and our advisory firm in this example is operating as a value chain.)
- A statement of the form that the resulting value (i.e., the outcome of what the organization is trying to achieve) takes (i.e., is it money, knowledge embodied in written articles, esthetic beauty embodied in paintings, stronger relationships with stakeholders, etc.)
- A statement of the organization's strategic intent[11]

The second tool is the effector plot. An ideal effector plot has a set of characteristics:

- The output resource (i.e., the resource form that embodies the value the organization is delivering) should be one of the left-most resources (i.e., one of the least influential).
- The output resource should also always be a value sink (i.e., appear under the x-axis that crosses the y-axis at $[0, 1]$). This is because a sustainable resource transformation system needs to generate more effort into the output resource than it must draw from the output resource to keep the system working. If this is the case, then there is an accumulation of effort in the output resource that can be used for other things such as, for example, influencing shareholders through paying dividends.

- The more influential an intermediary resource is (i.e., all resources except the output resource) the higher its effector ratio should be. This means that resources that have the highest influence on value creation should be best leveraged (managed). This also means that the more uninfluential an intermediary resource is (i.e., the further toward the left it appears in the effctor plot) the less critical becomes its position on the y-axis in the effector plot.
- The order in which resources are appearing is determined by the value-creating logic (see Chapter 1) of the organization. The most influential resource is the one that forms the basis for the organization's competitive advantage. Table 1.3, "Possible resources as a basis for competitive advantage in the different value creating logics,"

Case 3.10 ANSTO/ari: An Illustration of the IC Process Implementation

The following case study is a typical follow-up of the IC process which illustrates the necessary steps needed to fully execute the process, and describes associated benefits. The company in question, **ari**, had set a sales growth target of 10% and in order to achieve this, management needed to ensure optimum deployment of their resources, now and in the future. The IC process assisted them in accomplishing this. The outcome is depicted in simplified figures, including distinction tree, transformation matrix, IC navigator, and effector plots for present and desired situations.

The Australian Nuclear Science and Technology Organization (ANSTO) is Australia's national nuclear research and development organization and the center of Australian nuclear expertise. ANSTO Radiopharamaceuticals and Industrials (**ari**) is the commercial arm of ANSTO specializing in production of radioistopes for medical and industrial applications for domestic and international customers. As the market is expanding, **ari**'s business plan is based on 10% growth in sales. **ari** has about 80% of the hot-drugs market in Australia and is the only vertically integrated operator having the full range of capabilities from base material production in the reactor, purification, hot-drug chemistry, packaging, transportation, and also analysis. This means having staff with abilities relating to chemistry of the purification process which is dominated by routine, but employees also carry out custom syntheses to meet specific customer needs.

Given the complex balance between routine and custom jobs throughout the **ari** operation, **ari** needed an approach that allowed for a detailed understanding of how to deploy available resources in an effective way throughout the organization. The IC process was chosen to achieve this.

After defining the concept of value and outlining both the principle strategy and the key strategic logic, it became clear that since the production of radiopharmaceuticals is a relatively high cost activity, emphasis needs to be on activities that will increase customers' perceived value. This emphasis should be implemented with careful consideration of cost reductions that can be made without sacrificing quality and reliability of product provision. In addition, **ari** is moving from being a value shop organization to becoming a value chain organization (see Chapter 1 for more on value

Case 3.10 ANSTO/ari: An Illustration of the IC Process Implementation—cont'd

shops and value chains). This move is both desirable and necessary to improve performance of the organization. However, as there are aspects of value shop logic in product development and customized production, it is important for **ari**'s management to determine the interaction between the customized and the standardized side.

Following identification of the principle activity system and key success factors, **ari**'s management could outline necessary resources required for the organization to

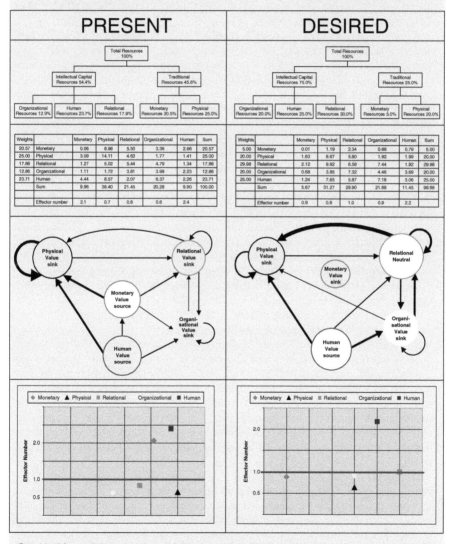

Graphical form of the present and desired situation (first iteration) defined by **ari**'s management.

Continued

Case 3.10 ANSTO/ari: An Illustration of the IC Process Implementation—cont'd

continue and improve its value creation activities. They also weighted the relative importance of these key resources based on **ari**'s ability to create value and created two distinction trees for the present and the desired future situation. Then **ari** identified its deployment structure (i.e., how resources are used) and the relative importance of these transformations for **ari**'s ability to create value. The outcome is presented in a simplified form in the figure opposite, showing distinction tree, transformation matrix and its graphic representation (i.e., the IC navigator), as well as effector plots for present and desired situations.

As can be seen, there are some differences between the present and the desired situation. The figure shows that the present organization focuses on physical (25%) and human resources (24%), with low focus on relational (18%) and organizational (13%) resources. This signifies an R&D organization reliant on both individual competence and physical facilities. One of the major problems with an organization like this is its lack of scaleability. It may well be effective but is normally not efficient. Both these statements were recognized by management as describing their present situation.

In the first iteration of the desired situation (depicted opposite), relational (30%) and human (25%) resources have high focus, closely followed by physical (20%) and organizational resources (20%). This illustrates a complex organization with parts that have completely different logics. The present need for investments in tangible reources is an explanation for the high monetary weighting (21%) in the present situation as compared to the first iteration of the desired situation (5%). In the present situation, human resources and monetary resources can be seen as prime sources of value, all other resources being value sinks that can be interpreted as unexploited value for **ari**. In the first iteration of the desired situation, only human resources is a value source. On the other hand, the effector values of both relational and organizational resources are higher.

As is seen from the preceding reasoning, the first iteration of the desired position was a move in the right direction, but the result was not good enough as it was a highly ineffective solution. This led to a second iteration that generated a better and final agreed desired position, which is depicted in the figure below. The focus has changed so that organizational (26%) and relational (24%) resources are seen as most vital for **ari**'s value creation whereas human resources (15%) are given much less emphasis than in the first iteration. This illustrates a value network scenario where organizational and relational resources are often the two most important resources and therefore the desired position is matching **ari**'s strategic logic. All resources excluding monetary resources can be seen as value sources that are being utilized by **ari**.

During the IC-process it became clear that **ari**'s strategy was feasible but needed to be executed better. The process showed **ari**'s management how to use its resources in an optimal way in order to be aligned with its strategy. It also showed that the optimal and most effective deployment of resources was not as management first expected it to be. The execution emphasis on increasing perceived value through, for example,

Case 3.10 ANSTO/ari: An Illustration of the IC Process Implementation—cont'd

branding, customization, service, quality, and innovation should be twice as high (in outcome terms) as the emphasis on cost reduction. In addition, it was apparent that the management team needed to create a more cohesive view of the future desired position as well as a better execution plan. As a result, **ari**'s management team have taken a number of steps, namely increased focus on innovative differentiated product offerings, invested in new process equipment, and streamlined operational processes. In addition, **ari** has succeeded in expanding into new markets.

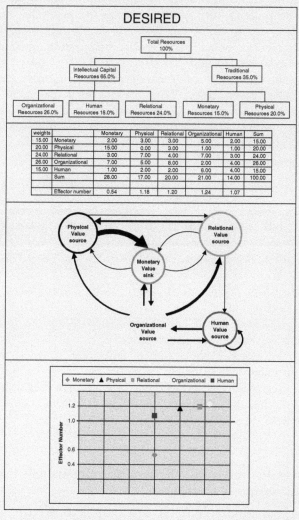

Graphical form of the desired situation (second iteration) defined by **ari**'s management.

Key Points in Chapter 3

- The essence of the intellectual capital management process is about the value-creating transformations that take place between the resources the organization has at its disposal.
- Two critical tools are provided for assisting in the analysis of the organization's resource transformation, and therefore also for assisting in improving the effectiveness of the way the organization deploys the resources it has at its disposal to create value. These two tools are:
- The intellectual capital navigator, a pictorial representation of the way the organization transforms its resources to create value
- The effector plot, a plot that allows for the identification of improvement potential in the way the organization transforms its resources to create value
- By linking these tools with the tools presented in earlier chapters and with some further presented insights into the development of the organization over time and an understanding of what drives value in a procurement situation, an analysis of actionable improvements in the way the firm transforms its resources to create value more effectively can be made.

If the book is being used as a workbook the following results should have been achieved so far:

- An intellectual capital navigator at least down to Level 3 should have been produced.
- Improvement conclusions should have been formulated based on this visual representation.
- A comparison of this ICN with the basic ICN for the dominating value-creating logics should have been done.
- Based on this comparison, a set of improvement hypotheses should have been formulated.
- An effector plot for (at least) Level 3 should have been drawn.
- Based on this plot, suggested improvement actions should have been formulated.

provides an overview of the possible combinations that exist, but the main conclusions are that:

○ In a value chain, human resource cannot be the right-most if the organization is in the business of making money.

○ In a value shop, physical resources cannot be the right-most if the organization is in the business of making money.

○ In a value network, you would expect some combination of organizational and relational resources to appear as the right-most if the organization is in the business of making money.

Given these ideal characteristics it is possible to verify and refine the improvement potential hypotheses formulated from the ICN.

In addition, a brief discussion with examples has been provided to illustrate the importance of taking into account the development phase of the organization in this analysis.

ENDNOTES

1. The term *navigator* has been used in many settings. It was first used in relation to intellectual capital by Leif Edvinsson in Skandia's intellectual capital supplement (1994). This original model was static and did not take into account the transformations—it was, in fact, a version of the balanced scorecard. The dynamic aspects were first introduced by Roos in Skandia's intellectual capital supplement (1996, p. 21) and elaborated further in G. Roos and J. Roos (1997), "Measuring your company's intellectual performance," *Long Range Planning*, 30(3), 413–426. This article formed the basis for what is now known as the intellectual capital navigator and the first detailed application was illustrated in the article G. Roos and K. Jacobsen (1999), "Management in a complex stakeholder organization: a case study of the application of the IC-process to a branch of the Commonwealth Public Service," *Monash Mt. Eliza Business Review*, 2(1), pp. 82–93.
2. The notion of strategic intent was first introduced by C.W. Hofer and D.E. Schendel (1978), *Strategy Formulation: Analytical Concepts*, St. Paul, Minn.: West Publishing; and further developed by G. Hamel and C.K. Prahalad (1989),"Strategic intent," *Harvard Business Review*, May-June, pp. 62–76.
3. In the early 1970s several major oil companies found that in areas where sealed competitive bidding was the method of acquiring leases, almost nobody who won one of these competitive bids seemed to make any money. The process around putting together the bids was as follows. The managers whose task it was to set bids on parcels in an impending sale ensured that there was a consensus property value put together by their experts. The only thing certain at this point was that the value was either too high or too low: it had no chance of being exactly the true value. Because the managers and their teams had long experience in the industry and this type of valuation we will assume that on average their value estimates were correct. Now consider a piece of land with exactly 10 billion barrels of recoverable oil. If you let five people in your own company interpret the seismic data, logs on nearby wells, and other sundry information, you will get five different estimates even though they all use the same basic information. The problem becomes more confounding if we look at the reserve estimates of five companies. They may each have different seismic data and different logs. It is quite likely that some companies will come up with estimates of more than 10 billion barrels and some with less. We have already admitted that though our estimates may be all right on the average, on any one tract they are going to be either too high or too low. In competitive bidding, the winner tends to be the player who most overestimates true tract value. This means that the bidder tends to

win a biased set of tracts: namely, those on which the bidder has overestimated value or reserves. This is called the winner's curse, and explains why nobody made any money. As a consequence of this insight, oil companies changed their bidding behavior. This learning has not yet penetrated all other industries, so the winner's curse is still quite prevalent and observable in competitive tenders. It has been formally shown that with sophisticated bidders adjusting for the winner's curse the maximum bid converges to the true value of the object at auction: a remarkable result when we realize that (ex ante) this true value is not known to anyone.

4. Some authors call this "blue ocean" strategy see e.g. W. Chan Kim and Renee Mauborgne, 2004, "Blue Ocean Strategy", Harvard Business Review, October, pp. 76–84.

5. The authors have developed a set of tools that assist in suggesting how the numerical and pictorial representation of the transformation matrix can be improved.

6. By making a set of reasonable assumptions (E.M. Rogers (1983), *Diffusion of Innovations*, 3rd Ed., New York: Free Press; and R.N. Foster (1986), "Timing technology transitions," in: *Technology in the Modern Corporation: A Strategic Perspective*, M. Horwich (Ed.), London: Pergamon), both technical progress and market diffusion through time can be expected to approximate a cumulative-logistic distribution (hence the term S-*curve*). The technology proceeds up an S-curve through regular innovation (Foster, 1986). As it proceeds up that S-curve it diffuses to fill the market circumscribed by the limits of the needs it can satisfy. The diffusion curve is also S-shaped (Rogers, 1983). The shape of the S-curve is predicated on the logic of two-step diffusion from a source to opinion leaders, and from the latter to the general population, whereas the leveling off at maturity is predicated on a finite target population of consumers. The graph of cumulative sales from early adopters to late adopters has an S-shape. From this it is possible to deduce that individual firms also will follow a lifecycle-type behavior.

7. Parts of this section draw on Da Silveira, G., Borenstein, D, F.S., Mass customization: Literature review and Research Directions, *International Journal of Production Economics*, 72, (2001), 1–13.

8. This taxonomy draws on the work by Winch, G. and Schneider, E. 1993: the strategic management of architectural practice. Construction Management and Economics, Vol 11, pp. 467–473.

9. This taxonomy draws on the work by Winch, G. and Schneider, E. 1993: the strategic management of architectural practice, Construction Management and Economics, Vol 11, pp. 467–473.

10. This taxonomy draws on the work by Winch, G. and Schneider, E. 1993: the strategic management of architectural practice, Construction Management and Economics, Vol 11, pp. 467–473.

11. The notion of strategic intent was first introduced by C.W. Hofer and D.E. Schendel (1978), *Strategy Formulation: Analytical Concepts,* St. Paul, Minn.: West Publishing; and further developed by G. Hamel and C.K. Prahalad (1989), "Strategic intent," *Harvard Business Review*, 62–76.

CASE 2 ENDNOTES

1. Recruit's RMS division provides Intellectual Capital, Human Resource Management and Economic Value Added Services. More information can be requested from www.recruit.co.jp.

2. Recruit's name for its IC process is "Value Creation Path".

CASE 4 ENDNOTES

1. K. Jacobsen and G. Roos (1999), "Management in a complex stakeholder organization," *Monash Mt Eliza Business Review*, 2(1), 82–93.
2. See Chapter 4 for further information on the IC index.

CASE 5 ENDNOTES

1. Recruit's RMS division provides Intellectual Capital, Human Resource Management and Economic Value Added Services. More information can be requested from www.recruit.co.jp.
2. Recruit's name for its IC process in "Value Creation Path".

CASE 8 ENDNOTES

1. L. Fernström, S. Pike, and G. Roos (2004), "Understanding the truly value creating resources: the case of a pharmaceutical company," *International Journal of Learning and Intellectual Capital*, 1(1), 105–120.

CASE 9 ENDNOTES

1. Recruit's RMS division provides Intellectual Capital, Human Resource Management and Economic Value Added Services. More information can be requested from www.recruit.co.jp.
2. Recruit's name for its IC process is "Value Creation Path".

4

Valuing and measuring intellectual capital

VALUING

Before discussing value and how organizations might be valued, there is a big step to take, which can be summarized with this simple question: Is it possible to value something that is characterized by having many parts, some of which are physical and some are not, and whose value depends on who you are?

The answer to the question is yes! If we were to answer "no" we would deny the validity of the free market as a forum and it would also mean that intellectual capital would have no real basis as a theory since it would fail the classical test of being testable (since testing requires measurement). The consequence is that intellectual capital is relegated to the level of a sometimes helpful curiosity. Many intellectual capital measurement systems fall into the category of sometimes helpful curiosities because they make no attempt to account for or value intellectual capital and no attempt to give it a predictive capability. Successful prediction of the results of scenarios in advance of them taking place is the ultimate test of a theory.

In addition to the argument in the previous paragraph, there are a number of other reasons why intellectual capital should be measured or evaluated. These reasons may be considered as broadly falling into one of two categories. The first is that valuation or evaluation will be useful in monitoring events inside the company, and the second is that there may be reasons to disclose results of an evaluation externally. Indeed, supranational bodies such as OECD[1] and EU[2] and regulatory bodies such as SEC,[3] FASB,[4,5] and ICAEW[6] are actively sponsoring work concerning disclosure of elements of organizational operations that are nonfinancial. The two reasons for measurement, internal and external, are quite different in purpose and lead to quite different forms of measurement.

There appears to be a wide variety of schemes available for recording intangible resources used by companies and a wide variety of justifications of such schemes. In 2003 the *Harvard Business Review*[7] published an excellent set of guides for the development of useful measurement systems for nonfinancial resource measurement. They list four mistakes common in business measurement systems:

1. Not connecting measurements to strategy (or what really needs to be measured)
2. Not ensuring there are causal links between the measure and the phenomena to be measured
3. Not setting the right performance metrics and targets
4. Measuring incorrectly

To these a fifth might be added, which is that the measurement system needs to be as compact as possible. Many companies have more performance measurements than they use and even know of. Many have developed independently to serve specific purposes and many become obsolete rapidly. Few are turned off. It is likely that most companies have considerable redundancy among their measurements and measurement schemes and thus sponsor costly activities whose uselessness is often very apparent to those close to the coal face. We chose to articulate this fifth point in the following way:

5. Not dealing with redundant or unwieldy measurement systems

When the purpose of measurement is to support the external publication of company performance, then there have to be some additional requirements on the measurement system. In our opinion, the further mistakes that are made include measurement systems that:

6. Are not auditable (by an independent third party) and consequently unreliable
7. Don't generate the information needed by shareholders, investors, or other relevant stakeholders

As with many philosophical issues, consideration of value and values stretches back to the ancient Greeks and, like many other things, seems to have lain largely dormant between the end of the classical period (300 BC) until renaissance times (1400 AD) in the West. In the nineteenth century the positivist movement sought to put science on to a firm philosophical (rather than technical) foundation. In the early twentieth century the logical positivists of the "Vienna circle" developed this further, admitting only theories, methodologies, or approaches that had either a basis in logic (such as mathematics) or could be proven experimentally (such as the other natural sciences). This second group can be problematic on the grounds of implied subjectivity. However, it can lead to the admission of axiology,[8,9] the study of value, into the fold of acceptability from the positivist point of view. What is clear is that an axiological approach has to be undertaken with rigor if it is to remain acceptable. To avoid disqualification on the grounds of subjectivity, a few simple precautions are required when employing axiology in practice. These are:

1. The object to be measured or valued is precisely defined.
2. The definition is inclusive of all opinions and requirements from all stakeholders.
3. All participants (stakeholders) have equal dignity or importance.
4. All participants are accountable for the veracity of their position.

Who are the stakeholders?

Since stakeholders are mentioned in the preceding paragraph, and since their identification can have a profound effect on the outcome of a value study, it is as well that they are chosen properly. A stakeholder is anyone who can affect an outcome that is valued by the organization. The framework developed by Agle, Mitchell, and Sonnenfield to nominate stakeholders[10] is a useful starting point and is shown in Figure 4.1. The framework uses the three criteria of power, legitimacy, and urgency to categorize stakeholders. The authors go on to categorize stakeholders by importance, stating that the most important stakeholders are definitive stakeholders. These stakeholders are characterized as having all the qualities identified: they are powerful, have legitimate claims and have an urgent need to be recognized. The next group in importance are dominant, dangerous, and dependent stakeholders, as shown in the figure. These stakeholders are characterized by having two of the three criteria that characterize definitive stakeholders. As such, these stakeholders have less claim. Even less demanding rights of claim are those of dormant, demanding, and discretionary stakeholders. Attaching importance to stakeholders, while it may be done as a piece of postprocessing to assist the manager in making decisions on courses of action, cannot be entertained during a value calculation as it infringes the third and possibly the second condition of axiology.

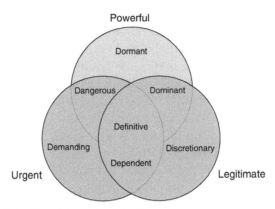

Figure 4.1. Stakeholder claim categorization.

In practice, it is for the problem owner to select the stakeholders whose views the owner wants to include. Opinions the owner does not want to hear can be excluded at this stage but with the risk that the picture that emerges will be incomplete and that some attributes of value may have been excluded. For example, a company manager may nominate analysts, investors, customers, suppliers, and regulators as stakeholder groups but exclude staff representatives. The measurement system that emerges will lack the value perspective that would be demanded by the missing group but more important is that decisions may be made that may be offensive to the missing group. Measures may be contemplated that would, in varying degrees, please all the chosen stakeholders but would lead to a strike the next day. Without a complete set of stakeholders, this crucial piece of advanced information is unavailable.

THE BASICS OF MEASUREMENT

Before embarking on a discussion of measurement, and especially the measurement of complex social phenomena such as businesses, a cautionary note should be sounded. Most of us are familiar with Garvin's[11] statement, "if you can't measure it, you can't manage it." This tends to act as a powerful incentive to managers to try to measure what they need to measure. And with an axiological perspective and the theories described in the following pages, they are well armed to achieve sensible measurement goals. However, if we ignore the theoretical underpinning of measurement or misuse the measures that result, then we are lost and will end up with the laughable measurement schemes that blight companies and many aspects of life. Public services seem especially prone to this. In Denmark, Petersen[12] has published several papers and books that illustrate the pitfalls brilliantly, with perhaps mischievous examples that rather than misuse theory, tend to ignore it altogether. While Petersen takes an academic approach to what he calls "unmeasurables" there are those who for one reason or another or perhaps for no discernable reason at all, believe that measurement beyond the physical or symbolic is not possible and that management by "gut feel" is the only possibility. For decision makers in management, this refusal to accept information amounts to an unnecessary degradation in the structure of problems they face (as defined by Simon[13]) perhaps also leading to difficulty in defining the nature of the problems in the first place. This is what Conklin and Weil[14] refer to as "wicked" problems.

What are we really doing when we take a measurement? Whether we want to measure the size of a room, weigh ingredients for a recipe, count money in the bank, or evaluate the value of a business, the process is the same. What we are trying to do is to measure the value of something which may be tangible or be made up of tangible and intangible elements. In all these cases, we are using a tool of some kind to transfer the characteristics of something in the real world into a numerical system that we can record, report, or use for some other purpose. In the preceding examples, a tape measure is used to measure the room, sprung scales measure the weights of ingredients, and money is already in a numerical system. The instrument used to measure the value of a business or components of it fulfills the same function and is bound by the same rules, but just happens to be a little more complex in form.

All proper measurements are underpinned by the same theory and that theory is, of course, measurement theory. Measurement theory is a branch of applied mathematics. Having introduced the theory, its full rigor will not be examined in detail in this book but the consequences that arise from the theory will be examined because they need to be considered when measuring anything. The requirement to adhere to the consequences of measurement theory is very important indeed, since deviations from it easily convert a useful tool to a dangerously inaccurate tool. For example, it is easily argued that a failure to follow measurement theory and value theory led to the design of accounting systems that, while they did not prohibit certain activities, clearly failed to measure important aspects of finance and allowed some large high-profile companies to follow their courses to spectacular crashes in recent years*. The collapse of Enron may be an example.[15]

---

*We here ignore any illegal activities and only refer to activities that where allowed within the prevailing accounting system at the time

Brief history of measurement

Measurement dates back to the first time humans needed to count something or evaluate one thing against another—flocks of sheep, for example. However, formalizing the theory behind measurement is a surprisingly recent event.

Serious thinking about measurement can be traced back to Eudoxus,[16] who grew up in the ancient Greek city-state of Cnidus located on the west coast of modern Turkey. His work on the theory of proportions addressed important issues with the practical use of simple measurement; for example, it was impossible to compare numbers (or, say, lengths) when they were irrational. But the ideas of the modern theory of measurement date only from the nineteenth-century work of Helmholtz[17] and others. Although most widely known for his work on electromagnetism, he began his academic career with physiology, optics, and philosophy. Throughout his life he tried to reduce all phenomena to simple physical principles. Measurement was therefore important to him. In the latter part of his career he published his famous work on counting and measurement, which laid the basis for one dimensional extensive relational measurement theory. This work was taken up by others in the nineteenth century.

As we have noted, the formalization of measurement theory is a surprisingly recent event. The primary motivation for the formalization of measurement theory was the need to understand what it means to measure things in the social sciences—things like preference, value, loudness, and so on. These attributes were obviously hard to measure, much as intangible resources would appear to be today. The catalyst for the formalization of measurement theory is generally accepted to be the psychologist S.S. Stevens,[18] with later interest from scientists in the field of quantum physics, but it was not until the 1970s that measurement was fully axiomatized with the publications of Scott and Suppes.[19,20]

What can we use measurement for?

Inevitably, rigorous measurement has the widest range of applications. The results of a value calculation can be used by themselves or in conjunction with other data (usually financial data, but also other things) and can be used in simulating value over time with or without other data. Some examples of the main applications of measurement are in the following lists:

Value results alone:

1. Value analysis of products, services, or objects
2. Value analysis of brands
3. Value analysis of companies or parts of companies
4. Value analysis of major functions in companies such as personnel, IT and knowledge management

Value results over time:

1. Monitoring the progress of management initiatives
2. Optimizing product or service replacement periods

Value and financial results:

1. Evaluating the value for money of candidate products or services
2. Evaluating the value for money of candidate investments in infrastructure
3. Evaluating the value for money of candidate investments in processes or services
4. Benchmarking
5. Disclosure (see Chapter 5) to the market or to others
6. Cost-benefit analyses
7. Finding cost reduction options with greatest impact and least value penalty

Value and financial results over time:

1. Through life value-for-money assessment
2. Evaluation of long-term strategic options

Value and other results over time (example):

1. With risk to assess value at risk over time

The sixteen points in the preceding lists are not exhaustive and should be seen as illustrative only. The key point is that managers have a reliable way of assessing the value of entities for which reliable measurement has hitherto been impossible. The actual applications that results from proper value measurement might be used in are numerous but will be peculiar to the circumstances of individual organizations.

What is measurement really about?

Measurement is about two things:

1. Representation
2. Ordering

Representation concerns itself with operations in which an attribute is represented by a measure; for example, 10 cm could be a numerical representation of a dimensional attribute of an object noting that a full description of the object requires that many other attributes are represented. Ordering is simple and concerns the amount of something an entity possesses and ensures—for example, that a 10 cm length object is always longer than a different object whose length measurement is 9 cm.

In practice, measurement theory keeps these two things separate. Entities or businesses in the real world to be measured are first represented in some way and then a numerical system is defined to handle the measurement in such a way that ordering requirements are maintained. This means that the process is a two-step one in which the entity in the real world to be measured is described in the first step and then a numerical system to describe it in numbers is created in the second step. The issue of ordering is handled within the second step and in the transition to it. This approach is known as relational measurement theory. A simple example is a child's toy building brick which has three orthogonal physical dimensions plus some others we may define to characterize it more accurately. These may include color, mass, or even taste! Obviously, measuring businesses is more complex, but the approach is exactly the same.

Businesses to be measured exist in the real world which theoreticians call an empirical relational space. There are three things that we have to worry about when we try to represent things. These are (1) the nature of the attributes we use to describe the business, (2) the relationships between them, and (3) the operations we may want to perform on them. In our case the object is the company and the attributes are the resources that collectively represent both the intellectual capital and the traditional resources of the company.

At this point we need to step back and take a broad view of what we are attempting to do. We are trying to build a measurement system or tool that can measure the value of something rather complex and express it from the viewpoint of different people. Here is where axiology, also known as the theory of value (which we discussed at the beginning of the chapter), and measurement theory come together. To them we need to add a third and final theoretical concept: multi-attribute value theory (MAVT).[21] MAVT allows for the representation of the value of complex entities using a hierarchical structure which can be made operational by the incorporation of mathematics to represent the subjective judgments made by stakeholders. For reliable use it requires that the internal mathematics are in all places compliant with measurement theory.

The basic steps in building a relational measurement system

1. The first and most important step in building a system is to define very precisely the scope of the object or business to be measured and to determine what the results are to be used for. This cannot be stressed strongly enough. Failures in measurement systems almost always have their origins here.
2. The second step is to determine who the stakeholders are.
3. With the problem scoped, work can begin on building an empirical relational system. In this third step, the basic axiological framework, MAVT, and measurement theory are used to build an empirical measurement system (i.e., a system containing all the attributes that, taken together, completely define the overall scope). There are two key tests at this stage and these are completeness and distinctness. The system is hierarchical and the statement about completeness applies at every level. Furthermore, at every level, the attributes must also be distinct from one another in terms of meaning. In this way the object or business to be measured is completely defined by attributes that are different from one another. The danger of double counting is therefore avoided. This process also requires that definitions of attribute meanings are rigorously recorded.
4. The empirical measurement system is a system showing what should be measured, and its development continues only until it is felt that there is a reasonable chance of the attributes actually being measurable in practice. When this point is reached, then a real working image of this empirical structure is built. This is the fourth step and it results in an isomorphic numerical measurement system: the ruler that we will use for measuring our object. Unfortunately, the process may require that proxies be found for some of the empirical attributes since it is usual that what one wants to measure often cannot be measured directly in practice. For example, we measure the gas temperature in the shockwave of a detonation by secondary observation of its effects rather than by direct measurements because the measuring equipment rarely survives the process. Proxy measures are subjected to a third test: agreeability. The key issue is that the

meaning of the attribute on the next level up in the numerical system is not changed by the substitution of the proxy.

5. Step five is to make the numerical relational structure active by inserting value and aggregation functions at the nodes of the structure. This is a simple step in that generic algorithms can be used over and over. However, when selecting algorithms for aggregation for the first time, a fourth condition must be satisfied, which is that the algorithms are preference independent. The test for preference independence requires that the operations used to aggregate value comply with the normal requirements of commutativity, associativity, monotonicity, positivity, and with the Archimedean condition.

6. The sixth step is to customize the settings of the numerical system to meet the preferences of the stakeholders. It is vital that no averaging is undertaken to get some mean stakeholder view. This is counter to the intent of axiology and mostly leads to a set of views that represent no stakeholder. The wealth of information that could come from stakeholders, especially if their views differ significantly, will be lost through averaging and will severely diminish the value of rigorous measurement. This customization process is best done in face-to-face discussions using techniques that assure unbiased weightings such as pair-wise comparisons. Other techniques may be acceptable as long as ratio-scale results are obtained. Step 7 explains ratio scaling.

7. The last step is to find the data needed to run the measurement system and actually do some measurement. Here the fifth and final requirement has to be met. Performance data must be commensurable, that is, normalized on a well-defined scale ranging from 0 to 1 and collected on a ratio scale. The definitions of 0 and 1 for each attribute must be recorded with the same rigor as the meanings of the attributes. Zero is usually taken to be the threshold of uselessness. This is the threshold where performance just starts to have some value. The meaning of 1 depends on the nature of the problem and the use to which the results are to be put. In most circumstances, 1 can either represent the strategic targets of the company if the results are to be used for internal measurement or management, the best in class if the results are to be used for external release or external comparison or the best imaginable if the results are to be used for strategic reframing.

Failure to weight or collect data preserving ratio or absolute scale data can invalidate many of the statistical processes that managers may wish to apply, or if the measurement system is being used as part of a larger simulation, it may invalidate the whole system. Fortunately, compliance is easy, but it must be done. Table 4.1 shows the categories.

Table 4.1. Description of Scales

Name of Scale	Typical Description	Transformations	Allowed Statistics
Nominal	A classification of the objects	Only those that preserve the fact that objects are different	(Descriptive) Frequencies, mode, information content; (Associative) Chi-square.
Ordinal	A ranking of the objects	Any monotonic increasing transformation, although a transformation that is not strictly increasing loses information.	(Descriptive) Median, quantiles and quartiles; (Associative) Spearman's rank-order correlation coefficient, Kendall's tau, rho.
Interval	Differences between values are meaningful, but not the values of the measure itself	Any affine transformation $t(m) = c * m + d$, where c and d are constants; the origin and unit of measurement are arbitrary	As above plus arithmetic mean, standard deviation
Ratio	There is a meaningful "zero" value and the ratios between values are meaningful	Any linear (similarity) transformation $t(m) = c* m$, where c is a constant; the unit of measurement is arbitrary.	As above plus geometric mean
Absolute	All properties reflect the attribute	Only 1-to-1 transformations	All

Case 4.1 Value Analysis for Carlton & United Beverages

The global drinks market is mature and crowded, with consolidation commonplace. However, while mergers and acquisitions offer an easier growth path compared to organic growth, there are major, if infrequent, opportunities with novel products. The rise of ready-to-drink beverages is the outstanding example of this. Companies in the drinks sectors are alive to the need to identify "white spaces," or niches for new product and packaging concepts.

In 2002, Carlton & United Beverages (CUB), part of the Australian drinks company Foster's Group, sought to undertake an analysis of drinks and drinking to attempt to find the white spaces where new beverages and selling concepts were most likely to succeed. Due to the complexity and crowding in the field, it was important that any data and later analysis of the field were as reliable and discriminating as possible. Furthermore, the analyses of the past were considered inadequate since they had already been used widely. To get the detailed background information required to determine what drinkers really valued, the company sought out a means of calculating value. For this reason the CVH approach was selected. The other useful features of the CVH were that it could handle multiple stakeholder groups (or even stakeholder groups at the individual level) and could compare across subsegments, such as across beer, wine, spirits, and ready-to-drink beverages.

The study sought to compare results through the segments to show, for each product class, or sets of classes, whether there are common sensitivities that are not filled by a product. If there were then these might indicate a white space. Market analysis would confirm its existence. Analyses through the classes will indicate whether, for each segment, there are any common sensitivities. This could point to the progression paths through products and hence whether drinks solutions would succeed and which products should be in them. These analyses are shown graphically in the left-hand figure that follows. The right-hand figure shows the secondary analyses carried out to incorporate financial issues, both for the drinker and the company. Thus the model provided comprehensive value and value for money results.

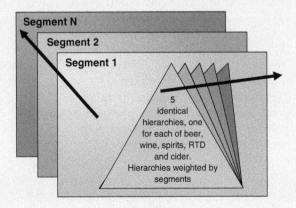

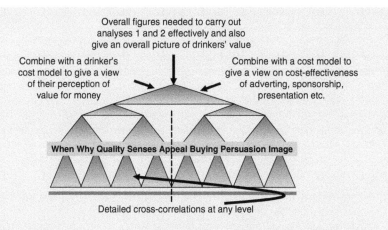

Overall figures needed to carry out
analyses 1 and 2 effectively and also
give an overall picture of drinkers' value

Combine with a drinker's
cost model to give a view
of their perception of
value for money

Combine with a cost model to
give a view on cost-effectiveness
of adverting, sponsorship,
presentation etc.

When Why Quality Senses Appeal Buying Persuasion Image

Detailed cross-correlations at any level

The hierarchical structure used to generate the results is shown, in a truncated form, in the following diagram. The structure appears to have 33 attributes, but the actual structure used comprised 84 attributes. The lowest level of attributes have been excluded for reasons of crowding, but the numbers to the left of the structure show the number of detailed and measurable attributes attached to the ones shown.

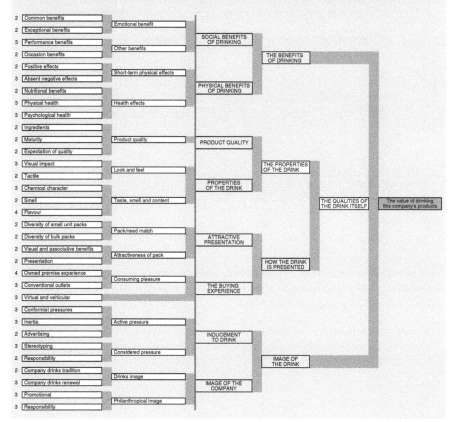

Continued

Case 4.1 Value Analysis for Carlton & United Beverages—cont'd

The working numerical isomorph was constructed by a survey which led to a number of distinct groups with similar drinking habits. The performance characteristics for the company's beverages and those of its competitors could be run through the value model and compared. The study showed that at least 30% of the attributes were of little importance to any group and could be excluded in a later and larger survey. Plots similar to the following one (for beer) were constructed for each drinker type and each drink type and showed where there was agreement or disagreement on the attributes. Not surprisingly, the majority were not issues of concern and were also issues where there was general agreement on the effect of changing performance. The analysis showed key areas where:

- Important attributes were agreed upon and represent attributes that must remain as they are (top left)
- Attributes that seemed unimportant but over which there was diversity of views, suggesting low priority consideration of the product portfolio (bottom right)
- Important areas where there was diversity in views, suggesting areas where the product portfolio should be expanded, possibly into a white space (top right)

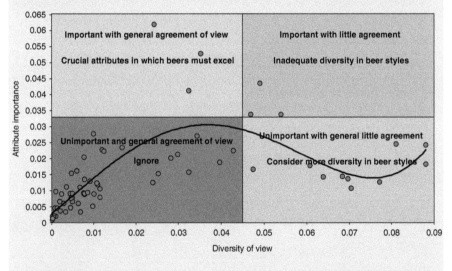

As expected in a category as mature as beer, there where only a few clear white spaces, but many improvement opportunities for either existing products to adopt to better meet changing consumer needs or new products to replace existing products through a better fit with existing consumer needs.

When the study was extended beyond beer and cross-correlations were undertaken between different drinks and specific segments of drinkers (based on communality of what they value in the drink), there appeared to be unserved combinations that could be filled with new offerings.

Existing systems and derived measures

When managers investigate the state of performance measurement in their companies they are often horrified at the sheer scale and cost of measurement taking place. It is not uncommon for the number of measurement systems of one kind or another to exceed 100 in large companies. Many of these will have been designed for purposes that no longer exist, many duplicate or are very similar to others employed elsewhere in the company, and many or most cannot be considered to be reliable systems with any attempt at compliance with measurement theory. Many or most can often be amalgamated or abandoned altogether with no significant loss in the supply of useful management information.

Instigation of a single system or one integrated from a number of semi-autonomous parts is a prospect that offers the possibility of streamlining what currently exists with the probability that the administrative overhead of running the redundant systems will be greatly reduced. Those being measured tend to dislike measurement when its purpose is unclear (and sometimes also when the purpose is clear). A single system offers the prospect of focusing the system of measurement (and perhaps management) onto what really matters to the company. It also changes behaviors. People have a natural desire to measure up well and will try to excel in measured areas even if those areas add little value to the company, whereas unmeasured areas may be much more important and are ignored by people who see no personal benefit in performing well in those areas.

Nevertheless, there may have been and continue to be reason for some measurement systems to be used as local indicators of performance or the value that is being added to the company. Obviously, the inclusion of such systems into a new company system is desirable. Alternatively, as existing systems are rarely compliant with measurement theory, a companywide system must have the capability of producing useful local derived measures where necessary. In this context, a derived measure is a measure that is taken from some combination of a limited number of attributes in the overall system to replicate the previously existing measure (or indicator).

In general, the decision to introduce a single theoretically compliant measurement system for what really matters to the company is an opportunity to reduce administrative costs, increase relevance, improve focus, and above all, supply managers with the data they really need.

Simplifying measurement systems

The danger in all measurement systems is that they get out of hand in terms of size. Hierarchical systems are particularly prone to this problem. At some point, the cost of obtaining the data outweighs the benefit in having it. If a measurement system branches into pairs at each level of granularity, then at 6 levels, the number of attributes requiring data is $2^6 = 64$, which is a manageable number. If the system branches into triples, then at 6 levels of attributes $3^6 = 729$ pieces of data are required, and that tends to be managerially unreasonable. Bearing in mind that most real structures are comprised of pairs and triples with the occasional quartet, the need to keep the measurement system in proportion is obvious.

In constructing working measurement systems the rule is that development of the structure stops at the first level where the builder believes that data for all attributes can be found. There is nothing to gain and much to lose from going to further levels of detail. However, once this level has been reached the process of finding the sources of data permits the use of agreeable proxy measures for things that cannot readily be measured. It is at this stage that consideration can be given to the possibility that the measurement system could be reduced by one level with all the advantages of a smaller system but with the disadvantage that a greater number of proxy measures will be needed. Provided that the proxies are acceptable, then the system can be simplified. The only other issue that requires consideration when embarking on this process is the possibility that some derived measures may no longer be available.

As with any measurement system, the tradeoff is between detail and utility against the cost and effort in collecting the data. The question facing companies is to decide whether they need to build a proper system that gives reliable results usable throughout the company or whether a simpler concept will suffice, albeit with more limited use. The next section deals with the difference between measurements and indicators. The two sections that then follow will illustrate the differences in capability and use by showing the construction of real systems with each approach, illustrated by real examples.

MEASUREMENT AND INDICATORS

Whether we realize it or not, valuation requires that an assessment is made which may be based on proper measurement at one end of the rigorousness scale and subjective judgment at the other. This is what is done whether one is calculating carefully before releasing auditable data on company performance or making a quick choice between two alternative products in a store. Obviously there are different levels and rigor with which these assessments are made, but the process is the same. Data, which may be hard or subjective, are collected and used with a measurement model, which may be formal and governed by hard rules, or ad hoc, to develop an answer that becomes part of the accounts or the choice between products. Providing certain conditions are met, either, but most likely the former example, can be called a proper measure whereas the latter is not. However, they may still be useful in making decisions or monitoring performance. This book labels nonrigorous assessments as indicators.

In the sections that follow, a distinction is made between (proper) measurement systems and other systems which will be referred to as indicators. At the outset, the distinction between measurement and indicators needs to be drawn clearly.

- Measures: A measure is a numerical representation of an object in which all the attributes of the object are included in the representation in a manner compliant with measurement theory and all measures and manipulations are also compliant with measurement theory.
- Indicators: An indicator is a roughly estimated representation of an object which may suffice for local needs but is prone to errors.

Comparing and using measurements and indicators

The decision to embark on building a measurement system or to use a set of indicators depends on the situation you face now and the situation you may face in time to come. Both measurements and indicators have their advantages and disadvantages, and Table 4.2 sets them out.

Both approaches require that nothing that would invalidate the system's use changes over the period that the system is to be used, such as a structural change in the company that makes a component of the measurement system or indicator redundant or something new that should be taken into account but is missing.

In the end, the choice of which route to follow boils down to the simple question: Do you want to measure what is going on accurately so you can be sure of the results and the decisions you may have to take, or can you be content with a group of indicators that monitor changes as they occur but cannot be used for decision making with safety? If you need

Table 4.2. Comparison of Proper Measurement and Indicators

	Measurement System	Indicators
Advantages	Accurate if built properly Produces a complete view of the object Data can be disclosed Results can be benchmarked Can be the basis of derived measures Can be used with other business models Transparent and auditable Takes multiple views of value into account	Quick to build Easy to operate
Disadvantages	Takes care and time to set up Data requirement can be large Data quality requirements are stringent	Purpose specific Cannot be bench-marked with safety Takes a single "average" view of value Cannot be built up to value complex objects Possibility of duplication

reliable information to make decisions about the future, then you must build a proper measurement system. If you want to monitor progress toward targets with moderate trust in the results, (that may, in practice, occasionally be compensated for by access to relevant and valid experience*) then use indicators.

ATTEMPTS AT VALUATION

At the time of writing (2005), there are hardly any measurement schemes available to measure intellectual capital that meet the criteria listed in the preceding section; this is particularly alarming given our long history of measuring business performance. It surprises many, even among academics,

---

*Relevant and valid experience is in fact a tacit measurement system embodied in the individual the problem tends to be around the relevance and validity due to a constantly changing world

when they realize that although we think of intellectual capital as a management approach born of the last decade, much of its important grounding was done in the 1950s[22] and its origins can be traced back to the work of economists in the United Kingdom and the United States in the early 1930s.[23,24] The real age of intellectual capital, or at least its forerunner, resource-based accounting, merely underlines the inability or unwillingness of academics and users to overcome issues in measurement.

It seems that many early exponents of the intellectual capital movement strove to make their individual approaches simple and distinctive at the expense of being able to do anything useful with the outcomes of their labors. However, it is very important to appreciate that "doing it right" doesn't mean that the process is inordinately difficult or time consuming; although there may be mathematics and a philosophical framework behind the measurement system, executing it in companies merely requires adherence to a few simple principles, some of which have already been touched upon.

The phenomenon that many early intellectual capital measurement and valuations schemes sought to explain and quantify was the difference between the apparent value of a company as expressed through its market valuation and the book value of the company as calculated by the accountants. The most famous example of this is the equation attributed to Edvinsson,[25] which is shown here:

$$\text{Market Value} = \text{Book Value} + \text{Intellectual Capital}$$

Many others followed Edvinsson's lead but substituted their own taxonomic methods of explaining how intellectual capital contributed to business performance and ultimately market value.

What should have become obvious from the preceding chapters is that the intellectual capital approach embodies a holistic approach to company management and is not something that one adds on to. Intellectual capital is an approach for managing the whole company and all its resources. Book value is just an expression of part of a company's resources; it is a snapshot of the magnitude of the physical and monetary resources only. There are three issues around linking intellectual capital and book value to market value. The first is the fact that book value and market value are measured using different units of measure, artificial money and real money respectively,[26] and this makes the whole exercise erroneous and meaningless to start with since you cannot add or subtract objects measured in different units. The second is that as the generation of value in a company is dependent on a complex interaction of resources, book value and intellectual capital are not the separable variables that the equation implies. Finally, market value is dependent on factors exogenous to the company and the value of the components of intellectual capital are dependent on the point of view of the observer. What this implies is that the context of value has to be defined very carefully; the simple intellectual capital measurement schemes envisaged by many early workers in the field simply did not have the care or the reach to deal with market value, an issue near and dear to the authors' hearts.

Some systems of measurement of intellectual capital predate Edvinsson's work, although the object under examination was often described in terms of independent measures or as groups of competencies. The most famous of these and by far the most widely used of all nonfinancial measurement schemes is the balanced scorecard. The logic for the balanced scorecard originated in France[27] as the *Tableau de Bord,* and later migrated to the United States. Second to this are the quality-oriented measurement systems in Europe and the United States. Both of these approaches suggest measures but require that the company precisely define the measures within predefined areas. This limitation has some severe implications for the usefulness of these approaches. There has been very little research on the actual effect of the balanced scorecard, but the research that does exist seems to indicate some disturbing results: most importantly that there is no positive affect on the firm's performance from its use.[28] This may be due to the fact that the balanced scorecard approach does not fulfill the requirement of being a measurement system and therefore has no predictive capability, and if decisions are made on its indications the outcome may not be the expected one. Benchmarking is the obvious "add on" that would allow one company to be compared with another. However, this is only meaningful in the limited situation where the two companies taking part have very similar scopes and intentions. Put simply, aiming for general measures that can be benchmarked decreases the relevance of the measures to the company(ies) being measured and compared. There are other problems associated with benchmarking (e.g., it generates a mental attitude of fast follower rather then leader). Perhaps the most problematic area associated with these popular approaches is that while both claim a causal linkage between the measure in the scorecard and the underlying business process, neither can demonstrate a causal link between the process and the value creation in the company that is the key to survival.

There are a small number of approaches that are financially based but that do not seek to connect the result to market value. The best known of these is the value added intellectual capital methodology (VAIC) in which the company is described as a set of processes and activities. A *process* is a value-creating or destroying step that begins with some input and ends with an output. Between the inputs and outputs, the process involves a number of activities, many of which will be common to several processes, but are carried out at a high level of granularity. To link the processes to financial data, each process is assessed in terms of a number of value ratios. The main problems are the degree of granularity required and the fact that while it derives its strength from its base of real financial data, it cannot be used predictively.

Despite this none too promising introduction to previous attempts at measuring intellectual capital—or perhaps because of it—interest in the subject has not waned. The European Union Information Society Technologies (IST) and Targeted Socio-Economic Research (TSER) has in recent years sponsored a number of studies on the subject, the most notable of which have been the PRISM[29] and MERITUM[30] studies. Both studies examined their closely related field in detail, reporting on the current state of knowledge. Critically, they both failed to make any significant headway on the question of measurement and indicators.

Over the last 10 to 15 years, a great number of systems have been devised to help managers with business performance and with a special emphasis on nonfinancial measures. According to Luthy (1998)[31] and Williams (2000),[32] methodologies may be categorized into four groups. These are:

1. **Direct Intellectual Capital Methods (DICM)** estimate the dollar value of intangible assets by identifying its various components. Once these components are identified, they can be directly evaluated, either individually or as an aggregated coefficient.
2. **Market Capitalization Methods (MCM)** calculate the difference between a company's market capitalization and its stockholders' equity as the value of its intellectual capital or intangible assets.
3. **Return on Assets Methods (ROA)** average pre-tax earnings of a company and divide them by the average tangible assets of the company. The result is a company ROA that is then compared with its industry average. The difference is multiplied by the company's average tangible assets to calculate an average annual earning from intangibles. By dividing the above-average earnings by the company's weighted average cost of capital or an interest rate, one can derive an estimate of the value of its intangible assets or intellectual capital.

4. Scorecard Methods (SC) identify various components of intangible assets or intellectual capital and indicators and indices are generated and reported in scorecards or as graphs. SC methods are similar to DIC methods, except that no estimate is made of the dollar value of intangible assets. A composite index may or may not be produced.

To which a fifth should be added:

5. Proper Measurement Systems (MS) take everything of value in or about the company and break them down into attributes that can be measured. These are built into a measurement system, usually a conjoint hierarchy, and real data are used to produce reliable calculations of value. These can be combined with financial data to provide value for money and related outputs.

MS is an approach that aims at completeness and reliability with an explicit treatment of all aspects of value. Of the others, the MCM and ROA approaches have an element of rigor in that they rely on financial figures which, if not perfect, are auditable. DICM, and to a lesser extent SC methods, offer the potential to create a more comprehensive picture of an organization's health than financial metrics, and they can be easily applied at any level of an organization. This is because they are directly aimed at management support and DIC is intended to be holistic.

ROA and MCM methods build on long-established accounting rules and are more easily communicated to those versed in the accounting profession. They attempt real valuations and may appear useful in M&A situations since they can give crude comparisons between companies within the same industry. However, for a detailed due diligence activity, they give far too little detail for an adequate comparison. Apart from a lack of detail to help managers, the ROA methods are very sensitive to interest rate assumptions. Several of them are of no use for nonprofit organizations, business units, government agencies, and not-for-profit organizations; this is particularly true of the MCM methods.

DIC and SC methods are more detailed and can be easily applied at any level of an organization. They measure intellectual capital resources from the bottom up and can therefore be faster and more accurate than ROA and MCM measures with respect to resources. Since they do not need to be measured in financial terms, they are very useful for not-for-profit organizations, business units, government agencies, and for environmental and social purposes. Their disadvantages are that the indicators are contextual and the meanings of the resource definitions can vary between each organization and each purpose, which makes comparisons very difficult. But perhaps the main problem is that they cannot be connected easily to financial results.

The MS methodologies, if done correctly, offer the possibility of not only reliable measurement but also of the proper combination of intellectual capital resources with financial resources. They do this by using dispassionate measurement as the starting point with the intention of applying it to company resources rather than making assumptions about the principle resources followed by an attempt to quantify them in some way. It is for this reason that almost all the methodologies noted, for example, by Sveiby, lead to indicators as the outcome rather than reliable measurements. Tables 4.3 through 4.6 are based on Sveiby's work and serve to briefly describe the approaches and the reasons that they fail to meet the standards required for reliable, auditable results.

In 2003, the preceding tables represented the extent of the conventional approaches to intellectual capital measurement and Pike and Roos[33] undertook an analysis of them.

One further methodology is listed by Sveiby and that is the IVM™ (Inclusive Value Manager), devised by M'Pherson.[34,35,36] Sveiby places it in the DIC group but it is completely different from them since, although it carries out direct evaluations of the components of intangible value, it is a true and generic measurement system similar to the CVH system described later in this chapter. IVM has been used in many different situations measuring the value and value-for-money of strategic options for companies through tactical options for companies down to detailed tradeoffs for products. CVH is also modular and can be used to assess value in company meta-functions such as knowledge management and in decision support.[37]

IVM and CVH bear a considerable outward similarity to each other in that both aim at true measurement using a conjoint hierarchy. Both are founded on axiology and employ measurement theory and multi-attribute value theory. Both take multiple stakeholder views. There are differences in how they operate internally in that the IVM uses a number of aggregation functions while the CVH has infinitely variable functions. There are also differences in the value functions they employ. These differences are crucial in that the use of inappropriate functions can lead to invalidation of the methodology with respect to the requirements of measurement theory. CVH is fully compliant with measurement theory. No other approach is. The single variable algorithm approach of CVH is better than IVM's four-algorithm approach as, at the time of writing, two IVM algorithms fail the associativity criterion and are noncompliant with the preference independence requirement and require intervention to assure accuracy in the results.

Table 4.3. ROA Methodologies[38]

ROA Methodologies	Originator and year of first publication	Description	Comment
Economic Value Added (EVA™)	Stewart (1997)[39]	Calculated by adjusting the firm's disclosed profit with charges related to intangibles. Changes in EVA provide an indication of whether the firm's intellectual capital is productive or not.	With the exception of VAIC, it is arguable that these are not really intellectual capital methodologies but simply a means of explaining a financial feature and attributing changes in them to the efficiency in the deployment of intellectual capital resources.
Human Resource Costing & Accounting (HRCA)	Johansson (1997)[40]	Calculates the hidden impact of HR related costs which reduce a firm's profits. Adjustments are made to the P&L. Intellectual capital is measured by calculation of the contribution of human assets held by the company divided by capitalized salary expenditures.	
Calculated Intangible Value	Stewart (1997)[37] Luthy (1998)[41]	Calculates the excess return on hard assets, then uses this figure as a basis for determining the proportion of return attributable to intangible assests.	These methodologies avoid direct comparison with market values but link to some of the factors that market makers use in their assessments of companies. Having said that, it is important to note that the attribution of value to the intellectual capital resources is "by infer-ence" in nature, there being no overt
Knowledge Capital Earnings	Lev (1999)[42]	Knowledge Capital Earnings are calculated as the portion of normalized earnings over and above expected earnings attributable to book assets.	
Value Added	Pulic (1997)[43]	Measures how much and how efficiently	

Intellectual Coefficient (VAIC™)		intellectual capital and capital employed create value based on the relationship to three major components: (1) capital employed; (2) human capital; and (3) structural capital.	causal link between the resources in use in the company and the calculated figures. Thus, the outcomes of these methodologies are indicators at best but with significant intra-sector comparability.
Accounting for the Future (AFTF)	Nash (1998)[44]	A system of projected discounted cash flows. The difference between AFTF value at the end and the beginning of the period is the value added during the period.	VAIC is different and more detailed in that there are links between the activities of the company, the resources used and the financial outcome. It appears to be the best of the ROA methodologies but fails as a measurement system due to internal difficulties with the distinctness and independence of the defined resources.

Table 4.4. MCM Methodologies[38]

MCM Methodologies	Originator	Description	Comment
Tobin's q	Stewart (1997)[39]	The "q" is the ratio of the stock market value of the firm divided by the replacement cost of its assets. Changes in "q" provide a proxy for measuring effective performance or not of a firm's intellectual capital.	This is the weakest of the five groups. To the weaknesses of the ROA group is added the further impediment of attempting to connect the figures to market value. The vagaries of the market can lead to considerable changes in intellectual capital value in a matter of hours! The problems of tracking market value in the way originally suggested by Edvinsson are described in this chapter. These approached lead to highly dubious indicators.
Investor assigned market value (IAMV™)	Standfield (1998)[45]	Takes the Company's True Value to be its stock market value and divides it into Tangible Capital + (Realized Intellectual Capital + Intellectual Capital Erosion + SCA (Sustainable Competitive Advantage).	
Market-to-Book Value	Stewart (1997)[39] Luthy(1998)[41]	The value of intellectual capital is considered to be the difference between the firm's stock market value and the company's book value.	

Table 4.5. DIC Methodologies[38]

DIC Methodologies	Originator	Description	Comment
Technology Broker	Brooking (1996)[46]	Value of intellectual capital of a firm is assessed based on diagnostic analysis of a firm's response to twenty questions covering four major components of intellectual capital.	Close inspection of the methodologies reveals that most fail several of the requirements of measurement theory and none are fully compliant. Their main failings concern the definitions of resources which have always been a weakness of the intellectual capital movement. Thus they are incomplete and indistinct with many concentrating on particular areas, notably intellectual property. While they may be agreeable proxies for desired measures, they are often populated by figures which are not collected on a ratio scale. Many can be made very useful as indicators by careful use in the areas where they can fail most easily.
Citation-Weighted Patents	Bontis (1996)[47]	A technology factor is calculated based on the patents developed by a firm. Intellectual capital and its performance is measured based on the impact of research development efforts on a series of indices, such as number of patents and cost of patents to sales turnover, that describe the firm's patents.	
The Value Explorer™	Andriessen & Tiessen (2000)[48]	Accounting methodology proposed by KMPG for calculating and allocating value to 5 types of intangibles: (1) Assets and endowments, (2) Skills & tacit knowledge, (3) Collective values and norms, (4) Technology and explicit knowledge, (5) Primary and management processes.	
Intellectual Asset Valuation	Sullivan (2000)[49]	Methodology for assessing the value of Intellectual Property.	A further problem with the issue of completeness is that whereas efforts can be made to include as many of the resources as possible, this tends only to address the area of intrinsic value leaving the area of resource use or instrumental value unaddressed.
Total Value Creation, TVC™	Anderson & McLean (2000)[50]	A project initiated by the Canadian Institute of Chartered Accountants. TVC uses discounted projected cash-flows to re-examine how events affect planned activities.	

Table 4.6. SC Methodologies[38]

SC Methodologies	Originator	Description	Comment
Human Capital Intelligence	Jac Fitz-Enz (1994)[51]	Sets of human capital indicators are collected and benchmarked against a database. Similar to HRCA.	The Intellectual Capital Index has been removed from Sveiby's original list and is discussed in a later section.
Skandia Navigator™	Edvinsson and Malone (1997)[52]	Intellectual capital is measured through the analysis of up to 164 metric measures? (91 intellectually based and 73 traditional metrics) that cover five components: (1) financial; (2) customer; (3) process; (4) renewal and development; and (5) human.	The SC methodologies are very similar to the DIC methodologies and apart from the ability to present results as a scorecard, they differ very little. Thus the comments that were made for DIC methodologies can be applied here.
Value Chain Scoreboard™	Lev (2002)[53]	A matrix of nonfinancial indicators arranged in three categories according to the cycle of development: Discovery / Learning, Implementation, Commercialization.	Apart from the Intellectual Capital Index, the Balanced Scorecard and the IAM of Sveiby himself deserve special comment.
Intangible Asset Monitor	Sveiby (1997)[54]	Management selects indicators, based on the strategic objectives of the firm, to measure four aspects of creating value from intangible assets. By: (1) growth (2) renewal; (3) utilization / efficiency; and (4) risk reduction / stability.	The Balanced Scorecard makes no pretence to measurement and is a system of indicators defined by the company with explicit causal links to the underlying processes but often not to the actual value creating

Intellectual Capital Navigator and Intellectual Capital Index	Roos and others (1997)[55]	Intellectual Capital is broken down into 3 areas: human, relational and organizational plus the conventional physical and monetary resources. These are all subdivided. Several user-friendly plots are produced including a navigator, a conceptual diagram of how the company works in IC terms. Indices are defined based on the key resources and resource transformations in the navigator.	processes. Nevertheless, it can cover the key perceived issues and is simple. Not surprisingly, it has achieved a level of usage far above all other methods.
Value Creation Index	Ittner and others (2000)[56]	Drivers of value are derived from an extensive literature survey and advanced statistics. Metrics are weighted and combined to give a Value Creation Index. The index is compared and combined with financial data.	The IAM does not look at resource use but it does look at the qualities of resources in a way not attempted by any other method except for the Intellectual Capital Index. It operates at a coarse level of granularity and so has limited diagnostic value from that stand-point but it can be made to be reliable in that its deviations from measurement theory can be minimized. It is also the basis for the popular management training simulation, "Tango", marketed by Celemi.
Balanced Score Card	Kaplan and Norton (1996)[57]	A company's performance is measured by indicators covering four major focus perspectives: (1) financial perspective; (2) customer perspective; (3) internal process perspective; and (4) learning perspective. The indicators are based on the strategic objectives of the firm.	

BUILDING REAL MEASUREMENT SYSTEMS

In this section, real examples will be used to illustrate the construction of measurement systems using our conjoint value hierarchy (CVH) system. The studies used as examples were all executed between 2000 and 2005; some have been anonymized.

Example 1: The Measured Company and the Results

In this example, an Australian third sector organization in the health sector sought to understand the value it provided its users and specifically the value its research function provided. It sought this understanding to assist with the formulation of better strategic development options. The purpose of this example is to demonstrate the definition of stakeholders and the building of an empirical relational system.

At twelve, the number of distinct stakeholder groups was numerous and included the federal and relevant state government, the parent organization, product user groups, staff representatives, patient support groups, raw material suppliers, service suppliers, regulators, dependent services, independent researchers and the media. In the end, the media declined to take part. This loss was regrettable in that valuable external opinion was lost and subsequent strategic options might have been pilloried in the press. Ultimately, however, the lack of media input was not a failing of the organization at the center of the study.

Over a two-week period, our researchers interviewed stakeholders to gain an understanding of the factors stakeholders felt to be important in the delivery of the organization's services and the services they might deliver in future. The forward-looking perspective was important in this example as the results were to be used to guide the formulation of strategic options. Thus, the measurement system would ultimately be required to evaluate business alternatives that were not part of the current portfolio. The large and diverse stakeholder group led to many revisions of the empirical structure, with completeness being the first priority. In the end, nine iterations were required to develop an initial hierarchy—developed from desk research to a final hierarchy—acceptable to all participating stakeholders.

The two-week process had two distinct phases. In the first phase, the initial 51-attribute hierarchy structure was allowed to grow to incorporate breadth of meaning. The concern at this stage was for completeness. The structure grew from 51 attributes at the outset to 55, then to 56, to 76, to 82, and finally to 96 attributes. At this stage the team were confident that the totality of the meaning of the value the organization gave and might give had been captured, but it was clear that there was duplication and overlap in the meanings of the attributes. The structure required rationalizing and the final iterations of structural change with expert stakeholders sought to retain the completeness but to ensure distinctness in attribute meaning. In steps, the structure size declined from 96 attributes to a final figure of 65 attributes.

The empirical relational measurement system that emerged was of moderate size. In practice, 20 to 25 attributes represent a small measurement system and more than 80 attributes represent a large one. Good and meaningful results can be obtained with measurement systems containing between 30 and 60 attributes, but in mathematical actuality there is no theoretical limit to size or complexity.

Due to the difficulty in reproducing even moderately sized structures on a printed page, Figure 4.2 shows a small and simplified structure used to demonstrate the value of a meteorology service. The hierarchical structure is obvious, but has been rotated to the right with the overall value being expressed in the box on the right. The two dashed lines across the structure show the demarcation between the axiological categories of intrinsic value (top), instrumental value (middle), and extrinsic value (bottom). Demarcation is unimportant except that it serves as a prompt to ensure that all possible or appropriate sources of value have been considered. The precise distinction between instrumental value (being of value because we value its use), intrinsic value (being of value because of what it is), and extrinsic value (being of value because others appreciate it) is the subject of axiological argument, with different academics defining categories differently. What is important in measuring value is that the attributes are complete and completely describe the object being valued and that they are distinct and are defined such that there is no element of meaning in one attribute that appears in any other.

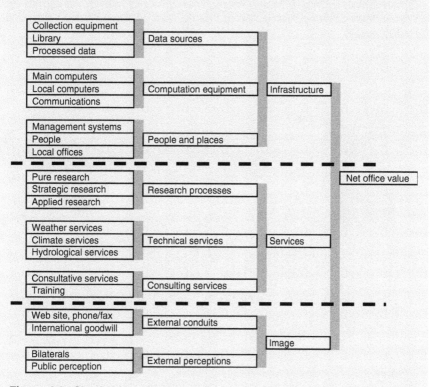

Figure 4.2. Simple hierarchial structure.

Continued

Example 1: The Measured Company and the Results—cont'd

The third sector organization with which we started this section then produced identical replica structures for each of the stakeholders and customized them by collecting weightings and other data through face-to-face interviews. They then had a set of well-formed and agreed-on structures and could undertake sensitivity studies to quantify the attitudes of the stakeholder groups and produce optimized strategic alternatives for further development. We see in the preceding sentence that the issue of data collection is absent. Sensitivity analyses can be undertaken without data, or at least by assuming the data can take user-defined values. Real data are not needed for this. The third example shows a wide range of the possible outputs from CVH, including sensitivity analyses.

Figure 4.3 shows the results of the sensitivity analysis for one of the stakeholders. The performance of the attributes is in the front-to-back axis and value is in the vertical axis. For each stakeholder the plot shows the attributes to which the stakeholder is most sensitive, that is, those with the largest value change and those to which the stakeholder is indifferent. Similar plots will be obtained for each of the other stakeholders and then comparisons can be made to find common ground or areas of difference. If the data were supplied through a business model, then the causal links could be backtracked to find the detailed reasons behind expressed differences.

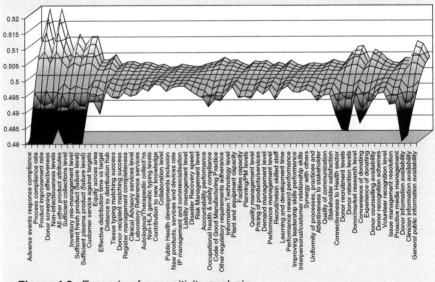

Figure 4.3. Example of a sensitivity analysis.

Example 2: Customization and Data Collection

Example 1 concluded with the construction of replica measurement systems, each customized to suit the preferences of a stakeholder group. There are two alternatives in carrying out the customization process in which weights, aggregation, and value functions are determined. The two basic processes are through face-to-face interviews or through a structured questionnaire.

Of these, the first is infinitely preferable and was the methodology used with the Australian third sector organization. Its advantage lies in the fact that understanding the definitions of attributes and the effects of other options in the customization process can be ensured when the expert and the subject are in the same place at the same time. CVH uses the pair-wise comparison methods of Saaty,[58] which are quite in line with the intentions of S. S. Stevens, with numerical data being calculated using a binary combination matrix (BCM). The BCM in our CVH model is possibly the largest available, capable of handling branches of 20 attributes at a time (12 is the largest freely available on the Internet), although structures requiring such heroic comparisons are valid only in specialist situations; otherwise, they are probably the result of a faulty structure. There are alternatives to pair-wise comparison and BCMs[59,60,61,62,63] but care is required that these methodologies may not lead to bias-free results on a ratio scale as required by measurement theory.

There are circumstances when the face-to-face approach cannot be used. Occasionally this occurs as a result of time constraints, population size, or geographical remoteness, in which case there can be recourse to electronically delivered questionnaires. The most common reason for using questionnaires is one of large numbers and interviewee accessibility. CVH was used to evaluate the value delivered by a European restaurant chain as seen by its customers and managers, and the role played by its brand. Almost 700 views were taken with the impossibility of grouping them other than by artificial demographic group. To accommodate this, each customer was considered to be in a stakeholder group of one with groupings applied later as a result of stated preferences rather than by preconceived notions of what groups should be or were likely to be. The ability to discriminate on the basis of value perception is unique and eminently suitable for market segmentation or product development/positioning type applications.

Questionnaires, on the other hand, rely on simplicity in use and clarity in explanation. In the case of the restaurant chain, completion of the questionnaire was done with the assistance of a tutor rather than without any assistance whatsoever. A properly executed face-to-face interview using pair-wise comparison and a BCM eliminates the possibility of hidden agendas influencing results. In the case of the large sample in the restaurant chain study, this was unlikely to be an issue and so the questionnaire process was used without much concern for bias. The questionnaire was also used on the managers of the restaurants in exactly the same way. A direct visual comparison of managers' and customers' sensitivities was obtained and demonstrated and quantified the not unusual difference between managers and customers in which managers believe only top performance is of any value while customers are actually rather more forgiving. Figure 4.4 shows the two plots on a common scale.

Continued

Example 2: Customization and Data Collection—cont'd

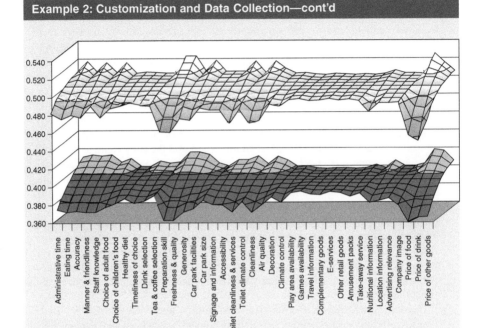

Figure 4.4. Sensitivities of customers (top) and managers (below) compared.

In addition to the sensitivity analysis described in both examples so far, subjective opinions of current performance were also taken, and Figure 4.5 shows performance (the dark line) superimposed on the surface plot of sensitivity. In general, performance data from direct observation, from a model, or from an expert would be used. In this case, customers were deemed to be experts! Clearly, if a current performance measure fell into one of the "valleys" on the plot then the company had a serious problem in that the CVH had identified an area where poor performance was having a very serious effect on the overall value perception of the restaurants. This general approach gives an instant and accurate picture of where real problems are occurring in the creation of value in the eyes of each stakeholder. Needless to say, since the results are based on reliable numerical data and the model gives the agreed value perceptions of the observer, reliable and prioritized lists of attributes in most need of performance improvements can be prepared. An example from this case is given in Table 4.7, in which the prioritized lists for performance improvement for four emergent customer groups are given. The numerical score shows the relative effectiveness of making a 10% performance improvement against the identified attribute.

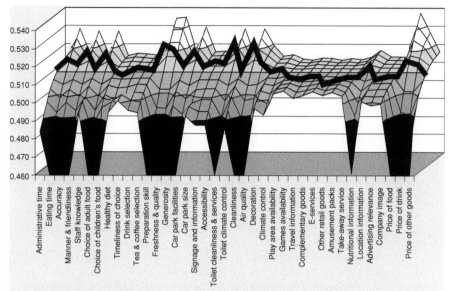

Figure 4.5. Sensitivity surface with current performance overlaid.

Table 4.7. Normalized Relative Effectiveness of a 10% Performance Improvement in Attribute Performance in Increasing the Perceived Value of a Restaurant Chain from four different customer segments point of view

REGULAR		IRREGULAR	
Preparation Skill	77	Preparation Skill	88
Freshness & Quality	77	Freshness & Quality	82
Eating Time	70	Cleanliness	67
Car Park Facilities	61	Car Park Facilities	64
Toilet Cleanliness & Services	59	Eating Time	62
Cleanliness	57	Toilet Cleanliness & Services	62
Accuracy	57	Manner & Friendliness	54
Manner & Friendliness	51	Generosity	50
Generosity	47	Accuracy	46
Administrative Time	43	Administrative Time	43

LAPSED		POTENTIAL	
Preparation Skill	75	Preparation Skill	100
Freshness & Quality	73	Freshness & Quality	86
Toilet Cleanliness & Services	62	Eating Time	60
Car Park Facilities	57	Administrative Time	60
Cleanliness	55	Generosity	57
Eating Time	52	Car Park Facilities	56
Generosity	49	Manner & Friendliness	55
Manner & Friendliness	41	Cleanliness	53
Administrative Time	41	Toilet Cleanliness & Services	46
Accuracy	34	Accuracy	39

Example 3: Strategic Issues

The third example is taken from an analysis of a large U.S. fast-food company. In this example, the context was the value of the company as a whole, but taking only the perspective of the (share price) market makers. Thus, the stakeholders were a group of analysts and were not investors themselves, nor were they in any other way connected to the company. The measurement system was constructed in the same way as for the previous two examples and the basic analyses shown in Example 2 were carried out.

The purpose of this example is to demonstrate the connectivity of the CVH system to other models. In this case the CVH was supplemented by a system dynamic business model of the company written using the Vensim[64] package. The selection of Vensim was driven by the ease of use of the package and that it could readily export results into other applications such as that in which the CVH had been operationalized for this example.

Four simulations using CVH and a system dynamics model were run with the system dynamics model generating performance outputs for both financial and nonfinancial attributes. The simulations ran over the period 1997 to 2002 to settle the model and demonstrate that it could track what actually happened. Then it was used predictively over the period 2003 to 2007. The four runs were:

1. A base run in which no parameters were altered
2. Scenario 1 in which advertising was cut by 15%
3. Scenario 2 in which there was a 40% cut in advertising and 62.5% of this saving devoted to training
4. Scenario 3 in which, in addition to the changes in Scenario 2, there was a one-off spend of 37.5% of the saved money applied to market research in the second year of the simulation and then that 37.5% saving was returned to shareholders in the third year and thereafter

These four runs constituted a logical comparable series. This means that the results from the three scenario runs could be compared against each other and also against the base run. Seven sets of stakeholder views were obtained which, together with the mean view gave a total of eight sets of outputs from the model, each (except for the mean) depicting the views and preferences of each separate stakeholder group.

The simplest output was a comparison of the overall intangible value outcome for the company over the five years of the analysis period for each stakeholder and for each scenario. Stakeholder data for each scenario were given in a single plot and the plots of value against time for each scenario are shown in the three graphs shown in Figure 4.6.

The first feature of note is the noticeable gain in value between the first and second years of the simulation in the views of the stakeholders, which can be attributed to the SD modeling settling from its original settings. This does not apply to the mean due to the different internal setting for the mean.

The second feature of note is that thereafter, none of three scenarios reflected growth but merely served to slow the rate of decline in value as seen by the stakeholders (with the possible exception of stakeholder (PN) in scenario 3. This result was expected and is typical of a "do nothing scenario."

Continued

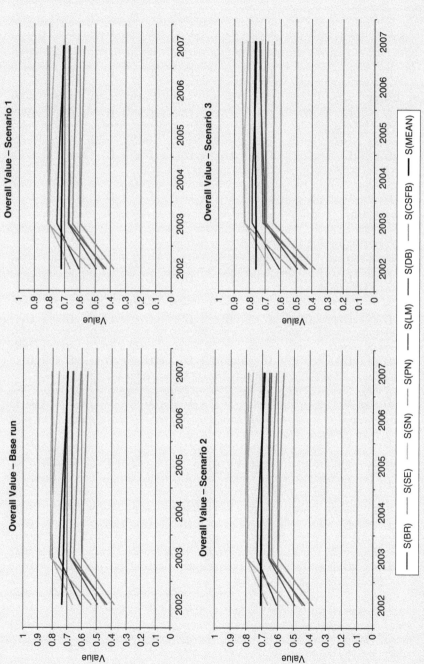

Figure 4.6. Basic predicted value outcomes for all stakeholders over 5 years.

Example 3: Strategic Issues—cont'd

The third feature of note is that there was a significant spread in the opinions of the stakeholders about the overall value of the company. This observation requires that further analysis be undertaken to understand the motivations of the stakeholders. Although sensitivity analyses can reveal stakeholder opinions in detail, it cannot explain why such positions are held.

The next level of analysis was that value outputs were plotted for each stakeholder and for each scenario over the same time period but at a lower level of granularity. The level used for this analysis was the key performance area level at which the single overall value figure had been broken down into six performance areas in the case of this company. The four sets of graphs in Figure 4.7 show the plots for the six key performance areas with one set per scenario.

The figures for the six key areas show there to be considerable commonality in the profile for all the stakeholders. The implication from this is all stakeholders were consistent in their valuation of performance. For example, the selection of a value function, apart from the peak function, has a consistent effect on the positioning of stakeholders with respect to each other.

The results from scenario 1 are shown in Figure 4.8. In this scenario, the corporate spending on advertising, but not the advertising carried out by the franchisees, is cut by $200 million.

The results from scenario 1 were disappointing since the cut in corporate advertising should have reduced the numbers of customers aware of the company and its offering. There is a mild downward effect seen after a lag of two years, but the decline at its worst is only a little over 1% but recovers to a near neutral position. This suggests that the other mechanisms for customer awareness, such as word of mouth, are overwhelmingly influential in attracting customers.

Scenario 2 involved a further $300 million cut in corporate advertising and this constituted the bulk of advertising. To compensate for this, the extra $300 million saved was applied to training staff to improve the service of customers. The results are given in the Figure 4.9.

Scenario 2 is interesting in that the extra expenditure on training yielded an improvement in the service area of close to 7%, depending on stakeholder view, and a 5%+ improvement on the qualities of the store, such as its cleanliness. On the other hand, the negative effects from the removal of the greater part of the funding from corporate advertising had a compensating negative effect on brand and operations which resulted in a near neutral to slightly negative overall effect on the value of the U.S. fast-food company's intangibles, with an effect ranging from +0.6% to −1.6%. It would appear that the improvement in service was more than counterbalanced by the loss in brand presence and that this had a negative effect on customer numbers and the top line.

The final scenario was complex, with advertising funds being devoted to staff training as in scenario 2 but with a one-off spend of $200 million in the second year being devoted to market research (leading to a financial neutral cost effect in that year) and an extra $200 million returned to shareholders in year three and thereafter. The results are shown in Figure 4.10.

Continued

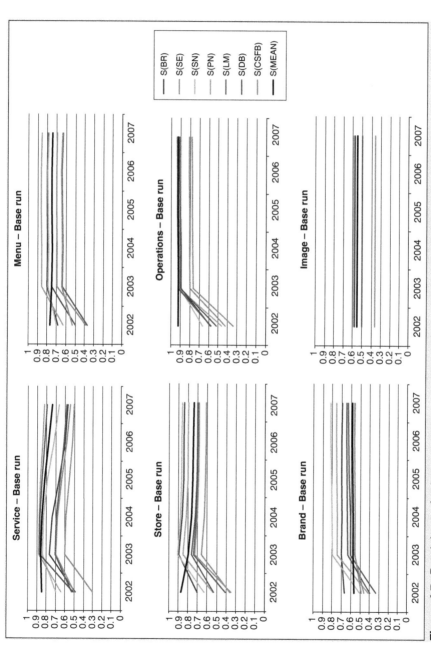

Figure 4.7. Breakdown of value perceptions into the six key performance areas for the base run.

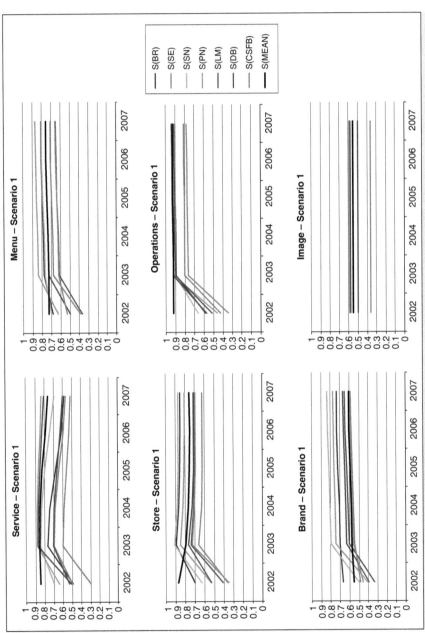

Figure 4.8. Breakdown of value perceptions into the six key areas for scenario 1.

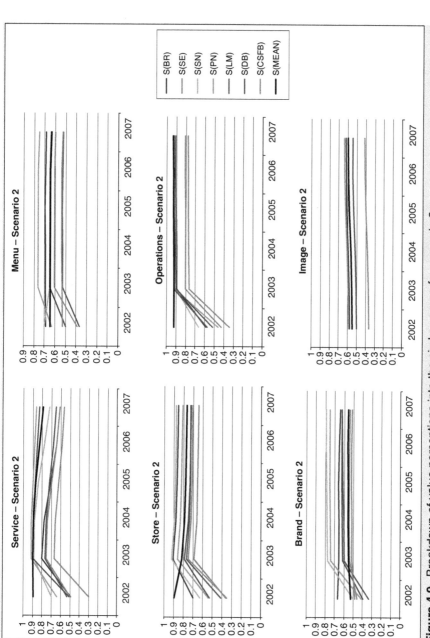

Figure 4.9. Breakdown of value perceptions into the six key areas for scenario 2.

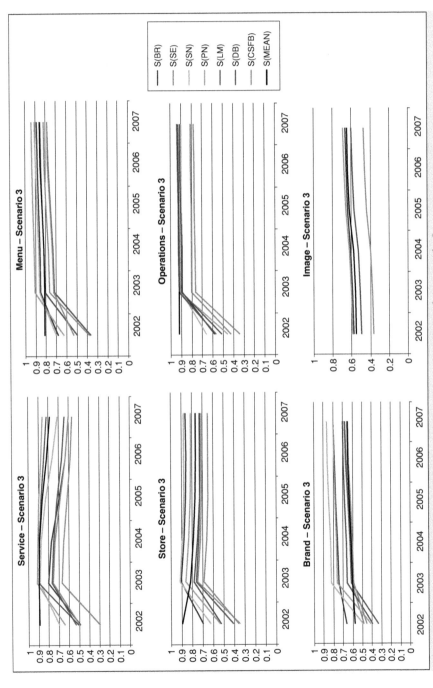

Figure 4.10. Breakdown of value perceptions into the six key areas for scenario 3.

Example 3: Strategic Issues—cont'd

As might be expected, the results show that there is a similar, although not so highly pronounced improvement in service and the qualities of the store. The lesser effect when compared to scenario 2 stems from the fact that in the latter years of the simulation, the level of discretionary funds was reduced to pay shareholders whereas it could have been used to maintain the improvement in service and store qualities. The money spent on market research seems to have been well spent, with increases also in the area of brand and menu. Operations remained neutral to slightly negative in terms of value contribution. Overall, the intangible value change for this scenario ranged from +4.66% to +7.98%, depending on the stakeholder.

As stated at the beginning of this section, the simulations carried out on the company model form a group of development options. This means that they can be compared against each other as if they were a set of development options being compared for efficacy. In particular, it allows for direct comparison of the cost of the options and the value benefits gained. This is a true calculation of value for money involving intellectual capital assets. The value for money plots for the company are shown in Figure 4.11. The plots show combinations of the financial output from the system dynamic model with the output from the CVH at the top level.

The top graph in each group shows the change in value for the scenario compared with the base run in which no action is taken. The middle graph shows the total revenue change between the baseline and the scenario in billions of dollars on the left-hand y-axis while the net saving for each scenario in millions of dollars is shown on the right-hand axis of the top graph. The lower graph of each scenario trio shows the quotient of the value change and the spending change.

It can be seen that there is an initial slight fall in value followed by a recovery. There is also a modest growth in income over the period of the simulation coupled with an overall discretionary spend saving over the period. Over the same period, as described previously, there is a very slight value change leading to a near-level value for money change. The second pair of graphs show the results for scenario 2 and show the loss of top-line benefit compared to scenario 1, stemming from the loss of brand presence. This is compounded by worse value results, leading to a negative value for money across the time period. Clearly this is a poor option. Finally, scenario 3 shows stronger top-line growth and a positive value for money change, making this the best value for money option of the three scenarios.

The basic philosophy in scenario 2 is similar to that in scenario 1. As shown in Figure 4.10, the same general profile of value change is expected although the recovery seen in scenario 1 does not occur for the reasons discussed above. This translates to a significantly worse value for money rating in the lower graph and this, coupled with the reduced financial top-line performance makes scenario 2 a poor option.

In the third scenario, shown in Figure 4.11, there is a noticeable improvement in the value of the fast-food company due to the changes made. In addition, there is a strong increase in revenue. The spending needed to achieve this is neutral for an extra year compared with the other scenarios, but then shows the strong change expected. This makes scenario 3 an acceptable scenario and the best of the three.

Continued

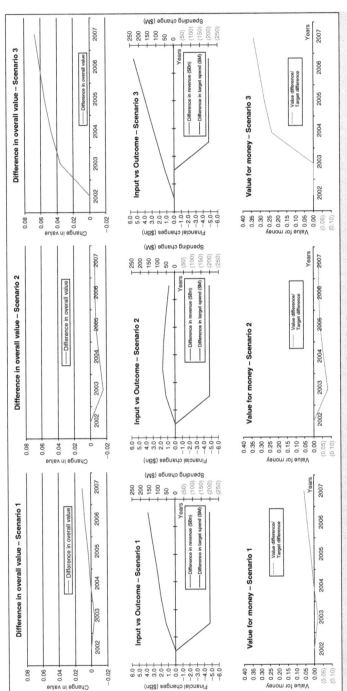

Figure 4.11. Value for money of the three scenarios compared to the base run.

Example 3: Strategic Issues—cont'd

Clearly, the CVH can differentiate between strategic options for real companies and express the results with meaningful calculations of value and value for money. In the example, the company would clearly not consider scenario 2 further due to the negative value for money outcome, and scenario 1 is probably too mild to make the meaningful improvement required. Scenario 3 would be investigated in further detail and with other changes to optimize the value for money outcome and to establish the robustness of the scenario.

BUILDING AN INTELLECTUAL CAPITAL INDEX SYSTEM

In this section, a real example of the construction of a set of indices using the intellectual capital index will be used to illustrate the general process. In contrast to the previous section, in which proper measurement was used to give auditable value and value for money results, the construction of indices is a much less demanding process and leads to results whose scope of use is small by comparison. While the CVH can deliver detailed results for use in either strategic or tactical situations, simple indices are restricted to broad-brush situations, often strategic in nature, since they lack the reliability to tackle detail problems.

Chapter 3 concluded with the construction of a number of simple plots that give managers a concise view of the importance of the deployed intellectual capital resources and how they interact with each other. This basic pool of data gives rise to the intellectual capital navigator (ICN) and the effector plots. The latter can be developed to show the robustness of the resources in use. In addition, the simple output is capable of detailed analysis to show how effectively and efficiently the company is performing and where, for the type of company being addressed, the danger areas exist.

The intellectual capital index (ICI) is an index system based on the intellectual capital navigator. Because the ICN and the underlying data are not based on the results from an actual and complete business model, but rather from the subjective strategic view of management, ICI systems cannot be used predictively in the way that the CVH can. Instead, index systems can, when correctly developed, be used with live or retrospective data to track progress toward a goal. This being said, it is possible to describe an intellectual capital resource and transformation outcome that the company would like to see, which could then be used as a target and the index system would chart the progress towards that goal. The obvious danger is that, unless some care is taken, there is no way the company can be sure that the goal is realistic or even desirable.

The first step in the process of developing an ICI is to define value. As stated in Chapters 3 and 4, no matter whether one is creating an index or a proper measurement system, the definition of the problem is critical. In the case of ICN based indices, the question of organizational boundaries is critical. It can require care over resource categorization, in that what is relational to a business unit may be organizational to the company as a whole. Similarly, monetary resources normally appear as sinks of value in a limited company if shareholders (a relational resource) are excluded, which they normally are on a business unit level. The consequences of sloppy work at this stage are possibly the creation of dangerously misleading indices.

The second step is to define carefully the desired end point for the company in the future. As stated previously, care and realism are required here. A particular danger is envisioning changes to the ICN that involve inadvertent damage or change to the business logic. For example, although changing the business logic from a value chain to a value shop is perfectly reasonable, it must be done as a clear intention and not as an inadvertent step on the way from the current position to the desired end point. Companies that have fallen into this trap usually suffer a "near death experience."

Assembling candidate measures

The starting point for candidate measures is the ICN because it shows what is influential in creating value in the company. The ICN *only* shows what is influential. This emphasis is crucial. Value may be created by the creation of a limited quantity of an influential resource or it may be created by the mass creation of something that, viewed individually, is not influential. This means that indices need careful construction and a balance between elements that track the resources (representing stocks of things) and the transformations (representing activities through which resources are created or depleted).

Activity maps become important because activities are real and measurable while the transformations of the intellectual capital navigator are, in general, not measurable directly. Measures need to be devised that follow from activities. Guidelines are:

- Devise 3 to 5 performance metrics for each of the critical activities such as perceived bottlenecks, weak points, choke points, or activities located along a critical path in the activity map.
- With the assistance of activity-based costing, devise 3 to 5 metrics for those activities that have the highest impact on delivered cost.
- With the assistance of stakeholder data, devise 3 to 5 metrics for those activities in which greatest value is added in the eyes of the stakeholder.
- Devise indicators that meet any regulatory requirements.

The list of measures may now be fairly extensive and need to be reduced to a practical level. The first test to apply is for reasonable compliance with some of the canons of measurement theory. In particular, measures should be distinct (to avoid double counting) and preference independent (to eliminate cross links in the index). Other tests that have to be applied to performance metrics are the practical ones of measurability and observability. If the index scheme is to be practical, it must use measures that are clearly meaningful with respect to the activity and can be accurately and repeatably taken.

Performance measures that remain are now aligned with the ICN of the present and the ICN of the future. The involvement of the ICN of the future is most important because the difference between these two intellectual capital navigators will show which resources and transformations have to be built up and which have to be reduced. What is often overlooked is that the efficiency with which a company creates value may be more easily improved by stopping an activity that is wasteful of resources rather than trying to improve one that is already near capacity. This is really only a tactical step, but it will mean that some indicators will be designed to show a decline—a profile often distasteful to the casual observer but important nonetheless.

It is possible to separate resource measures and transformation measures and combine them separately into resource group indices and finally combine them into an overall index. This is only possible if the performance metrics are all clearly to do either with a transformation or to do with a donor or recipient resource. If this separation is not done in the performance metrics, then it is not possible to produce independent resource and transformation indices. In this case, these resource indices must be discarded since the intellectual capital management process is based on the premise that value is created through the use of resources, not through the ownership of the resources (especially noting that not all, or indeed many, intangible resources will be actually owned by the

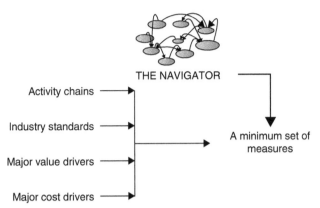

THE NAVIGATOR

Activity chains ⟶

Industry standards ⟶

Major value drivers ⟶   A minimum set of
                                         measures

Major cost drivers ⟶

Figure 4.12. The input for Selecting appropriate Intellectual Capital Index metrics.

organization). In addition, at the highest level filtration of the ICN—that is, the simplest ICN that shows only the key transformations—the performance metrics can be used to produce a single performance index. The step-wise logic is illustrated in Figure 4.12–4.15.

The four inputs on the left in Figure 4.12 are the usual obvious sources of metrics but the ICN with its insight into what is strategically significant is a key determinant of metrics.

Metrics must be minimal, as too many lead to accusations of micro-management, cause a large overhead and irritate those being measured. Metrics must be appropriate as the wrong metrics instil unwanted behaviours. It is in the nature of people to try to improve performance against metrics but if the metrics are wrong, the important things go unattended and the unimportant (and possibly counterproductive things) are "improved".

Figure 4.13 shows examples of transformation measures. Transformation-orientated metrics are the most important since value is created when resources are used (transformed) rather than through the mere fact of their ownership.

Using combinatorial mathematics (see below), metrics can be combined in a logical way to provide indices that can be tracked over time.

As intimated earlier, it is wholly wrong to combine metrics because, for example, two of them happened to be sub-resources of human capital. The key to determining which metrics are combined is to follow the transformation pathways in the ICN. In this way, single strands leading to cash or some other value sink are calculated. Note that there will often

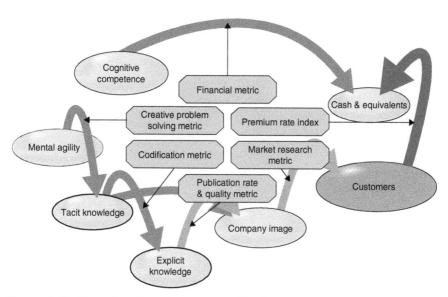

Figure 4.13. Examples of metrics suggested by the navigator.

be more than one route to the end which is knowledge intensive. For example, sales staff may be the ultimate step in the transformation of a product into cash while the administrative (behaviours) leading to a better customer experience may also contribute but in an unrelated way, it should therefore be considered separately. This logic is illustrated in Figure 4.14.

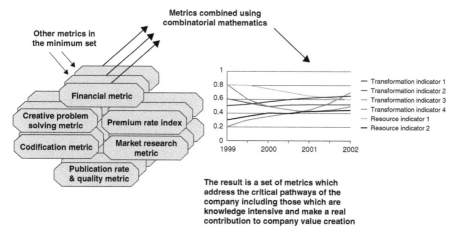

Figure 4.14. Constructing an Intellectual Capital Index metrics.

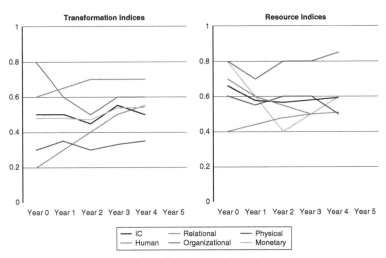

Figure 4.15. Examples of Intellectual Capital Indices.

Figure 4.15 illustrates two plots of intellectual capital indicators produced using the ICI and plotted over 5 years. The plots cover the transformation and resource measures. In each plot, the development of the level 1 resource categories are plotted along with an overall index of intellectual capital.

As the focus and means of operation of the company changes, such as an investment in e-business, changes would be expected in the relative balance of IC resource categories. The ICI allows these to be followed along with the more traditional and ever-present drive for improved performance.

Metrics can be assigned to the transformations of the intellectual capital navigator and also to the resources if the distinction made above has been adhered to. There should not be more than about three metrics per transformation or resource. Metrics for individual transformations or resources are combined. This is done using an appropriate combination algorithm, which is usually a simple weighted mean. The general form is shown in Figure 4.16.

Armed with reliable measures for resources and the transformations between them, combinations can be produced to meet the current need. There are several purposes for which different combinations are used. In increasing levels of complexity, a typical set would be:

1. Resource or transformation metrics which are used as indicators as they are

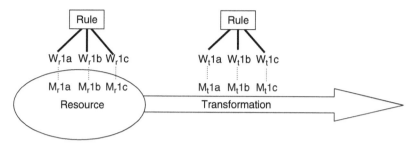

Figure 4.16. Resource and transformation combinations.

2. Combinations of resource metrics into a level 1 figure which can be benchmarked internally or externally
3. Combinations of resource and transformation metrics on critical transformations which have either to be built up or reduced
4. Combinations of resource and transformation metrics on extended and critical value creation pathways in the company

The first type are not really combinations at all and so are the simplest possible indicators. Their only disadvantages, but they are big ones, are that they have a "so what" factor and that they still do not reflect the important activities that are always more complicated than the simplicity of these indicators can accommodate.

Combinations of the second type are also simple since all they require is that the metrics for resources in a group are weighted according to their importance and combined using an additive algorithm. No further effort is needed. They suffer from the same disadvantages as indices of the first type, and although they have resulted in a set of just five numbers to follow, detail has been lost that may be important.

The third type of combination gives an intellectual capital perspective and allows the monitoring of the changes to critical resources and their transformations. This means that the mindset is definitely an intellectual capital one with trust being placed in the intellectual capital navigator with the activities that underlie the transformations submerged (out of view). To calculate the index, the best course of action is to combine the indicators for the connecting transformation and resources at the beginning and end of the transformation. If the assumptions are made that both the transformation and the starting resource have to score well for generation of the finishing resource to be effective and that if either the starting resource or the transformation should perform very badly then the whole fails, then the combination is nonadditive. In these cases, a weighted multiplicative algorithm is used.

Key Points in Chapter 4

- To be able to measure and value complex objects such as businesses that consist of both tangible and intangible attributes, you have to accept the assumption of axiology (value theory) that everything can be measured so long as the object to be measured is meticulously defined and the stakeholders are identified (that is, from whose perspective the measurement should be made).
- Measurement of intellectual capital is mainly done for two reasons: internal performance measurement or external reporting. In the latter case, the results have to be reliable and auditable and they have to satisfy the information needs of external stakeholders.
- There is a clear process to follow in order to build a proper measurement system that follows the foundations of measurement theory and fulfills a set of requirements.
- To introduce a single theory-compliant measurement system that measures what really matters in a company and provides the managers with the information they really need usually means reduced administration costs, increased relevance, and enhanced focus.
- There is an important distinction between measures and indicators. *Measures* are the results of rigorous measurement and are suitable when the output needs to be completely reliable. *Indicators* are more subjective assessments which are suitable for internal performance tracking locally.
- A large number of initiatives on valuation of intellectual capital have been taken over the past years. They can be divided into direct intellectual capital methods, market capitalization methods, return on assets methods, and scorecard methods. The CVH methodology is the only one to date that fully complies with the requirements of a valid proper measurement system.
- The ICI index is a system of indicators that can be used when the requirements on the reliability and precision of the output is limited, and the focus is on trends and rough decision support for management.

The fourth type of combination is the most complex but most the useful since if follows the key value-creating processes of the company from a reasonable starting point to a conclusion. To construct such an index, the general process described for the third type is followed, except that the whole process is extended by the undoubted complexity of the value-creating pathways. Where the pathway is linear, then a multiplicative algorithm is used such that if one link in the chain fails then the whole chain fails. Where there are branches in the pathway with secondary resources contributing through branches, then a weighed additive algorithm is used.

The result is a complex algorithm that is calculated only once; thereafter, only data are required, with the index being produced as a result. This is then followed over time and can be compared with an "ideal" trajectory based on the starting and finishing intellectual capital navigators.

ENDNOTES

1. *Measuring and Reporting Intellectual Capital: Experience, Issues and Prospects* (1999), Amsterdam: OECD.
2. C. Eustace (2000), *The Intangible Economy: Impact and Policy Issues*, EU.
3. L. Turner (2001), A speech entitled "The Times, they are a-changing," SEC.
4. Financial Accounting Standards Board, 2001, FAS141 – Business Combinations, available at: www.fasb.org
5. Financial Accounting Standards Board, 2001, FAS142 – Goodwill and Other Intangible Assets, available at: www.fasb.org.
6. ICAEW library reading list on intangibles (2004), available at: http://www.icaew.co.uk/.
7. C. Ittner and D. Larcker (2003), "Coming up short on nonfinancial performance measurement (HBR OnPoint Enhanced Edition)," *Harvard Business Review*, 89–95
8. R. Frondizi (1971), *What is Value*, La Salle, Ill.: Open Court Publishing.
9. N. Rescher (1969), *Introduction to Value Theory*, Eaglewood Cliffs: Prentice Hall.
10. B. Agle, R. Mitchell, and J. Sonnenfield (1999), "What matters to CEOs? An investigation into stakeholder attributes and salience, corporate performance and CEO values," *Academy of Management Journal*, 42(5), 507–525.
11. D. Garvin (1993) In: "Building a learning organization," *Harvard Business Review*, 71(4), 78–91.
12. V. Petersen (2000), "Common chairs and chimerical measures, CREDO working paper," Aarhus, Denmark. Also available at: http://www.credo.asb.dk/pdf/CommonChairs.pdf.
13. H. Simon (1960), *The New Science of Management Decision*, New York: Harper & Row.
14. E. Conklin and W. Weil (2000), "Wicked problems: naming the pain in organisations," Group Decisions Support Systems Inc. Working Paper.
15. J. Chatzkel (2003), "The collapse of enron and the role of intellectual captial," *Journal of Intellectual Capital* 14(2), 127–143.
16. For a biography of Eudoxus, see *Encyclopaedia Britannica*. A useful review can be found at: http://www-groups.dcs.st-and.ac.uk/~history/Mathematicians/Eudoxus.html
17. H. Helmholtz (1887), "Zahlen und Messen," in: *Philosophische Aufsatze*, Leipzig: Fues's Verlag, 17–52. Translated by C.L.Bryan (1930), *Counting and Measuring*, Princeton, NJ: Van Nostrand.
18. S.S. Stevens (1946), "On the theory of scales of measurement," *Science*, 103.
19. D. Scott and P. Suppes (1958), "Foundational aspects of theories of measurement," *Journal of Symbolic Logic*, 23(2), 113–128.
20. D. Krantz, R. Luce, P. Suppes, and A. Tversky (1971), *Foundations of Measurement, Vol 1: Additive & Polynomial Representations* (1971), *Vol 2: Geometrical, Threshold & Probabilistic Representations* (1989), *Vol 3: Representation, Axiomatization & Invariance* (1990), New York: Academic Press.
21. R. Keeney, H. Raiffa, and R. Meyer (1993), *Decisions with Multiple Objectives: Preferences and Value Trade-Offs*, Cambridge: Cambridge University Press.
22. E. Penrose (1959), *The Theory of Growth of the Firm*, Oxford: Blackwell.

23. E. Chamberlin (1933), *The Theory of Monopolistic Competition*, Cambridge, Mass.: Harvard University Press.
24. J. Robinson (1933), *The Economics of Imperfect Competition*, London: MacMillan Press.
25. L. Edvinsson, M. Malone (1997), *Intellectual Capital: Realizing Your Company's True Value by Finding its Hidden Brainpower*, HarperCollins Publishers.
26. In A. Justice (1707), "A general treatise of monies and exchanges," London- it is stated, "Money in general is divided into two sorts, imaginary and real."
27. See, for example, P. Lauzel and A. Cibert (1962), *Des Ratios au Tableau de Bord*, 2nd Ed., Paris: Enterprise Moderne D'Editions.
28. A. Neely, M. Kennerley, and V. Martinez (2004), *Does the Balanced Scorecard Work: An Empirical Investigation*, Cranfield, Centre for Business Performance, Cranfield School of Management.
29. C. Eustace (Ed.) (2003), *The PRISM Report 2003: Research Findings and Policy Recommendations*, EU(IST).
30. *MERITUM: Guidelines for Managing and Reporting on* Intangibles (Intellectual Capital Report) (2004), EU(TSER).
31. D. Luthy (1998), *Intellectual Capital and its Measurement*, Proceedings of the Asian Pacific Interdisciplinary Research in Accounting Conference (APIRA), Osaka, Japan.
32. M. Williams (2000), "Is a company's intellectual capital performance and intellectual capital disclosure practices related? Evidence from publicly listed companies from the FTSE 100," Paper presented at McMasters Intellectual Capital Conference, Jan 2001, Hamilton Ontario.
33. S. Pike and G. Roos (2004), "Mathematics and modern business management," *Journal of Intellectual Capital*, 5(2), 243–256.
34. P. M'Pherson and S. Pike (2001), "Accounting, empirical measurement and intellectual capital," *Journal of Intellectual Capital,* 2(3), 246–260.
35. P.K. M'Pherson S. Pike, and G. Roos (Oct 2001), "Strategic analysis adapted for IC networks and e-business networks," presented at the Strategic Management Society (SMS) 21st Annual International Conference, San Francisco, California.
36. P.K. M'Pherson and S. Pike (2001), "RACE for Faster, Better, Value," INCOSE 2001, Melbourne, Australia.
37. S. Pike and G. Roos (Jan 2001), "Measuring and decision support in the knowledge society," presented at The 4th World Congress on Intellectual Capital, 22nd McMaster Business Conference, 2nd World Conference on E-Commerce, Hamilton, Canada.
38. Table 4.3 is based on the table in Pike, S. and G. Roos "Mathematics and Modern Business Management", Invited Paper for the Performance Management Association Symposium, INSEAD, July 28-29, 2003, Modified paper presented at the Cranfield Centre for Business Performance PMA IC 2003 SYMPOSIUM, October 1st, 2003 and in further modified form at 25th McMaster World Congress Managing Intellectual Capital, Hamilton, Ontario, Canada, January 14–16, 2004 and published in the Journal of Intellectual Capital, Vol. 5, No.2, 2004. pp. 243–256.
39. Stewart, T., (1997), Intellectual Capital: The New Wealth of Organisations, Doubleday, New York.
40. Johansson, U., (1997), A model illustration and implications, Journal of Human Resource, Costing and Accounting, Vol. 2, No.1.
41. Luthy, D.H., (1998), Intellectual Capital and its Measurement, Proceedings of the Asian Pacific Interdisciplinary Research in Accounting Conference (APIRA), Osaka, Japan.
42. Lev, B., (1999), Seeing is Believing - A Better Approach To Estimating Knowledge Capital, CFO magazine, April 2000.

43. Pulic, A., (2000), An Accounting Tool for IC Management. Available online: <http://www.measuring-ip.at/Papers/ham99txt.htm>
44. Nash, H., (1998), Accounting for the Future: A Disciplined Approach to Value-Added Accounting, (in draft).
45. Standfield., K, (1998), Extending the Intellectual Capital Framework. Available at: http://www.knowcorp.com/article075.htm.
46. Brooking, A., (1996), Intellectual Capital: Core Assets for the Third Millennium Enterprise, Thomson Business Press, London, United Kingdom.
47. Bontis, N., (2000), Assessing Knowledge assets: A review of the models used to measure intellectual capital. Working paper, Queen's Management Research Centre for Knowledge-Based Enterprises.
48. Andriessen, D., Tiessen, R., (2000), Weightless Weight - Find your Real Value in a Future of Intangible Assets. Pearson Education, London.
49. Sullivan, P., (2000), Value-driven Intellectual Capital: How to convert intangible corporate assets into market value. Wiley.
50. Anderson, R. and McLean, R., 2000, Total Value Creation, CR-ROM available from CICA (Canadian Institute of Chartered Accountants).
51. Fitz-Enz. J., (1994), How to Measure Human resource Management. McGraw-Hill.
52. Edvinsson, L., Malone, M., (1997), Intellectual Capital: Realizing your Company's True Value by Finding Its Hidden Brainpower, Harper Business, New York, New York.
53. Lev, B., (2002), Intangibles: Management, Measurement and Reporting, Brookings Institution, Washington.
54. Sveiby, K., (1997) The New Organizational Wealth: Managing and Measuring Knowledge Based Assets, Berrett Koehler, San Francisco.
55. Roos, J., Roos, G., Dragonetti, N., Edvinsson, L., (1997), Intellectual Capital: Navigating in the New Business Landscape. Macmillan.
56. Ittner, C., Kalafut, P., Larcker, D., Sean Love, S., Low, J., Park, J., Siesfeld, T., Zito, S., (2000), Measuring the Future: Value Creation Index, Available at: <http://www.ca. cgey.com/news/invisible_advantage_mediakit/vci.pdf>
57. Kaplan, R., Norton, D., (1996), The Balanced Scorecard: Translating Strategy into Action, Harvard Business School Press.
58. T. Saaty (1980), *The Analytic Hierarchy Process*, New York: McGraw Hill.
59. D. von Winterfeldt and W. Edwards (1986), *Decision Analysis and Behavioural Research*, New York: Cambridge University Press.
60. J. Hammond, R. Keeney, and H. Raiffa (1999), *Choices: A Practical Guide to Making Better Decisions*, Boston: Harvard Business School Press.
61. W. Edwards and F. Barton (1994), "SMARTS and SMARTER: improved simple method for multi-attribute utility measurement," *Organisational Behaviour and Human Decision Processes*, 60, 306–325.
62. J. Yao (2002), "Applications of a new bar and range procedure and swing weighting procedure in predicting best picture award," unpublished but available at: http://www.psych.upenn.edu/~jyao/research.pdf.
63. A. Salo and R. Hämäläinen (1992), "Preference assessment by imprecise ratio statements," *Operations Research,* 40(6), 1053–1060.
64. Vensim is marketed by Ventana Systems Inc., Harvard, Mass. See: http://www. vensim.com

5

Reporting on intellectual capital

Having looked at what intellectual capital is, why it is important, and how to analyze, manage, and measure it, we have now come to the inevitable issue of disclosure. As described in Chapter 1, all listed firms ultimately have an interest in reporting on *all* their value-creating resources, including intellectual capital resources, since they do have an impact on share price performance and it is desirable to avoid information asymmetry to the greatest extent possible. Leaders of these listed companies can only ask to truly understand the drivers of future value and how to manage these for the desired effect on the share price. This is even more important for firms that operate as either value shops or value networks (e.g., eBay) and therefore do not base their competitive advantage on monetary or physical resources. However, not only is there a growing need for firms to understand and disclose intellectual capital from a management point of view, but there is also increasing pressure from authorities and pressure groups, the Sarbanes-Oxley Act currently being the most influential for listed firms. This chapter sets out to more closely examine the issue of disclosure, presenting some of the initiatives taken to provide assistance for firms in achieving high quality disclosure of intellectual capital.

The area of intellectual capital disclosure is still very much in an immature phase where a lot of suggestions for solutions are presented from scholars, practitioners, authorities, and other influential bodies. This chapter hence describes the situation as the authors see it at the time of writing (early 2005). The outline of possible methods to use is therefore not to be considered as comprehensive but as a sample of approaches developed that have had some impact on the area of disclosure of intellectual capital.

WHY REPORT ON INTELLECTUAL CAPITAL?

As discussed in Chapter 1, the nature of the U.S. economy and the economy of the Western world in general have clearly changed. Chapter 1 presented a number of proofs that the economy of today to a great extent relies on intangible elements and primarily leverages intellectual capital resources for value creation. Firms are not only relying to a greater extent on different resources than they used to (i.e., intellectual capital resources such as human, organizational, and relational resources) rather than traditional resources (monetary and physical), but they also largely rely on business logics that are different from the conventional value chain logic.

A major survey of the issues involved in the disclosure of company information on intellectual capital to the investment community was carried out in 1999 (Rylander et al., 1999)[1]. The principal issues at the time were:

- The information asymmetry gap is growing as the proportion of company value attributable to intangible assets increases.
- Long-term information, particularly on strategic intent and execution, was lacking from company reporting but was considered to be of particular importance to external stakeholders, especially the investors.
- Standards and comparability relating to the disclosure of intellectual capital would remain a major issue.
- Value creation models could provide information to complement traditional reporting required by law.

Since the publication of that report in 1999, there have been a number of developments along the lines foreshadowed in the paper. However, there have been neither solutions nor concrete proposals. Hence, the problem remains the same.

A recent survey executed by a large international consulting[2] firm shows that 94% of managers in the United States and Europe think that it is important to understand and manage intangibles and intellectual capital, and 50% of them claim that it is among the top three challenges facing managers (13% state that it is the most important issue facing management). The reason stated was that managers who are good at managing intangibles and intellectual capital will be rewarded with higher shareholder value. Simultaneously, 49% of the managers say that they view intangibles and intellectual capital as the most important source for long-term value creation for owners and other stakeholders. Finally, 48% believe that the stock market rewards firms that invest in intangibles and intellectual capital. All these numbers pointing at how important intellectual capital is need to be contrasted with the alarming fact that 95% of managers claim not to have a robust system for measuring these intangibles and intellectual capital and a third say that they have no system at all for this purpose.

As shown in Chapter 1, firms that invest in and manage intellectual capital will reap the rewards in the form of better value creation, whether expressed as total shareholder returns or increased stakeholder commitment. The problem is that when firms embark on investing in intellectual capital, traditional accounting based disclosure models can no longer capture and track success or failure in the same way as before. These models were developed for dealing with monetary and physical resources and the disclosure of these is now standardized enough for there to be a fairly general understanding of how to read and interpret financial reports such as annual reports. Again, these traditional models were developed to capture monetary and physical resources in a value chain–world based on historic events and are therefore not future driven. Thus, they work well for establishing a basis for managing the current value component of a firm's share price, but when it comes to capturing the future value component of the same firm's share price they do not apply. This also explains why the intellectual capital approach presented in this book is particularly relevant if the *current* value component of the firm's share price is low, while the existing or potential *future* value component of the firm's share price is high.

Disclosure is about the mechanisms of information transfer to outside stakeholders and the extent to which this can take place without compromising the security and the competitive position of the company. There is a growing body of evidence[3] that careful disclosure of information, even strategically sensitive information concerning research and development intentions, is beneficial in terms of market value.

FINANCIAL VERSUS IC REPORTING

The IC perspective is about value creation, thus IC disclosure must take a form that enables reporting on value creation. This may seem obvious, but the standard form of corporate reporting of today, namely financial accounting, only measures *value realization*. The challenge then lies in creating a way to measure and report on value creation (i.e., on value that is potentially available for realization). Disclosure of IC does not replace traditional reporting but it does add a new and important dimension to it (see Figure 5.1).

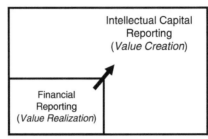

Figure 5.1. Financial reporting and the new dimension of IC reporting.[1]

Then again, financial reporting has some self-evident advantages. Embedded in this standard is 120 years of experience of modern accounting, building on a 500-year-old bookkeeping tradition. The input numbers are based on third-party transactions, and financial accounting provides a universal language. Finally, since practically all private sector firms are obliged to use this standard, both management and stakeholders are used to this type of data.

As for IC reporting, there is still no standard and the business community has *at most* 15 years of experience of managing and reporting IC, including the pioneers. The input numbers are based on indicators with varying reliability and relevance, and there is no standardized common language (e.g., there is no formal consensus on what organizational capital is). Finally, fewer than 1% of private sector firms have experience from IC reporting. Nevertheless, there are a number of clear benefits of IC reporting. It can, for instance, address and to some extent resolve the following problems associated with traditional disclosure:

- **The risks of insider trading:** Information asymmetries are not as strong in firms that depend more on tangible, observable assets. The higher the reliance on esoteric know-how for competitiveness, the more difficult it becomes for the average outside investor to assess the true value of IC and the larger the gains to be made by insiders from this information asymmetry.
- **Higher costs of capital:** Companies with more intangible and fewer tangible assets may find it harder to raise capital than companies with more tangible assets, which investors or bankers may regard as security.
- **Overvaluation of intangibles leading to misallocation of capital:** Unregulated disclosure of information about intangible assets makes it possible for companies to manipulate perceptions of their value, leading investors to overvalue them.

- **Dulled incentives for knowledge workers and entrepreneurs:** Better information about the value of people and their ideas would reduce the information asymmetry between managers and workers, which managers in theory can exploit to their advantage.
- **Increased volatility:** Inadequate disclosure concerning the quality of intangible assets may feed volatility and uncertainty in capital markets.

There are further incentives specific to institutional investors with IC reporting. Increased transparency and lower information distortions will allow fund managers to reconcile theory and practice to construct portfolios with the defined ideal risk/return tradeoff and diversification risk reduction benefits. It also has the potential to allow the establishment of a formalized connection between:

- The **past** (past financial performance, financial policy, accounting changes, corporate governance history, management experience and track record);
- The **present** (current results, strategic changes, communication skills); and
- The **future** (management vision and promises, perception of risks and challenges, match between management quality and contingencies)

Figure 5.2 sets out the financial indicators of most and least importance to investors respectively, as identified in a classic study from 1997.

The 10 most valued non-financial indicators, beginning with the most valued indicator	The 10 least valued non-financial indicators, beginning with the least valued indicator
1. execution of corporate strategy	1. compensation ratios
2. management credibility	2. use of employee teams
3. quality of corporate strategy	3. environmental and social policies
4. innovation	4. process quality awards
5. ability to attract employees	5. product quality awards
6. market share	6. quality of published materials
7. management experience	7. quality of customer service departments
8. quality of compensation policies	8. number of customer complaints
9. research leadership	9. experience of investor relations personnel
10. quality of processes	10. employee turnover rates

Figure 5.2. What investors view as important.[4]

As for management, the incentives lie in creating transparency about the use of private and public funds and explaining the achievements of research, for example, and their benefits to stakeholders. Disclosure of IC also allows for illustrating the development of the intangible assets of the company and revealing leverage effects and externalities. Moreover, it provides a vehicle for communicating organizational values and demonstrating their competitiveness. The ultimate benefit is that the company gets valued at a more accurate level than is possible without the disclosure of the performance of intangible assets.

The next section looks at the development around disclosure of nonfinancial information in the United States and initiatives taken in Europe.

DEVELOPMENTS IN THE UNITED STATES

One important driver of how firms deal with the reporting of both tangible and intangible asset information is the regulatory environment. Much of what firms report to the external world is required by regulation, and it is unlikely that major movements toward intangibles reporting will take place without regulatory action. That is, however, not to say that going down the regulatory route is the best way to proceed within this field (see the last section of this chapter, Recommended Guidelines for the Future). This section looks at regulatory developments in the United States.

Sarbanes-Oxley and the new regulatory environment[5]

For U.S. firms and those reporting in the United States, the U.S. Sarbanes-Oxley Act of 2002 (SOX) is the single most important external influence on financial and nonfinancial reporting. The drafting of this act came as a consequence of numerous corporate scandals, including Enron, Tyco, Global Crossing, and WorldCom. SOX essentially amends the U.S. Securities Exchange Act of 1934, tightening up rules on disclosure, specifically prohibiting certain acts and conflicts of interest, establishing a new level of governance for public accounting firms, and making CEOs and CFOs (and other officers and board members) criminally liable for fraudulent and misleading statements within their public financial filings. Severe penalties are included for willful violation. SOX applies to publicly traded companies in the United States, including each of their divisions and all of their wholly owned subsidiaries, and any non-U.S. public multinational company whose securities are registered with the U.S. Securities and Exchange Commission (SEC).

Sarbanes-Oxley consists of eleven Titles, and in simple terms, the objectives of SOX include:

1. Increasing the accountability of management of public companies
2. Improving corporate governance
3. Increasing the oversight of public accounting firms
4. Restoring investor confidence in capital markets

The SOX act largely focuses on corporate governance and controllability of accounts, and there is little that explicitly requires a formalized disclosure of intangibles. There is, however, Section 408, which provides power to the SEC to review disclosures made by issuers (including Form 10-K) for the purpose of scheduling reviews, among other factors such as:

1. Issuers that have issued material restatements of financial results
2. Issuers that experience significant volatility in their stock price as compared to other issuers
3. Issuers with the largest market capitalization
4. Emerging companies with disparities in price to earning ratios
5. Issuers whose operations significantly affect any material sector of the economy
6. Any other factors the Commission may consider relevant

Section 408 therefore provides that the SEC may single out for further examination the largest companies with the highest levels of performance and the highest degree of intangible assets, since those are likely to be the firms with the highest relative price to earnings (P/E) ratios.

Section 409 requires issuers to disclose to the public, on an urgent basis, information on material changes in their financial condition or operations. These disclosures are to be presented in terms that are easy to understand and supported by trend and qualitative information, and graphic presentations, as appropriate. This begins to suggest a requirement for reporting on intellectual capital resources (assets and capabilities), though the language is too broad for anyone yet to understand its full implications.

In general, it is fair to speculate that many firms in the United States have not yet understood the significance of Sarbanes-Oxley and its implications for their management information systems. Many do not yet comprehend the requirements for identifying the processes that have an impact on their financial statements, the key issues and risks associated with and embedded in these processes, and the degree of documentation creation and retention. Nor have the extended responsibilities for operational reporting been picked up on. It is likely to be several years before there is sufficient clarity on these issues. There is little doubt that new horizons in financial and nonfinancial reporting are opening up in the United States, but to date there is little clarity about how to move forward successfully.

Financial Accounting Standards Board

In parallel with the Sarbanes-Oxley Act, other regulatory bodies have been pressing and moving toward the mandatory disclosure of certain elements of intangible resources and the recording of elements of goodwill in mergers and acquisition. The most important of them are FAS 141 and 142, stipulated by the Financial Accounting Standards Board (FASB).[6] FASB works to put in place and enhance standards of financial accounting and reporting for the guidance and education of the public, including issuers, auditors, and users of financial information. The organization is recognized as authoritative by the Securities and Exchange Commission.

FAS 141 concerns the reporting of intangibles in business combinations, triggered by the fact that intangible assets were already becoming an increasingly important economic resource for many companies and hence an increasing proportion of the assets acquired in many mergers and acquisitions. There are two basic methods to use for this purpose: the purchase method and the pooling method. The first recognizes all intangible assets acquired in a business combination (either separately or as goodwill), whereas the latter only recognizes those intangibles previously recorded by the acquired entity. Two different methods made it difficult for analysts to make comparisons, which is why the standard was established that only the purchase method should be used in business combinations.

Closely linked to FAS 141 is FAS 142, which is about "Goodwill and Other Intangible Assets." This statement deals with how to account for intangible assets that are acquired individually or with a group of other assets (excluding those acquired in a business combination). It also addresses how goodwill and other intangible assets should be accounted for after they have been initially recognized in the financial statements. It is important to remember that the definition of intangible assets in the financial accounting community is rather different from the wider notion of intellectual capital resources used in this book (see Chapter 1).

Other initiatives

One initiative for intangible assets measurement, monitoring, and reporting was taken jointly by the Brookings Institution and the Stern School of Business with Baruch Lev as the motor behind it. It set out to initiate a national discussion in the United States about better ways of measuring, monitoring, and reporting on critical intangible sources of wealth. It carried out a literature study to establish what was already known within these areas with regards to academia, practice, and policy, and finally presented a number of recommendations for policy changes. The result of this project is a book published by the Brookings Institution.[7]

A U.K. initiative was taken by CEST (Centre for Exploitation of Science and Technology) in 2000. It took a pragmatic approach to the problem of information asymmetry in a collaborative project, Valuing the New Intangibles,[8] with the goal of understanding the field of disclosure and the needs of the external and company communities. CEST adopted the approach of running two complementary and alternating forums, one engaging company representatives and the other engaging City of London investors. As with the other initiatives, the key areas where more and reliable information is required are the long-term prospects and intentions of the company.

In Europe, the EU-project PRISM aimed at creating a coherent pan-European community of practice out of the fragmented academic and other interest groups currently working on issues relating to business intangibles. The PRISM action group assembled academics and practitioners from all over Europe, facilitating more work and research in the area of IC management and disclosure. In the PRISM final report on accounting and financial reporting[9] a proposal for a framework for convergence is presented. The report stresses that before defining a regulatory framework a number of issues have to be discussed, especially the problem of drawing the boundaries between intangibles that can be disclosed and those that cannot: trade secrets have to remain secret, even if they might constitute key intangible assets for the firm, because otherwise the firm would divulge too much to its competitors. Other issues include industry-specific versus general reporting, status versus flow, absolute versus relative measures, and quantitative versus narrative reporting. The framework proposed is based on nine principles (or postulates), as follows:

1. Position
2. Evolution
3. Cost
4. Tactility
5. Results
6. Category
7. Sustainability

8. Conservatism

9. Materiality

Given these nine principles, PRISM suggests that two intangibles reports could be appropriate: the Status and Flow Report, and the Sustainability Report.

APPROACHES TO DISCLOSING INTELLECTUAL CAPITAL

Initiatives on how to report on intellectual capital have come from various academics, practitioners, authorities, and interest groups. In general, initiatives for solutions—especially as related to intellectual capital rather than intangibles—have tended to come from Europe rather than from the United States. This section presents a sample of approaches that have earned a place in the discourse on disclosure of intellectual capital.

The MERITUM project[10]

MERITUM (measuring intangibles to understand and improve innovation management) was a joint research project made up of nine research groups from six European countries (France, Spain, Norway, Denmark, Finland, and Sweden) funded by the EU through the TSER Program. The project commenced as a consequence of an OECD initiative in 1996.[11] The project was executed in the period 1998–2001. The research was premised on the assumption that firms and organizations were facing important changes linked to nonfinancial resources, and especially knowledge. These changes would generate substantial challenges since it is difficult to define, measure, and report these nonfinancial resources. Another assumption underpinning the project was that there was a need to develop a common framework for defining and classifying nonfinancial resources and guidelines for measuring, managing, and reporting these resources. The researchers who took part in the project were interested in understanding how different firms managed and controlled their nonfinancial resources and how they could produce a set of guidelines for management and reporting.

The project was divided into four work streams[12]:

1. **Classification of intangibles[13]:** Defining and classifying concepts such as nonfinancial resources and intellectual capital. At the time of the project there was no common classification of intellectual capital. There existed almost as many definitions as there were authors writing about the topic, even though many components were common

between them. A classification was proposed that divided intellectual capital into human capital, structural capital, and relational capital. This was basically a compromise between the classification proposed by Leif Edvinsson in Skandia[14] (human capital and structural capital) and Roos and Roos in their writings[15,16,17] (human capital, organizational capital, and relational capital).

2. **Management control:** Investigating how management controlled nonfinancial resources. One of the most important findings was the difference between the different countries when it came to experience, measurement, disclosure, and management of intellectual capital. It was relatively easy to find firms with experience in Denmark and Sweden but not in Spain and France. Another important conclusion was the identified relationship between measurement and reporting on the one hand and management on the other. It turned out that measurement of intellectual capital without clear guidelines for management of intellectual capital was a waste of time.

3. **Capital market study:** This work stream investigated the consequences for the capital markets of poor information relating to the nonfinancial resources of firms. The research supported the claim that intellectual capital is highly relevant for financial markets. Based on econometric analysis, it was shown that both R&D and qualitative human capital was related to the value of the firm.

4. **Drafting and testing guidelines:** The last of the MERITUM work streams produced a suggestion for guidelines relating to managing and reporting intellectual capital. The proposal was based on the findings from the three preceding work streams and was refined through a Delphi process involving representatives for European firms, politicians auditing firms, employee organizations, and so forth. The general view was that the guidelines were basically in order but needed some further development. There were two concrete suggestions:

- A suggestion for phases a firm needs to go through when developing a management system for intellectual capital (formulate a vision, identify critical components of intellectual capital, measure the critical components)
- A suggestion for a set of supporting processes that are important to ensure that the measurement and reporting turns into action by management.

The final deliverable of the MERITUM project was a reporting model for intellectual capital. The MERITUM Guidelines[18] recommend that the following information should be included in such a report:

- The firm's vision
- A summary of the intangibles of the firm and the firm's activities
- A set of indicators

The Danish disclosure initiative[19]

Denmark was the first country to impose the requirement that firms provide a disclosure statement for intellectual capital in addition to all other regulatory disclosures. The Danish Financial Statements Act that came into force in 2003 requires two documents in addition to the annual report. One is a description of the firm's intellectual capital, should these resources be of importance to the firm's future value creation. The other is a description of the firm's environmental impact and its objectives for reduction/prevention of negative environmental impacts (see also the section on the Triple Bottom Line).

The Danish initiative for disclosure of intangibles is made up of four elements that together are intended to provide a transparent picture of the firm's business. These elements link the customer of the firm's offerings to the firm's need for knowledge resources. This includes both a mapping of the need for knowledge management and a set of indicators that are used for identification, measurement, and tracking of interventions.

The first element is known as a knowledge narrative. It expresses the firm's intent of improving the value received by a user/customer from the firm's offerings. This value can be called user value. In order for this value to be created, the firm is assumed to need a set of knowledge resources. The essence in this disclosure document is that the firm identifies the knowledge resources needed for generating the user value that the firm wants to generate. As understood from the name, this is a narrative that links the firm's resources with the customer. In this way the knowledge narrative is used to illustrate how the firm's knowledge is used to provide the customer with improvements.

Summary of the questions to answer in the knowledge narrative:

- What is the firm offering?
- In what way is the firm making a difference to the customer?
- Which knowledge resources are necessary for providing the customer offering?
- How are the knowledge resources and the user value interlinked?

The second element is a set of management challenges that indicate which knowledge resources need to be enhanced, either through internal development or external acquisition. This could include improved cooperation with customers who are early adopters or development of further competence in a given area. These types of management challenges are assumed not to change very rapidly and are closely linked to the knowledge narrative and the role played by the individual knowledge resources within the firm. The starting point of the management challenges is to make use of the existing knowledge resources, followed by the identification of needs that require the development of knowledge resources that are currently not present in the firm.

Summary of the questions to answer in the management challenges:

- What existing knowledge resources are to be strengthened?
- What new knowledge resources are needed?

The third element is a set of activities or interventions that should be initiated to address the management challenges. The activities are primarily about how to interconnect, develop, and acquire the necessary knowledge resources and about how to trace the scope and effect of these activities. This could include activities such as invest in IT, employ more development engineers, commence education in the firm's processes, or increase the social activities to enhance employee satisfaction. The activities have primarily a short time horizon. It is assumed that the portfolio of activities is to be observed from year to year even though an individual activity can extend beyond 12 months. Interventions are concrete actions under the responsibility of identified actors.

Summary of the questions to answer in the activity statement:

- What activities are to be initiated?
- What activities are to be prioritized?

The fourth element is a set of indicators that enable the tracking of whether activities have been initiated or not and whether management challenges are addressed or not. These indicators make the activities measurable, which makes it possible to evaluate the initiated activities and their impact. Some indicators can be directly linked to activities (e.g., number of training days or amount invested in IT). Others can have a more indirect link to a given activity. Examples of indicators are shown in Figure 5.3.

	What exists	What has been done	What has been achieved
Employees	Qualified university degree	Training per employee	Lower turnover
Customers	Existing customer pool	Customer survey	Customer satisfaction
Business processes	IT-costs	Good and best practice	Knowledge building and sharing
Technology	R&D costs	Focus groups	Shorter time to market

Figure 5.3. Examples of indicators within different areas.

Summary relating to indicators:

- What indicators can be used for the different activities?
- Is the indicator supposed to measure impact, activity or resource mix?

These four elements together make up an analysis of the firm's knowledge resource management. The four elements are clearly interlinked and they are solely relevant when viewed together and in context. Once the analysis is done the four elements can be presented in the model in Figure 5.4.

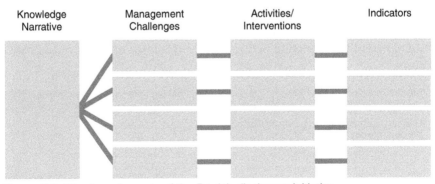

| Knowledge Narrative | Management Challenges | Activities/ Interventions | Indicators |

Figure 5.4. The four elements of the Danish disclosure initiative.

As can be seen, so far many of these approaches are inspired by the balanced scorecard thinking. The MERITUM guidelines and the Danish guidelines where developed at approximately the same time and are similar in that both are tools for management to create value and to communicate how value is created for stakeholders. Both of these guidelines are also premised on the firm's being a knowledge based system. The Danish guidelines view the intellectual capital guidelines as part of the firm's knowledge strategy in addition to communicating the targets, initiatives, and results of knowledge management. Both guidelines emphasize the importance of reporting, and the Danish guidelines are taking this furthest since they see reporting as a way of improving corporate governance.

Case 5.1 Coloplast[20]

Coloplast is a Danish company that produces medical consumables. It has since 1998 reported its intellectual capital in accordance with the Danish disclosure guidelines. The firm has been involved in this initiative since the original development project in 1997, as one of the 19 original firms. This development project was supported by the Danish Department of Industry. The information in Coloplast's intellectual capital report is aimed for four stakeholder groups: owners (stockholders), customers, employees, and society. In the annual report for 2002/2003, as many as 18 of the 55 pages are dedicated to a set of indicators relevant for each of these groups. This is the sixth consecutive year that the firm has produced such an additional disclosure document. The following table shows examples of indicators within each stakeholder group.

Customers	Employees	Society	Stockholders
• Collaboration with healthcare and users • Complaints • Customer satisfaction	Job rotation • Turnove • Absence • Unsollicited job applications	• Water • Process waste • Accident frequency • New jobs	• Patent applications • Patent rights • New products' share of revenue • Operating profit per employee

---

Guidelines for additional information on value creation

The Norwegian Association of Financial Analysts has developed a set of guidelines for voluntary reporting of nonfinancial information. The background to the work was an admission that the present methods for reporting provide insufficient information compared to the information needs of the firm's stakeholders and that real value creation is insufficiently reported through the existing historical cost based accounting models.

The idea behind the project is to provide guidelines to the management and boards of companies wishing to report information above and beyond that required by law. As a consequence, the understanding among the firm's stakeholders for the way the firm creates value would increase and thereby create less information asymmetry as relates to the firm's value creation. Ultimately, this should help reduce volatility in the firm's share price.

The main message in the guidelines is that the firm should report externally the resources that are used for the internal management of the firm. Information and measures to be disclosed should relate to value-creating activities within the perspectives of relations and customer capital, human capital, structural capital, and innovation. This can be viewed as a mixture of the balanced scorecard and the guidelines discussed earlier in this chapter.

The following premises are established for the guidelines[21]:

1. Reporting is voluntary
2. The aim is to create as correct a picture as possible of the firm through this reporting and this means that the information provided must be correct, consistent, and assurable.
3. The objective is to inform about activities and resources that contribute to the firm's value creation, and this means that all information provided must be linked to the firm's strategy and value creation.
4. Quality takes precedence over quantity. The report must be as correct as possible using firm' specific information.
5. Measurability, consistency, and continuity are important. The intent is that the reporting firm is to show development over time and measure itself against itself. The information reported must therefore be consistent and complete over time. This means that definitions or indicators cannot be changed once selected for disclosure. It is accepted that due to external or internal changes the relevance of reported indicators my go down and at some point it may make sense to abolish them, and likewise it may make sense at some time to include new indicators, but the reasoning and grounding for such changes should be made explicit.

The guidelines assume that value is created by firms in either value chains or value networks. Based on this assumption, value creation is dependent on:

1. External boundary conditions and the opportunities and threats that this poses
2. The firm's strategy for value creation, its resources and its activities

As can be seen, the model follows the same principle as the previous models. However, a difference from the previous models is that these guidelines have a category called *innovation*. Under this heading are issues such as improvements and new developments. This includes new products, new services, and new business concepts to new or existing markets. It also includes issues around taking existing offerings to new markets. Process improvements and the like fall under structural capital.

ARCS's intellectual capital report

Austrian Research Centers Seibersdorf (ARCS) is the largest research organization in Austria. It has developed its own method for reporting on intellectual capital and has done so since 1999. As a research organization, it is particularly important that it can communicate its performance against a set of knowledge goals to its stakeholders. Because it is financed with public funds, it is important to the organization to be transparent as to how the money is used.

ARCS has published five intellectual capital reports,[22] and the reports now show a good degree of continuity. The reports are based on three categories of intellectual capital: human, relational, and structural capital. Through the reports, the organization communicates how well they perform against a set of knowledge goals, with indicators presented in the three different categories of capital (where applicable). These goals may change slightly over time

In addition to the three categories of capital, the reports address the key processes of independent research and contract projects. What sets this approach aside from others is the use of four further categories of results within the areas of finance, economy, research, and society (Figure 5.5).

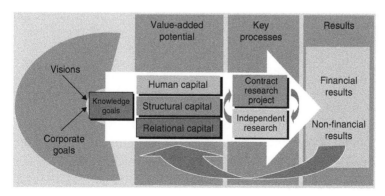

Figure 5.5. The intellectual capital reporting model of ARCS.[23]

In their 2002 Intellectual Capital Report, ARCS disclosed performance indicators against the following knowledge goals:

1. Knowledge transfer: Between knowledge and application oriented research as well as between science and government authorities
2. Interdisciplinarity: Successfully link different research disciplines for interdisciplinary solutions
3. Research management: Best practice project and research management
4. Internationality: Become successful in the international research market
5. Spin-offs and investments: Facilitate market-oriented exploitation of R&D results

Performance against these goals is presented both in a brief narrative and in figures. Examples of indicators for the interdisciplinarity goal include "Staff with more than one degree (% of researchers)" within the human capital category, and "Interdepartmental projects (% of all new projects)" within the relational capital category.

There have also been developments within the Austrian regulatory landscape. The Austrian Ministry for Education, Science and Culture has recognized the importance of efficient use of IC for university performance and has therefore adopted the idea of IC reporting to enhance transparency, to foster the management of intangible resources, and to set incentives for performance orientation. According to a revised university law,[24] all universities will have to issue annual IC reports by 2006. Within this IC report, each university will have to publish input, output, and performance indicators for research, teaching, and other forms of IC. The IC report should serve as a management tool for the university as well as a communication vehicle between universities and the Ministry.

Triple Bottom Line

The triple bottom line (TBL) has over some years achieved interest among managers, consultants, investors, and academics. The idea behind the TBL is that an organization's success is not only dependent on the traditional financial bottom line but also on social/ethic and environmental outcomes. Supporters of the TBL claim that organizations have a duty to society, employees, customers, suppliers, and other stakeholders, and that social/ethical and environmental outcomes are to be measured, calculated, audited, and disclosed in the same way as financial outcomes. This approach has some similarities to some of the thinking of the intellectual approach but differs in several important dimensions.

The TBL can be viewed as a framework for tracking and reporting of a corporate performance by, in addition to financial results, using indicators for social, societal, and environmental outcomes. The triple bottom line is also viewed as a concept that captures a wide range of values, challenges, and processes that an organization must take into account to minimize unwanted outcomes from the organization's activities and capturing the wanted outcomes in the financial, social, and environmental dimensions. This requires honesty as relates to the organization's intent and requires that the interests of all relevant stakeholders are taken into account (e.g., shareholders, customers, employees, partners, public sector, local government, and the general public).[25] It is not easy to find an agreed, clear and concise definition of what the TBL concept actually means and there is no clear methodology or formula for arriving at the TBL. Some of the organizations using the TBL are accordingly rather vague when describing the methodology or defining the concepts.

If we, for example, look at the indicators for social outcomes, these can be tracked by using standard indicators of diversity (e.g., percentage of managers who are women, percentage of employees who are handicapped, etc.), health and safety (number of fatal accidents at work, program for healthy living, etc.), and society (share of profit fed back to society, corporate social responsibility program, etc.). Based on these indicators, a bottom line for the company's social responsibility can be calculated. These indicators all belong to different categories of intellectual capital.

However, there is, as was mentioned, no generally accepted method for calculating the TBL, which makes it difficult to interpret the information disclosed in the form of a TBL and compare to other companies' TBLs. One can only speculate on the significance of an indicator increasing or decreasing over time. With the literature on TBL readily available today, there is no means to find out. Moreover, the TBL cannot be linked to the financial accounting framework since the information in a TBL is not additive.

In the same spirit as the TBL, many large corporations today publish corporate social responsibility reports. Diageo is one such company.

They publish both global and country-specific "Corporate Citizenship Reports" showing investments made into responsibility and sustainability programs. However, these types of reports resemble marketing material more than anything that can be linked to the financial reporting routines of the companies.

Disclosing information on social and environmental responsibility and sustainability may be worthwhile for certain companies. Studies have, for example, shown that investors use environmental reports in their analyses and that reporting on environmental issues can improve the valuation of a firm.[26] Still, TBL is clearly not a well-developed method for this purpose.

The Balanced Scorecard

The idea of the balanced scorecard (BSC) is most often attributed to Robert Kaplan and David Norton,[27] even though the principal model had been used for several decades in France under the name *tableau de bord*[28] when Kaplan and Norton published their first work on the model. The literature on the *tableau de bord* was for decades only available in French, which in practice limited its application to the French speaking academic and business community. Then, when Kaplan and Norton introduced the principal model in the English-speaking world of business, it rather quickly gained attention and popularity. The most important objective with the concept was to move beyond managing the company solely with traditional financial indicators and start applying indicators within three further perspectives: customers, processes, and learning and growth. These are all based on the company's vision and strategy. The four perspectives are then transformed into objectives and key performance indicators.

The balanced scorecard was from the start meant as a measurement system for nonfinancial values, but has since been put to use in a number of other areas and for other purposes. Some companies use the model as a central framework for their management processes. The model is also applied for the following purposes:

- Clarify the strategy and unify the organization around it.
- Communicate the strategy to the company.
- Harmonize objectives of units and individuals.
- Link strategic objectives to long-term goals and yearly budgets.
- Identify and harmonize strategic alternatives.

- Carry out periodical and systematic strategic analyses.
- Get feedback in order to increase knowledge and enhance the strategy.

Figure 5.6 shows the balanced scorecard model in graphic form and the four perspectives on which the model is based are described in the following sections.

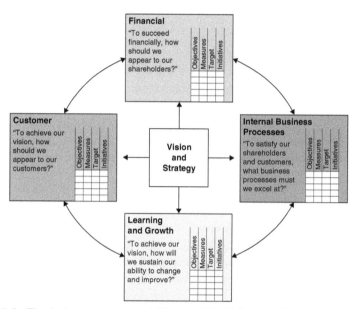

Figure 5.6. The balanced scorecard (Source: The Balanced Scorecard Institute).[29]

The financial perspective

The balanced scorecard includes the financial perspective since financial figures are important when it comes to estimating the financial consequences of actions and activities that have already been carried out. The financial key performance indicators show whether the company's strategy and implementation is contributing to increasing the profit. Figures used within this perspective are about profitability and include, for example, profit, return on capital, economic value added, cash flow, and increase in revenue.

The customer perspective

This perspective is about following up on the company's target market segment through a set of indicators on things such as customer satisfaction, probability for repurchase, handling of new customers, profitability per customer, market share within the chosen segments, and so forth. There should also be concrete indicators for the products and services the company provides to its customers.

The process perspective

Within this perspective, the most important processes for company success are identified. In this perspective, there are elements that set the balanced scorecard apart from conventional approaches. For example, traditional models for financial control usually aim at controlling and improving existing processes. The balanced scorecard instead focuses on the identification of new processes that the company must master to achieve its financial and customer related goals.

The learning and growth perspective

This last perspective is all about the infrastructure needed for the company to create long-term learning and growth. As mentioned in the preceding sections, the customer and process perspectives identify the factors critical to the company's future. It is, however, unlikely that the company will achieve its long-term objectives with today's competence and technology. The organizational learning and growth comes from three sources: people, systems, and routines. Hence, this perspective follows up on how well the company is equipping itself for the future with indicators for each of the three sources of renewal.

In short, the balanced scorecard is about turning the vision, mission, and strategy of the organization into objectives and key performance indicators based on four different perspectives. The final product of a balanced scorecard is a set of key performance indicators that are relevant for achieving the organization's vision and strategic objectives.

The BSC has been criticized for being a rigid framework and by those who believe the four perspectives are not enough to describe the totality of the organization.[30] The identification of only four perspectives in the BSC introduces a certain element of rigidity, given the suggestion that key success factors and indicators can be found by looking at the company through the lens of only the four perspectives. The given perspectives in the BSC can therefore be limiting in themselves as certain aspects of management may fall outside these. Further critique lies in that the balanced scorecard only looks after a sample of stakeholders such as customers and owners/stockholders, but shuts out employees, suppliers, partners, and the community.

In general, the balanced scorecard is intended as a management model but is widely applied as an internal communication tool for strategy implementation. Its application for external reporting is very limited.

The Skandia model

The Swedish insurance company Skandia was one of the first large companies to adopt the thinking around intellectual capital, spearheaded by their Director of Intellectual Capital, Leif Edvinsson. The group became the first company ever to issue an Intellectual Capital Supplement to their annual financial report in 1994, in which the company explained their work with visualizing IC and its value-creating potential internally. In order to do this and to create a framework for measuring the progress in this area the Skandia Navigator was created, a further development of the balanced scorecard of Kaplan and Norton as described above.

The Skandia model describes the building blocks of a firm's market value and illustrates the different components of the intellectual capital.[31] This was an attempt to explain the difference between book value and market value. Hence, intellectual capital in this framework was defined as the difference between the market value and the financial capital (i.e., the book value).[32] Given the discussion in Chapters 2 and 4, we now know that this is not a valid definition.

The Skandia model divides intellectual capital into human capital and structural capital, which in turn is divided into customer capital and organizational capital. The latter is then split into innovation and process capital. These categories are roughly comparable to the resource categories used throughout this book: human, organizational, and relational.

The categories in Figure 5.7 formed the basis for the Skandia Navigator, which is a hybrid of the balanced scorecard and a simplified version of the IC navigator presented in Chapter 3. The thoughts around intellectual capital in the company provided the groundwork for their reporting system. This system contains a number of key performance indicators with the aim of providing a more holistic picture of the company's performance and ability to achieve its goals. There are many similarities with the

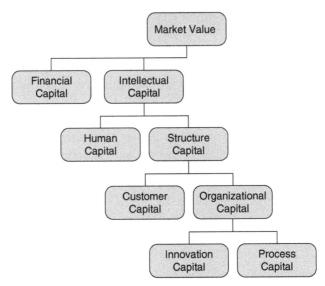

Figure 5.7. The Skandia market value scheme.[33]

balanced scorecard, but the Skandia model has five focus areas (see Figure 5.8) instead of four: the financial, customer, and process focus areas are the same as in the balanced scorecard and the renewal and development focus area is comparable to that of learning and growth in the balanced scorecard. The addition in the Skandia model is the human focus area in which knowledge and knowledge building is visualized. Each of these five areas is in turn part of a value-creating process.

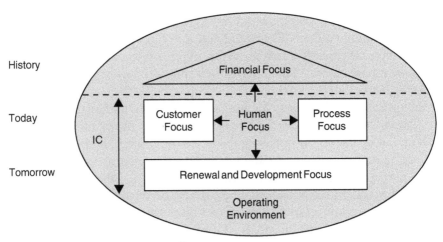

Figure 5.8. The Skandia Navigator.[34]

Critics claim that Skandia's work with intellectual capital and their reporting on this lead to a significant overvaluation of the company in the mid 1990s. In the early years of the new millennium, major scandals in the company were uncovered. This shows that the misuse of this type of information can result in a culture in which the wrong type of behavior is rewarded and that the company in many cases did not have substantiation for the claims they made on their intellectual capital. Most importantly, the intellectual capital reports were never audited by a third party, meaning that they were not subjected to the same scrutiny as financial reports. This, in addition to the fact that the indicators did not have any real meaning since nobody knew how to interpret them, meant that the management at the time could get away with exploitation and manipulation, as seen elsewhere in the cases of Enron and WorldCom.[35]

The longest experience of intellectual capital reporting is found among companies in Scandinavian countries (Denmark, Norway, Sweden, and Finland). Danish companies obviously have to comply with the narrative model of the Danish Guidelines, whereas other companies use one or a combination of the approaches described preceding sections of this chapter. Australian companies have also been early movers when it comes to disclosure of nonfinancial information, and the frequency of doing so is high[36] (see e.g., Morgan & Banks Limited Annual Review 1998). There are other alternative models used for the purpose of disclosure such as IC Rating™ [37] or the Intangible Assets Monitor.[38]

A recent study in the United Kingdom[39] showed that external reporting of intellectual capital does exist but is still very immature in terms of how it is done and how it is used. None of the 95 knowledge intensive listed companies in the study specifically accounted for intellectual capital resources although they did report on it in a descriptive albeit unstructured way. The most frequently reported intellectual capital resource by far was relationships, followed by organizational and human resources (even though these terms were not necessarily used).

Case 5.2 Example of an anonymized excerpt from an ICN and ICI based disclosure document

In 1997, CONTRACT RESEARCH (CR) management undertook a review of the strategic aims of CR using the new management perspective of intellectual capital. The intellectual capital perspective allowed them to look at the resources at their disposal, both traditional and intangible, and determine the relative importance of them as factors which could influence the achievement of the strategic aims of CR. The approach was just as relevant for the organization in its role as "technology house". The best expression of the intellectual capital approach is in the development of an "intellectual capital navigator". Intellectual Capital Navigators show how the classes of resource, both traditional and intangible should interact to create value.

The intellectual capital navigator developed in 1997 and shown below looked forward to the present time and showed that human resources (the people) were most important. Human resources were followed by relational resources (the interaction with customers and suppliers), then monetary resources, organizational resources (processes, knowledge and intellectual property) and finally the physical resources of the organization. Value is created by using resources to further the strategic development and this means for the organization to fulfill the role for its customers. The most important utilization of resources is indicated by the thickness of the link.

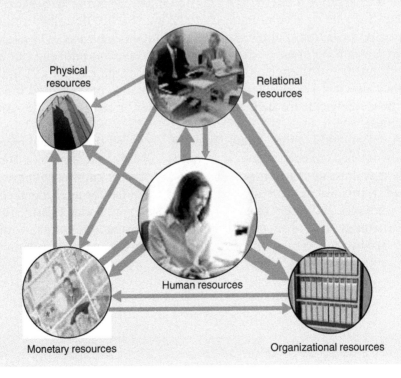

Physical resources

Relational resources

Human resources

Monetary resources

Organizational resources

The chart shown below shows the performance measured using these indicators over five years. For convenience, the thirty measures have been combined into seven main areas and an eight which combines the seven. The seven areas are:

1. Visibility to the customer, industry and wider community through teaching, conferences and visits.
2. Visibility to the customer, industry and wider community through staff exchanges to and from academia.
3. Tangible outputs from activities.
4. Reports and presentations arising from assignments for our customers.
5. Publications in the scientific and popular press to reinforce our scientific standing.
6. Use of CR as a source of authoritative statements and seminars.
7. Potential in existing patents and the qualification of staff as the basis for future organizational development.

These main areas cover the strategic aims of developing our markets, enhancing customer relations, maintaining quality and developing our knowledge base.

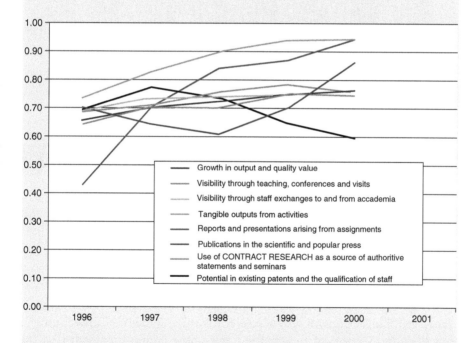

The first group in the chart below is the summary position and shows an upward trend over the period from 1996 to 2000. This is an excellent result since it has to be achieved against a backdrop of change in which some indicators are purposely left to decline. The most significant increases have been in the areas of the reporting and

Continued

Case 5.2 Example of an Anonymized Excerpt from an ICN and ICI Based Disclosure Document—cont'd

publications, CR's authority and the potential for the future vested in its people and their knowledge. These changes are in line with the strategic aims set out above. On the other hand, there has been a minor decline in the more physical, or tangible type of output.

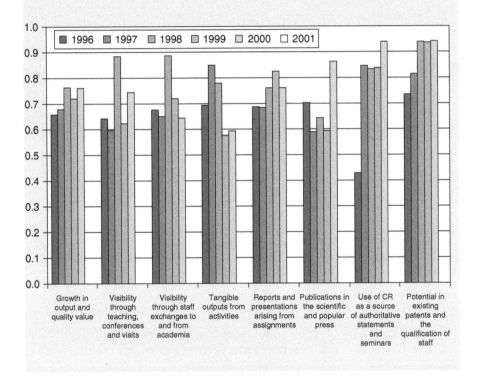

PROS AND CONS OF REPORTING ON IC

Whether it is possible in practice to measure, value, and disclose intellectual capital in a coherent way across companies, industries, and countries has been the subject of debate for a long time. Some point out that the lack of theoretical underpinnings for this purpose cannot be ignored. Compared to traditional financial reporting, the reporting of intellectual capital is more speculative. This is a problem for companies in an era where big financial scandals make almost daily news (Enron, WorldCom, Skandia, etc.).

Another issue is that of what a firm is actually prepared to tell the world about. From a commercial standpoint, there is information that the company may wish to keep secret for a little longer in order to prevent competitors from taking advantage of it. Potential partners may also use the information disclosed to find out how important they are in the future development of the company and then use that information in a negotiation situation.

A Dutch study involving three knowledge intensive companies and four financial analysts reported the following advantages and disadvantages for reporting intellectual capital.[40]

Advantages

1. Increase transparency to the financial market which may result in lower weighted cost of capital and therefore a higher market capitalization
2. Help create trust among employees and other stakeholders
3. Support the long-term vision of the company since intellectual capital reporting is about long-term perspectives
4. May be used for marketing purposes

The last point, however, is not endorsed by the authors of this book. Purposely using the intellectual capital reporting for marketing purposes will undermine the credibility of the report. Still, there may be marketing benefits coming out as a byproduct of the intellectual capital reporting. This byproduct may be beneficial but one should not be tempted to intentionally use the intellectual capital reporting as a marketing vehicle.

Disadvantages

1. Reveals sensitive information that competitors may use to their advantage
2. May enable the manipulation of information so that solely the positive information is disclosed
3. May create liability risks for executives if presenting future-related information that cannot be substantiated
4. Increases costs as a consequence of new regulations and bureaucracy that the firms must comply with
5. Reduces the freedom for management and may lead to higher expectations which may prove difficult to live up to

Despite the advantages expressed in theory by the analysts mentioned previously, there is a lot of reluctance among financial analysts to the disclosure of intellectual capital value in companies' external reporting. One reason for this is that analysts have developed their own models for determining the value of a firm's intellectual capital and if they were proved accurate they could be very valuable.[41] They would only stay valuable, though, as long as information on intellectual capital is not publicly disclosed. In addition, as seen before in this chapter, analysts use their contacts to talk directly to the firms that they value, and the information they extract from these conversations gives the analysts significant advantages over regular investors.[42]

THE CVH: THE NEXT STEP FOR DISCLOSURE?

So far, the approaches described in this chapter have been around for quite a while and some are well used (the balanced scorecard globally and the Danish Guidelines in Denmark) and fill some purpose. None of them is perfect, however; they all have flaws in some way. In this section, we present a novel model that takes disclosure of intellectual capital to the next stage in terms of rigor and comparability, while still protecting sensitive data. Thus, this model actually addresses and solves some of the disadvantages with intellectual capital disclosure mentioned in the preceding section. The underlying model has been around for quite some years,[43] but its application in reporting has been limited thus far.

Analysts need a model that describes the value context of the investors. This is still dominated by financial considerations, but intellectual capital, specific ethical positions, and the ability of management teams make significant contributions. A model that combines the attributes of value from the standpoint of the investor and analyst will have a limited range of applicability but one that will allow it to be used across a market segment while not being specific to any individual company in that segment. All the analysts require then is input.

The company needs a measurement scheme and model that embodies the management principles they wish to follow. The model must not impose a large measurement overhead; it must facilitate strategic and tactical management; and it must generate the information needed by shareholders and investors. The most difficult to meet are the last two, which require the strategic input and the consequent generation of useful information. However, these requirements align exactly with the needs of the external community. The model and methodology must therefore expose and measure the real routes to value creation in the company and include the areas of uncertainty and risk. As there have to be strategic levers, the model must be forward looking.

As the company would have both the internal model and the external model, management would have the opportunity to see in advance the possible effects of their strategic options on the stakeholder groups as well as the long-term effects on the make-up of their companies. There would inevitably be a tendency to investigate the most favorable solutions, but such is the real diversity of stakeholder groups that solutions that please everybody are usually impossible.

Chapter 4 described the measurement of intellectual capital and concentrated on the process of building proper measurement systems. This led to the identification of just one or two measurement systems that were truly reliable in that they met all the requirements of measurement theory. What this compliance does is confer reliability and repeatability on the results. In short, the results can be trusted.

It is not an unreasonable assumption that companies competing in the same market segment will be very similar in general makeup and the market will be basing its valuations on very similar criteria. An example of this is the supermarket chains in the United Kingdom. The U.K. food retail sector is dominated by five large retailing chains differentiated by geography and market positioning, but in other respects very similar. Another example is motor manufacturers where there are again geography based differences and differences in the part of the market on which they concentrate. The common factor between the car manufacturers and the supermarket chains is that both have shown considerable degrees of standardization in operational approaches due in large part to the common market forces each sector faces. With further thought, many other reasonably homogeneous groups will be found.

At present, financial performance targets and the expectation that company managers will be able to deliver the targets over time form a large part of the assessments made which directly influence market value. As usual, the possession, control, and deployment of the intellectual capital resources upon which performance actually depend do not feature in any overt or reliable way in assessments of companies. At best, nonfinancial factors may be assimilated into assessments as indicators (as opposed to measures). The main problem with the disclosure of intellectual capital information is that it can be very revealing of general company health and strategic intent. Naturally, no company would be willing to disclose such information and it is unlikely that any regulator would attempt to force it. On the other hand, the reduction of information asymmetry is important. The issue then boils down to two things:

1. How it can be standardized in limited market sectors to permit comparison?
2. What should be revealed and how can sensitive company information be protected?

Measurement systems such as the CVH, whose general properties were outlined in Chapter 4, offer a means to do this.

Comparison

Figure 5.9 shows a simplified CVH hierarchy for a supermarket. In the gray boxes are six key performance areas that will be common to all companies in the sector. Obviously, entities at this level are standard and results from one supermarket can be compared with those from the others. At a level of detail below it is likely that there will be between 12 and 20 attributes which again, entirely make up the non-financial elements of the supermarket and again, are likely to be applicable to all supermarkets in the sector.

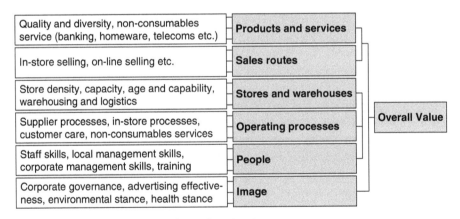

Figure 5.9. A simple supermarket value structure.

At this stage, it must be recognized that some of the factors involved in valuation analyses are absent—most notably, the financial projections. Those are collected or evaluated separately.

CVH usually uses a taxonomy that culminates in real measurable activities at its most detailed level rather than in the language of intellectual capital resources and the transformations between them.

Developing a measurement structure that uses the language of intellectual capital is difficult, but broadly speaking, the following general comments can be made.

Image is largely concerned with customers and the perceptions they have of the processes of the company. Thus, this section would contain relational and organizational resources plus some of the transformations between them. In the central section of the structure are found attributes such as people, processes, and physical entities. Obviously, the resources here are broadly human, organizational, and physical with very few inter-resource transformations. This section is basically the intrinsic value area—that is, value derived from what the company has. Finally, the top section is all about the delivery of services and is instrumental in character. This is where value is derived from what a company does, and therefore is dominated by resource transformations of all types.

Protecting data

There are two areas in which data must be protected from disclosure. The development of structures such as that in Figure 5.9 so that performance measurements can be used as input will inevitably cross into the discomfort zone of the company where real business models hold sway and the inner workings (efficiencies and effectiveness) of the company are laid bare. Clearly this is undesirable from the company perspective. Happily, revealing it is not required. Data, which must be auditable for veracity by an accredited third party auditor, can be input by the company and revealed in publications or briefings only at the relatively highly aggregated levels suggested in the figure. Thus, while useful and reliable data are provided, the underlying business is not unduly exposed.

Although the company has legitimate desires to keep certain things private, so too does the analyst. The measurement structure is common across the sector and may even be common across the analyst community since it should be a complete description of the company, including everything that every stakeholder believes to be a constituent of value. From the analyst's perspective, what is most definitely private are the internal combination settings and the weightings used, since it is these that embody the personal assessments of each analyst regarding what is important and what is not. These differences in perception are the origins of their competitive advantage. Happily, there is no reason why these should ever be revealed, although for the sake of understanding, an analyst's preferences may be shared with the company itself; but this is optional.

The entire schema of disclosure using the CVH is shown in Figure 5.10.

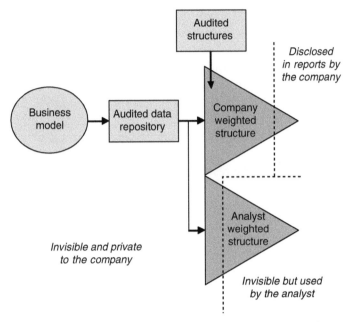

Figure 5.10. Schema for the disclosure and protection of intangible data.

PROACTIVE EXTERNAL COMMUNICATION

We have throughout the previous chapters shown the importance of understanding, managing, and measuring intellectual capital resources. It is clearly getting increasingly important for companies to be proactive when it comes to reporting. Up until now, external communication has predominately been a reactive function, since the focus has been on past transactions and historic financial information. The intellectual capital is becoming more and more critical to the future profitability of a firm and deals with leading indicators (whereas traditional financial accounting uses lagging indicators). This must be reflected in external communications to a greater extent than it is today. The key is to satisfy the needs of the investors for nonfinancial information. The problem today is that financial analysts pay little attention to the intellectual capital reporting initiatives taken so far. One of the most important reasons for this is that there is no standardized way in which to report, rendering the information difficult to interpret and use as a basis for comparisons.

Long term, it may be that companies can only optimize their share prices by looking beyond the bottom line. If the management in addition can identify, manage, measure, and report on their nonfinancial performance they may be able to capitalize on the third of investment decisions that are made based on intellectual capital in some way or the other.

In 2003, a consulting company carried out an experiment involving fund managers of a large fund.[44] The consulting firm used the annual report of Coloplast, one of the Danish companies subject to the Danish Guidelines, and stripped it of all quantified nonfinancial information. The resulting document was in accordance with Danish reporting regulations including the knowledge narrative, but it did not contain Coloplast's own indicators that related the operational indicators to the financial result. The consulting company then gave the two versions to the fund managers: half of them got the full report and the other half only got the financial information. The name of the company was kept secret for both groups. The fund managers were then asked to estimate turnover and profit for the coming two years as well as give a stock recommendation based on the information they had at hand. They all had two hours to do this and did not have access to any other information. The result showed, as expected, that the fund managers with the complete report came up with lower but more accurate estimates than those who only had the financial data. The group with the full report was also much more positive toward the company and gave a buy recommendation to a greater extent than the other group. The latter were less enthusiastic and almost 80% gave the stock a sell recommendation. This little experiment points at the benefits of transparency in giving the market a better understanding of the company and its operations. Higher revenue estimates with large volatility are not as attractive as a more consistent and accurate estimation of the value of the company.

The message is clear: investors use nonfinancial information in their analyses whether or not the companies are strategic about their efforts. Company executives who effectively manage, measure, and communicate their efforts and performance may not only contribute to a better valuation of the company but may also improve the company's ability to attract capital, employees, and partners.

RECOMMENDED GUIDELINES FOR THE FUTURE OF IC DISCLOSURE

This chapter has presented a number of approaches and methods for reporting on intellectual capital. Even if the frameworks and tools as such are different in their design, they also have a lot in common. They all have the same objective of creating a new language that can allow both internal parties (employees, management, board) and external parties (customers, banks, regulatory bodies and authorities, financial analysts, etc.) to better understand the processes around intellectual capital. There is a clear need for this new language since there today is information asymmetry between different stakeholders when it comes to intellectual capital.

Even though we are on the path to finding a common solution, there are still a number of issues around measurement and disclosure of intellectual capital. What is the fundamental objective with the type of guidelines presented in this chapter? To what extent should regulatory authorities be involved? Is there a need for compulsory external reporting of intellectual capital such as the view taken by the Danish government? Is it possible to develop global guidelines for reporting of intellectual capital when there is such a plethora of cultural differences to take into account?

All these questions are undoubtedly important, but there are as of yet no generally accepted answers and solutions to them. What is evident is that the work on intellectual capital has resulted in the development of methods, models, and approaches that have already been put in practice in companies in a number of countries, some with good results and some with not so good results.

For companies realizing the value of reporting on their intellectual capital and who are about to embark on the journey of finding a suitable model for doing this, we would give the following recommendations.

- Finding a suitable model for disclosing intellectual capital information is a challenging and costly task since it is about changing both internal and external stakeholders' ways of thinking and views of the company. It is also about turning something that is complex and dynamic in nature into something simple and practical. Therefore, it is of utmost importance that the value of the new ideas and methods is laid bare in order to gain support within and outside of the organization.

- In order to find a suitable model to use, the organization first must assess and define its own needs and how to address them. This is about predicting changes and their consequences, so make sure the management team fully supports the idea and make sure the model is aligned with the strategy of the organization. Moreover, the organization should take its own and others' experiences and insights into account and establish critical success factors as well as barriers to success. It is not recommended to launch into a measurement system without having a sound understanding of the grounding principles of measurement. You need sound and clear mental models to be able to develop effective management systems.
- The implementation is best done step by step. That way, feedback from internal and external stakeholders can be integrated along the way. In deciding which approach to take and which content to go for, the strategy of the company must be taken into account and be used as a basis for the decision. Finally, the key performance indicators are defined and existing data is mapped. This is the stage where stakeholders get to comment on a draft reporting model.

In general, it is the view of the authors that it is still too early to regulate on reporting of intellectual capital. Doing that now will only force companies into costly reporting routines based on models that are inaccurate or difficult to interpret and do not add the value intended. The models of today are very far indeed from working in the same way as traditional accounting and reporting models. Instead, companies should be given amnesty for yet some years to encourage experimentation in this area. At the same time, more unified research is required on the subject, working for an overarching framework for intellectual capital and value creation. Academic research and experimentation in practice will in the end allow for regulation based on a well-grounded, tried and tested model that has been proved to work for all stakeholders involved.

The only alternative that we can see being regulated in the near future would be one where a synthesized stakeholder is assumed and a model is built around this assumption. Such a model will have to be rigorous, auditable, and well grounded in measurement theory. The only starting point would then be the CVH as presented in the preceding section.

Key Learning Points in Chapter 5

- Traditional financial accounting and reporting is well suited for monetary and physical resources but is not designed for and cannot handle intellectual capital resources in a credible way. There is therefore a need for finding new models for this purpose since the IC resources often are of critical importance to the organization's ability to create value.
- There are a number of approaches and methods for reporting on intellectual capital, of which the Danish Guidelines, the Austrian Research Centre's model, the balanced scorecard, the Skandia Navigator, and the CVH are some.
- CVH is the only model capable of solving the problems of standardization of IC reporting and enabling comparisons within industries without laying bare the sensitive information of companies.
- Advantages of IC reporting
  - Increased transparency to the financial market which may result in lower weighted cost of capital and therefore a higher market capitalization
  - Helps create trust among employees and other stakeholders
  - Supports the long-term vision of the company since intellectual capital reporting is about long-term perspectives
- Disadvantages of IC reporting
  - Reveals sensitive information that competitors may use to their advantage
  - May enable the manipulation of information so that solely the positive information is disclosed
  - May create liability risks for executives if presenting future-related information that cannot be substantiated
  - Increases costs as a consequence of new regulations and bureaucracy that the firms must comply with
  - Reduces the freedom for management and may lead to higher expectations which may prove difficult to live up to
- When developing a model for reporting on intellectual capital, the following should be kept in mind:
  - Visualize the value of the new ideas and methods to gain support for them both internally and externally.
  - Assess and define the organization's needs and how to go about addressing them.
  - Implement one step at a time.

ENDNOTES

1. Rylander, A., Jacobsen, K. and G. Roos "Towards Improved Information Disclosure on Intellectual Capital", International Journal of Technology Management, Autumn 2000, pp. 715–741.
2. M.J. Molnar (2004), "Executive views on intangible assets: insights from the Accenture/Economist Intelligence Unit Survey, research note," *Intangible Assets and Future Value*, 1(April 13), pp. 1–4.
3. V. Narayanan G. Pinches, K. Kelm, and D. Lander (2000), "The influence of voluntary disclosed qualitative information," *Strategic Management Journal*, 21(7), 707–722.
4. Mavrinac, S.C., and T. Siesfeld 1997. Measures that Matter: An Exploratory Investigation of Investors' Information Needs and Value Priorities. Working Paper No.97–10. Richard Ivey School of Business, Research and Development Office: London, Ontairo.
5. J.G. Harris, R.J. Burgman, and T.H. Davenport (2005), "New frontiers of operational reporting," Accenture Research Note, 2 February, Issue 6.
6. Financial Accounting Standards Board, www.fasb.org.
7. B. Lev (2001), *Intangibles: Management, Measurement, and Reporting*, New York: Brookings Institution Press.
8. CEST, The Centre for Exploitation of Science and Technology (2000), http://www.cest.org.uk.
9. S. Zambon (2003), "Accounting, financial analysis and audit in the intangible economy," PRISM Final Report, 31 March.
10. More information available at http://www.fek.su.se/home/bic/meritum/.
11. More information available at www.oecd.org.
12. MERITUM (2002) as described in L. Cañibano, P. Sanchez, M. Garcia-Ayuso, and C. Og Chaminande (Eds), *Guidelines for Managing and Reporting on Intangibles*, Fundaciōn Airtel Mōvil.
13. Despite the attempts of MERITUM to create a generally accepted classification framework, there are still conflicting opinions on the subject. There is, however, consensus enough on the principle of three categories of intellectual capital: one that has to do with human resources, one that captures the intangible resources in the organization as such, and one that deals with the relationships of the organization.
14. Skandia (1994), "Visualizing intellectual capital in Skandia, Supplement to Skandia's Annual Report."
15. Roos G and J. Roos (1997), "Measuring your company's intellectual performance," *Long Range Planning*, 30(3), 413–426.
16. G. Roos and J. Roos (1996), "Measuring intellectual performance," Paper presented at the Knowledge in Action Conference in Israel, October.
17. J. Roos (1997), "Intellectual capital – the next generation," *Financial Times, Mastering Management*, The Reader No.1, May.
18. "Guidelines for managing and reporting on intangibles (intellectual capital report)." Project report available at http://www.pnbukh.com/ PDF_FILER/MERITUM%20Guidelines.pdf.
19. This part is to a large extent based on the document "Videnregnskaper – den nye guideline," published in Danish by the Danish Ministry for Knowledge, Technology and Development; and J. Mouritsen, H.T. Larsen, P.N. Bukh, and M.R. Johansen (2001), "Reading an intellectual capital statement: describing and prescribing knowledge management strategies," *Journal of Intellectual Capital*, 2(4), 359–383.
20. Based on the article "Hidden treasures" by Ben McLannahan, CFO Europe, Dec 30th, 2003. More information available at www.coloplast.dk.
21. More on this model is available on www.finansanalytiker.no (mostly in Norwegian).

22. More information and all reports available on www.arcs.ac.at.
23. ARCS, Intellectual Capital Report 2002: Knowledge Shapes the Future, available at www.arcs.ac.at.
24. Universitaetsgesetz 2002 – UG 2002, available in German at http://www.bmbwk.gv.at/universitaeten/recht/gesetze/ug02/Universitaetsgesetz_2002_inh.xml.
25. W. Norman and C. MacDonald (2004), "Getting to the bottom of 'triple bottom line,'" *Business Ethics Quarterly*, 14(2), 243.
26. D. Cormier and M. Magnan (2002), "The contribution of environmental reporting to investors' valuation of a firm's earnings: an international comparison," Working paper 13-2002, Centre de Recherche en Gestion, Universite du Quebec a Montreal.
27. R.S. Kaplan and D.P. Norton (1996), *The Balanced Scorecard: Translating Strategy into Action*, Cambridge, Mass.: Harvard Business School Press.
28. See e.g. P. Lauzel and A. Cibert (1962), *Des Ratios au Tableau de Bord*, 2nd Ed.; M. Epstein and J.F. Manzoni (1998). "Implementing corporate strategy: from tableaux de bord to balanced scorecard," *European Management Journal*, 16(2), 190–203; A. Bourguignon, V. Malleret and H. Norreklit (2004), "The American balanced scorecard versus the French tableau de bord: the ideological dimension," *Management Accounting Research*, 15(2), 107–134.
29. Available at www.balancedscorecard.org.
30. N. Bontis, N.C Dragonetti, K. Jacobsen, and G. Roos (1999), "The knowledge toolbox: a review of the tools available to measure and manage intangible resources," *European Management Journal*, 17(4), 391–402.
31. L. Edvinsson and M. Malone (1997), *Intellectual Capital: Realizing Your Company's True Value by Finding Its Hidden Brainpower*, New York: Harper Business.
32. This definition has later been proved misleading (see Chapters 2 and 4 of this book for a more detailed discussion).
33. Edvinsson, L. and Malone, M.S. (1997) Intellectual Capital: Realizing Your Company's True Value by Finding Its Hidden Brainpower, New York: Harper Business.
34. Skandia Intellectual Capital Report, 1998.
35. Skandia no longer works actively and explicitly with intellectual capital, but part of the business was spun off and today works with scorecards for intellectual capital.
36. A. Wyatt, Z. Matocsy, and D. Stokes (2001), Capitalisation of intangibles: review of current practice and regulatory framework, *Australian Accounting Review*, 11, 22–38.
37. For more on IC rating, se www.intellectualcapital.se.
38. The Intangible Assets Monitor was developed by Karl-Erik Sveiby; see www.sveiby.com.
39. D. Gray (2004), "Reporting on intangibles," *Perspectives on Performance*, 3(1/2), 22–23.
40. Jeltje van der Meer-Kooistra og Siebren M. Zijlstra: "Reporting on intellectual capital," SOM-theme E Financial markets and institutions, available at the library of the University of Groningen: http://www.ub.rug.nl/eldoc/som/e/01E50/01E50.pdf.
41. S. Zambon (Coordinator) (2003), "Study on the measurement of intangible assets and associated reporting practices," prepared for The Commission Of The European Communities Enterprise Directorate General, University of Ferrara.
42. E. Amir, B. Lev, and T. Sougiannis (1999), "What value analysts?" working paper available at http://papers.ssrn.com/sol3/papers.cfm?abstract_id=193428.
43. See Chapter 4.
44. B. McLannahan (2003),"Hidden treasures," CFO Europe, Dec 30th, 2003.

6

Other applications of the intellectual capital approach

The first five chapters of this book have sought to introduce the subject of intellectual capital beginning with a description and an explanation of its importance. Chapter 2 sought to demonstrate a process by which intellectual capital resources in a company could be described, and the next chapter showed the relationships, or transformations, between the resources and the insights that could be gained from the process. Then the book addressed the measurement of intellectual capital and, finally, the difficult issues of the disclosure of information about companies' intellectual capital resources and how they are used. At numerous points case studies have been used to show how this is done in practice. These examples have tended to involve whole companies and straightforward analyses.

Real life is more complex and there are many scenarios in which a company could find itself where approaches drawing on the principles discussed earlier could be useful. This chapter addresses the two common scenarios of managing mergers or acquisitions and managing divestment. Both scenarios concern strategic changes planned by companies (although in special cases such as through government or regulatory action, divestments can be forced) and both are attended by significant failure rates in which the desired outcomes were either achieved more slowly than expected or not at all. The application of intellectual capital techniques provides very powerful addition to the conventional approaches of legal and financial due diligence supported by ad hoc analyses.

Finally in this final chapter, we address the application of the intellectual capital approach to areas that receive considerable attention in their own right. These areas are the management of human resources and knowledge management. This book seeks to show how the intellectual capital perspective is applied to each and can serve the vital task of integrating these areas meaningfully within the strategic framework of the company.

MERGERS, ACQUISITIONS, AND JOINT VENTURES

Mergers and acquisitions result in a permanent size increase, whereas joint ventures may be of limited life. In simple acquisitions, all aspects of the acquired company are subsumed into the acquiring company and it is usual that many of the processes, customs, and culture of the acquired company are replaced by those of the acquiring company, although such a stark fate is not always the case. Mergers and joint ventures require more careful integration.

Mergers and acquisitions have become a well-institutionalized phenomenon for executing corporate strategies and reallocating resources in the global economy. Many companies today find it quicker and cheaper to acquire, or at least acquire access to, the intellectual capital resources they need via these processes than to develop them themselves through organic growth. In the past, monetary or physical resources motivated such deals, but increasingly now deals aim for the transfer of knowledge either with or without its human element, relational resources, strategic capabilities, and technology that give firms advantageous competitive opportunities as they move outside their current strategic, organizational, and cultural contexts.

Being able to anticipate the likelihood of success of a merger, acquisition, or joint venture before it is actually carried out is increasingly becoming a critical capability for senior managers. Being able to predict the success or failure of an alliance is particularly difficult, and reliable tools or methods for doing so have yet to be developed where key opportunities for value creation are likely to arise from leveraging the newly combined intellectual capital resources. Common due diligence frameworks and approaches largely ignore intellectual capital, because it is more difficult to identify and assess than tangible assets. The common cause here lies in the causal ambiguity associated with intangible resources and the time constraints imposed by an impending deal. It is for this reason[1,2] that, when mergers acquisitions and joint ventures occur, it is the intellectual capital that is most at risk of being lost or destroyed and the venture failing to achieve its objectives.

The importance of mergers and acquisitions in competitive strategies demands a framework that identifies the factors that contribute to their survival or success. The intellectual capital perspective is invaluable in these situations since it brings structure into the complexities involved and, by focusing analysis at a resource level, increases the clarity given to the process through which merging organizations can successfully capitalize on synergies based on their resources. This extends the traditional legal and financial due diligence frameworks commonly used in mergers, acquisitions, and joint venture operations. Focusing on the unique intellectual capital that underlies competitive advantage in participating firms enables managers to link the desired results with the processes through which the results are to be achieved over time. Furthermore, the intellectual capital perspective can be used to identify and exploit synergies not easily identified and communicated through traditional due diligence approaches. Because the intellectual capital perspective values and prioritizes both tangibles and intangibles, new ways of extracting value can be discovered. The intellectual capital perspective is fundamentally more detailed and more focused on long-term potential.

Motives

The motives behind mergers and acquisitions are diverse in detail and can be explained as complex phenomena forced by various patterns of motives. We can distinguish between actions initiated to increase shareholder value in the short term, which primarily involves *value capture,* and actions initiated for strategic long-term value creation and the strengthening of competitive performance, which involve *intellectual capital deepening* and *intellectual capital extension.* These longer-term actions are clearly the ones of interest since they require much more skill and planning to execute successfully, and this book continues by looking at them rather than the simple and predatory value capture mergers.

With respect to the strategic value creation logic of a firm, depicted by the intellectual capital navigator and introduced in Chapter 1, intellectual capital deepening can be said to represent a *path-dependent* M&A motive, whereas intellectual capital extension represents a *path-breaking* M&A motive. Mergers and acquisitions whose objectives involve firms retaining similar intellectual capital bases can be referred to as path-dependent. Merging firms accumulate resources as a result of path-dependent actions of learning, investments, and other organizational activities the firms take over time. Merging firms can then build on similar intellectual capital instead of exploring new areas, and pursue a strategy to develop and effectively exploit a distinct intellectual capital resource. Where expansion incentives and competitive pressures outweigh path-dependence, the merger and acquisition objective prescribes a strategic path-breaking change. Here merging firms retain their own intellectual capital bases separately. There might be an incentive for this in changing environments where the retained intellectual capital bases may provide the merged organization with potential competitive advantages in the future. This form of merger or acquisition forces the pursuit of greater degrees of coordination and integration.

The value of each merger and acquisition strategy depends on the context within which the strategy is implemented. Although all strategic mergers and acquisitions share the underlying motivation of long-term value creation, mergers and acquisitions differ in their relation to corporate strategy and by the kind of intellectual capital that is involved for achieving synergies. Each of these strategies emphasizes a distinct dimension important in the IC perspective, and each has consequences for the nature of the acquisition decision making process and for the challenges in the integration process.

Case 6.1 Joint Venture Assessment

In 2001 a due diligence exercise was undertaken by two companies considering forming a semi-independent joint venture company between them. Both were telecommunications companies and the purpose of the joint venture was to undertake mutually beneficial R&D in the mobile telecommunications field. One company was based in Europe and the other in the Far East.

In common with many telecommunications companies at the time, both were very profitable but both faced the same technological challenges stemming from the development of new third generation technology (3G) mobile telephony. A joint venture was attractive because it both split the costs and brought the full spectrum of technological skill together, which neither company alone possessed.

The companies were both aware of the statistics on the success rate of mergers and acquisitions, and because the stakes were high, the failure of the joint venture to launch and operate successfully would be damaging to both companies. Because the traditional financially dominated due diligence process would be unlikely to reveal problems, that approach would actually contribute little to the process.

What was required was an approach that looked at how the companies used their resources and how their different cultural backgrounds might affect the formation and operation of the joint venture. To investigate how resources, especially those of an intangible nature, are used in both companies and how they might be used in a joint venture, a practical working means of analyzing and measuring intellectual capital was required. Of particular use was the IC navigator since this gave a simple but useful visualization of the modes of use of the resources and would highlight any serious incompatibilities in value logic. Further analysis using the effector analysis would reveal quality synergies, complementarities, and gaps.

The study was carried out in the early part of 2001 with wide-ranging but managed access to key documents concerning company structure, business processes, and strategies. From the documents and reports, a picture of the nature, volume, and quality of the resources proposed for use in the joint venture was built. This led to the creation of detailed distinction trees in which the resource categories were fully defined and quantified. More importantly, the business process information and strategic documents gave a clear picture of how they were used at present. The two navigators for both companies at level 1 (the coarsest level of granularity) are shown in the following figure.

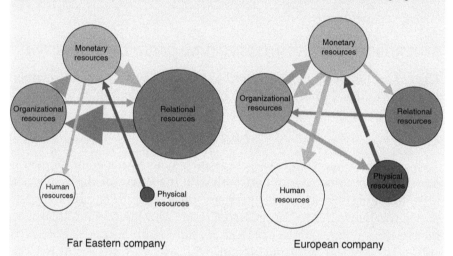

Far Eastern company   European company

The differences between the two companies are obvious. The Far Eastern company is typical in that it operates a network of alliances that supply ideas, manufacture components, and assemble. Thus relational resources are large and influential. The human resources of the company are of lesser importance and serve to forge and hold partner alliances as well as integrate ideas in equal measure. The principal use of financial resources is to support suppliers and partners. By contrast, the European company is a typical value shop but with an in-house manufacturing capability. Here, customers' demands and company human resources fuel product development and new (organizational) ideas. The organizational resources (IP, processes, and plans) drive the physical resources, which then lead to income.

It was clear that the two modes of operation were not immediately compatible and since the joint venture would have to follow the value logic of one or the other parent, a successful joint venture could not be put in place quickly, if at all. The main problem is that if the Far Eastern company were to adopt the more in-house approach to R&D, this would deeply offend the relationships it had forged over the years. On the

Continued

Case 6.1 Joint Venture Assessment—cont'd

other hand, the European company had few such relationships to contribute since its R&D was concentrated in-house. If it were to adopt the R&D strategy of the Far Eastern company, its own R&D capability would be rendered irrelevant which would have consequences for its non-joint venture operations.

Given the serious differences at this level of analysis and the lack of time to make meaningful and acceptable changes, the recommendation was that the joint venture should not be entered upon. This is the course of action that was followed. Had more time been available or if the differences in value logic had been less marked, then the analysis would have continued with a more searching investigation at the next level of granularity coupled with an investigation into the quality of the resources through the effector and hot-spot analyses.

SYNERGIES FROM THE INTELLECTUAL CAPITAL PERSPECTIVE

The concept of synergy has evolved to become the holy grail of mergers and acquisitions. Conceptually, the benefit of synergy can be understood using the oft-repeated illustration:

$$2 + 2 = 5$$

To assess and understand issues regarding synergies, a common taxonomy is required that corresponds well with the nature of the managerial task. Most classifications of synergies fail to provide insight into how these synergies are to be achieved and what the issues regarding their realization are going to be. Indeed, the conditions under which synergy arises are not well understood, and synergies are a concept that many managers seem to understand but have a difficult time putting into practice.

In the intellectual capital perspective where firms are viewed as systems of tangible and intangible resources, synergies can be conceptualized as a value creation benefit arising through the interaction between two systems of resources.[3] In other words, a synergy in intellectual capital terms can be defined as the *interaction* of two or more resources from previously sovereign organizations that creates an enhanced combined effect to value creation and competitive performance, which is greater than the sum of their individual effects.

There are three categories of benefits from mergers and acquisitions:

1. **Automatic benefits:** Automatic benefits do not require any interaction of resources from merging firms and require very little postacquisi-

tion activity. They stem from transaction cost reduction (i.e., increased efficiency), increased market power (increase relational capital), coinsurance and risk diversification—purely financial capital rationales—to reduce the probability of bankruptcy for the combined firm.

2. **Economies of fitness:** Economies of fitness represent synergies that are achieved by combining different but complementary intellectual capital. Gains from resource interactions between firms stem from the existence of complementarity between resources throughout the value creation model and exist when the joint use of two different sets of resources can potentially yield a higher total return than the sum of returns that can be earned if each set of resources is used independently of the other. The joint use does not have to prevent either set of resources from being used simultaneously or sequentially with other resources that also exhibit complementarity with them.

3. **Economies of sameness:** These synergies are achieved through accumulating similar intellectual capital. They include benefits from economies of scale, which are common in strategy literature. Here the focus is usually on a value adding resource, which covers a key factor for success in the business. In this case, intellectual capital from one firm strengthens the competitive position of the other. The two value creation models in the firms are not identical, but are similar in some parts. Synergies can only be achieved by an active combination, integration, and reconfiguration of the former independent parts—for example, merging sales personnel and manufacturing capacities. It is possible that resources and their interactions combine destructively to decrease value generation to levels below either of the previously sovereign levels. In these circumstances, divestment of the least important resources and interactions (which together represent a set of business activities) is a course of action that should be considered.

An analysis of the nature of the possible synergies requires a two-stage approach using the intellectual capital process. The first stage involves a high-level assessment of the strategic fit of the intellectual capital value creation models. This step involves assessing and comparing the navigators for the merging firms. The second step involves a deeper and more detailed qualitative analysis of the merging resources to assess the readiness and inertia of the merging resources. We now discuss each step in further detail.

Case 6.2 Cloetta Fazer Confectionery: Innovation Process as a Success Factor in the Fast Moving Consumer Goods Business

Cloetta Fazer Confectionery is the Finnish sales and marketing company of Cloetta Fazer, a merger of the Swedish Cloetta and Fazer Konfektyr of Finland. Cloetta Fazer is the Nordic region's leading confectionery company, and has well-established brands such as Fazer Blå, Dumle, Kexchoklad, Center, Marianne, Fazermint, Bridgeblandning, Tyrkisk Peber, Plopp, and Sportlunch. Year after year, Cloetta Fazer is able to maintain its market leader position and keep consumers satisfied. The success of the company is based on long history and family traditions as well as on the personnel's ability to anticipate and translate consumer needs and preferences into delicious products and strong brands.

The management of Cloetta Fazer Confectionery is committed to the notion of continuous improvement, which manifests itself above all in personnel and process development. Being in the business of fast-moving consumer goods, one of the key success factors of the company is cross-functional innovativeness enabled by visionary and professional personnel and efficient work practices to develop ideas into commercially successful products. The challenge for the management was to understand how innovations come about and how this process could be integrated into the personnel development and strategic planning processes. In addition, tools were needed to manage the innovation process. An IC approach provided an appropriate framework for a resource based view to meet the needs of management.

First, the innovation process was mapped and divided into development, execution, and exploitation phases. Each phase was further divided into subprocesses such as idea generation, idea handling, and idea approval to cover all critical steps necessary from idea generation to sales of a new product. In the next step, existing concrete tasks and practices within the various process phases were identified. Finally, the necessary and critical human, structural, and relational resources were identified and allocated to each task, giving a comprehensive view of the intangibles generating product innovations.

The analysis provided the management a structured and comprehensive picture of the existing activities and intangible resources generating innovation, and also disclosed some gaps where improvements could be made. The IC view on the innovation process broken down into human, structural, and relational capital disclosed necessary and critical competences, work practices, procedures, processes, and external partners that were involved in the process steps. For instance, the structures and practices to filter ideas in the idea handling phase turned out to be too weak, resulting sometimes in inefficient allocation of resources.

Also, insight was gained on the importance of all categories of intangibles and the need to have a balance between human, structural, and relational capital resources. For instance, the exercise revealed that relational capital (e.g., customers, partners) could be engaged more in the idea generation phase. Next the management would like to synchronize the innovation process with the company's strategic planning process. The framework will also provide information on what should be measured and followed up. In addition, it allows for analyzing critical interfaces between teams and functions and thus improving exchange of knowledge and communication.

For the HR function and personnel development, the approach provided insight as to how personal characteristics could be taken into account in work assignments and various innovation related tasks and how these issues could be discussed in performance appraisals and employee evaluations.

HIGH-LEVEL ASSESSMENT OF THE STRATEGIC FIT OF INTELLECTUAL CAPITAL

Strategic fit is largely dependent on a match between types of business models or the type of intellectual capital resources. A strategic fit in a merger or acquisition can be judged by the degree to which combining firms augment or complement each other's strategy in terms of industry, market, or intellectual capital base. This involves assessing and comparing the individual value creation models as depicted by the intellectual capital navigators introduced in Chapter 3.

Synergies are assessed by inspecting and quantifying the adherence to one of the three basic business logics; value shop, value chain, or value network. Inspection shows the predominant mode, and the matrix of interactions that provides the data for the intellectual capital navigator is used to quantify the degree of adherence. To do this, the sum of the value-creating transformations among the core resources is compared to the sum of the whole. Generally speaking, a combination of resources (together with their transformations) can be a considered a strength if they are in line with the strategic logic and are being leveraged. Similarly, weaknesses in a value creation model are represented by apparent lapses and qualitative shortcomings in the IC navigator model. Based on this distinction between strengths and weaknesses, the first dimension in assessing the strategic fit calls for a conjunctive review of the strengths and weaknesses in the merging value creation models. The second dimension examines whether or not the value creation models currently fit together or can be brought into line in the future according to strategic merger/acquisition objectives. Most businesses are not based on a single pure logic but often have elements of two or more logics. It is this that often permits a meaningful assessment of how combining resources in their logics can be reconfigured. A merger or acquisition will only be successful if the new resulting value creation model after integration can leverage intellectual capital more effectively and efficiently than the sovereign value creation models that were used before the merger or acquisition. If we assume that strategic intent and the industry opportunities and threats are taken into consideration in a strategic due diligence, then assessment of the strategic fit of intellectual capital involves two dimensions: the two dimensions of strategic fit and the strength of the creation model. A matrix of possible outcomes from such analyses can be drawn up for a quick view of the degree of difficulty likely to be encountered in merging two businesses. This may lead to a decision to abandon a merger or acquisition at this stage.

Strategic fit of the value creation models

- **Low Strategic Fit:** If the underlying strategic logics are different and have little common ground, they have low strategic fit. If there is no chance of overcoming this deficit even with the help of integration management, there is low strategic fit and there is a problem with the merger and acquisition.
- **Medium Strategic Fit:** If the logics are different but there is synergy in secondary business logics, the value creation models have a medium strategic fit. If there is no clear fit in the present situation but there are reasonable prospects for achieving an appropriate fit in the future, the partners should also be analyzed with respect to possible reconfigurations in the value creation models so that the two partners can grow together and reach a satisfactory strategic fit. This also leads to an evaluation of a medium level of strategic fit. However, particularly in these cases, the dangers have to be analyzed thoroughly and the presumed benefit of the synergy compared with the expected costs of conversion and integration management.
- **High Strategic Fit:** A strategic fit is considered to be high if the present value creation models already fit together and no significant deterioration is to be expected.

Strengths of the value creation models

- **Low Strength:** When the value creation models of both organizations show apparent weaknesses, a merger or acquisition does not have to be ruled out but it does require considerable care. If there are weaknesses in the same areas of the navigator, a negative reenforcement can be expected. On the contrary, two weak partners can support each other if the weaknesses are of a different nature through economies of sameness.
- **Medium Strength:** The value creation models are considered to be of medium strength if at least one of the partners can be classified as

strong. If one model is stronger, a reconstruction might take place by investing in or combining intellectual capital. If the strengths are on the part of the less dominant firm, the dominant firm can profit from this. In areas of high strategic fit a reduction of one's own weaknesses is possible. If the less dominant firm posses strengths in areas that do not fit with the dominant one, a possible removal of intellectual capital can be taken into consideration.

- **High Strength:** The value creation models are of high strength if both partners possess fairly well-developed value creation models and core intellectual capital. If they also go together well, the prerequisites for a "superdeal" are perfect, otherwise, intellectual capital stripping may be thought of.

Taking a high-level approach that considers value creation strengths and the strategic fit of the value creation models yields potentially important insights and implications for postdeal integration management of the concerned intellectual capital. While the analysis so far has been useful, it must be continued by undertaking a more detailed analysis and qualitatively assessing the individual intellectual capital resources. Fundamentally, the qualitative assessment process is the same as described in Chapter 3 for a single-firm context, but in a merger or acquisition a qualitative assessment is undertaken for each resource base to be integrated (see Figure 6.1).

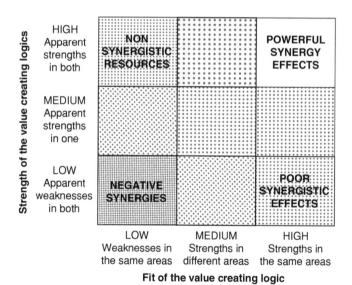

Figure 6.1. Detail assessment of resource bases.

The assessment of resources falls into two basic categories: the first looks at the resources themselves and the second at the inertial effects that may hinder the integration of the resources into their new context. Expressed as an equation we have:

$$\text{Value creation potential} = f(\text{conditions for trading and leveraging IC; transformation inertia})$$

Conditions

There are five conditions that determine whether intellectual capital has the potential for synergy and whether that potential can be fully leveraged. A simple scoring system to give a fitness index is all that is required in this assessment. In the descriptions of the conditions given in the following paragraphs, the resources are rather generic in character, which means that practitioners in real situations should use these as a guide while developing their own measures that follow the spirit of the general examples.

1. **Criticality:** All resources in the intellectual capital navigator are strategic because they are required for the strategic logic of the companies in question. However, when value creation models are reconfigured to form a new model of value creation, strategic needs may require a change in resource circumstances. With regards to the strategic logic, we already distinguished between intellectual capital deepening, which involves firms retaining similar intellectual capital to the existing intellectual capital, and intellectual capital extension, which involves firms retaining intellectual capital distinct to the existing intellectual capital. A strategy of IC deepening is represented by a path-dependent change in the strategic logic whereas a strategy of IC extension is represented by a path-breaking change in the strategic logic. Depending on the strategy followed, intellectual capital that has been valuable in the past does not necessarily have to be valuable in the new strategic logic. The metric therefore applies to important resources only and a high score is given to those resources that have high importance in the merged organization.

2. **Flexibility:** For intellectual capital resources to have potential for synergy, the underlying resources and transformations must have the ability to create multiple outputs.[4] They have to be flexible. In other words, intellectual capital must possess strategic substitutes for it to

possess synergy potential. Ultimately it is the flexibility of the resources and transformations that provide this potential. The flexibility of intellectual capital resources can increase on one of the following dimensions:

○ IC flexibility increases as the range of uses to which IC can be applied effectively increases. Intellectual capital resources such as intellectual property, systems, and skills vary in their degree of flexibility regarding their usage. For example, the range of uses the Coca-Cola Company can associate with the Coke™ brand is limited to a greater extent than the range of uses the Walt Disney Company can associate with the Disney™ brand (theme parks, cartoon characters, toys, videos, movies).

○ Resource flexibility increases as the time required to switch a resource from one use to another decreases. Flexible intellectual capital has more than one use and can be switched from one use to another quickly and efficiently. For example, training an employee in a new skill might require longer than installing a new software on an IT system. Here the IT system is the more flexible resource.

○ Resource flexibility increases as the switching cost from one use to another decreases. For example, in a bank merger the high cost of adapting one intranet to that of the dominating merger partner might justify replacing the intranet completely.

3. **Accessibility:** Intellectual capital resources must be accessible before they can be leveraged for synergy. Although the condition of accessibility might seem logical for physical resources, it cannot always be taken for granted for intangible resources, and resource accessibility is critical for synergies based on knowledge based resources.[5] With human resources, this is often an organizational culture issue, and where this is the case a deeper analysis of the prevalent organizational cultural systems is warranted.

4. **Capacity Constraint:** Intellectual capital resources must have the capacity to be leveraged as a synergy. In other words, all value creation must be within the capacity of intellectual capital for synergy to be realized.[6] Physical resources have clear capacity constraints to value creation. Raw materials, fixed assets, and network delivery systems present a fixed capacity limit. Because intellectual capital resources are nonrivalrous, an assessment of the current and future leveraging capacity is important. For example, where a knowledge-based synergy effect is dependent on the teaching of knowledge, organizations differ in their capacity to engage in different types of

learning.[7] A common factor discussed in the literature as affecting capacity for learning is the *absorptive capacity* of an organization.[8] Here it is argued that a necessary condition for a firm's successful exploitation of intangible resources outside its boundaries is the development of the ability to absorb such resources within the firm. The people involved need to have the critical mass of intellectual ability to use and apply what has been traded. It must be stressed that intellectual capital resources often do not have a direct capacity constraints, but constraints lie in the mechanisms that leverage the resources and, hence, the resource transformations.

5. **Coordination Flexibility:** Coordination flexibility refers to the ability of managers to coordinate new strategic uses for flexible intellectual capital resources by redirecting, reconfiguring, and redeploying the resources. Style and ability to integrate the management of the two firms are critical variables for success; therefore the capacity to manage interdependences correctly is a key determinant for value creation in mergers and acquisitions.[9] Similarly, just as intellectual capital resources are required to be flexible in their use to allow for synergies, the coordination management of these resources and transformations is essential to using these flexibilities of a company's resources advantageously in a dynamic setting. The coordination flexibilities of companies arises from the companies' abilities to change their strategic logic, management practices, and intellectual capital when it becomes strategically advantageous to do so. The inflexibilities of the least flexible element will act as a bottleneck that limits the overall flexibility of the firm as a system to respond to change.

Transformation inertia

The second dimension to analyzing the transformations associated with a trade of resources concerns the barriers and obstacles that inhibit the transformations during the trade of intellectual capital. Based on the definition, a resource transformation is "the process of engendering a fundamental change in one or more resources." Inertia is the strong persistence of existing forms and functions. Clearly, transformation inertia can inhibit the rate at which synergies are realized.

The causes of inertia will vary from instance to instance, but five of the common causes of inertia are described in the following paragraphs.

1. **Differences in Epistemological Viewpoints:** Differences in the epistemological viewpoints of people are directly correlated to the transformation inertia associated with the trade of knowledge intensive intellectual capital. Epistemology is the study of knowledge, and epistemological viewpoints refer to how knowledge is developed in a company and individuals. Knowledge transfer through intercompany links has primarily focused on the existence of an underlying latent construct of ambiguity surrounding the trade.[10, 11] For example, Attewell[12] states, "Far from being readily or easily transferred from the originator to the user of a technology, knowledge faces barriers and is relatively immobile." Such a view is shared by others,[13] who warn that knowledge is not as mobile as it has often been assumed, and who point to the "inertness of knowledge."

   In knowledge intensive organizations, the concept of intellectual capital path-dependency can be extended to account for the underlying epistemological viewpoints surrounding the value creation model. In the case of merging firms, success in the merger is more likely to occur if the crucial knowledge based value-creating pathways that are to be brought together have the same epistemological type. The key to this is the nature of the knowledge mechanisms in the companies. This means both the explicit systems embedded in information technology (IT) and the human based knowledge. Whereas IT systems can easily be changed, high value knowledge in the humans depends on their epistemologies, and this cannot be readily changed. Three cognitive distinctions exist[14] between knowledge viewpoints: cognitivist, connectivist, and autopoietic epistemologies. They are briefly described as follows:

   ○ Cognitivist organizations are considered as open organizations that develop increasingly accurate pictures of their worlds through the assimilation of new information. As the brain is seen as a machine of logic and deduction, knowledge is developed according to universal rules, hence the context of the incoming information is important. Cognitivists consider the identification, collection, and central dissemination of information as the main knowledge development activity.

   ○ Connectivist organizations share many similarities with the cognitivist approach, but one crucial difference is that there are no universal rules. Rules are team-based and vary locally. Organizations are then a group of self-organized networks dependent on communication. They make no distinction between the elements that store and process information since both are embedded in the connections between people. The connectionists believe that knowledge resides in the connections and hence focus on the self-organized dispersed information flow.

○ Autopoietic organizations are fundamentally different because the context of information inputs is unimportant; it is seen as data only. The organization is a system that is simultaneously open (to data) and closed (to information and knowledge). Information and knowledge cannot be transmitted easily since they require internal interpretation within the system according to the individual's rules. Thus autopoietics develop individual knowledge and respect that process in others.

The transfer of tacit knowledge and its effect on interfirm links has already been the subject of some debate. For example, in the case of strategic alliances, knowledge tacitness limits knowledge transfer due to the impact of tacitness on the instability of cooperation. In the context of hybrid organizations, technology transfer agreements, whose purpose is the exchange of tacit knowledge and expertise, tend to break down more often than those involving the exchange of formalizable technology. Theoretically, transformation inertia regarding tactiness equates the degree of resource tacitness to the extent of its nontransferability. The consequence of a large discrepancy in the epistemological modes between the merging companies is transformation inertia and leads to a very significant challenge for those charged with integration

2. **Intellectual Capital Complexity:** Complexity refers to the number of interdependent resources and transformations linked to core intellectual capital. As the complexity of core intellectual capital increases, it becomes more and more difficult to replicate all parameters involved. When the resources and capabilities that generate competitive advantage are complex networks of relationships between individuals, groups, and technology, imitation can be difficult. Hence, the complexity of core intellectual capital is positively correlated with the inability of others to imitate core intellectual capital.

3. **Experience with Changing Resource Transformations:** Based on empirical research, the level of experience a company has with changing the contexts of resource transformations is negatively related to the transformation inertia associated with the trade. Researchers[15] have found that tacit knowledge accumulated from prior acquisitions influences postacquisition performance if experiences are highly homogenous.

Experience in collaboration is essential to manage a diverse portfolio of collaborative ties and to accumulate the intellectual capital to benefit from the resulting interdependencies. Some blame the main source of problems and failures in collaborations on ignorance and lack of experience in dealing with changes associated with collaborations. Some have shown that past experience leads to the emergence of a distinct form of collaborative know-how that helps achieve greater benefits in subsequent intercompany links. In a significant way, this collaborative know-how affects the ability of companies to understand and adopt proper procedures for information gathering, interpretation, and diffusion. Companies traditionally involved in the purchase of technology from outside sources will develop appropriate routines to deal with this activity based on the accumulation of operating experience. Such understanding of collaborative mechanisms and trade processes favors the resource transformations during resource trade by eliminating many of the unnecessary tasks and disruptive noise of cooperation.

4. **Organizational Slack:** It has been found[16] that companies that allowed some slack in the postacquisition integration situation were not being sloppy but, instead, had found a way to deal with operating and strategic difficulties at the operating and business unit levels. Slack provides both protection and maneuvering room, preventing premature fixation on short-term results when the merged company does not immediately meet performance expectations. Organizational slack is an important concept in strategic management and organization theory and is referred to as "[the disparity] between the resources available to the organization and the payments required to maintaining the coalition." The availability of organizational slack is significantly influenced by postmerger integration management and is hence difficult to evaluate. Particularly where synergies involve human intellectual capital, the requirement for organizational slack and discretionary resources is high. Other transformation inertia factors act as major barriers to change and the synergy effects will not be realized immediately.

5. **Organizational Cultural Distance and the Atmosphere for Trade:** Organizational culture concerns symbols, values, ideologies, attitudes, and assumptions that operate, often in an unconscious way, to guide and fashion individual and business behavior. Organizational culture represents a significant source of complexity in postmerger integration, and organizational literature stresses the need for a culture fit as a necessity for the success.[17] The message they convey is that just as

culture is as fundamental to an organization as personality is to the individual, the degree of culture fit that exists between combining organizations is likely to have a direct effect on the value creation potential of the merger. The fundamental change may be a strategic redirection, but it always includes structural change and a dramatic alteration in the behavior of individuals. Where the strategic motivation of mergers requires the trade and integration of resources, success becomes heavily dependent on synergy effects between human capital and organizational capital resources. The integration process is one that, depending on the strategic requirements, can call for a significant amount of change. Culture strongly inhibits change, and especially strong cultures are particularly resistant to change.[18] In a merger and acquisition integration process, the sociocultural integration of two previously discrete organizational cultures is a major ungluing and regluing job. The ensuing changes lead to numerous challenges for the combined organization such as threatening of individual interests and power bases; challenging of existing ideologies, norms, values, traditions, rules, and procedures; creation of personal stress; and so on. For the most part, these potential disruptions motivate people to resist change and defend the status quo, unless they see some personal or organizational benefits to be gained from the changes.

Case 6.3 Analysis of the Merger of Two Consultancies

In the autumn of 2000, a large management consultancy/accountancy firm commenced the acquisition of a small specialist consultancy/think tank. The motivation of the large company was that it needed the know-how and methodologies of the specialist company to bolster its market offerings and give it a competitive advantage over its competitors. Although the liaison was sought by both companies and might be called a merger, due to the disparity in sizes, the intention of the large consultancy was the total integration of the specialists into its structure, making this more of an acquisition. The specialist company, while accepting that this was a takeover and initially apprehensive, felt that the large company would be able to leverage their methodologies and give them international visibility in a way that they could never achieve themselves.

A financial and legal due diligence activity was initiated by the large company, who were eventually satisfied that there were no apparent barriers to acquisition. At the time, the methodologies described in the preceding section to analyze an acquisition were not available, and so the acquisition went ahead without a methodology and in a way entirely in line with the common practice of the time. A stepwise acquisition was planned with the large company acquiring the specialists with share ownership increasing with the passing of managerial milestones.

Toward the end of 2001, the requirement to separate accounting and consulting activities led to the break-up of many of the large consulting/accounting firms. This event led the consulting entity to undertake a strategic realignment away from management and toward information technology: hence, there was now no longer any need for the acquisition. The stepwise acquisition was halted. It is arguable that the acquisition and integration was not going well and that if an intellectual capital analysis had been undertaken as described in the preceding section, then either the acquisition would have been managed differently or some other form of cooperation would have been negotiated in place of an acquisition.

This case study uses the process described in the preceding sections to show what would have emerged in this case.

The motives of the two companies have already been touched upon, and the mode is clearly one of intellectual capital deepening, which implies path-breaking. The issue of size disparity can be overstated since the companies are what they are. In general, the benefits occur in fitness and are worth pursuing. The benefits for the two organizations are as shown in Table 6.1.

Expected IC Synergies

	For the large company	For the specialist company
Automatic benefits	Low due to size disparity	High due to size disparity
Economies of fitness	High due to large influx of specialist forms of human and organizational capital	High due to large influx of specialist forms of relational and organizational capital
Economies of sameness	Low due to size disparity	High due to size disparity

The high level analysis requires that intellectual capital navigators are constructed for the two companies, and these are shown in Figure 6.2. The navigators have some outward similarities such as the irrelevance of physical resources and the pattern of transformation linkages. However, the navigator also shows the big difference between the companies. In the large consultancy, the resource that affects the customer (a relational resource) and the cash (a monetary resource) is the standard portfolio of deliverable processes, which is the major component of the organizational resources. In short, the large consultancy sells and delivers standard processes and is efficient in this. The human resource is used just to deliver engagements, and should there be a loss in human resources, those losses could be made good quickly by recruitment. Even if this occurred during an engagement, the damage would not be serious because the replacement people simply continue the engagement according to the prescribed process. The key value generating resource in the specialist company is the human resource. Although the codification of ideas into processes is still important, more important is the ability of the people to address and solve nonstandard customer problems. Thus, when they

Continued

Case 6.3 Analysis of the Merger of Two Consultancies—cont'd

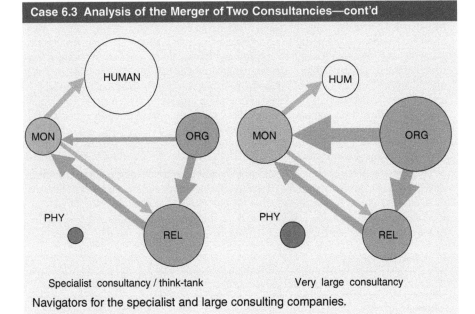

Specialist consultancy / think-tank   Very large consultancy

Navigators for the specialist and large consulting companies.

are hired on an engagement, the key earning process is through the sale of that ability.

Since the strategic models have significant differences in that the specialist is a true value shop while the large consultancy has a strong bias towards being a nonmanufacturing value chain, their strategic fit cannot be said to be high. At best it is medium. Both models are robust and work well, and so the strength of the value creation model might be judged as high. However, it cannot really be counted as a super deal because the strength of the specialist consultancy is in an area where the dominant big consultancy logic has no real need for strengthening. While this is a point which must be the focus of the detailed analysis, at this point it serves only to impose a slight reduction in the strength of the value-creating models. Figure 6.3 is a copy of Figure 6.1 but now showing the assessed position of this merger.

The detail assessment of the merging companies is given in Table 6.2. The assessment is undertaken in two parts, each being evaluated separately in the first place. This results in two figures whose product is the instantaneous value-creating potential. Because the second element, transformation inertia, is time-dependent, evaluations of the inertia will change in time and thus affect the overall value creating potential.

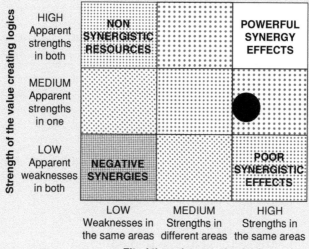

High level assessment.

The mean of the conditions section would be a mid-range score. The means of the transformation inertia section would be a low score. It would be expected that the initial value creation levels would be low.

It is also clear from the analysis that the key area for the acquiring managers to focus on was finding a way to integrate the autopoietic specialists without degrading their abilities and output with rules or, in the extreme, without triggering their departure. Furthermore, and more difficult, the acquiring managers had to convince the ultra-conservative client managers to try the acquired methodologies on clients. Due to the market circumstances at the time, this was probably the more difficult task.

The conventional due diligence exercise was carried out without a hitch and without highlighting any causes for concern. The intellectual capital analysis showed that the acquisition was reasonably attractive at a high level but the more detailed analysis showed two areas where the acquisition could run into serious problems. This would have given those managers charged with acquisition and integration the information they needed to plan the best integration pathway. They did not do so, however, as exogenous events intervened and the acquisition was terminated.

Continued

Case 6.3 Analysis of the Merger of Two Consultancies—cont'd

Detailed Analysis

Conditions	Comment
Criticality	Low score since the important human resources of the specialist company will not be critical in the new circumstances.
Flexibility	High score as the critical human resources are inherently flexible.
Accessibility	Mid score since although human resources are generally accessible, cultural issues may override this.
Capacity constraint	High score. The capacity to absorb the processes of the specialist may be considered high due to the general recruitment of high quality staff.
Coordination flexibility	Low score. In the prevailing market conditions, managers have great difficulty in applying the new resources through client managers unwilling to innovate.

Transformation Inertia

Epistemological differences	An epistemological assessment of the companies and key groups within them showed the big consultants to be connectivist/cognitivists (team players but with a strong process bias) while the specialists were autopoietic (individualists). Low score due to a large mismatch.
IC complexity	High, as the operational logic of both companies was simple.
Experience	Low score. The track record of successful assimilations of specialists into the large company was mediocre.
Organizational slack	Medium score. The large consultancy aimed at very high utilization, and this meant that the best people were rarely available to facilitate the integration.
Cultural distance	Low score. The specialists were egalitarian and chaotic in the eyes of the large consultancy. They were seen as rigid and impossibly structured by the specialists.

DIVESTMENTS

Divestment does not seem to have attracted the same level of academic interest as mergers and acquisitions. Nevertheless, mishandling a divestment can cause as much difficulty as a mishandled merger or acquisition. It has been noted[19] that even in the United Kingdom when divestment levels were at their peak the 1980s, there were few analyses or studies concerning the motives or mechanics of divestment. The first studies on divestment date from the 1970s, and were related to the growing number of nationalizations in developing countries, which translated into the forced divestment of some industrial companies. In the 1980s, studies on divestment focused on joint ventures' instability and barriers to integration. Finally, during the 1990s, studies allied the relationship between cultural, social, behavioral, and empirical experiences arising from foreign expansions of multinational companies and their consequent divestments.

Before entering a discussion of divestment, it is important that the scope of the term is defined. Broadly, divestment includes any action that implies a lower level of commitment to the functional scope of the subsidiary. This is in line with the definition developed by Benito and Welch[20] (which also includes de-internationalization). Divestment ranges from the mildest interpretation of "lower commitment" to the most extreme forms of divestment, which is the closure or sale of a subsidiary. Another view of divestment situations is to consider them as an adjustment process by which companies attempt to find their *good* level of diversification. In addition, success with divestment appeared to depend of two main factors. The first of these was the level of exogenous shock and the level of diversification encountered, and second was the adjustment promptness, the latter point being in line with the time needed to build new relational resources. Companies shed business units for a variety of reasons. The three most commonly cited are as follows[21]:

1. Markets demand the improvement in near-term earnings and divesting low performing business units as a way to improve the performance of the remainder, to raise cash to maintain dividends, to fund critical capital expenditure and repay debt makes a compelling case. This reason can also be reversed in situations where the HQ is the underperforming entity.
2. Splitting a major company into two or more "pure plays" promises to unlock value for shareholders. This is similar to the first reason, but without the stigma of poor performance.

3. Following a merger or acquisition, the acquiring company recognizes that some of what it has bought is not needed for the strategic development of the company and so it is divested or spun off as soon as possible.

Setting aside the circumstances that lead to forced divestment (nationalization, confiscation or seizure), divestment makes sense only as part of a sound, long-term strategy in which the company constantly reviews, replenishes, and trims its portfolio as its markets change and evolve. That is very different from selling a poorly performing unit at an unattractive valuation, which is an all too common response to difficult economic times.

Statistically, for every successful spin-off or divestment, there are two that fail to live up to their potential. This rather dismal figure suggests that boards of directors, executives, and especially senior managers charged with the management of the divestment are lacking something and are therefore unable to develop and execute strategies that will fulfill the promise. It appears that a successful spin-off requires the following three steps[22]:

1. **Ensure that both parent and Spin-off have viable business and financial structures.** A company's decision to divest a division is often triggered by the parent's poor performance. On average, divesting companies underperformed the S&P 500 by 5% in the two years before the announcement. Their lagging financial performance frequently persuaded parent companies to improve their own balance sheets by burdening their offspring. Divested companies are more likely to fall into bankruptcy than the parent because the parent saddles them with excessive debt, onerous contracts, or impaired assets.

2. **Continue growth beyond childhood.** Growth appears to be a more considerable challenge for divested companies than for other publicly traded companies.

3. **Meet or exceed earnings expectations.** Markets seem to allow a year or two for divested companies to settle before settling on a view of the quality and reliability of the newly independent company's management team. Analysis suggests that during this critical period, an earnings shortfall has a somewhat greater effect on the stock price of a divested company than on the average publicly traded company's stock.

Inspection of the preceding criteria reveals perhaps the cause for the dismal failure rate of divestments, especially in the divested entity. It is plain that the criteria are aimed at financial performance rather than taking the wider perspective that intellectual capital allows. The CFO may see the company as a hierarchical structure of cost and profit centers within strategic business units and that these are all part of a whole with HQ at the top. Following on from this would be the not unnatural assumption that distinct sections of the financial structure can be divested with little difficulty as they are already, or could become, (semi)autonomous accounting units.

Of course, the reality of the situation is usually very different. While subsidiaries, let alone strategic business units, may appear to be readily separable, the actual operational links between them and other parts of the company are manifold and diverse. It is the inadvertent rupture of these links that lead to problems as new relationships take time to be forged, and during this time financial performance is poor. There are undoubtedly other issues along the lines of those described in the section on mergers and acquisitions which an already stretched management team has to address.

The following example illustrates the pitfalls of divestment from an intellectual capital perspective. The advantages of taking a resource based view on company development was, of course, studied in the 1950s and it was demonstrated that different company resources allied to the environment in which they are deployed conferred advantages in different ways for different companies and that a strategic action map or other preparation was required The example concerns a company that designs and manufactures widgets in a Western country. Over recent years, the relocation of the manufacturing to countries where the (wage) cost base is much lower has been very common. In addition, for some companies whose designs have been obviously excellent and whose designs are modular in nature, there has been another option. This involves the divestment of the manufacturing activity while the remainder of the company concentrates on design. The divestment looks reasonably easy from a financial perspective as the facilities used by the manufacturing part are separate from the research part and manufacturing is a separate accounting unit. The business plan for the divested part would be that it would continue to manufacture for the original designers and would be free to contract in manufacturing for other widget companies and would be able to expand their manufacturing portfolio to maximize the utilization of their plant and people. From such a rough basis, a post-separation growth plan for the manufacturing part is perfectly possible to envisage. The design part would also have a growth plan in that they would not be in any way constrained by the capabilities of their manufacturing plant and would simply be selling excellent widget designs to other widget companies with other manufacturing capabilities and would also be able to extend their business by extending into new areas of widget use. Again, an entirely plausible growth plan can be envisaged.

Prior to divestment, the intellectual capital navigator of the whole company would typically be as shown in Figure 6.4.

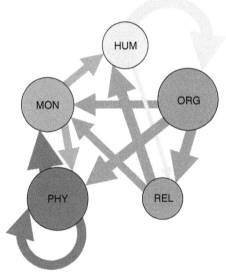

Figure 6.4. Intellectual capital navigator of the undivested company.

The navigator is quite typical of a "hybrid" manufacturing company and shows the two distinct organizational forms of a value chain (manufacturing) and a value shop (design). In the manufacturing value shop, raw materials or components are purchase (monetary to physical), manufacturing occurs (physical to physical) using a manufacturing process (organizational to physical), and the product is sold (physical to monetary). At the same time, humans are devising new design recipes (human to organizational), taking cues from external sources and the customers (relational to human), and customers are attracted by the excellence of the designs (organizational to relational) and buy the designs (relational and organizational to monetary).

Viewed very simply, the manufacturing value chain part is basically linear (physical to physical to monetary) while the design value shop is triangular (relational to human to organizational to relational). However, even excluding the physical and monetary resources, there are critical links that will be broken on divestment and new ones will have to be built to complete the new organizations. Figure 6.5 shows the two divested organizations side-by-side for comparison.

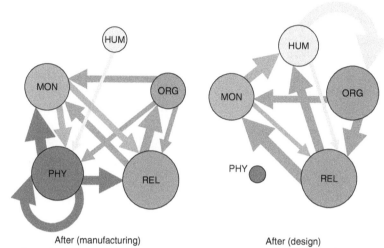

After (manufacturing)   After (design)

Figure 6.5. The divested organizations in functioning form.

Even starting with the same basic resources, their importance has changed in the two organizations, as has the importance of the resource transformation links. New links have had to be forged in both companies to make them viable.

In the manufacturing company the value chain is unchanged. However, in place of the manufacturing recipes provided by the design part, they are now dependent on winning new contracts from new customers. Thus their physical capabilities will affect the customers (new link) and those customers will be supplying the business recipe (the contractual requirement in the order), so relational resources will affect the organizational ones. Monetary resources will accrue through the strength of these relationships and the quality of the physical product. Thus relational and physical capital affect monetary capital. Humans are incidental in what is assumed to be a highly automated manufacturing process. While the fundamental value chain is intact and obvious, a whole new set of relationship has to be built if the newly devolved company is to grow or even survive.

In the new design company there is no need for physical resources, so they have effectively disappeared from the navigator. As with the manufacturing company, the basic value-creating pathway, the triangular value shop, is intact, but other things now have to replace the missing link to manufacture. After divestment, the money generating transformations arise from the transformation of customer capital and the new product (organizational capital) into monetary resources. Crucial again is the attraction of a new type of customer (relational capital) since the product now being sold is a process rather than a physical object. In both new organizations, monetary resources will be needed to build this new customer base, and money is the key resource in maintaining the flow of ideas round the value shop.

In both new companies there are surprising changes in the navigators, principal among these is the different type of customer needed in both navigators. In manufacturing, new customers with new requirements that can be translated into organizational capital must be found. This is a two-resource type search. For the design company, new customers with new needs are required.

While both companies can survive on legacy products and processes at a lower level for a while (the designers must find customers to sell their old process to, other than their former manufacturers and the manufacturers must manufacture with the possibility of new competitors using their old processes), something must be done quickly. The time, effort, and expense involved in generating a new client base of a different type from the one that existed previously is never to be underestimated. Aside from any other cultural or financial problems that may have been inherited at divestment, the need to rebuild the navigator is paramount, and it is this that is underestimated. While a simple-minded division of the financial cake might be thought to indicate the existence of a viable divestment, as suggested in the first bullet point in the preceding list, divestment ought to be preceded by an analysis using an intellectual capital navigator followed by a build-up of new resources and transformation in the six months before divestment. One suggested model[23] is an eight-stage structure of development for viable subsidiaries with specific guidance for the subsidiary management team at each stage. The key recommendation from this research is that subsidiary managers need to change their mindset from one of obedience to HQ (what the research terms "boy-scouts") to one of being proactive initiative takers (subversives). This has to be undertaken from all perspectives and not just the HQ perspective.[24] It is likely that the failure rate of divestments is, in part, caused by a failure to do this properly.

HUMAN RESOURCE MANAGEMENT

This section aims to understand the impact human resource management approaches have had on overall business performance. This section charts the development of human resource management through the twentieth century and culminates with an explanation of the benefits of the intellectual capital perspective. It demonstrates the application of the methodology explained in Chapters 2 and 3 and shows how this gives insight; with the addition of the measurement methodologies from Chapter 4, it shows how these may be quantified.

History of human resource management

For as long as one person has been engaged or employed in furthering the aims of another, the employer has been concerned with ways of motivating the employee to maximize the effectiveness of the enterprise. Perhaps the most obvious example of this is to be found in the military world. In the commercial field, there is early but unreliably documented evidence of work on improving the conditions and effectiveness of employees in both France and the United Kingdom. In France the work most often cited is that of Jean Randolph Perronet, who studied the processes in the manufacturing of pins in the 1760s. In the United Kingdom, Thomas Mason in the Old Derby China Works published studies in 1792. The best documented early work is that of Robert Owen, a high capitalist but widely regarded as the father of socialism in the UK, who contributed greatly to the 1802 and 1819 Factory Acts (of Parliament) in the United Kingdom.

At the company level, the work of Fayol[25] in France and Taylor[26] in the United States represent the earliest attempts to put management on a more scientific standing and improve the efficiency of companies through better management of their resources and operations. Both Fayol and Taylor tended to concentrate on the activities and processes of companies, but their recognition of the employee is visible. This is especially true of Fayol, whose five roles of management are underpinned by fourteen general principles. Four of Fayol's principles have an almost modern feel while a fifth is reminiscent of recent Japanese employment principles. These are:

1. **Specialization of Labor:** Specializing encourages continuous improvement in skills and the development of improvements in methods.

2. **Remuneration:** Employees receive fair payment for services, not what the company can get away with.
3. **Equity:** There must be equality of treatment (but not necessarily identical treatment).
4. **Esprit de Corps:** Harmony and cohesion must exist among personnel.
5. **Personnel Tenure:** Limited turnover of personnel and lifetime employment for good workers were expected.

Through the remainder of the twentieth century there has been a general consensus on the stages of development of the human resource practice. Commentators have tended to partition the development of human resource management into about five periods. If the first of these is the early work, then the second may be labeled the welfare phase, and is exemplified by the experiments on working conditions by Mayo at the Hawthorne Works of Western English Electric Company. The third is the cost-center phase, the fourth is the internal market, and the last, so far, is strategic human resource management.

After the 1960s HR departments tended to become more of a branch of the administrative functions of companies. Typically, the HR department was a division of corporate HQ charged with providing services aimed at providing a fair, equitable, and high quality working environment for employees. It also dealt with pay and promotion structure and all other administrative procedures to do with hiring, firing, conduct, welfare, and so on. In the 1980s, however, there was a growing realization that the centralized approach was not a flexible and sustainable model of operation, especially as companies merged and became more international. A common response to this was the devolution of the HR function to strategic business units, with the central HR function being reduced to policy setting only. In this way, the subtlety of meaning in mission and vision statements emergent at this time could be interpreted more effectively by companies. It could be argued, however, that the function of the HR department retained its traditional nature in terms of day-to-day operation. It had become more efficient as it had lost its old status as a simple cost center. Because devolved HR depended on users buying "on-demand" service, HR had become part of an internal economy subject to the forces of internal markets.

The shift away from being a cost center to being a player in an internal market heralded a new phase in large company HR in which accountability to the company was of prime importance. Coinciding with this change was the rise of the intellectual capital perspective. It was now not enough for the HR function of the company to just "pay its way" as an integral operational part of the company. From now on, its role was to be strategic, and the concept of strategic human resource management (SHRM) was born.

The role of SHRM

Some believe[27] that SHRM "should be concerned with the determinants of decisions about human resource practices, the composition of the human capital resource pool, the specification of required human resource behaviors, and the effectiveness of these decisions given various business strategy and/or competitive situations." The distinction between traditional HRM and SHRM is that SHRM links human resource management practices with the strategic management process of the organization, whereas HRM has concentrated in the past on being a technically correct service.

The traditional HR function[28] is perhaps the last bastion of bureaucracy in many companies and is frequently viewed as a development roadblock by much of the rest of the organization. While some need for this role occasionally remains, especially in the implementation of legislation, much of the HR role is transforming itself. To make the changed function effective and relevant requires considerable change since the trend in successful organizations is to become more adaptable, resilient, quick to change direction, and customer centered.

Effective human resource management is no longer concerned with simply executing a standard set of policies and procedures. Rather, it requires questioning and understanding the relationships between choices in managing people, the strategies and goals of the organization, and the possibilities presented by the external environment. The future of HRM does not lie in progressive initiatives unconnected to business goals or organizational and environmental realities. Neither does it lie in the production of standardized sets of best practices. Rather, it lies in ensuring that the choices made in managing people are made sensibly with clear strategic purposes in mind. Clearly, its role[29] is now pervasive and highly interlinked, and the intellectual capital navigator should be extremely useful in mapping and explaining this.

In Japan[30] companies have been described as communities bound together by a common fate rather than as functional organizations. This suggests that management in Japan must analyze and define the types of HRM that will be needed in the future. They must put in place the means of measuring performance and rewarding people to encourage performance.

Since the early 1990s[31] there has been a lot of work investigating and researching business process architectures and models. Research has tended to describe the need to develop more formal systems engineering based approach for modeling HRM practices from a business process viewpoint.[32] It has pointed out that there is considerable confusion over the classification of HRM models and this can be seen best by contrasting the work of several mid-1990s viewpoints.[33,34,35] The literature describes the four most commonly accepted models. These are:

1. The Michigan Model[36] published from Michigan Graduate School of Business, which consists of strategic management and environmental pressures and the human resource cycle.
2. The Harvard Model[37] published from Harvard Business School, which consists of two parts human resource system and a map of the HRM territory.
3. The Guest Model,[38] devised by David Guest, involves four policies to achieve four main HR outcomes. These outcomes will lead to desirable organizational outcomes. This model is similar to the Harvard Model.
4. The Warwick Model,[39] developed by Warwick University, consists of inner and outer context and has more emphasis on strategy. Again, it is based on the Harvard Model.

Impact of HRM on company performance

In the literature there is surprisingly little that actually connects HRM practices with the performance of the business overall. Arguments are made in research connecting current and potential human resources to the development and execution of its strategic business plan. The work that has been carried out has tended to be statistical in nature, connecting the use of modern HR practices in companies with financial measures by means of techniques like factor analysis. The explanation for this is that the means by which HRM practices affect companies are very complex and reliable causal models are thus very hard to construct. The challenge is worthwhile; benefits most often cited include comprehensive employee recruitment and selection procedures, incentives, compensation and performance management systems, and extensive employee involvement and training. This, it is argued,[40] improves the knowledge, skills, and abilities of current and potential employees, increases their motivation, reduces absenteeism, and enhances retention of the best employees while encouraging nonperformers to leave the firm.

In 1995 a study was undertaken that sought to evaluate the links between these practices and company performance by means of a survey in the United States of nearly one thousand companies.[41] The assumption was that more effective systems of HRM practices are sources of sustained competitive advantage. Unfortunately, very little empirical evidence supported this, and what empirical work does exist has largely focused on individual HRM practices and not on the overall HRM system. It was contended[42] that human resources are frequently underutilized because employees often perform below their maximum potential, and that organizational efforts to elicit discretionary effort from employees are likely to provide returns in excess of any relevant costs. The argument was that HRM practices can affect such discretionary effort through their influence over employee skills and motivation and through organizational structures that provide employees with the ability to control how their roles are performed.

It was also noted that there was theoretical and empirical justification for a clear positive link between the adoption by organizations of a variety of progressive HR practices and both individual and organizational performance.[43] However, the nature of this link is still not well understood. In fact, there are a number of theories that have been proposed to account for the hypothesized affect of HR practices on performance. Particularly important in this respect are arguments derived from expectancy theory and from various behavioral theories of HRM. These suggest that progressive HR practices have a positive affect on performance primarily by enhancing employee skills and motivation as well as their overall level of satisfaction and identification with the organization. When the impact of complementary human resource management (HRM) practices on innovation performance was investigated, it was supposed that if there was a close connection between knowledge possessed by company personnel and the companies' products and services, it would be expected that a company's ability to produce new products were linked to how it organizes its human resources.[44]

Scorecard approaches linked to business performance

In the preceding section, the connection between the use of sets of HRM practices and improved business performance is demonstrated, but the connection to the processes is weak. It can be concluded that the there are useful HRM models and that their use improves business performance, but it is not known how in detail.

The strategic labor allocation process (SLAP),[45] is a resource based model with value creation in the market as its ultimate aim. The model applies equally to companies in the private sector and to nonprofit organizations in the public sector. In the SLAP model, distinctive competencies are the crucial elements of the organization's business idea and can be directly linked to the labor allocation process.

Two important points about the SLAP model can be made. First, a business idea and the associated distinctive competencies are not static entities. Changes in the external environment may not only have effects on the labor allocation process of the organization itself, but may also affect the degree of distinctiveness of its competencies in either a positive or negative way. Second, the SLAP model describes a more indirect feedback relation between the qualitative ways labor is allocated and the strengthening or weakening of the organization's distinctive competencies. From a methodological point of view, the SLAP model represents an intermediate step between the more traditional models described in preceding sections and the possibilities of an intellectual capital approach.

Intellectual capital is a holistic approach to business management and includes human resource management, integrating it in its proper places in the map of value creation in the company. Despite this holistic viewpoint, a large number of attempts to measure human capital in isolation have been made. Because of the narrowness of their viewpoint, they will be unable to account for the true role human capital and subsequent HRM plays in improving business performance since they cannot explain all the salient links without going outside their area. The result of this is that most of the attempts to measure human capital in isolation have no defensible mechanism to underpin them and consequently rely on scorecards, often backed up by benchmarking, to assess the state of human capital management and human resource management in companies.

Arguably, the most important of these approaches is that of the Saratoga Institute.[46] This lays a foundation for a methodology for measuring the return on investment (ROI) of human capital by suggesting the ways in which such capital interacts with other aspects of intellectual capital to optimize the effectiveness of an enterprise. To estimate the ROI of human capital, the Saratoga approach relies primarily on quantitative metrics, but also incorporates some perceptual measures into a scorecard model. This provides guidance on the design of objective and perceptual metrics at the enterprise level and claims that changes revealed by these metrics are a function of five indicators: cost, time, volume, errors, and human reactions. These indices can be compared with metrics for functional unit service, quality, and productivity to discover links between them, and they provide some examples of the effects of change on several performance indices.

A more process-orientated approach is that devised by Human Capital Capability Incorporated[47] and Cognitive Technologies Group.[48] The end result of this is a scorecard, but underpinning the scorecard structure is a three-tier model that has at its base human capital enablers (learning, governance, job design, and time), resources (investment, staff, technology, and content), and operations (process feedback, staffing, competency development, and retention). These produce intermediate outcomes (workforce proficiency, workforce engagement, employee satisfaction, manager proficiency, customer satisfaction, turnover, time to competence, and revenue from new products). At the top of the model is company financial performance, which comprises income, sales growth, market share, and stock performance. Whereas such a structure undoubtedly sets it apart from other scorecard approaches in that it can have the ability to predict the effects of HRM actions, its inputs are incomplete with respect to the breadth of managerial actions available to the management team. Only the holistic structural models found in an intellectual capital system can do this.

The final scorecard-based approach of note is the human capital index devised by Watson Wyatt.[49] Watson Wyatt carried out research using data from 400 U.S. and Canadian companies that were publicly traded, had at least three years of shareholder returns, and had a minimum of $100 million in revenue or market value. They asked a wide range of questions about how the organizations carried out their human resources practices, including pay, people development, communication, and staffing. Responses were matched to objective financial measures, including market value, three- and five-year total returns to shareholders (TRS), and Tobin's Q. Publicly available data from Standard and Poor's Compustat database were used to access the financial information needed.

To investigate the relationship between human capital practices and value creation, a series of multiple regression analyses were conducted, identifying a clear relationship between the effectiveness of a company's human capital practices and shareholder value creation. Thirty key HR practices were associated with a 30% increase in market value. Summary HCI scores were created for individual organizations so that results could be expressed on a scale of 0 to 100. An HCI score of 0 represents the poorest human capital management, whereas a score of 100 is ideal. The survey was extended to Europe and repeated in North America with an even larger sample in 2001. Companies could be ranked and compared against each other. The results showed a clear connection between HRM practices, the index developed, and the shareholder consequences. In this case, because the underlying structure is relatively simple, predictive and analytical work cannot be conducted.

The intellectual capital perspective

A company's employees provide a unique source of competitive advantage that is difficult for its competitors to replicate. Drawing on the resource based theory of the firm,[50] it is contended that human resources can provide a source of sustained competitive advantage when four basic requirements are met. First, they must add value to the company's production processes; levels of individual performance must matter. Second, the skills the firm seeks must be rare. Since human performance is normally distributed, this suggests that all human resources must meet both of these criteria. The third criterion is that the combined human capital investments a company's employees represent cannot he easily imitated. Although human resources are not subject to the same degree of imitability as equipment or facilities, investments in firm-specific human capital can further decrease the probability of such imitation by qualitatively differentiating a firm's employees from those of its competitors. Finally, a company's human resources must not be subject to replacement by technological advances or other substitutes if they are to provide a source of sustainable competitive advantage. Since these criteria and those used in the effector analyses of Chapter 3 are based on the resource based theory of the firm, they at once connect mainstream HR research with the intellectual capital approach.

By the same token, many of researchers cited in the preceding discussion have sought to look at systems of practice and the interconnections between HR management, strategic implementation, and future business performance. Once again, these align exactly with the intentions of the intellectual capital movement as a whole.

To discover the current interactions between human resources and all other resources important in running the company, all that is needed is to follow the processes in Chapters 2 and 3. In these, an intellectual capital navigator is produced which shows the importance of human resources and their value-creating interactions within the company. A numerical estimate of their importance relative to the company as a whole can be obtained from the underlying intellectual capital navigator matrix of transformations by summing the transformations and comparing them to other major functions of the company as a whole. It must be remembered that the navigator is a plot of what is important and is not a plot of value creation. This arises because equal value can be created in a range of ways stretching from a small but crucially important activity at one end to a large but not that important activity at the other.

In addition to this first analysis, it must be recalled that the intellectual capital approach is strategic and often requires that navigators depicting future desired states are also constructed. The difference between HR resource importance and resource transformation now and those of the desired future states shows where the key areas of development have to take place. It also shows which activities, and hence resources, need to be curtailed or halted. Thus the navigator plots instantly set out a strategic plan for HR management that is wholly aligned with the overall strategy of the company. It is a sad fact that many functional areas in many companies are charged with the development of their own local strategy, totally ignorant of whether it aligns with the corporate intent or any of the other subsidiary strategies.

While the intellectual capital navigator sets out the strategy for the HR managers, it can only hint at the implementation plan. It does this by showing which resources and transformations are to be subject to the greatest changes. More detail is gathered from the effector and hot-spot analysis. In the effector plot (Figure 6.6), the ratio of the transformation direction importance is plotted against the absolute importance of the resource.

In the plot, the lighter shades represent the evaluation of the resources as they stand, and the darker plots show the resources if the strategy is executed. The arrows clarify the changes. Clearly, some care has to be taken with the execution of the subsidiary HR strategy as the human resources move into the danger zone. The action required here is that the analysis is repeated at a lower level of granularity (Level 2) to understand exactly what the cause of this is, whether an alternative strategy should be considered, or what can be done within the existing strategy to mitigate the risks.

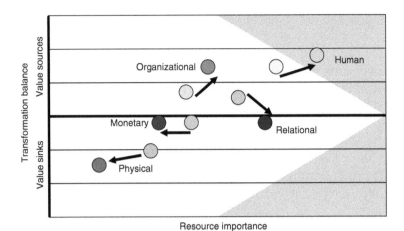

Figure 6.6. Effector plot of current and future resource returns.

The analysis can and should be continued with a hot-spot analysis. In this analysis, the qualities of the resources are evaluated and plotted. This is shown in Figure 6.7.

In this plot, the color codes of the resources are replaced by a "robustness" figure. Resources colored red are vulnerable in some respect, those colored green are robust, and those colored orange lie in between these limits. The plot shows the same strategic development but estimates the robustness of the resources if current strategies are pursued. Assuming

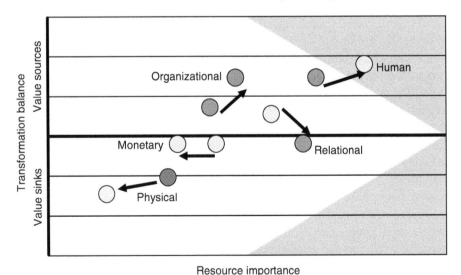

Figure 6.7. Hot-spot analysis.

the example is one of a company divesting its physical (manufacturing) resources to concentrate on more knowledge intensive activities, we can see the following:

1. The vulnerable physical resources are declining in importance (moving right to left) and the vulnerability of those that have to be retained improves overall. It is assumed that the most vulnerable are being divested.
2. Monetary resources are also declining in importance as some elements of expenditure such as reinvestment in manufacturing equipment are no longer required.
3. Organizational resources are becoming more important (moving left to right) and it is hoped that they will become more highly leveraged (moving up). Their robustness stays the same, which assumes continues investment in image, brand, IP, and so on.
4. Relational resources are becoming more important (moving left to right), but there is more investment in winning and retaining them (moving down). Their robustness is improving with the investment.
5. Human resources are becoming more important (moving left to right), with a slight increase in leveraging in their new role (moving up), but robustness is declining because nothing is being done in the strategy to improve it. They are also now in the danger zone. Again, the overall human resource bundle must be analyzed in more detail to find the aspects of human resources that are really in danger and the aspect of robustness that is degrading the overall figure. It is a poor strategy where the most important resources are vulnerable to some environmental change.

The preceding example demonstrated the use of the navigator. Of course, HR strategy specific indicators (the IC index) can be devised using the methodology in Chapter 4 to chart the progress as the strategy is implemented.

The alternative to indices is a full measurement exercise using CVH, again as described in Chapter 4. In common with the intellectual capital navigator approach, a CVH value calculation cannot be carried out in isolation from the rest of the company. However, detailed HR issues can be developed separately in what is termed a conflation level. In its most highly developed form, this can be used to address the performance of teams or individuals under the conditions extant during the strategic changes. This can even be used as a transparent way of awarding compensation or, at least, performance-related bonus pay.

KNOWLEDGE MANAGEMENT

Knowledge management has become an important activity in companies and in some has achieved a status that rivals human resource management or some other critical function. It has generated a new role for individuals—the chief knowledge officer—and companies now have knowledge management strategies in the same way that there are human resource strategies. In addition, knowledge management budgets are large, with many billions being spent worldwide on software solutions, underlying information technology hardware, and consultancy fees.

The following discussion will show that knowledge management shares many of the characteristics of human resource management in its contribution to success and making a difference to companies in creating value. It differs only in that it is less easy to localize. Human resource management is concerned with people and their interactions within the company to create value, the rules by which they operate and are rewarded, and so on. But the starting resource is always the tangible person. Knowledge, on the other hand, is more nebulous. Sometimes it is vested in people, sometimes it is recorded (or codified) and appears as an organizational resource; it can even be embedded in processes. Thus, while it shares many of the characteristics of other meta-activities, its diversity makes it more difficult to deal with. Nevertheless, the intellectual capital approach can be used to demonstrate how it creates value, how it should be managed strategically, the degree to which investment should be made, and even the nature of that investment.

Basics of knowledge management

If we adopt a contemporary inclusive definition of knowledge management (KM) we would probably say that KM has been practised for only 10 years or so. But this would be misleading, since most or even all of the elements of the practices that are bundled and called KM stretch back to the ancient Greeks and have always been followed in some form in the West. Undoubtedly, KM practices stretch back over a similar period in China and India, but their form and legacy is little researched or understood in the West.

The emergence and impact of the global market and the attendant pressures on the older elements of the economies of the West were highlighted by forward thinkers in the 1980s[51] and 1990s,[52] both decades' work offering similar perspectives in many ways. They showed how successful companies, societies, and economies would have to operate in future to meet the changed circumstances and this, in turn, highlighted the special place KM would play. If it is generally accepted that KM is not a fad,[53] then it is therefore to be taken seriously by companies and governments. Given this attitude, it is disappointing to find that very few companies think that their investment in KM was a success while between 16% and 36% felt it was a failure.[54] The reasons companies (or individuals for that matter) invest in KM are:

1. It gives a temporal or a functional or an efficiency advantage over their competitors.
2. They do it to try to negate the advantages of others.

Many dress up the decision to invest in KM in softer terms, but the underlying motives remain simply advantage or survival.[55,56]

Before considering KM, it is worth very briefly investigating exactly what it is that is being managed. There is considerable latitude among the human race as to what knowledge is, what it means, and consequently, how it should be managed, if at all. A grounding in epistemological issues, the study of knowledge, is required. This is not an esoteric excursion; it is fundamental. If managers try to impose a model of knowledge and then attempt management on a basis foreign to the workforce, they will fail. Epistemological classes have been described by researchers for many decades, but particularly in the 1980s[57] and also 1990s[58] as KM and the wider subject of intellectual capital became more prominent, The three classes of epistemology are illustrated in Figure 6.8. Individuals show varying tendencies to one type or another.

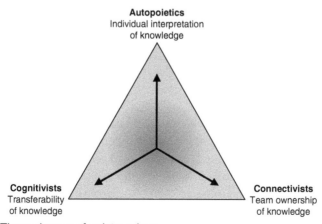

Figure 6.8. Three classes of epistemology.

A further fundamental distinction arises concerning value (in truth or knowledge) and whether it can be meaningfully discussed or whether it is emotional, making discourse meaningless. This boils down to the philosophical beliefs of the workforce, and the simplistic distinction is between a strict logical positivist view[59] and an axiological view in which discussions of value can be admitted into the bounds of acceptability from a positivist perspective.[60]

With an understanding of what the workforce believes about knowledge, it is then possible to look at how organizations deal with the practicalities of creating, managing, and using knowledge. It is convenient to look at the mechanics of knowledge management using some framework. Although a number of cyclical schemes exist,[61] Boisot's[62] 6-step social learning cycle is a useful tool for explaining the life-cycle of knowledge. The steps are: scanning, problem solving, abstraction, dissemination, absorption, and impact, and they are shown in Figure 6.9.

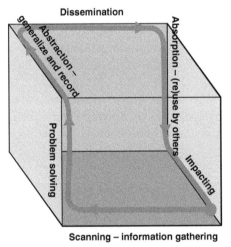

Figure 6.9. Boisot's social learning cycle.

Within this general framework, there are a variety of different mechanisms available for each step, and the applicability of these mechanisms is idiosyncratic to the individual application. Failure to understand the complex nature of the "life of knowledge" and the adoption of a one-application-fits-all mentality is a major contributor to the statistics of failure.

The first stage of learning is scanning, which is concerned with the acquisition of material with which a solution is synthesized and often involves relational to human resource transformations. It also includes self-generation in fundamental research and thus also has a human to human component. This is a mechanistic stage whose aim is first to discover whether a problem's solution already exists and if not, what is known in contributory areas. The parallel to the early stages of the classical scientific method is clear.[63] This step can be either a team or an individual activity, and the potential for success is dependent on several elements. Supporting IT (physical and organizational resources) that gives access to the widest range of material is necessary but not sufficient. Some argue for the importance of the network,[64] while the more straightforward demands on organizational memory for optimum ultimate new product performance and creativity is argued by others.[65]

The second stage of the Boisot SLC is problem solving and is not usually considered to be a feature of knowledge management since it concerns creativity, which is regarded by many to be a human attribute and one in which human-to-human interactions dominate.[66] However, technological aids can support the transition between steps 1 and 2, and the classical example is TRIZ[67], first outlined in Russia in 1956. The outcome of the second stage of the SLC is a problem, solved using knowledge that was already available or was created. It is at the end of this stage, where the solution exists in the mind of the individual or team, that modern IT-intensive knowledge management looms large.

The third stage of the SLC is abstraction, in which the latter stages of the scientific method are carried out and the new knowledge made available. This occurs in two steps as, first, the new knowledge from the solution of problems in stage 2 is generalized and, second, it is recorded for use by others. This is the transformation of a human resource to an organizational one. It is at this stage that there exist a great many "KM software solutions." However, this step is only one of six and many[68] explain that reliance on IT is insufficient for a complete approach to knowledge management. However, the desirability of making an electronic record of everything is questionable, with many[69,70] explaining the importance of tacit knowledge. Others show how concepts are internalised in personal languages such as I-language[71] or Mentalese[72] which cannot be transferred. Others have specifically highlighted the more practical problems of disseminating tacit knowledge effectively around the organization.[73] Whatever the balance between tacit and explicit knowledge in the company, a full appreciation of the way in which information is passed between people and understood requires a basic understanding of ontology and semiotics. Ontology is the study of the nature of being and dates back to Aristotle, but in more modern applications researchers tend to concentrate on investigating onto-logical mismatches as a basis for the creation of new knowledge.[74] Semiotics is the study of human communication, for example.[75]

The fourth stage of the SLC is dissemination. In the past, this was simply by personal communication or the printed word. Thus, the Renaissance scientist's communication time frame was of the order of months. Now it is milliseconds, but the reason for dissemination is the same. Here, organizational resources are converted to themselves with the aid of a physical resource.

The fifth step in the social learning cycle is absorption which, within the confines of the company, has to go hand-in-hand with the third step of the SLC, abstraction. Absorption is the step in the SLC where infor-mation (or knowledge) is (re-)used by others. In the field of tacit knowl-edge exchange, Nonaka and Takeuchi's work stands preeminent, but others have built on this, some with specialized applications such as tech-nological knowledge.[76] In essence, explicit knowledge (an organizational resource) backed by the tacit knowledge (a human resource) of the orig-inator are transformed into the tacit knowledge of the recipient, but bearing in mind that the tacit knowledge of the recipient may well be dif-ferent from that of the originator since the recipient will have a different cognitive framework into which the new knowledge must be integrated.

The final step in the social learning cycle is impacting. This step con-cerns the outcome of the use of knowledge. Here is a point of major interaction with the rest of the company since it concerns the uses to which the knowledge may be put and the modes of use. The SLC assumes that knowledge generation is a cyclical process, but a value shop requires that the customer is influenced by the new knowledge and is instrumental in the next loop round the social learning cycle.

The intellectual capital perspective

The use of Boisot's social learning cycle has been very convenient since it has enabled a translation directly into the language of intellectual cap-ital resources and transformations. The only shortcoming of the expla-nation is that it has concentrated on the knowledge itself without concern for the rest of the organization or the people, usually the cus-tomers, who are influenced or affected by the new knowledge.

It is helpful to express the SLC now in terms of intellectual capital resources at the second level of granularity to show where it fits in rela-tion to the rest of the value shop. For convenience and clarity, some of

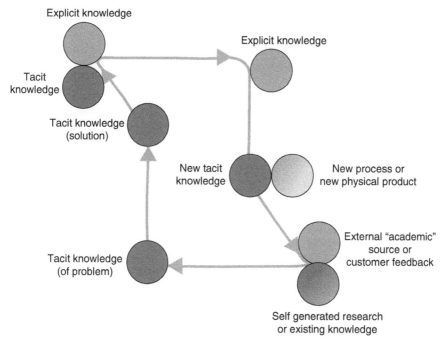

Explicit knowledge

Explicit knowledge

Tacit
knowledge

Tacit knowledge
(solution)

New tacit
knowledge

New process or
new physical product

Tacit knowledge
(of problem)

External "academic"
source or
customer feedback

Self generated research
or existing knowledge

Figure 6.10. The SLC described using intellectual capital resources.

the company's resources have been left out. Figure 6.10 shows the intellectual capital navigator.

Figure 6.9 can be compressed into tacit knowledge (human), explicit knowledge and processes (organizational), and customer knowledge (relational), and then it can be seen to fit into the classic triangular think-tank or university structure. What should also be apparent is that, like human resource management, it is part of a larger whole and so there is a definite link between knowledge management and the strategic development path for the company as a whole. With company strategy as the starting point, subsidiary strategies such as HR or KM naturally emerge and are in all ways consistent with the company strategy and any other subsidiary strategies.

In the same way as for human resource management, indicators of progress toward strategic goals for KM can be developed using the methods in Chapter 4. Likewise, if proper measurement of the value of knowledge management is required, the CVH can provide that. (See the section on human resource management, with the suggestion that the CVH could be used to determine rewards.) The analogue for knowledge management is value for money calculations for IT and systems investment and operation. Given the knowledge of what resources are actually involved in knowledge management and how they actually interact with one another, then value for money calculations using CVH are perfectly possible for knowledge management.

Key Points in Chapter 6

- Common due diligence frameworks and approaches largely ignore intellectual capital because it is more difficult to identify and assess than tangible assets. However, merely looking at financial and legal factors when evaluating the potential of a merger or acquisition often lead to unsuccessful deals and/or integration trouble. With the IC perspective it is possible to predict the success and synergy potential of the merger.
- Prior to the merger, an assessment of the strength of and the match between the involved companies' respective value-creating models needs to be carried out.
- A number of conditions need to be fulfilled for the intellectual capital to have a sound potential for future value creation. These include the criticality of the intellectual capital, its flexibility, its availability, its capacity, and its coordination flexibility.
- There are many potential causes for transformation inertia (counter-productive forces in a merger) such as differences in epistemological viewpoints, the complexity of the intellectual capital, lack of experience of merger and acquisition situations, lack of organizational slack, and cultural distances.
- An IC analysis is as important in divestments as it is in merger and acquisition situations to ensure that you do not unintentionally loose resources that actually create value and that the divestment gets the highest cost reducing effect while also having the least value reducing effect.
- Intellectual capital often ties closely into human resources management (HRM) in people's minds. That is not the full picture, but intellectual capital thinking and the resource based approach may provide the key to quantifying the links between HRM and business performance, although work to date has proved that it may not be possible to clearly separate HRM from other management actions to quantify the effects of HRM. The CVH approach involving rigorous measurement may, however, be used for this purpose.
- Intellectual capital and knowledge management (KM) are also closely related fields. The social learning cycle in KM can be translated into IC language and explained through resources and transformations. Before any KM investment, one has to assess which type of knowledge viewpoints the people in the organization have (cognitivist, connectivist, or autopoietic) for the investment to be effective.

ENDNOTES

1. T. Chi (1994), "Trading in strategic resources: necessary conditions, transaction cost problems and choice of exchange structure," *Strategic Management Journal*, 15(4), 271–290.
2. S. Lippman and R.P. Rumelt (1982), "Uncertain imitability: an analysis of interfirm differences in efficiency under competition," *Bell Journal of Economics*, 13, 418–438.
3. P.C. Haspeslagh and D.B. Jemison (1991), *Managing Acquisitions: Creating Value through Corporate Renewal*, New York: Free Press.
4. G. Easton and L. Araujo (1996), "Characterizing organizational competences: an industrial networks approach," in: R. Sanchez, A. Heene, and H. Thomas (1996), *Dynamics of Competence-based Competition*, Kidlington, Elsevier Science.
5. A.C. Inkpen (1998), "Learning and knowledge acquisition through international strategic alliances," *Academy of Management Executive*, 12(4), 69–80.
6. T.S. Gruca, D. Nath and A. Mehra (1997), "Exploiting synergy for competitive advantage," *Long Range Planning*, 30(4), 605–611.
7. M. Makhija and U. Ganesh (1997), "Control and partner learning in learning-related joint ventures," *Organization Science*, 8(5), 508–527.
8. W.M. Cohen and D.A. Levinthal (1990), "Absorptive capacity: a new perspective on learning and innovation," *Administrative Science Quarterly*, 35, 128–152.
9. P. Haspeslagh and A.B. Farquhar (1987), "The acquisition integration process: a contingent framework," written for presentation at the seventh Annual International Conference of the Strategic Management Society, Boston, MA, 14–17 October.
10. B.L. Simonin (1999), "Ambiguity and the process of knowledge transfer in strategic alliances," *Strategic Management Journal*, 20, 595–623.
11. D.C. Mowery, J.E. Oxley and B.S. Silverman, B.S. (1996), "Strategic alliances and interfirm knowledge transfer," *Strategic Management Journal*, 17 (Winter Special Issue), 77–91.
12. P. Attewell (1992), "Technology diffusion and organizational learning: the case of business computing," *Organizational Science*, 3(1), 1–19.
13. B. Kogut and U. Zander (1992), "Knowledge of the firm, combinative capabilities and the replication technology," *Organizational Science*, 3(3): 383–397.
14. G. von Krogh. J. Roos, and D. Kleine (1998), *Knowing in Firms: Understanding, Managing and Measuring Knowledge*, London: Sage Publications.
15. H. Singh and M. Zollo (1998), "The impact of knowledge codification, experience trajectories and integration strategies on the performance of corporate acquisitions," Working Paper 98–24, The Wharton School, University of Pennsylvania.
16. R.M. Cyert and J.G. March (1963), *A Behavioural Theory of the Firm*, Englewood Cliffs, NJ: Prentice–Hall.
17. J. Veiga, M. Lubatkin, R. Calori, and P. Very (2000), "Measuring organizational culture clashes: a two-nation post-hoc analysis of a cultural compatibility index," *Human Relations*, 53(4), 539–557.
18. Cartwright, C. and Cooper, C.L. (1993), "The role of culture compatibility in successful organizational marriage," *Academy of Management Executive*, 7(2), pp. 57–70.
19. M. Haynes, S. Thompson, and M. Wright (2000), "The determinants of corporate divestment in the UK," *International Journal of Industrial Organization*, 18, 1201–1222.
20. G.R.G. Benito and L. Welch (1997), "De-internationalization," *Management International*.
21. F. León-Darder and A. Dasí-Coscollar (2001), "Perspectives of foreign subsidiary detachment from the MNC: Spanish evidence," Working Paper Universitat de Valància Avgda dels Tarongers. Available at: www.sses.com/public/events/euram/complete_tracks/managing_multinational_companies/dasi-coscollar_leon-dorder.pdf

22. C. Lucier, J. Dyer, and G. Adolph (2002), "Breaking Up Is Hard to Do—and Manage," *Strategy + Business*, 28(Third Quarter), 14–17.
23. E. Delany (1998), "Strategic development of multinational subsidiaries in Ireland," in: Birkinshaw and Hood (Eds), *Multinational Corporate Evolution and Subsidiary Development*, London: Macmillan Press Ltd.
24. R. Griffin and J. Fairhead (1999), "Power in and about the Irish subsidiary," presented paper, IAM Conference, 9–10 September, University of Limerick, Ireland.
25. Fayol, H. (1916), Administration industrielle et générale, Bulletin de la Société de l'Industrie Minérale, No. 10, pp. 5-164, Regular re-editions by Dunod since 1918.
26. Taylor, F.W. (1911), The Principles of Scientific Management, Harper and Row, New York, NY.
27. P.M. Wright and G.C. McMahan (1992), "Theoretical perspectives for strategic human resource management," *Journal of Management*, 18(2), 295–320.
28. Heathfield, S.M., 2002, http://humanresources.about.com/library/weekly/aa051400a.htm.
29. M. Armstrong (1997), In: A.J. Price, Human Resource Management in a Business Context, International Thompson, 168–169.
30. S. Komatsubara and Y. Mizuta (1997), "Strengthening management by restructuring the HRM system," *Journal of Mitsubishi Research Institute*, 31 (English summary), Tokyo
31. M. Hamme and J. Champy (1993), *Re-engineering the Corporation*, New York: Harper Colin.
32. F. Cakar and U.S. Bititci (2001), "Human resource management as a strategic input to manufacturing," Presented paper, International Working Conference on Strategic Manufacturing, 26–29, August, Aalborg, Denmark.
33. K. Legge (1995), *Human Resources Management Rhetorics and Realities*, London: Macmillan Press.
34. S. Tyson (1995), *Human Resource Strategy: Towards a General Theory of Human Resource Management*, London: Pittman Publishing.
35. J. Storey (1995), *New Perspectives on Human Resource Management*, London: Routledge.
36. C.J. Fombrun, N.M. Tichy and M.A. Devanna (1984), *Strategic Human Resource Management*, New York: John Wiley.
37. M. Beer, B. Spector, P. Lawrance, D. Quinn Mill, and R. Walton (1984), Managing Human Assets: A general managers perspective. New York: Free Press.
38. D.E. Guest (1987), "Human resources management and industrial relations," *Journal of Management Studies*, 24(5), 503–521, Table 11, pp. 516.
39. C. Hendry and A. Pettgrew (1992), " Patterns of strategic change in the development of human Resourcermanagement," *British Journal of Management*, 139–156
40. Jones and Wright (1992), U.S. Department of Labor.
41. M.A. Huselid (1995), "The impact of human resource practices on turnover, productivity, and corporate financial performance," *Academy of Management Journal*, 38(3), 635–672.
42. T. Bailey (1993), "Discretionary effort and the organization of work: employee participation and work reform since Hawthorne," Working paper, New York: Columbia University.
43. D. Guest and R. Peccei (2002), *Trust, Exchange and Virtuous Circles of Cooperation: A Theoretical And Empirical Analysis of Partnership at Work*, The Management Centre Research Papers, London: King's College.
44. K. Laursen (2000), *The Importance of Sectoral Differences in the Application of New HRM Practices for Innovation Performance*, LINK, Department of Industrial Economics and Strategy, Copenhagen Business School.

45. E.H. Bax (1999), *The Strategic Labor Allocation Process: A Model of Strategic HRM, SOM-theme A*, University of Groningen Library.
46. J. Fitz-Enz (2001), *The ROI of Human Capital: Measuring the Economic Value of Employee Performance*, New York: AMACOM.
47. Human Capital Capability Inc, http://www.hcc-scorecard.com.
48. Cognitive Technologies Group, http://www.cognitive-technologies.com/#.
49. Watson Wyatt, http://www.watsonwyatt.com.
50. J. Barney (1991), "Firm resources and sustained competitive advantage," *Journal of Management*, 17, 99–120.
51. A. Toffler (1985), *Future Shock*, New York: Bantam Books.
52. P. Drucker (1994), *Post-Capitalist Society*, Butterworth-Heinemann.
53. KPMG (2000), *Knowledge Management Research Report* 2000.
54. CTP (1999), *The Knowledge Paradox: How to Manage your Most Strategic Asset*.
55. M.R. Lyles and C.R. Schwenk (1992), "Top management, strategy and organizational knowledge structures," *Journal of Management Studies*, 29(2), 155–174.
56. G. Huber (1990), "A theory of the effects of advanced information technologies on organizational design," *Academy Management Review*, 21(1), 47–71.
57. J. Habermas (1984), "Translator's introduction," in: J. Habermas, *The Theory of Communicative Action,* Vol. 1, Cambridge: Polity Press.
58. G. Von Krogh, J. Roos, and D. Kleine (1998), *Knowing in Firms*, Sage.
59. A.J. Ayer (1936), *Language, Truth and Logic*, New York: Dover Books (Original publication – but see later reprints).
60. N. Rescher (1969), *An Introduction to Value Theory*, Englewood Cliffs: Prentice Hall.
61. T. Savolainen (2000), "How organizations promote and avoid learning," *Journal of Workplace Learning*, 12(5/6), 195–204.
62. M. Boisot (1995), Information Space: *International Thompson Business,* London.
63. E. Wilson (1952), *An Introduction top Scientific Research*, London: McGraw Hill.
64. M. Augier and M. Thanning-Vendelo (1999), "Networks: cognition and management of tacit networks," *Journal of Knowledge Management*, 3(4), 25–26.
65. C. Moorman and A. Miner (1997), "The impact of organizational memory on new product performance and creativity, *Journal of Marketing Research*, February, 91–106.
66. I. Nonaka and T. Nishiguchi (2000), *Knowledge Emergence*, New York: Oxford University Press.
67. G. Altshuller (1956), *And Suddenly the Inventor Appeared*: TRIZ, the Theory of Inventive Problem Solving. Worcester, MA: Technical Innovation Center. (Originally published in Russian in 1956, translated in 1996 by Shulyak, L.).
68. T. Davenport (1997), *Information Ecology*, Oxford University Press.
69. I. Nonaka and H. Takeuchi (1995), *The Knowledge Creating Company*, New York: Oxford University Press.
70. M. Polanyi (1966), *The Tacit Dimension*, London: Routledge.
71. N. Chomsky (1986), *Knowledge of Language*, New York: Praeger.
72. J. Fodor (1975), *The Language of Thought*, New York: Crowell.
73. T. Haldin-Herrgard (2000), "Difficulties in diffusion of tacit knowledge in organizations," *Journal of Intellectual Capital*, 1(4), 357–365.
74. N. Fridman Noy and C. Haffner (1997), "The state of the art in ontology design: a survey and comparative review," *AI Magazine*, 18(3), 53–74.
75. D. Chandler (1995), http://www.aber.ac.uk/media/Documents/S4B/sem0a.html.
76. A. Reuithe and S. Aberg (2000), "The tacitness of codified knowledge," Paper presented at the 18th Annual IMP Conference, Bath, UK.

Index

Page numbers followed by *t* and *f* indicates tables and figures, respectively.

For Product Safety Concerns and Information please contact our EU
representative GPSR@taylorandfrancis.com
Taylor & Francis Verlag GmbH, Kaufingerstraße 24, 80331 München, Germany

www.ingramcontent.com/pod-product-compliance
Ingram Content Group UK Ltd.
Pitfield, Milton Keynes, MK11 3LW, UK
UKHW042201240425
457818UK00011B/325